D0492224

# Input and interaction in language acquisition

# Input and interaction in language acquisition

*Edited by*

## Clare Gallaway

*Centre for Audiology, Education of the Deaf
and Speech Pathology
University of Manchester*

and

## Brian J. Richards

*Department of Arts and Humanities in
Education
University of Reading*

CAMBRIDGE
UNIVERSITY PRESS

Published by the Press Syndicate of the University of Cambridge
The Pitt Building, Trumpington Street, Cambridge CB2 1RP
40 West 20th Street, New York, NY 10011–4211, USA
10 Stamford Road, Oakleigh, Melbourne 3166, Australia

First published 1994

*A catalogue record for this book is available from the British Library*

*Library of Congress cataloguing in publication data*

Input and interaction in language acquisition / edited by Clare
Gallaway and Brian J. Richards.
   p.    cm.
Includes bibliographical references and index.
ISBN 0 521 43109 3 (hardback) – ISBN 0 521 43725 3 (paperback)
   1. Language acquisition – Parent participation. 2. Social
interaction in children. I. Gallaway, Clare. II. Richards, Brian J.
P118.5.I56 1994
401′.93 – dc20   93–5482 CIP

ISBN 0 521 43109 3 hardback
ISBN 0 521 43725 3 paperback

Transferred to digital printing 1999

CE

# Contents

# Figures

# Tables

# Contributors

MICHELLE E. BARTON
Division of Social Sciences, New College of USF

GINA CONTI-RAMSDEN
Centre for Educational Guidance and Special Needs, School of Education, University of Manchester

ALAN CRUTTENDEN
Department of Linguistics, University of Manchester

CLARE GALLAWAY
Centre for Audiology, Education of the Deaf and Speech Pathology, School of Education, University of Manchester

PETER GEEKIE
School of Policy and Technology Studies in Education, University of Wollongong

ELENA V. M. LIEVEN
Department of Psychology, University of Manchester

JULIAN M. PINE
Department of Psychology, The University of Nottingham

BRIDIE RABAN
Education Department, University of Warwick

BRIAN J. RICHARDS
Department of Arts and Humanities in Education, University of Reading

CATHERINE E. SNOW
Graduate School of Education, Harvard University

JEFFREY L. SOKOLOV
Department of Psychology, University of Nebraska at Omaha

MICHAEL TOMASELLO
Department of Psychology, Emory University

MARJORIE BINGHAM WESCHE
Second Language Institute, University of Ottawa

BENCIE WOLL
Centre for Deaf Studies, University of Bristol

# Preface

The motivation for this volume came about in late 1989 when the editors were putting together a research proposal concerned with input. We realized that, in spite of the dramatic increase of studies in this area, there were few survey articles covering the most recent developments. Above all, no single source existed to which we could conveniently refer which would set out the complex arguments now surrounding input issues and which also included important new directions appearing in the late 1980s. In particular, we noticed that no attempt had been made to produce a sequel, as it were, to Snow and Ferguson (1977).

Our aim in producing this book, therefore, has been twofold: firstly, to provide a survey of both classical and recent input and interaction studies, including studies concerning particular types of learner and particular types of context in which language is acquired; and secondly, to provide a detailed assessment of the theoretical issues and controversies in the area. We believed that this daunting task would be best tackled by sharing it with others directly involved in the field.

The book is organized as follows: the scene is set by the Introduction, in which the development of the research area over the years is described, the main body of text consists of chapters on specific issues grouped into three broad areas, and a synthesis of the findings and general implications of the research can be found in the final chapter.

We would like to acknowledge the contribution of our chapter authors to the organization and final scope of the book; we would like to feel that, with their help, we have arrived at a reasonably comprehensive coverage of the issues. Any omissions, of course, remain our own responsibility.

Our thanks are also due to Veronica Butcher, Al Matthews, and Maureen Underwood for their valuable comments on some of the drafts, and of course, to our families for their patience and support throughout this project.

The order of editors was decided by the toss of a coin.

CLARE GALLAWAY and BRIAN J. RICHARDS

# Introduction

# Beginning from Baby Talk: twenty years of research on input and interaction

*Catherine E. Snow*

## 1      Introduction

Research on the nature of linguistic input to language-learning children has a longer history than "modern" child language research (the era whose beginning I take to be marked by the publication of Brown and Bellugi 1964). Anthropological linguists and fieldworkers were publishing papers in the 1950s and 1960s about the phenomenon of "Baby Talk" as a special register of the languages they had studied. They documented Baby Talk primarily as an interesting sociolinguistic phenomenon, but often reported as well the local beliefs that it aided children in learning to talk. Even in the earliest moments of the "modern era" of child language research, analyses of input were never ignored. For example, Brown and Bellugi identified "expansion," a maternal response, as one of the three processes involved in language acquisition in their 1964 work.

Despite this early and consistent interest, the accumulation of information about the nature of adult speech to language-learning children was fairly slow until the mid 1970s. During the 1970s and 1980s, in contrast, the amount of work on interaction expanded enormously. There have been dozens of papers on this topic published in the *Journal of Child Language* since its inception in 1974, as well as in the journal *First Language*. At least half of the papers selected for publication in conference volumes following each of the last three meetings of the International Association for the Study of Child Language (held in 1984 in Austin, Texas, in 1987 in Lund, Sweden, and in 1990 in Budapest, Hungary) have been devoted to studies of input and interaction. Several monographs have been published focusing on the topic of how adults' language might help children learn to talk, as have countless chapters in edited volumes. It has become standard even in research directed primarily to analyses of children's own output to incorporate analyses of how their interlocutors are talking to them, if only to exclude imitative child utterances from further analysis. If ubiquity and frequency are the criteria, then the field called "social interaction as related to language

3

acquisition" has certainly come into maturity during the last twenty years.

However, this work has consistently been viewed by many as peripheral to mainstream thinking about language acquisition. The central questions of importance have been defined as if they are questions only about what goes on inside children's heads – questions about universal grammar, learning strategies, operating principles, cognitive constraints on language development, and so on. From this inside-the-head perspective the nature of the social interaction children engage in evidently seemed too much like noise, random variation in the system. For those who assume that the important aspects of language acquisition are all the product of universal, innate grammar, of course study of the input to children offers little interest. For example, in his 1986 keynote address to the Boston University Child Language Conference, Noam Chomsky characterized all child language research as falling into one of three categories: wrong, trivial, and absurd. Needless to say, he put attempts to relate aspects of acquisition to the input squarely in the third category. Fortunately, many theorists have now come to an alternative formulation, in which information about input is seen as central to constraining hypotheses about what is inside children's heads. The controversy about the need for and existence of negative evidence falls into this category. Some researchers even of a relatively cognitivist bent are now acknowledging that we need real data about input and the child's linguistic environment to integrate into the determinants of learnability, though many still dismiss work on interaction as descriptive and tangential to work on language acquisition.

It will be my goal, in this brief introduction to a collection of chapters which brings the field up to date on the topic of input as related to acquisition, to give a bit of historical context to the work reviewed in this book. In addition, I will present and discuss four ways in which I think future work on language acquisition done from a social interactionist perspective will differ from that done so far. If I am right, then future analyses of input and interaction will be able to contribute to our understanding of the nature of language acquisition much more powerfully than has work done along these lines so far.

## 2     A modest beginning

In 1974 a group of about thirty researchers converged on Brookline, Massachusetts for a conference on Input and Language Acquisition, for which the inspiration and the work of securing funding had been the responsibility of Charles Ferguson. Ferguson had been a leader in the study of Baby Talk from the traditional, descriptive perspective, and was quick to recognize the value of relating that work to the work being done on input by people who called themselves developmental psycholinguists. The conference was the first explicitly to bring linguists with an interest in specialized registers such as Baby Talk together with developmental psychologists who did research on the social context of language development. It had grown out of discussions at two previous conferences – the AILA (Association Internationale de Linguistique Appliquée) meeting in Copenhagen in the summer of 1971, and the International Child Language Meeting in Florence in the summer of 1972. In Copenhagen I went to hear Charles Ferguson present a paper on Foreigner Talk, and was amazed to hear him relate that phenomenon to recent studies of mothers' speech to children, none of which had yet been published. (Jean Berko Gleason has told me that Ferguson heard her present her paper "Code-switching in children's language" at a conference in Buffalo in 1971, and pursued her down a hallway to have the chance to tell her about the other people he knew were doing similar analyses.) In Florence the program committee had juxtaposed papers by Helen Remick, Jacqueline Sachs, and me – all of us, strangers to one another, reporting on our recently collected data showing that mothers talk in distinctively simple, clear, and repetitive ways to young children! At about the same time, Juliette Phillips, Patricia Broen, Jean Berko Gleason, Susan Ervin-Tripp's groups of students, and others surfaced, all with data suggesting that linguistic input to language-learning children was worthy of direct empirical study. Charles Ferguson was evidently tracking these efforts and decided their quantity and ground-breaking character merited bringing the various researchers together at a conference; accordingly, he convinced the Social Science Research Council to fund a three-day meeting.

The 1974 meeting in Brookline was pleasant but not, if I remember correctly, bursting with energy. There was little controversy, perhaps because the emphasis was on description rather than explanation. Heavily freighted issues, such as learnability, the existence and role of negative evidence, whether input served as a source of cumulative learning or as a trigger, and the impossibility of recovery from too simple hypotheses, had not yet emerged. Foreshadowings of these issues were certainly present in the conflict between the findings reported by Elissa Newport and those of Toni Cross, both present at the conference and both contributors to the volume that derived from it (Snow and Ferguson 1977); however, in 1974 Cross was still concentrating on analyzing child effects on maternal speech, and only in 1975 at the International Association for the Study of Child Language meeting in London did she report effects of mothers on children (Cross, 1978).

The wealth of research on input as related to acquisition carried out between 1977 and the present is documented in the chapters in the present volume, *Input and interaction in language acquisition*. Julian Pine's and Alan Cruttenden's chapters (this volume) review the basic descriptive research on input language comprehensively. Vast quantities of data have accumulated since the early 1970s, filling out the picture of how adults talk to children both by adding detail and by expanding the horizon of phenomena included in the descriptions. First, and perhaps most crucially, a much more truly interactive model for analyzing input is now widely applied. Rather than just analyzing adult utterances to assess their complexity, their correctness, their vocabulary choice, and their redundancy, researchers started also attending to the relations between adult and preceding child utterances (Cross, 1978), as well as between adult utterances and child gaze (Collis 1977) or child gestures and object-related actions (Goldfield 1987). Thus, the analysis of input moved from being located in the study of registers to being located in the study of discourse analysis.

Accompanying the shift from corpus analysis to conversational analysis came a rise in attention to the pragmatic and social functions of adult utterances, rather than just to their lexical and grammatical characteristics. Pragmatic analyses made clear that the speech addressed to young children was simple and restricted in the variety of communicative intents expressed, in that hints, irony, sarcasm, and other forms of indirect speech were avoided, and in the mapping between pragmatic functions and forms (e.g. Ninio 1992). These pragmatic and communicative forms of simplicity may be as crucial in making adult utterances usable to language-learning children as their structural or semantic simplicity.

The kinds of analyses applied to child-directed speech have expanded, as have the populations studied. The speech of parents to children with language delay and other developmental disabilities, as well as to children who have visual or hearing impairments, has been extensively studied (see Conti-Ramsden this volume; Gallaway and Woll this volume). Speech of mothers who are depressed or themselves impaired in hearing or vision has been studied (Tingley 1990; de Villiers 1985; de Villiers, de Villiers, and Hoban 1993). Analyses have been extended to encompass the speech of preschool teachers, as well as teachers in primary classrooms (see Geekie and Raban this volume). Though the vast majority of the data available still comes from Anglo-American parents, some expansion of interest to other cultures and to minority groups within the United States and Great Britain has occurred (see Lieven this volume). The focus on maternal and teacher input in relation to language development has been expanded to include interest in the impact of various sorts of input on preliteracy and literacy development as well. Analyses of speech addressed to second language learners, both children and adults, has replicated the shift in research paradigms that occurred in child language studies; whereas twenty years ago one studied "Foreigner Talk" primarily as a sociolinguistic register analogous to "Baby Talk," now work in second language acquisition emphasizes adaptation of input to the learner's level, its informativeness and comprehensibility, and its usefulness as a basis for learning (see Wesche this volume).

Already by 1977, when the book *Talking to children: language input and acquisition* that was based on the 1974 conference appeared, the field of child language research in the United States was getting large and complex enough to be subdivided by topics (e.g. syntactic *versus* pragmatic development), by researchers' disciplines (e.g. linguistics *versus* psychology), by burning issues (e.g. finding universal grammar *versus* remediating language delays), and by sociometrics (e.g. attendance at the Stanford *versus* the Boston University child language meetings). In Europe, fortunately, the separations were less extreme, perhaps because local associations and meetings maintained contact across theoretical or disciplinary divides in the smaller national or regional child language communities. Fractionations like those seen in North America may be inevitable in any successful and growing field, but they come at a cost. In the field of child language, unfortunately, the cost has been particularly high because many of the fracture lines coincided, thus creating groups of people interested in the same phenomenon who almost never talked to one another. Researchers trying to understand how children understood and learned language from adult utterances and utterance–context co-occurrences were classified as interested in social interaction, whereas those trying to identify reflexes of universal grammar in child language data were classified as interested in grammatical development. In fact, of course, both groups were trying to do precisely the same thing – figure out how children use the information available to come to be able to produce grammatical and interpretable sentences. Different assumptions about the relative importance of innate and interactive sources of insight closed off contact between these two groups of researchers to an unnecessary extent. Our understanding of the full complexity of language development has suffered as a consequence. Perhaps the chapters in this volume will serve to establish a starting point of shared knowledge that could reopen mutually informative dialogue.

## 3    Future possibilities

The basic descriptive work on the nature of linguistic input to language-learning children has still not been finished, primarily because of the neglect of most of the world's cultures and languages in the work done so far. Beyond expanding the list of groups studied, though, there is reason to hope that research done in the next twenty years might be different from the last twenty years' worth in qualitative ways. Four advances in our thinking and in the tools available to us make the next era of research on social interaction particularly promising.

## 3.1    Large-scale analyses

A basic question has dominated research and generated controversy about simplified and facilitative language input, namely, is it available to all children? One of the obstacles to carrying out truly convincing research speaking to issues of the general availability and usability of information about language structure from input was purely practical: collecting and transcribing interactive data is time-consuming and labor-intensive. Most researchers worked with transcripts from just a couple of time points and a handful of children. The relatively very large longitudinal corpora collected by Brown, by Kuczaj, by Sachs and a few others over-represented middle-class children with academic parents, and large amounts of transcript data from cultures other than Anglo-American ones were inaccessible as a basis for generalization.

At least for English-speaking children, though, enough transcript data have now accumulated from many different laboratories and research efforts that very large-scale analyses have become possible. Such large-scale analyses enable us not only to talk about the generality of phenomena of interest, but also to find individual or group differences in access to the input that might facilitate language learning. The willingness of researchers to donate their transcripts to the Child Language Data Exchange System (CHILDES) (MacWhinney 1991; MacWhinney and Snow 1985, 1990) has made feasible cross-child, cross-age, and cross-national analyses that would have been quite impractical even a few years ago. One example of such a large-scale analysis is the thesis research of Jeffrey Sokolov (1990), in which more than 150,000 utterances from three different corpora were analyzed. Obviously, analyzing such large datasets depends on the availability not just of lots of data, but also of automated analyses; Sokolov developed a program, called CHIP (Sokolov and MacWhinney 1990), which compares adjacent utterances for degree of lexical overlap, and thus can automatically identify adult imitations, expansions, and reductions of preceding child utterances (see Sokolov and Snow this volume). Analyzing lexical overlap at the corpus level rather than utterance by utterance, Gleason and her colleagues have used the CHILDES transcript archive and CLAN programs to show how the number of different words used by mothers increases as their children get older (Hu in press). Such large-scale analyses on massive databases are now feasible for anyone with a personal computer; the time when single case studies dominate the child language literature is probably behind us.

## 3.2 Focus on rare events

It is traditional in analyzing input data to present findings in terms of percentage – 30 percent of adult utterances are expansion, 47 percent are semantically contingent, 6 percent are direct corrections, and so on. Perhaps we should be thinking about the occurrence of interesting events in the linguistic environment of the child from a more ecologically valid perspective: how often does an average child hear an expansion? A directive? A clarification question? How often do potentially very useful events like occasions of language teaching or explicit correction occur? Even the most intensively studied children have been recorded for only an hour or two a week – let us say two hours out of about eighty waking hours per week, assuming the best case in which children sleep twelve hours a night. So observing even just one or two instances of potentially useful adult utterances, explicit language teaching, negative feedback, modeling the correct utterance in an hour's transcript could be extrapolated to over 400 chances per year for the child to hear such an utterance. Of course, in most one-hour observations there are considerably more than one or two potentially instructive adult responses. The potential value of rare events in language acquisition has been pointed out and argued for by K. E. Nelson (1980, 1981), but only with the accumulation of a fairly large amount of transcript data can these rare events actually be tabulated and their impact assessed.

The general tendency to report results in terms of percentages also, of course, runs the risk of obscuring differences in children's language experiences that relate to the amount of talk they hear. One of the more sophisticated analyses of input effects on language acquisition so far reported, that by Huttenlocher, Haight, Bryk, Seltzer, and Lyons (1991) utilizing Hierarchical Linear Modeling, found that *amount* of maternal talk during the observation was the best predictor of children's growth in vocabulary. Hoff-Ginsberg (1992) has reported significant differences between working-class and middle-class children, not in distribution of their mothers' talk over various interactive categories, but in the amount of maternal talk they hear. Such differences deserve considerably more attention than they have so far typically received in the theorizing about input and acquisition, because these differences in amount accumulate to produce enormously divergent language environments for different groups of children.

## 3.3    *Targeted relationships*

In the early and eager attempts to find relationships between aspects of input and children's language acquisition, a fairly scattershot approach was used. It was assumed that high-quality input, however that was defined, would result in generally faster or better acquisition as reflected in nonspecific measures such as mean length of utterance. This assumption reflected the unexamined notion that language development is a relatively undifferentiated process, within which various markers of development all operate more or less together. For example, reliance on mean length of utterance (MLU) as the major index of language development instantiates the view that various aspects of the language system are acquired together; computation of MLU in effect collapses over semantic, syntactic, and morphological growth such that gains in any of them can be reflected in higher scores (see Richards this volume for a similar point).

One of the disappointments of the first wave of research on interaction and language acquisition was the difficulty of finding clear relationships. Indicators of quality in the input could not consistently be shown to relate to speed of development, perhaps because the research seeking such relationships was often plagued by small and heterogeneous samples (e.g. Newport, Gleitman, and Gleitman 1977) as well as by differences in interpretation of the findings that did emerge (see, for example, Furrow, Nelson, and Benedict 1979, the response by Gleitman, Newport, and Gleitman 1984, and the further response by Furrow and Nelson 1986). However, searches for more targeted relationships between features of the input and aspects of development have been quite successful. Thus, for example, Keith Nelson has carried out a series of studies in which he has shown that provision of information about specific structures – the passive, or relative clauses – has an impact on the child's control of those particular structures (K. E. Nelson 1981). Acquiring control over one such grammatical structure may, of course, not radically affect global indices like MLU. But such incremental acquisitions may better approximate the way language is learned than the model of undifferentiated growth that is presupposed by global developmental indices.

Furthermore, most research seeking evidence for impact of input on acquisition has also looked only at two time points – essentially using difference scores to assess child language growth. Two time points are a very weak basis for assessing growth; a much better model requires having several waves of data so that robust growth models can be developed. It could be argued on theoretical as well as statistical grounds that rate of change is a much more sensible outcome variable than is status at any particular age; theoretically, rate corrects for late starters and reflects quality of input more sensitively, and statistically rate reflects all the available data points and thus is a more reliable measure. Multiple waves of data generating solid estimates of rate of change should be the standard model in seeking the effects of input on acquisition, but this model has been utilized very rarely. Newport, Gleitman, and Gleitman's (1977) study, for example, had only two waves of data, as did Furrow, Nelson, and Benedict's. The Huttenlocher *et al* (1991) study that found robust relationships between density of maternal speech and vocabulary growth used as an outcome growth rate based on several measurement points. We can only hope that future researchers will take work like this as a model (see Richards this volume for a similar point).

## 3.4     *Vulnerable populations and unbuffered skills*

A further reason why effects of input on acquisition are hard to find is that the normally developing child is well buffered against variation in the input. We know that children acquire at least the basics of their language in a wide variety of social and linguistic settings, and that in general the success rate is very high at least for phonology, morphology, and syntax. One could argue that the skills associated with connected discourse and with pragmatic appropriateness are somewhat less evenly distributed in the population, but clearly there is a central set of language skills, the acquisition of which is very likely to be successful. By definition, then, it is extremely difficult to observe effects of the environment on these acquisitions; buffering implies either that only a relatively small amount of social support of the right sort might be necessary, or alternately that any of several different environmental events might be sufficient for some bit of learning to occur. Under these circumstances, variations at the margin in the quality of the linguistic environment a child is exposed to might not have any measurable effect on the speed or the ease of language acquisition.

However, many children have to learn language without some of the buffering normally developing children enjoy. Children with hearing impairments, for example, or even those with transient but recurrent hearing loss due to *otitis media*, may be missing a good percentage of the potential learning experiences normal children enjoy. Children with visual impairments hear language around them, but have considerable difficulty making semantic mappings between utterances and objects or events. Children with perinatal brain injuries, with Down's syndrome or other forms of mental retardation, children who were born premature or small for date or very sick, and children with specific language impairment all display a diminution of the buffering normally developing children enjoy. They are at considerable risk for delayed or deviant language development. Such children may be considerably more dependent on the availability of optimal input if they are to show normal language acquisition than are normally developing children. It may be that we will identify the features of parent–child interaction that most robustly support language learning even for normally developing children by focusing our attention more directly on these developmentally disadvantaged groups.

## 4    Conclusion

The contributions to this volume provide an invaluable overview of what has become a complex and multi-faceted field of research. Comparing the reference list from the 1977 volume *Talking to children: language input and acquisition* to the reference list at the end of this book makes clear how much more we now know about the social context within which children learn language. The most powerful questions that have guided this research, though, are paradoxically not yet answered: is access to usably simplified input universal? Is input fine-tuned to aspects of the child's competence? Are differences in the quality of the input associated with differences in speed, ease, or pattern of language development? What are the most crucial and facilitative features of input to children learning language? These questions remain with us, to be answered by research undertaken in the next twenty years.

NOTE

This chapter was prepared with support from the NIH through HD223338.

# Part I

General issues

# 1    The language of primary caregivers

*Julian M. Pine*

## 1    Introduction

It has been clear since the late 1960s and early 1970s that there are systematic differences between speech to children and speech among adults (Snow 1972; Phillips 1973; contributions to Snow and Ferguson 1977). Child-directed speech (CDS) tends to consist of short, well-formed utterances, to contain fewer false starts or hesitations, and to include fewer complex sentences and subordinate clauses (Snow 1972; Phillips 1973). It is characteristically higher in pitch, more exaggerated in intonation, and slower in tempo than speech among adults (Garnica 1977). It is also highly redundant, as reflected in the incidence of part or whole repetitions (Broen 1972; Snow 1972), much more closely tied to the immediate context (Phillips 1973; Snow 1977a), and employs a number of special discourse features which serve to involve the child in interaction and to clarify and upgrade the child's own contributions (Cross 1977; Snow 1977b).

Given that these differences appear to constitute adaptations to the child's limited linguistic ability, they have often been seen as a way of shifting the burden of explanation away from the sort of innate language acquisition device proposed by Chomsky (1965). However, while it is certainly true that any adequate theory of language acquisition must specify the way in which children make use of the input they receive, it has become increasingly clear that the relationship between child-directed speech and the child's acquisition of language is much less straightforward than a generally facilitative model of CDS would lead us to assume.

The present chapter will review the current state of our knowledge about CDS with reference to the following questions: Why is CDS used? In what sense is it facilitative? Most importantly: what can it tell us about the language acquisition process? As has already been implied, the answers to these questions turn out to be rather complex. However, it will be argued that the study of CDS remains important for a number of reasons: firstly, it provides information about the language which the child is actually hearing; secondly, it allows us to investigate the way in which this input interacts with the child's own language-learning mechanisms; and, finally, such effects as can be demonstrated serve to constrain hypotheses about the way in which children manage to construct a language of their own from the input they receive.

## 2    Why is CDS used?

The first systematic studies of speech addressed to children were undertaken in response to the claim that, like the language used among adults, the language heard by children was grossly defective – full of false starts, grammatical errors, and misleading pauses – and, as such, represented a very poor sample of the language which the child must eventually learn (Chomsky 1965). These studies showed that speech addressed to children was largely clear, well formed, and semantically and syntactically simpler than speech addressed to adults and led some researchers (e.g. Levelt 1975; Moerk 1976, 1983) to argue that, in simplifying their speech, mothers were presenting their children with graded language lessons which could bear at least some of the burden of explanation for the child's remarkably swift progress in language learning. However, this view of CDS as a syntax-teaching language has proved untenable for a number of reasons.

Firstly, as Newport, Gleitman, and Gleitman (1977) point out, given the opacity of grammatical relations, the implicit assumption that mothers have some effective notion of how syntax might be taught serves only to replace a very strong claim about the child with a very strong claim about the mother, and could be argued to entail an even more radical form of nativism than that proposed by Chomsky. Secondly, it is not at all clear that CDS is well adapted for teaching syntax. For example, Newport *et al.* (1977) suggest that in teaching a new language one might reasonably proceed by presenting the learner with canonical sentences first and then gradually broadening the range of sentence constructions. However, not only are declaratives much less common in CDS than in speech to adults, but they actually increase in frequency as the child gets older while the range of sentence types narrows. This means that, in certain respects at least, CDS is actually rather complex in comparison with adult speech. Thirdly, several studies (e.g. Cross 1977; Newport 1977; Newport *et al.* 1977) have shown that the syntactic complexity of mothers' speech is not "fine-tuned" to the child's current level of productive language. This not only suggests that CDS may be shaped by factor other than the desire to teach language, but also raises the import question of what it might mean to characterize CDS as a simplified speech register. That is to say, although CDS clearly reflects some kind of adaptation to the child's limited communicative abilities, it is not immediately clear what it is about the child that the mother is responding to and thus whether this process of adaptation should make the task of syntax acquisition easier or not.

Newport et al. (1977) contrast the notion of CDS as a syntax-teaching language with a multi-factor functional model according to which CDS arises in response to a variety of different constraints imposed by the need to communicate with "a cognitively and linguistically naive child in the here-and-now" (Newport et al. 1977, p. 124). This view has a number of advantages over an explicitly pedagogical model. Firstly, it accords much more closely with our intuitions about the nature of interactions between mothers and young children in the real world. That is to say, although mothers can often be seen attempting to teach their children language – for example, training them in politeness forms (Moerk 1976) or eliciting labels (Ninio and Bruner 1978) – it seems unlikely that such attempts take precedence over more mundane matters like getting them to put on their shoes, clear away their toys, or eat up their greens. Secondly, it can account for the fact that many features of CDS are not restricted to the speech of adults to language-learning children, but also appear in speech to foreigners (Ferguson 1975; Wesche this volume), in speech to dogs (Hirsh-Pasek and Treiman 1982), in speech to three-month-old infants (Snow 1977b), and in the child-directed speech of children themselves (Shatz and Gelman 1973; Sachs and Devin 1976; Barton and Tomasello this volume). These similarities are much more readily explained as the by-product of attempts to communicate with a noncompetent speaker than they are as the result of a motivation to teach language. Thirdly, it takes account not only of the way adults talk to children, but also of the rather narrow set of semantic relations which are typically expressed in their speech. Indeed several researchers (e.g. Cross 1977; Snow 1977b) have argued that the apparent syntactic simplicity of CDS is best understood as an artifact of its semantic simplicity, with short MLUs reflecting a predominance of single-term utterances and increases in MLU reflecting increases in the amount of information being communicated. Finally, a multi-factor model fits much better with the data on fine-tuning. That is to say, although several studies have failed to find evidence of fine-tuning at either the syntactic or the semantic level (e.g. Newport 1977; Newport et al. 1977; Snow 1977a; Retherford, Schwartz, and Chapman 1981), the results of those studies which have found relationships between maternal speech characteristics and children's current language level have tended suggest, firstly, that such effects are stronger for word choice and content than they are for syntax (Chapman 1981) and, secondly, that mothers are more sensitive to the child's comprehension level than they are to her productive language level (Cross 1977; Clarke-Stewart, Vander-stoep, and Killian 1979).

These findings reinforce the claim that the syntactic simplicity of CDS may be best understood as an artifact of its semantic simplicity (Cross 1977; Snow 1977a). However, they also suggest that global relationships between children's current language level and the average complexity of their mothers' speech may reflect adult responsiveness to signs of non-comprehension on the part of the child. Indeed Bohannon and Marquis (1977) have shown that children do tend to signal communicative failures after long complex sentences and success after short simple utterances and that adults react to these signals in a very stereotypical fashion, simplifying after failures and using longer, more complex utterances after successes. Such an analysis provides us with a useful model of how relationships between children's comprehension level and the complexity of maternal speech may actually be mediated. However, it also serves to remind us that global measures such as maternal MLU necessarily mask utterance-by-utterance changes in the complexity of the speech which mothers address to their children. That is to say, even the most "finely tuned" mother is presenting her child with some utterances which are within her/his current level of comprehension together with others which may be well beyond it. This suggests that, from the child's point of view, the language which s/he hears is actually only very roughly tuned to her/his current linguistic abilities. On the other hand, as Chapman (1981) points out, it is probably unnecessary for children to receive input which is very finely tuned to their current language level since their limited comprehension abilities will in any case automatically filter out complexity beyond a certain level.

Bohannon and Marquis's (1977) feedback model clearly provides us with some important insights into the relationship between CDS and the child's current level of language ability. However, by emphasizing the role of the child in determining the nature of the language to which s/he is exposed, it also underlines the need to consider the interactive context in which CDS occurs if we are to understand exactly how it operates. Indeed Newport *et al.*'s (1977) multi-factor model of CDS is considerably strengthened by the insight that, as Snow (1986) puts it, "mothers do not talk at children, but with them" (Snow 1986, p. 80). Snow points out that a large proportion of maternal utterances are responses to child utterances, and almost all maternal utterances are directly preceded and followed by child utterances. That is to say, mothers are not simply communicating information to their children but are attempting to engage them conversation. Moreover, the fact that the roles of mother and child in such conversations are necessarily very unequal provides a means of accounting for several characteristics of CDS which are difficult to explain outside an interactive framework. Thus, not only can the semantic simplicity of CDS be seen to reflect the fact that much of the mother's speech is shaped by the child's ideas, interests, and cognitive and linguistic abilities (Snow 1977a), but also the high proportion of questions in maternal speech can be seen as a way of passing the conversational turn to the child, and the use of expansions and verbal reflective questions (i.e. questions which repeat or paraphrase the child's previous utterance) as attempts to clarify and upgrade the child's own limited contributions (Snow 1977b).

This kind of analysis is clearly a powerful means of integrating many aspects of CDS within a single framework. On the other hand, it also raises the question of the extent to which these characteristics of CDS are determined by communicative pressures, and the extent to which they reflect a particular culturally defined view of the language-learning child. In fact, as Snow (1986) herself points out, it has become increasingly clear in recent years that different cultures see language-learning children in rather different ways and that this can have quite far-reaching implications for the way in which caregivers interact with young children (e.g. Schieffelin 1979; Ochs 1982; Heath 1983; Lieven this volume). This suggests that interactive approaches to CDS need to be defined rather more broadly than would seem to be implied by a simple conversational model. Moreover, this may be necessary not only in order to understand crosscultural differences in CDS, but also in order to understand the full range of variation in the language to which children are exposed in our own culture (e.g. Lieven 1978a, 1978b).

There is now a general consensus that speech adjustments to young language learners are motivated by a desire to communicate rather than to teach language (Brown 1977; Newport et al. 1977; Shatz and Gelman 1977; Snow 1977a, 1977b). For example, Brown (1977) argues that such adjustments have two main functions: the facilitation of understanding and the direction and sustaining of attention. However, it is also worth noting that this kind of communicative model of CDS is open-ended enough to permit a range of possible interpretations. Indeed, whereas Snow (1977a, 1977b) tends to emphasize the conversational nature of CDS, Newport et al. (1977) stress its role in directing and controlling the child's behavior. Such differences of interpretation reflect the fact that both the nature of CDS and the level at which it is pitched are actually determined by a number of different factors operating at a variety of different levels. Thus, although it is certainly true that CDS can only be properly understood by putting it back into the context in which it occurs, it is also clear, as Durkin (1987) points out, that this "context" is itself multifaceted and extends far beyond the dyad itself, not only to the family in which the child is growing up, but also to the culture or subculture of which it forms a part.

## 3      Effects and non-effects of CDS

The relationship between CDS and language acquisition has most often been understood in terms of a question about the extent to which maternal speech modifications facilitate language development. This question has generally been addressed by examining the relationship between individual differences in the relative frequency with which mothers use particular speech modifications and variation in their children's subsequent language growth. However, the results generated within this kind of framework have been rather inconclusive (see Richards this volume).

One of the first studies to use this kind of correlational approach was Newport *et al.*'s (1977) study of fifteen mothers and their daughters aged 1;0 to 2;3 in two sessions spaced six months apart. Correlations were computed between characteristics of the mother's speech in session 1 and language growth in their children between sessions 1 and 2. However, since the children were of different ages and since neither variation in maternal speech nor variation in child growth rate is independent of differences in initial age and language level, both the children's age and initial level of advancement on the dependent language measure were partialled out of each of the correlations (see Richards this volume). Newport *et al.* (1977) found no relationship between the syntactic simplicity of maternal speech and any measure of language progress. Moreover, they argued that the pattern of relationships which did emerge suggested that the use of CDS was largely irrelevant to the process of language acquisition. That is to say, although several relationships were found between individual differences in maternal speech characteristics and growth in language-specific features, such as the number of auxiliaries per verb phrase and the number of inflections per noun phrase, no relationships were found between such differences and growth in what they saw as universal properties of language, including the number of noun phrases and the number of verb phrases per utterance. These findings were interpreted as consistent with a nativist model of language acquisition, according to which universal properties of language are innately specified and only the acquisition of language-specific properties depends on t' nature of the input. However, they were soon challenged by the resul* a further study by Furrow, Nelson, and Benedict (1979) in which rel* nips were found not only between maternal MLU and children's sub-sequent language growth, but also between certain features of maternal speech and precisely those aspects of children's language growth which Newport *et al.* had singled out as language universal.

The motivation for Furrow *et al.*'s (1979) study was a statistical and conceptual critique of Newport *et al.*'s (1977) work in which it was argued that, since CDS is likely to have qualitatively different effects on the child at different ages and linguistic levels, real effects were likely to have been obscured by equating age and language level statistically when those ages and levels were not in fact equal. Furrow *et al.*'s solution to this problem was to avoid the need for any partialling procedure by basing their analysis on a homogeneous group of seven children at the one-word stage of development who were all 18 months old at the first recording session. Moreover, although this approach has itself been criticized for ignoring potential diffferences between children at MLU = 1.0 (Barnes, Gut-freund, Satterly, and Wells 1983; Gleitman, Newport, and Gleitman 1984), the fact that it resulted in such a different pattern of results from the previous study appeared to suggest that Newport *et al.*'s original conclusions may have been rather premature. Indeed one of the most striking features of Furrow *et al.*'s data was the extent to which they appeared to show facilitative effects for precisely those aspects of mothers' speech which differ from speech to adults, and in the predicted directions. That is to say, although, as Furrow *et al.* themselves acknowl-edge, the fine detail of these results was not always easy to interpret, the overall pattern tended to suggest that the relative simplicity of mothers' speech did have facilitative effects on the child's subsequent language development.

It is clear that Newport *et al.*'s and Furrow *et al.*'s findings suggest two very different accounts of the relationship between CDS and language acquisition, and this conflict has led to a prolonged and at times rather acrimonious debate (Gleitman *et al.* 1984; Furrow and Nelson 1986). Firstly, Gleitman *et al.* (1984) argue that Furrow *et al.*'s (1979) finding of a positive relationship between simplicity of input and children's lan-guage growth must be spurious since it is theoretically inexplicable. This view is based on a particular kind of learnability model (i.e. Wexler and Culicover 1980) which assumes that the child uses the input to formulate hypotheses about the structure of the input language which are revised only when disconfirming evidence becomes available. According to such a model, the child is likely to formulate oversimple rules if the speech to which she is exposed does not display the full range of complexity in the adult language. However, although it derives some rather limited support from a significant positive correlation found in Gleitman *et al.*'s reanalysis of Newport *et al.*'s original data (between maternal MLU and children's auxiliary verb growth), this relationship was only present for their younger subgroup of children and has not been replicated in subsequent research. In contrast, Barnes *et al.* (1983) suggest that the most facilitative input to young language-learners is likely to be neither too simple nor too complex. That is to say, although it must obviously fall within the range of the child's current processing capacities, it must also be far enough in advance of the child's own linguistic abilities for her to be able to learn something from it. This view receives support from several more recent studies which have replicated Newport *et al.*'s original (1977) finding of no relationship between maternal MLU and children's language growth despite restricting their analyses to children within a much narrower range of linguistic abilities (Barnes *et al.* 1983; Hoff-Ginsberg 1985; Scarborough and Wyckoff 1986). On the other hand, as Bohannon and Hirsh-Pasek (1984) point out, this does not rule out the possibility that there may be a role for input simplicity in the very earliest stages of language development when children's processing capacities are particularly limited, and it is worth remembering that Furrow *et al.*'s sample as a whole is probably the least advanced group of children which has been studied in the literature to date.

A second area of disagreement between Newport *et al.* (1977) and Furrow *et al.* (1979) was Newport *et al.*'s attempt to distinguish between input-sensitive and input-insensitive aspects of language structure. Furrow *et al.* argued that their data provided no support for such a distinction and this conclusion appears to have been borne out by more recent studies in which further relationships have been found between maternal speech characteristics and what Newport *et al.* refer to as universal properties of language. These include Hoff-Ginsberg's (1985) finding of significant positive relationships between maternal expansions and self-repetitions and growth in the number of verb phrases per utterance in children's speech. In fact, whether or not such relationships emerge appears to depend, at least in part, on the extent to which such structures are developing during the period which is under investigation. Thus, Hoff-Ginsberg and Shatz (1982) argue that Furrow *et al.*'s finding of relationships between maternal speech characteristics and the development of language-universal structures may reflect the fact that it is precisely these basic structures which Furrow *et al.*'s subjects were likely to be in the process of acquiring. They go on to note that this suggestion is consistent with the fact that more correlations were found for verb phrase development than for noun phrase development, since children were particularly likely to be working on the former, whereas the development of the latter was likely to be already well under way. Moreover, such an interpretation is also consistent with the results of Hoff-Ginsberg's (1985) study in which relationships between maternal speech characteristics and children's growth in the number of verb phrases per utterance appeared to reflect the fact that growth in verb phrases was a particularly good indicator of children's general progress in language development over the period in question. This suggests that Newport *et al.*'s distinction between input-sensitive and input-insensitive aspects of language structure may have resulted from their failure to restrict their analysis to children at a particular language level. On the other hand, it is also worth noting that at least one study (i.e. Scarborough and Wyckoff 1986) has also failed to find any such relationships despite restricting their analysis to children within a very narrow range of linguistic abilities. Moreover, although this study has been criticized for using Newport *et al.*'s (1977) controversial split-half reliability procedure, it is clear that the pattern of results obtained is quite different from that found in either Newport *et al.*'s (1977) or Furrow *et al.*'s (1979) studies. That is to say, not only did Scarborough and Wyckoff (1986) fail to find evidence of any significant relationships between maternal speech characteristics and children's growth in noun and verb phrases per utterance, but they also failed to find any of the language-specific effects reported by Newport *et al.* (1977) themselves.

This lack of consistency between the results of different studies illustrates the degree of uncertainty which still exists in the literature regarding the effects of CDS. However, it has also had the effect of raising awareness of the theoretical and methodological problems involved in this kind of approach to the investigation of the relationship between CDS and language acquisition (see Richards this volume). Firstly, it has become increasingly clear that the potentially facilitative effects of CDS may not be as straightforward as is implied by a simple correlational model. For example, individual differences in some features of CDS may turn out to be largely unimportant once some minimum threshold is exceeded, and some aspects of CDS may bear a nonlinear relationship to children's language growth which would not show up within a correlational analysis (Bohannon and Hirsh-Pasek 1984).

Secondly, even when relationships are found, there are methodological problems which need to be overcome before any correlation can be viewed as a direct effect of input on the child's language growth. These include the need to control for relationships between mothers' speech and the child's initial age and language level (Newport *et al.* 1977; Furrow *et al.* 1979); the need to control for variation in subsequent growth which is due to differences in the child's initial status (Newport *et al.* 1977; Barnes *et al.* 1983; Richards 1991); and the need to rule out indirect effects such

as apparent effects of the mother which are actually mediated by relationships between different aspects of maternal speech at time 1 or by
relationships between the child's language at time 1 and the child's
language at time 2 (Schwartz and Camarata 1985; Yoder and Kaiser
1989). It seems likely that some of the correlations reported in both
Newport *et al.* and Furrow *et al.* may actually be mediated by relationships between different aspects of mothers' speech in the first recording
session.

This brings us to a third area of difficulty: namely, the problems of
interpretation which are created by a simple correlation approach to
maternal speech effects. That is to say, since few studies start out with
specific *a priori* predictions about the potential effects of CDS, there is a
great temptation to indulge in *post facto* theorizing once the results are in.
Moreover, the assumptions behind such theorizing are seldom made
explicit, with the result that relationships between those effects which are
found and more general theories of language development often remain
unclear. Furrow *et al.*'s (1979) results provide a good example of this
problem since, as Hoff-Ginsberg and Shatz (1982) point out, several of
the correlations are extremely difficult to interpret in any meaningful way.
It is clearly a mistake to argue, as Gleitman *et al.* (1984) do, that because
of this difficulty such findings are necessarily "garbage" and can be safely
ignored. However, it is equally true that, in the absence of some kind of
mechanism by which particular speech modifications can be argued to
support acquisition, the claim that CDS is somehow facilitative is theoretically rather vacuous (Pinker 1979).

This has led some researchers (e.g. Hardy-Brown 1983; Scarborough
and Wyckoff 1986) to argue that the number of significant relationships
reported in the literature, and the extent to which they have proved
replicable, may be no more than would be expected by chance. Although
this suggestion might be regarded as somewhat extreme, it is certainly true
that the level of agreement between studies has been far from impressive.
However, it is probably also the case that part of the problem has been the
implicit assumption that the relationship between CDS and language
acquisition should be the same regardless of the child's current level of
linguistic ability. Thus, Snow (1986) points out that some of the differences between Newport *et al.*'s and Furrow *et al.*'s findings may be readily
interpretable once one accepts that the tasks facing language-learning
children are rather different at different stages of development. For
example, if the task in the earliest stages is to learn a basic vocabulary and
effective ways of expressing simple semantic forms and pragmatic functions, then very simple CDS may well be the most facilitative. On the
other hand, as the child's task shifts to the acquisition of morphological

and syntactic rules, it will probably be the case that more complex input is required. This underlines the need to specify *a priori* which aspects of CDS are likely to support which kinds of learning procedure and at which points in development, and reinforces Gleitman *et al.*'s (1984) conclusion that the effects of CDS must be understood in terms of the language-learner's "own dispositions as to how to organise and exploit linguistic stimulation" (Gleitman *et al.* 1984, p. 76). However, it also implies that framing the relationship between CDS and language acquisition in terms of a general question about whether CDS is or is not facilitative is ultimately unlikely to be very productive. That is to say, since it is clear that children make use of the language which they hear in different ways at different points in development, the crucial question is not how facilitative CDS might turn out to be, but rather how it is actually used by the child at particular points in the acquisition process.

## 4      How is CDS used by the child?

One of the features of Newport *et al.*'s original (1977) study was their attempt to explain several of the relationships which they did find in terms of the kind of procedures involved in children's analysis of their input. Thus growth in children's auxiliary verb use was unrelated to the total frequency of auxiliaries in maternal speech but was strongly related to the frequency of *yes–no* questions in which the auxiliary is typically preposed (e.g. *Can you sing?* as opposed to *You can sing*). This was taken to reflect the increased perceptual salience of sentence-initial auxiliaries to the child, who was seen as having a processing bias in favor of attending to the beginnings of utterances.

Similarly, a significant positive correlation was found between children's growth in the use of noun inflections and the frequency of deictic utterances in mothers' speech, and a significant negative correlation between the same measure and mothers' use of positive imperatives. These were taken to reflect the influence on syntactic growth of the child's use of a referent-matching strategy. That is to say, it was assumed that children were trying to find the referents of words in input strings and that this was easier to do for deictic utterances which make the relationship between words and referents particularly explicit and much harder to do for positive imperatives which, it was argued, "rarely map onto the non-linguistic context" (Newport *et al.* 1977, pp. 140–1).

Finally, a significant positive correlation was found between children's growth in auxiliary verb use and the frequency with which mothers expanded their children's utterances. This was taken to reflect a special case of referent matching in which the mother "produces a construction when the child's attention is fixed on the notion that construction refers to in the language" (Newport *et al.* 1977, p. 141).

Of course Newport *et al.*'s explanations of these relationships are necessarily *post hoc*. However, in attempting to use relationships between CDS and children's language growth as a means of looking at the way in which children make use of the input which they are receiving, they not only suggested a potentially more illuminating approach to the study of maternal speech effects, but also provided a set of hypotheses which could be investigated in subsequent research. Moreover, further research has added to Newport *et al.*'s findings in a number of ways. Thus several studies have found input effects on auxiliary development (e.g. Furrow *et al.* 1979; Barnes *et al.* 1983; Hoff-Ginsberg 1985), though the frequency of *yes–no* questions in mothers' speech has not always been the crucial variable. Others have found positive relationships consistent with the notion of a referent-matching strategy. For example, Furrow *et al.* (1979) found positive effects of the frequency with which mothers used nouns as opposed to pronouns in their speech, though the fact that this was correlated with children's growth in verb phrases per utterance makes it difficult to interpret. Finally, a number of studies have found positive effects for mothers' use of expansions (Nelson, Carskaddon, and Bonvillian 1973; Nelson 1977a; Cross 1978), though there is also evidence that the mother's use of extensions (i.e. utterances which incorporate the child's topic, but add new information) may be equally facilitative (Cross 1978; Barnes *et al.* 1983).

This brings us to a basic problem with this kind of approach to the question of maternal speech effects: namely, that the kind of relationships reported can often be explained in a variety of different ways. Thus, whereas it is certainly possible that positive imperatives may present problems for children using a referent-matching strategy, Hoff-Ginsberg and Shatz (1982) point out that many such imperatives (e.g. *Eat your dinner* or *Pick up your toys*) contain nouns which map quite well onto visible referents. On the other hand, many others (e.g. *Come over here* or *Get down from there*) contain no nouns at all. It is therefore unclear to what extent this relationship is a result of difficulties in referent matching and to what extent it is a result of the number of noun inflections actually heard by the child. Alternatively it may reflect other more general relationships between maternal speech style and children's language growth. For example, McDonald and Pien (1982) reported negative relationships between mothers' use of directives and mothers' use of conversation-eliciting devices such as real questions (information-seeking questions to which the speaker does not have the answer), report questions (those which comment upon the world and provide new information), and verbal reflective questions (see above). It may therefore be that negative relationships between maternal imperative use and children's language growth simply reflect differences in the extent to which mothers are adopting a "conversation-eliciting" style of interaction.

Similar problems arise with respect to the positive effects of maternal expansions. That is to say, since the semantic content of maternal expansions is generally the same as that of the child's previous utterance, it is possible that this effect may be a further result of ease of referent matching. Indeed, this interpretation derives some support from the fact that several studies have found that the most powerful predictor of children's linguistic ability is the proportion of maternal utterances which are semantically related to preceding child utterances (e.g. Cross 1978; Wells and Robinson 1982; Barnes *et al.* 1983). On the other hand, it is also possible that expansions might illustrate syntax for the child by filling in elements omitted in the child's previous utterance or "by dropping and adding structurally cohesive groups of words" (Hoff-Ginsberg and Shatz 1982, p. 10). Indeed there is some evidence that children may be able to make use of such information not only in the form of expansions of their own previous utterances, but also in the form of two contiguous utterances spoken by the mother. For example, Hoff-Ginsberg (1985) found relationships between certain categories of self-repetitions and expansions in maternal speech and child growth in verb phrases per utterance which suggested that children were sensitive to pairs of utterances in which the second utterance broke the first at a major constituent boundary. This implies that the positive effects of expansions may not only be due to ease of referent matching but may also reflect the fact that children are able to make use of structural information in the input in order to advance their linguistic system.

Finally, Hoff-Ginsberg and Shatz (1982) point out that the relationship between maternal use of *yes–no* questions and children's growth in auxiliary verb use is also open to a variety of different interpretations. Thus it may be that children have a processing bias in favor of attending to the beginnings of utterances. However, it is also possible that sentence-initial auxiliaries are simply more easily heard by the child because they are less likely to be contracted and more likely to be stressed. Compare, for example *Have you been sleeping?* with *You've been sleeping* or *What've you been doing?* In a later paper, Gleitman *et al.* (1984) appear to modify their original proposal in order to combine these two ideas in what has come to be known as the "Auxiliary Clarification Hypothesis" (Richards 1990a). However, even this revised model of the positive effects of *yes–no* questions does not rule out the possibility of other alternative explanations. For example, it is also possible that examples of preposed auxiliaries are important as data for distributional analysis, serving to illustrate either auxiliary movement or the fact that auxiliaries participate in subject–verb inversion. According to such a view, what is important is not the frequency of *yes–no* questions *per se* in the child's input, but rather the fact that, in combination with other forms, such as declaratives and *wh*-questions, they provide the child with information about how the auxiliary participates in a range of different sentence constructions. This "Variable Position Hypothesis" (Shatz, Hoff-Ginsberg, and MacIver 1989) is consistent with Hoff-Ginsberg's (1985) finding of a relationship between auxiliary growth and the frequency of *wh*-questions in mothers' speech. However, it is not supported by the results of Shatz *et al.*'s (1989) own experimental study, in which it was found that, in terms of their auxiliary growth, children benefited significantly more from input in the form of pairs of *yes–no* questions than they did from input in the form of mixed pairs of *yes–no* questions and declaratives, though neither group was significantly different from a control group who participated in play sessions in which the input was not manipulated.

A third possibility is that the positive effect of *yes–no* questions may reflect the way in which questions operate in conversation. That is to say, questions may be more salient to the child because they require an answer, or *yes–no* questions may have a specific influence on the kind of language which the child practices because, in contrast to other types of questions, they provide the child with material from which to formulate a response. Compare, for example, the lexical and syntactic overlap in the following exchanges taken from Hoff-Ginsberg and Shatz (1982): *Can you throw the ball? – Yes, I can*, and *What's in here? – A ball*.

Finally, the frequent use of questions may be associated with a particular kind of conversation-eliciting speech style which is conducive to rapid language learning for a variety of different reasons. For example, Hoff-Ginsberg (1986) found relationships between auxiliary growth and mothers' use of real questions and verbal reflective questions, which have both been implicated as features of a conversation-eliciting style of interaction (McDonald and Pien 1982). According to this view there may be no specific relationship between *yes–no* questions and growth in children's auxiliary verb use, but the former might simply reflect more general differences in maternal style and the latter represent a particularly good measure of children's language progress over the period under investigation (Richards 1990a).

As Hoff-Ginsberg and Shatz (1982) point out, these explanations are not necessarily mutually exclusive. Indeed, in a recent reanalysis, Hoff-Ginsberg (1990) found evidence that the effects reported in her previous work (Hoff-Ginsberg 1985, 1986) could be understood both in terms of the generally facilitative nature of a conversation-eliciting style and in terms of specific relationships between beneficial utterance types and the particular aspect of syntax predicted by their use. On the other hand, if maternal speech effects are to prove useful for inferring the kind of procedures which children bring to the analysis of their input, it would seem necessary to identify specific dependencies between input and acquisition rather than rely on global characterizations of maternal style. That is to say, on the one hand, general relationships between mothers' interactional behavior and children's language growth would appear to be rather uninformative as regards possible mechanisms of acquisition, whereas, on the other, even such general relationships may well be mediated by differences in the structure of the input to which different interactional styles actually give rise. This suggests the need, firstly, to look more closely both at those features of the input which have been found to predict children's linguistic growth and at those aspects of language growth which they have been found to predict; and, secondly, to derive specific testable hypotheses which are capable of differentiating between alternative explanations of these relationships. This is an approach adopted by two recent studies of maternal speech effects, namely Farrar's (1990) study of the relationship between maternal discourse features and children's early morphological development and Richards' work on the relationship between *yes–no* questions and children's auxiliary and copula verb growth (Richards 1990a, 1990b; Richards and Robinson 1993).

Farrar (1990) takes as his starting point the uncertainty which exists in the literature as to the potentially facilitative effects of maternal discourse features on the child's subsequent language growth. However, rather than looking for generally facilitative effects, he examines the relationship between the different ways in which mothers model grammatical morphemes and their children's subsequent acquisition of those same morphems over a six-month period. This approach has two advantages over previous approaches to this issue: firstly, it attempts to draw specific links between maternal discourse adjustments and the particular grammatical morphemes which are modeled within them; and secondly, it attempts to determine which aspects of maternal discourse adjustments are actually responsible for their facilitative effects. Thus Farrar (1990) identifies four properties of recasts which could conceivably play a facilitative role in the child's morphological development. These include simply following the child's utterance, maintaining the semantic topic of the child's utterance, expanding the child's utterance while using some of the child's own words, and reformulating the child's utterance by adding to or correcting a particular noun or verb phrase. He then constructs four discourse models in which these properties systematically vary and looks at the relationship between these models and children's acquisition of particular grammatical morphemes.

Farrar's results suggest not only that specific relationships do exist between the acquisition of particular grammatical morphemes and their presence in certain kinds of maternal utterances, but also that the refor- mulation component of recasts may have a unique role to play in the acquisition of specific grammatical morphemes. On the other hand, the fact that such relationships were only found for plural and present progressive markers suggests that the effects of recasts are selective and that they should not be seen as all-purpose facilitators of language acquisition. Indeed Farrar (1990) suggests that recasts may be most beneficial to the child in allowing her to identify and extract grammatical morphemes as meaningful units (see also Peters 1983). However, prior to the time that children are cognitively ready to extract a morpheme, or once they have successfully extracted it, recasts may not play a unique role in acquisition. This may well account for inconsistencies in the results of previous research in which some studies have reported strong facilita- tive effects for expansions and recasts (e.g. Newport *et al.* 1977; Howe 1980; Wells 1980) whereas others have found no such relationships (e.g. Hoff-Ginsberg 1985; Scarborough and Wyckoff 1986). Whatever the case, it seems clear that by identifying specific relationships between morpheme acquisition and maternal discourse adjustments this study shows how the investigation of relationships between maternal speech adjustments and differences in children's language growth can provide information about the way in which children are using the input which they are receiving in the acquisition of particular linguistic forms at particular points in development.

A second example of this kind of approach to maternal speech effects is Richards' work on the relationship between *yes–no* questions and aux- iliary and copula verb growth (Richards 1990a, 1990b; Richards and Robinson 1993). Richards points out that, despite its currency as an explanation of the positive effects of *yes–no* questions, the "Auxiliary Clarification Hypothesis" is problematic for a number of reasons. Firstly, as we have already seen, it is not the only possible explanation of the relationships found. Secondly, as Fletcher (1985) has shown, sentence- initial auxiliaries, even in utterances addressed to children, vary consider- ably in degree of phonological reduction and stress and therefore do not actually clarify the auxiliary to anything like the extent predicted by the "Auxiliary Clarification Hypothesis." Thirdly, although several studies have found positive relationships between *yes–no* questions and auxiliary verb growth (e.g. Furrow *et al.* 1979; Barnes *et al.* 1983; Hoff-Ginsberg

1985), others have failed to find any such relationships (e.g. Hoff-Ginsberg 1986; Scarborough and Wyckoff 1986). Moreover, even those relationships which have been reported have tended to be between auxiliary growth and "intonation only" rather than inverted *yes–no* questions. This means that none of them actually supports the "Clarification Hypothesis."

These observations appear to cast serious doubt on the validity of the "Auxiliary Clarification Hypothesis." However, the picture is complicated by methodological differences between studies which often make comparison and interpretation difficult. These include differences in the age and language level of the children concerned, differences in the time intervals between the first and subsequent recordings, and differences in the way auxiliaries are actually classified. In fact, when Richards (1990a) reanalyzed Barnes *et al.*'s (1983) data using slightly different coding procedures, he found that their original findings were actually reversed. That is to say, although, as in Fletcher's (1985) study, only a minority of the fronted auxiliaries heard by the children were both stressed and uncontracted, it was now inverted rather than "intonation only" *yes–no* questions which were found to predict children's auxiliary verb growth. This suggested that, whether or not phonological clarification played a role, the beneficial effects of *yes–no* questions were associated with the occurrence of the auxiliary in sentence-initial position.

Richards (1990b) and Richards and Robinson (1993) followed up this reanalysis of Barnes *et al.*'s data with a further study of the effects of *yes–no* questions on auxiliary and copula verb growth in thirty-three children selected for their similar ages and MLUs at time 1. This study aimed not only to eliminate some of the methodological problems associated with Barnes *et al.*'s original study, but also to evaluate the relative strengths of three alternative explanations of the positive effects of *yes–no* questions at four different points in development. Thus the "Clarification Hypothesis" was addressed by testing for specific effects of auxiliary or copula inversions on auxiliary or copula verb growth; the "Variable Position Hypothesis" (Shatz *et al.* 1989) was addressed by examining the contribution of auxiliaries or copulas in tag questions, which illustrate both medial position and inversion (e.g. *He can do it, can't he?*); and the "Conversation-Eliciting Hypothesis" by correlating all auxiliary input measures with all child copula measures and *vice versa* and testing for the specificity of relationships between copulas and auxiliaries in the input and the child's copula and auxiliary verb growth.

Richards' results tend not only to support some form of the "Clarification Hypothesis" over both the "Variable Position Hypothesis" and the "Conversation-Eliciting Hypothesis," but also suggest that it can be extended to a consideration of children's copula verb growth. That is to say, significant relationships were found between auxiliary development and the frequency of auxiliary inversions, and between copula development and the frequency of copula inversions, whereas relationships were less consistent between the frequency of either auxiliary or copula tag questions and children's copula and auxiliary verb growth. This suggests that the positive effects of *yes–no* questions are more consistent with the notion of the salience of sentence-initial position than with their potential role in illustrating auxiliary inversion. Moreover, there was also specificity in all correlations but one in the pattern of relationships between copulas and auxiliaries in the input and the child's copula and auxiliary verb growth. That is to say, although significant relationships were found between copula inversions and children's auxiliary verb growth, no relationships were found between children's copula gains and any of the auxiliary measures in the input. This suggests that the positive effects of *yes–no* questions cannot be explained in terms of a more general "Conversation-Eliciting Hypothesis." Indeed, Richards argues that even the relationship between copula inversions and auxiliary growth may not so much cast doubt on the specificity of input relationships as raise questions about the degree of dependence between copula and auxiliary verb learning at this stage of development. That is to say, these effects may reflect the fact that children are operating with a single composite category in which copula and auxiliary BE forms are not differentiated. Of course such a suggestion is necessarily rather speculative. However, by raising the question of the kind of categories which underlie the child's auxiliary growth, it does underline the fact that maternal speech effects can only be properly understood if we have a relatively good idea of what the child is actually learning at any given point in development. This suggests the need to integrate the study of maternal speech effects with a more fine-grained analysis of the way in which particular aspects of the child's language system are changing over the period which is under investigation.

To summarize, both Farrar's (1990) and Richards' studies (Richards 1990a, 1990b; Richards and Robinson 1993) represent good examples of how the investigation of maternal speech effects can provide important insights into the way in which children make use of the language which they are actually hearing. However, they also illustrate the need for a much more sophisticated approach to the question of the relationship between CDS and language acquisition. That is to say, if such speech effects are to be properly understood, it is necessary not only to look beyond general frequency effects towards a more detailed analysis of the relationship between what the child is hearing and what the child is actually saying, but also to give more careful consideration to the question of precisely how the child's system is changing over the period under investigation. This suggests that there is a need to move beyond quantitative measures such as rate of language development towards a more qualitative analysis of the nature of the child's early language. It also brings us to a final area of research: namely, the investigation of relationships between differences in maternal speech and stylistic differences in children's early language development.

## 5     CDS and stylistic differences in early language development

The most commonly used dimension of stylistic variation in children's early language development is Nelson's (1973) referential–expressive distinction. Attempts to relate such variation to differences in maternal speech style date back to Nelson's (1973) original study, where a significant negative relationship was found between maternal direction and referential vocabulary at fifty words. This finding has been replicated in subsequent research (Della Corte, Benedict, and Klein 1983), and significant positive relationships have also been found between children's referential style and maternal object-referencing (Klein 1980; Furrow and Nelson 1984); referential style and maternal common noun usage (Klein 1980; Hampson 1989); and referential style and maternal description of the immediate environment (Della Corte *et al.* 1983; Hampson 1989). However, while it seems increasingly likely that important links can be drawn between differences in maternal behavior and stylistic variation in early language development, investigators have been slow to appreciate the potential of research in this area for inferring the kind of procedures which children bring to the analysis of their input.

One reason for this is that, as in the literature on CDS and effects on children's rate of language development, relationships can often be explained in a variety of ways. Thus, K. Nelson (1981), in her review of the individual differences literature, distinguishes between four sets of factors which might account for strategy differences in early language development. These are differences in individual makeup, differences in type of input, differences in the type of speech expected by the environment, and differences in children's perception of speech function. Although these sets of factors are obviously theoretically distinct, they are clearly very difficult to disentangle in practice. For example, differences in individual make-up are likely to influence the environment within which children learn to talk, while differences in maternal style would seem capable of exerting effects not only directly through input differences, but also indirectly through differences in the type of interaction in which mothers tend to engage their children. Moreover, although some attempt has been made to distinguish between differences which are related to the language-learning environment and differences which are related to the child's own predispositions (e.g. Goldfield 1987; Hampson 1989), the problem of how environmental effects are actually mediated has been largely ignored. Thus it is unclear, for example, whether the relationship between referentiality and maternal description of the immediate environment is a result of different patterns of dyadic interaction over objects, of differences in the extent to which children are being provided with models of the referential functions of language, or simply of differences in the form or content of descriptive as opposed to other kinds of speech. This suggests the need to develop testable hypotheses capable of differentiating between these alternative explanations. However, this is something which previous research has, by and large, failed to do.

A second problem has been the degree of confusion which exists about the nature of the differences which are in need of explanation. It goes without saying that any attempt to explain or predict variation in children's language will depend crucially on the way the investigator chooses to characterize such variation. However, there are several problems with the way stylistic differences have been defined in the literature, which inevitably cause problems for the investigation of possible relationships between maternal and child language styles. Perhaps the most important of these is the question of whether such differences should be viewed in formal or functional terms. Although often ignored or glossed over in the literature, this issue has important implications for the investigation of the relationship between strategy differences and differences in maternal language style. That is to say, whereas the view derived from Nelson (1973) that differences between children are essentially functional in nature has tended to lead researchers to focus on the pragmatics of maternal speech (e.g. K. Nelson 1973, 1981; Della Corte *et al.* 1983), a more form-based view of the nature of vocabulary differences would tend to imply the need for a rather different level of analysis.

It has often been argued in the literature (e.g. McShane 1980) that Nelson's original claim that she had classified vocabulary in terms of its functional, as opposed to its formal, properties is difficult to sustain. Indeed, in a recent study, Pine (1992a) found that individual differences in vocabulary composition at fifty words were not related to the pragmatics of children's spontaneous speech. Moreover, Lieven, Pine, and Dresner-Barnes (1992) have shown that differences in vocabulary composition may best be captured by a "common-noun/frozen-phrase" distinction which operates at a relatively formal level of description. This suggests that variation in lexical style should not be seen in terms of differences in the way language is used, but rather in terms of variation in the type of units which children are extracting from their input (Peters 1983), and implies that hypotheses about the nature of maternal speech effects should focus not so much on global differences in interactional style itself, as on the implications of different modes of interaction for the nature of the input which any given child is receiving. For example, Tomasello and Todd (1983) have argued that by focusing specifically on patterns of attentional regulation in mother–infant dyads, variation in early vocabulary development can be seen as a product of the interaction between differences in the structure of the input and processing mechanisms which are common to all children. That is to say, their analysis of episodes of joint attention appears to indicate that maternal directiveness has an effect not so much on the child's overall assessment of the function of language, as K. Nelson (1981) has argued, but rather on the learning conditions surrounding the acquisition of particular vocabulary items.

This kind of approach has the advantage not only of avoiding making unwarranted assumptions about form–function correspondences in children's "one-word" speech, but also of addressing the issue of underlying mechanisms much more directly than has been done hitherto. However, research on the "Attentional Regulation Hypothesis" (Tomasello and Todd 1983; Tomasello and Farrar 1986; Tomasello, Mannle, and Kruger 1986; Akhtar, Dunham, and Dunham 1991) illustrates a further problem with the way variation in lexical style has been defined in the literature: namely, the tendency to measure referentiality in such a way as to confound genuine stylistic differences in vocabulary composition with differences related to increases in referential vocabulary which occur in all children as a function of increases in vocabulary size. Thus, whereas Nelson's original referential vocabulary measure was based on a fixed number of vocabulary items (i.e. fifty words) and therefore captured differences between children at roughly equivalent levels of development, many subsequent studies have used cross-sectional measures based on vocabulary totals which vary quite substantially across children (e.g. Tomasello and Todd 1983; Tomasello and Farrar 1986; Bates, Bretherton, and Snyder 1988; Hampson 1989; Akhtar et al. 1991). The effect of this has been to confuse relationships between maternal speech characteristics and stylistic variation with relationships between maternal speech characteristics and children's general progress in language development. That is to say, since Pine and Lieven (1990) have shown that age-defined cross-sectional measures confound strategy differences with differences in children's rate of language acquisition, it is unclear to what extent the kind of speech effects demonstrated relate to stylistic differences in children's speech and to what extent they simply reflect relationships with differences in children's overall rate of vocabulary development.

The above greatly diminishes the utility of Nelson's original distinction as a dependent variable in the investigation of maternal speech effects since it has the effect of creating an evaluative attitude, according to which "nonreferential" children are seen as exhibiting a deficient or inferior language style, and their mothers as providing unhelpful or impoverished input. However, as Pine and Lieven (1990) have pointed out, not only did Nelson herself find no differences in the age at which her referential and expressive groups of children reached fifty words, but the significant correlations between referentiality and vocabulary size which have been reported since (e.g. Bates, Bretherton, and Snyder 1988; Hampson 1989) are almost certainly a direct result of the kind of age-defined cross-sectional measures which have been used in subsequent research. This would seem to suggest the need for a new approach to the question of the relationship between maternal speech and individual differences in early language development in which not only is an attempt made to document specific relationships between differences in children's language and differences in the structure of the input which they are receiving, but such relationships can be viewed as reflecting genuine stylistic differences between children as opposed to differences in the speed with which different children are acquiring language. Such an approach would not only allow researchers to move away from quantitative measures such as rate of language development, but would also permit a more detailed analysis of the relationship between particular features of maternal speech and the way in which different children's language is developing.

To summarize, consistent relationships have been found between differences in CDS and stylistic differences in children's early language, particularly negative relationships between referentiality and maternal directiveness, and positive relationships between referentiality and maternal description. These relationships are still far from being properly understood. However, if they are to throw light on the kind of procedures which different children bring to the analysis of their input, there is a need, firstly, to define stylistic variation much more carefully than has been done hitherto, secondly, to differentiate relationships between CDS and stylistic differences from more general effects on children's rate of language development, and, finally, to derive testable hypotheses capable of distinguishing between the many alternative explanations of the relationships which have been found.

## Conclusion

his chapter has attempted to show how current research on the relationship between CDS and language acquisition has shifted away from an
emphasis on demonstrating facilitative effects for their own sake towards
an attempt to use maternal speech effects as a way of inferring the kind of
procedures which children bring to the analysis of their input. This shift
reflects the realization, firstly, that, since the nature of CDS is determined
at a variety of different levels, its relationship to the process of language
acquisition is likely to be complex rather than simple, and, secondly, that
continuing to see this relationship in terms of a question about how
facilitative CDS might turn out to be is ultimately unlikely to be very
productive. On the other hand, it is also clear that the speech which
children hear does have implications for the way in which they acquire
language. Indeed certain relationships have been found which have been
replicated with sufficient regularity for us to be confident that they do
represent real phenomena. This suggests that the challenge for future
research is, firstly, to provide a more detailed account of these effects in
terms of specific relationships between particular features of the input and
the acquisition of particular aspects of the language system, and,
secondly, to specify how such relationships are actually mediated and
hence what implications they might have for more general theories of
language development.

# 2    The changing role of negative evidence in theories of language development

*Jeffrey L. Sokolov and Catherine E. Snow*

## 1    Historical origins

The current stage in thinking about the role of negative evidence in language development is the product of many twists and turns in the history of this topic. Prior to the Chomskian revolution in linguistics and the simultaneous cognitive revolution in psychology, language acquisition was explained by behaviorist models within which feedback (or reinforcement) was the only mechanism available to effect learning (Skinner 1957; Staats 1974). The influence of these behaviorist views even on current thinking about feedback emerges in assumptions that feedback has its effect through reinforcement rather than through information value.

An alternative behaviorist view held that the primary mechanism available to child language learners was imitation (see social learning theorists such as Whitehurst and Vasta 1975; Bandura 1977), which could be shaped in the direction of adult-like forms using feedback. Thus, environmental language was assumed to have two roles: firstly, in modeling the imitations, and secondly, as a reaction to imitative attempts.

## 2    The paving of the nativist road

Chomsky's earliest theory of language acquisition (1965), which was intertwined with his theory of transformational grammar, argued that transformations were structure-dependent. In other words, the applicability of a transformation depended on the structure surrounding the to-be-transformed element(s). Chomsky also argued that these transformations were specific to language (but see Simon [1962] for a discussion of the possible generality of transformations to complex hierarchical structures). Crucially, the structure dependence of transformational rules is not clearly revealed in the input that children receive from their parents. Since children are not able to learn about structure dependency from the input they receive, Chomsky argued that they must possess an innate language acquisition capacity; otherwise it would be impossible to account for the fact that children do, in fact, learn grammar. Although Chomsky did not in that formulation specify exactly what he thought was innate, he suggested that the first place to look was universal grammar. These views are concisely discussed in the following quote:

the discussion of language acquisition in previous sections was rationalistic in its assumption that various formal and substantive universals are intrinsic properties of the language-acquisition system, these providing a schema that is applied to data and that determines in a highly restricted way the general form and, in part, even the substantive features of the grammar that may emerge upon presentation of appropriate data. (Chomsky 1965, p. 53)

This quote prompts a question about the nature of "appropriate data." Chomsky regarded the language of adults as deformed and degenerate, thus clearly not appropriate data. He described linguistic input as including hesitations, self-corrections, and ill-formed utterances, and as failing to display the structure of sentences at the abstract level.

This view constituted a challenge to early child language researchers. Initial interest in the characteristics of maternal speech arose in direct response to these rather extreme and unsubstantiated claims that Chomsky incorporated into his argument for an innate Language Acquisition Device (LAD). His boldness in making claims that speech to young children was error-ridden, ungrammatical, highly complex, and a very poor database from which to deduce linguistic structure aroused several psychologists to begin more or less simultaneously collecting samples of maternal speech and analyzing their characteristics (Remick 1971; Broen 1972; Snow 1972). Of course, it was discovered that the maternal speech samples were in general quite simple, repetitive, grammatical, and adjusted semantically to the child's comprehension level and interests (see also Cross 1977, 1978). Subsequent nativist responses to these reports argued that the very simplicity of maternal speech constituted a barrier to language acquisition: the simple speech would justify too simple hypotheses about the nature of language, and thus lead children along a garden path from which only corrective feedback could rescue them (Wexler and Culicover 1980).

At around the same time, Gold (1967) demonstrated mathematically that only finite-state or regular languages are learnable from Text Presentation (i.e. positive data or "good models") alone. In order to learn the class of languages that include natural languages, Gold argued that the learner would need Informant Presentation (i.e. both positive and negative data, information that some structures are wrong as well as good models). Gold's proof highlights the learnability tradeoffs that exist between the form of the input that children may receive and the constraints that may exist on the types of allowable grammars. Simply stated, even if children do not receive negative data, learnability can be demonstrated by constraining the range of grammars that they hypothesize during learning.

The Gold analysis posed a clear and testable question: do children receive negative evidence, for example, information that a particular utterance contains an error? If they do not, then theories of language acquisition will have to propose constraints on the types of grammars that child language learners hypothesize; to the extent that they do receive negative evidence, then those constraints can become less limiting and less severe. In 1970, Brown and Hanlon examined transcripts of mother–child interaction to determine if mothers provided explicit feedback to their children based on the grammaticality of their speech. Candidates for positive feedback were statements such as *Well done* or *That's right* following grammatical utterances and *No* or *That's not right* following ungrammatical ones. They discovered that parents did not provide children with explicit feedback that was contingent upon the grammaticality of their speech. Instead, the feedback that parents provided to their children was contingent on the truth value of the child's speech. For example, when the child Adam produced *Draw a boot paper*, his mother responded positively to the truth value of the utterance with *That's right. Draw a boot on the paper* while seemingly ignoring its ungrammaticality.

It was thus generally accepted that:

1 language is too complex and abstract to be learned from conversational interaction;
2 non-finite-state languages are not learnable without negative evidence;
3 children do not receive explicit negative feedback from their parents.

These findings paved the road for the nativist revolution in child language research. The nativists could argue that since natural languages are not finite-state automata and since the input that children receive is not sufficient for language to be learnable, certain aspects of language must be innate.

### 3     Parallel roads: nativist and empiricist accounts

With no evidence for negative evidence (and coincidentally no evidence concerning the efficacy of any feature of the input language), nativist theorists pursued the development of competence models with relatively few constraints from data about how children talk and essentially no constraints from data about how adults talk to or respond to children. The linguistic structures of greatest interest to nativist theorists were structures of relatively low frequency in children's spontaneous speech:

complex clauses, anaphors, reflexives, and so on. Acquisition of such structures was primarily addressed through comprehension studies, and then typically only with children over three years of age. It is worth noting that, more recently, some studies have used spontaneous speech to analyze phenomena like pro-drop (Hyams 1987), verb argument structures (Pinker 1989), and the emergence of functional categories (Radford 1990).

Competence models that emerged during this period of study postulated a series of constraints on possible grammars. These constraints were presumed to be innate and specific to the problem of language acquisition, rather than being general constraints on learning (Wexler and Culicover 1980). Two early constraints include the Binary Principle and the Freezing Principle. The Binary Principle prevents transformations from analyzing more than one level down from that reached in the cycle, while the Freezing Principle prevents transformations from analyzing nodes dominated by frozen nodes, the latter being nodes that immediately dominate configurations which could not have arisen as the result of a base rule. In addition, the Subset Principle (Berwick 1985) has been proposed. It states that the learner should choose the simpler grammar when input is ambiguous between a simple grammar and a more complex one. The Uniqueness Principle (Pinker 1984) informs the learner that the same form cannot be used for more than one meaning. This eases learning by constraining the surface structures onto which a given deep structure can map. Within the parameter-setting framework, several researchers have argued that because children do not receive negative evidence from the environment, they must set the initial parameters so that positive evidence alone will lead them to the correct grammar (Hyams 1987; Wexler and Manzini 1987). For example, Wexler and Manzini have argued that children must set the initial binding parameter for reflexives (e.g. *himself*) to allow only local binding (i.e. within the governing category), because children could not retreat from a grammar with both local and global binding in the absence of negative evidence.

Meanwhile, empirically oriented researchers were traveling a parallel road, pursuing questions about early language acquisition during the period before syntax was a major problem. For example, Bruner (1975) argued that the study of communicative precursors to formal language was important and quite independent of the nature–nurture controversy. Dore (1974), Bates (1976), and Ninio and Bruner (1978) responded by characterizing the communicative intents of prelinguistic children. In addition, researchers who were examining transcripts of spontaneous speech, typically from children interacting with their parents, were struck by the wealth of helpful responses parents give – expansions, extensions, corrections, clarification questions, and repetitions. Considerable effort was expended in descriptive work, on child language and on the input to children, without much attention until the 1980s to specific links between the input and the speed or course of acquisition.

Work relating the nature of the input to the rate of acquisition generated considerable controversy. While some of the predicted relationships were confirmed (Furrow, Nelson, and Benedict 1979), others attacked the analyses and failed to replicate the results (Gleitman, Newport, and Gleitman 1984; see also Furrow and Nelson 1986 for a response). The internal complexities of such analyses are now obvious (see Richards this volume): for example, since we do not expect that a feature of maternal speech that is facilitative at one stage will still be helpful some time later, the child's developmental state is crucial but has often been ignored in attempts to find connections (Bohannon and Hirsh-Pasek 1984); several maternal mechanisms may have the same effect, so absence or low frequency of one of these mechanisms may not reveal itself in outcome data; and so on. However, experimental studies in which features hypothesized to be helpful were actually shown to promote syntactic acquisition (Nelson, Carskaddon, and Bonvillian 1973; Nelson 1977a; Baker and Nelson 1984; Nelson, Denninger, Bonvillian, Kaplan, and Baker 1984) provided incontrovertible evidence in support of the value of appropriate input. Aspects of the input that were the most powerful in the training experiments were recasts: responses to child utterances that provided corrected or alternative versions, demonstrating clearly that feedback can be used by children.

Thus, child language research in the mid 1980s could be characterized as following a number of parallel pathways, with little contact among researchers who were pursuing their own lines of work – as if the various researchers were studying quite different phenomena. Work on maternal speech to children was trying to use characteristics of excellent *versus* average language-learning environments in order to understand the nature of the learning mechanisms available to children. Such work was also seen as relevant to the design of therapy for language-delayed children and of optimal preschool classrooms. A basic assumption of this work was that children's social and communicative skills were more precocious than their language skills, and could thus serve as a facilitative source for language development. Negative evidence in this view could derive from frustration of the child's communicative attempts, since any failure to achieve one's intended communicative end constitutes information that one's utterance was flawed. Furthermore, the language system was seen as a system in which the child could be working in a variety of separate problem spaces.

Nativist work during the same period started from the assumption that the acquisition of grammar could not be explained from analyses of input to different populations of children in different situations or cultures. This is because nativists believed the essence of language to be the universal characteristics of grammar. Therefore differences between children in speed or course of acquisition were considered uninteresting, as these probably reflected social differences. Syntactic acquisition was the core of the problem for children, and it was seen as a single process, every increment of progress in it characterized by a thoroughly renovated grammar.

Perhaps one place where these two research traditions converged was in the work on errors of overgeneralization, such as overregularized plurals, past tenses, and past participles. Studying children's overgeneralizations involved looking closely at spontaneous speech data. It was generally assumed that such overgeneralizations represented child initiatives – in fact, the relative abundance of overgeneralizations in the verb system raised the question of why there were not more overgeneralizations elsewhere in child language, and supported the notion that children were limited by innate constraints on the kinds of hypotheses they could formulate. Clearly, overgeneralizations were not simple imitations of input, since adults in general do not make such errors. But they might well be influenced by the frequency of certain forms in the input that produce, in effect, paradigms for overgeneralization (Slobin 1985a). Furthermore, morphological overgeneralizations generate many opportunities for negative feedback, but might also represent a domain where positive evidence (hearing others' nonregularized forms) is sufficiently strong to motivate learning without negative evidence.

## 4    The empiricist road upgraded

More recently, changes in the views of communication, language, and the child as learner have made empiricist models of language acquisition increasingly attractive. In the early 1970s, pragmatics began to reemerge as a viable research topic, due in large part to the pioneering work in speech acts carried out by Austin (1962) and Searle (1969) and the work in conversational postulates conducted by Grice (1975). With the advent of the notion of speech acts, the connection between prelinguistic communicative intents and early language became more transparent. Child language researchers once again became interested in the communicative intent of the speech of both parents and their children, for reasons elegantly stated by Michael Halliday: that "[children are] surrounded by language, but not in the form of grammars and dictionaries, or of

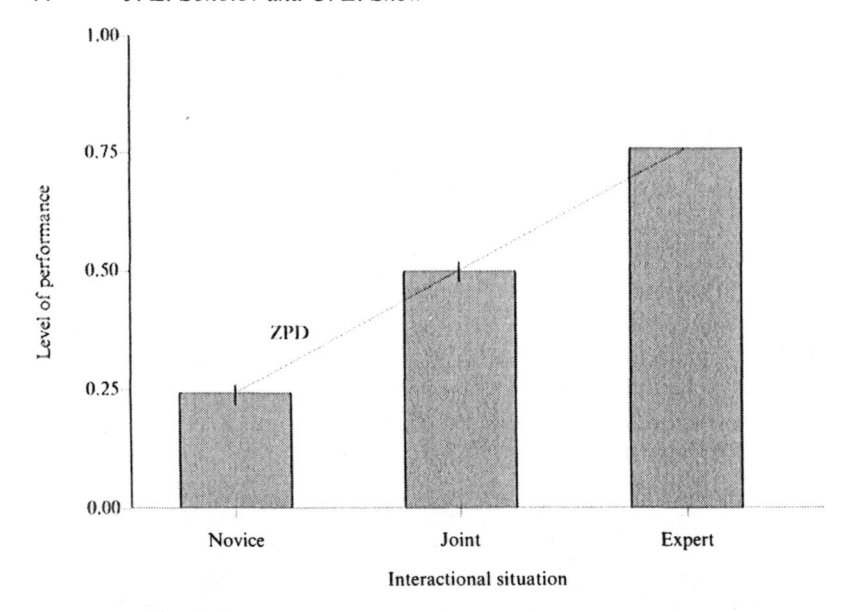

Figure 2.1  A graphical depiction of Vygotsky's zone of proximal development in which the level of solitary child performance (the novice) is raised by joint collaboration with the parent (the expert)

randomly chosen words and sentences ... what [they] encounter is 'text,' or language in use" (Halliday 1975, p. 20). The implications of the insight that what children acquire and encounter is "language in use" are that communication should be central in the study of acquisition, that the study of language should be conducted in the context of conversational interaction, and that data from controlled experiments must be complemented by observational studies of children in their natural environments.

The renewed emphasis on mother–child interaction in language studies and other domains of development spawned or revived some powerful metaphors. For example, Vygotsky (1978) used the term "zone of proximal development" (ZPD) to characterize the role of mother–child interaction in development (figure 2.1). Within the ZPD, a parent can help to raise the level of the child's performance interactively, generating improvements in performance that become permanent as the child internalizes them. Bruner introduced the notion of "scaffolding" to describe the manner in which mothers aid and support their children's development, for example by fine-tuning their speech to the child's level. Finally, the notion of "cognitive apprenticeship" (Brown, Collins, and Duguid 1988; Rogoff 1990) suggests that children learn about thinking and problem-solving "from *actively* observing and participating in culturally-defined problems with more skilled members in their society" (Rogoff 1990, p. 7). The common theme behind all these metaphors is that parents, as the more skilled performers and the more sophisticated inter-actional partners, facilitate their children's growth in important ways. During early development, parents are the social agents that best under-stand children's intentions and thus can best provide the scaffolding that they need. These metaphors and the move to study communication and pragmatics in child language (as evidenced in the quote from Halliday) characterized the lively empiricist tradition in the 1980s. As we will see in the next section, this empiricist activity is exemplified by the research challenging the no-negative-evidence claim.

A concurrent shift in thinking within linguistics brought linguists studying language development closer to empiricists. In the late 1970s and 1980s, lexicalist alternatives to the transformationalist account of lan-guage were being proposed (Bresnan 1982; Pollard 1985) that placed the structure of the language less in global rules than in lexical frames. It is not hard to imagine how very young children could acquire lexical frames from the input. The connection between the linguistic description of the target grammar and development in the child became much more visible, located as it was in the role of the verb or the grammatical head within the structure of the sentence rather than in abstract, structure-dependent rules.

A fourth important shift occurred as the cognitive revolution brought the study of learning to the forefront once again. One of the major goals of cognitive science (as reviewed in Kaplan and Simon 1989) was to understand the learning process. Protocol analysis (Erikson and Simon 1984) became an accepted means for understanding sequential learning processes. In addition, computer scientists interested in building learning machines invested great effort in exploring the efficacies of different learning mechanisms (see chapters in Michalski, Carbonell, and Mitchell 1983, 1986). Developmental psychologists once again became interested in developmental continuity and transitional mechanisms (Sternberg 1984). Finally, connectionism contributed two profound insights:
1 Much of learning can be performed by general learning mechanisms.
2 These mechanisms excel at learning from noisy input when presented with similar information repeatedly.

As a direct result of the cognitive revolution, the study of probabilistic learning, which had been pioneered years earlier by Bruner (Bruner, Goodnow, and Austin 1956; Estes 1959; Levine 1963), was revived. Models of language development incorporating mechanisms based on probabilistic learning were proposed, for example, the acquisition of word classes based on distributional analyses of the input (Maratsos and Chalkley 1980) and an updated notion of pivot grammar proposed by Braine (1991). Perhaps the most detailed of these models was the competition model (Bates and MacWhinney 1979). Within the competition model, children acquire language by discovering the ways in which different surface cues map onto different grammatical functions. Since cues sometimes compete with one another in the expression of grammatical functions, children must learn which cues are the strongest and use these to comprehend and produce language. The mechanism underlying the acquisition of these cue strengths is competition – cues compete with one another but those which are frequent and reliable in the input eventually win out. A major tenet of this model is that form–function mappings and thus the relative strengths of various cues will be different for different languages, a hypothesis which has been confirmed in a large number of studies (see MacWhinney and Bates 1989 for a review).

These four changes – increased emphasis on language as a communicative rather than a formal system, recognition of the role of the local expert in helping the learner, the availability of lexicalist grammars, and the increased viability of learning models that relied on probabilistic learning mechanisms – have enabled us to think about language acquisition in a very different way. However, the basic problem of the poverty of the stimulus – the unavailability within the input of information about the abstractions of the grammar – had not disappeared. The poverty of the stimulus would lead to incorrect grammars which could be corrected only with negative evidence. Linguists and learnability theorists persisted in the position that negative evidence was crucial to successful language learning in the absence of comprehensive innate structures (based on Gold 1967) and that it was unavailable (based on Brown and Hanlon 1970). The time was ripe for child language researchers to reopen the question of whether negative evidence is available to the language-learning child.

## 5     The existence of implicit negative evidence

A major cornerstone of the argument in favor of specifically linguistic innate constraints lies in the supposed non-existence of negative evidence. However, several recent studies have discovered that parents *do* respond differentially to the grammatical and ungrammatical utterances produced by their children. These differential responses could be enough to signal an error to the child. For example, Hirsh-Pasek, Treiman, and Schneiderman (1984) found that parents tend to repeat more of their children's ill-formed utterances than well-formed ones. They also discovered that these repetitions often include corrections. Demetras, Post, and Snow (1986) discovered that the most common response to a well-formed child utterance was to continue with the conversational topic, while the most common response to an ill-formed utterance was a clarifying question. In addition, Warren-Leubecker, Bohannon, Stanowicz, and Ness (1986) noted that parents differentially used repetition to respond to syntactic errors (well-formed = 18 percent, ill-formed = 21 percent) and to phonological errors (well-formed = 13 per cent, ill-formed = 29 percent). Furthermore, this effect was modified by the length of the child's utterance. There was more of a tendency for parents to repeat longer utterances than shorter ones. In addition, repetitions tend to occur more often when only one child error was produced (Bohannon and Stanowicz 1988). This indicated that parents most often provided children with differential feedback when only one error was produced and when their utterance was at the upper boundary of their abilities. In addition, it was discovered that a large percentage of repetitions following child errors include specific grammatical corrections. Examples of implicit corrections have been discovered for subcategorization errors (Hirsh-Pasek, Golinkoff, Braidi, and McNally 1986), bound morphemes (Farrar 1990), and closed-class verbs (Sokolov in press).

In fact, even in the examples that Brown and Hanlon (1970) used to illustrate the actual uses of *explicit* approval and disapproval by parents (table 1.12, p. 49), it is possible to find examples of parental responses providing *implicit* negative evidence. For example, in that table, Brown and Hanlon provide an example in which when Adam says *Draw a boot paper* and his mother responds *That's right*. Brown and Hanlon provide this interchange as an example of a parent providing *explicit* feedback about the truth value of their child's speech rather than its well-formedness. However, if one looks closely at the sequence of utterances preceding this interaction, there are repeated examples of Adam's mother recasting his incorrect utterance into *Draw a boot on the paper*.

Recasts of children's errors are also useful for their data-providing characteristics (Hoff-Ginsberg 1990). This point can be illustrated with a short description of two possible learning scenarios based on the following snippet of parent–child conversation:

C:   Fix Lilly.
M:   Oh ... Lilly will fix it.

The first scenario involves the learning of new grammatical knowledge, while the second involves strengthening or modifying previously acquired knowledge. The communicative context for his example is an apparent request by Adam to have Lilly fix something. The mother's response is an affirming statement incorporating a modal verb which grammaticizes the appropriate tense and aspect and also reorders the subject and main verb. Finally, the response adds a direct object.

Although several learning scenarios are possible, each one must assume that Adam and his mother share a similar (but not necessarily identical) representation of the situation. For the first learning scenario, we will assume that the child has not yet acquired a lexical frame for the modal *will* but is familiar with all of the other items in the mother's response. Learning in this case might involved the abduction of the unknown lexical item via a fast-mapping procedure (Au and Markman 1987; Rice 1990). In fast-mapping, the child uses the functions of known lexical items and the nonlinguistic context to predict the functions of unknown items. For example, in this case, Adam would have to abduce that *will* encoded some aspect of an intention or a future activity in the context of a request and then create a lexical frame for *will* which included these observations (Pinker 1984). Although fast-mapping can be an extremely useful learning mechanism, it is known to be error-prone. Children sometimes store information that is irrelevant to the lexical item. For example, in this case, Adam might erroneously undergeneralize the function of *will* believing it must be associated with a request.

For the second scenario, we will assume that Adam has acquired a lexical frame for *will* but, for whatever reasons, is not producing the item in this context. Learning in this case might involve competition (Bates and MacWhinney 1987; MacWhinney 1987). This would involve updating or strengthening the elements of the lexical frame for *will* which match the current linguistic and nonlinguistic context. Through repeated presentations, a competitive learning mechanism is able to correct the inaccuracies created by fast-mapping. This is because correct form–function mappings are strengthened, leading to the relative weakening of incorrect mappings. For the present example, this would mean that those aspects of the lexical frame for *will* which encode a future activity would be strengthened. Of course, since we are describing the same example, the context of a request would also be strengthened but since this is not the only use of *will* that Adam hears, he will eventually learn to generalize *will* to other future contexts.

The point of this discussion is not that children learn from this example in the exact manner proposed but that parental input has important data-providing characteristics. In this case, the lexical addition of a modal provides Adam with useful information. This is especially true when the additions are fine-tuned to the child's ability and repeated many times. This is because children are provided with useful information at the time when they need it the most.

It should be pointed out, of course, that the demonstration that middle-class American children receive negative evidence hardly proves the case that negative evidence is available to all children. Considerably more research is needed on culturally diverse populations to demonstrate that (see Lieven this volume on crosscultural comparisons). However, work with laterborn children in rural working-class families in the southern United States (Post 1992) essentially replicated the results of Demetras *et al.* (1986) concerning the universally greater probability that clarification questions or amended repetitions follow ill-formed child utterances while normal conversational responses follow well-formed child utterances. In addition, these rural southern mothers did much more explicit correcting than middle-class mothers do with firstborns.

## 6    Beyond the existence proof: the effects of negative evidence

As several learnability theorists have argued (Grimshaw and Pinker 1989; Morgan and Travis 1989) it is not enough simply to show that negative evidence is present in the input to children. Child language researchers must test the possibility that children attend to the information provided to them and are able to utilize that information in acquiring language. Although this is clearly an area in which more research is required, there are three types of evidence which support the notion that children attend to and learn from negative evidence.

The first piece of evidence, based on correlational data, is only suggestive: a positive correlation exists between maternal expansions and child language development (Newport, Gleitman, and Gleitman 1977; Cross 1977, 1978; Furrow *et al.* 1979; Barnes, Gutfreund, Satterly, and Wells 1983; De Villiers 1985; Hoff-Ginsberg 1985). The second piece of evidence, from a study by Farrar (1992), is that children are two to three times more likely to imitate the correct grammatical morpheme following corrective recasts (i.e. implicit negative evidence) than following any form of positive evidence. Evidently children attend to the information provided to them by parental responses. The third piece of information is the most convincing: numerous training studies have demonstrated that enriched input facilitates the development of precisely those aspects of the language system to which the training is directed (Nelson *et al.* 1973; Nelson 1977a; Baker and Nelson 1984; Nelson *et al.* 1984; Roth 1984; Shatz, Hoff-Ginsberg, and MacIver 1989). Thus not only do children receive rich and informative input, they also appear able to use this input to advance their linguistic skills.

## 7    Issues in defining negative evidence

The exact characterization of negative evidence has been slowly evolving over the last two decades. For Skinner (1957), negative evidence meant an overt correction by parents of their children's grammatical error. For Gold (1967), negative evidence was defined in terms of *Informant Presentation*. Gold's Informant Presentation was characterized by the presence of an information source which explicitly told children whether their utterance was grammatical or not. Although Brown and Hanlon (1970) suggested that "repeats of ill-formed utterances usually contain corrections and so could be instructive" (p. 43), they did not pursue this notion in their definition of contingent approval. Therefore, these definitions of negative evidence were more or less accepted until 1984 when Hirsh-Pasek *et al.* provided an alternative based on implicit evidence.

According to the Hirsh-Pasek *et al.* (1984) alternative, parents may "be more likely to *repeat* incorrect than correct utterances" (p. 82) and that this tendency may provide children with distributional information concerning their errors. Even more importantly, these parental repetitions may include corrections of child errors. The empiricist research (e.g. Demetras *et al.* 1986; Bohannon and Stanowicz 1988) following this study generalized the notion of negative evidence to include *any verbal cue that differentiated ill-formed from well-formed child speech*. These researchers argued that any distributional cue which distinguishes ill-formed from well-formed child utterances may ultimately be informative. Within the competition model approach (MacWhinney 1987; Bohannon, MacWhinney, and Snow 1991), negative and positive evidence are functionally similar. Any verbal cue that enhances the strength of correct hypotheses without supporting incorrect ones may be considered informative. If negative and positive evidence lead to similar developmental results, then concerns over the presence of negative evidence may be misplaced. As we will see in the next section, this new characterization of negative and positive evidence as equivalent does not entirely eliminate the need to explore the role of innate biases. However, it does have an effect on the centrality of such biases in language acquisition theory. In addition, it calls into question the need to attribute innate constraints to the child on the basis of the negative evidence argument alone. The important empirical questions then change from whether negative evidence is present to what the exact character of the input is and how the child learns from it.

## 8    A multiple factors framework

In 1980, Wexler and Culicover set out to construct a formal model of language development which would achieve learnability. As was dis-

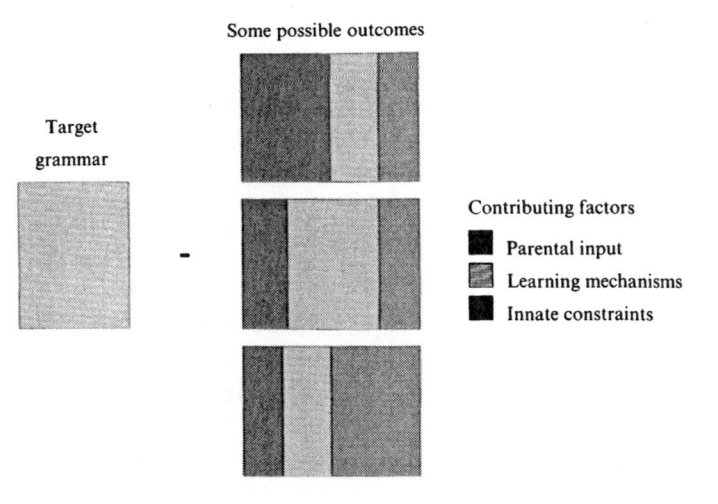

Figure 2.2 A graphical depiction of a multiple factors framework for language development

cussed in the introduction, the *no-negative-evidence* claim was central to their chain of argumentation. At around the same time, Baker (1979) discussed the role of negative evidence in the logical problem associated with the learner's ability to recover from overgeneralizations. Within both these theoretical discussions, the question about the availability of negative evidence determined the answer to the question about innateness. Without negative evidence, languages were unlearnable unless initial hypotheses were innately constrained. With negative evidence, natural languages could be learned without innate constraints.

We propose instead a "multiple factors" framework of learnability, in which learnability can be viewed as an equation with four unknowns. The larger the contribution of one variable, the smaller the other variables would need to be while still achieving learnability. We expect that empirical research should set the value of each of the variables (and perhaps find evidence for additional components). As illustrated in figure 2.2 the four components include:

1 a characterization of mature language competence;
2 the innate constraints built into the child;
3 the learning procedure utilized by the child;
4 the role of parental input.

This proposal is an extension of Snow, Perlmann, and Nathan's (1987) multiple routes model and Bohannon *et al*.'s (1991) notion of *an equation with three unknowns*, adding the learning mechanisms available to the language-learning child. Proposing a different characterization of language competence is clearly beyond the scope of this chapter (but see Van Valin 1992 for such an attempt); however, the second and third components are central to the present argument. We have already discussed the role of negative evidence in the input to children; let us now move on to discuss the third component, learning mechanisms.

## 9     Robust learning mechanisms

One of the more important problems associated with traditional learnability theory is that the learning model upon which it is based is too brittle. As Valian (1990) notes, parameter-setting models "portray the child as a device which *deterministically* sets the correct value of each parameter" (p. 107). She also correctly argues that deterministic learning mechanisms are extremely weak and because they make all-or-none decisions have trouble recovering from errors. There is evidence from decades of research in learning theory that people can learn from probabilistic information (see Bruner *et al.* 1956; Estes 1959; Levine 1963). With this in mind, child language researchers need to propose and test a learning model based on well-specified and psychologically plausible learning mechanisms operating within normal parent–child communicative situations (Snow 1989). The claim that children cannot learn from noisy input (Wexler and Culicover 1980) has not held up. Robust learning mechanisms for different aspects of language have been proposed by researchers working within the parallel-distributed processing framework (Rumelhart and McClelland 1986; MacWhinney, Leinbach, Taraban and McDonald 1989; Plunkett and Marchman 1991).

Since these models indicate that learning does not come from a single example but from a large collection of interactional patterns with multiple cues, we would hypothesize that children process the learning opportunities provided by their parents and utilize them to the best of their abilities at the time they are produced. There is evidence that children receive a large number of informative parental responses during the course of language development. For example, Sokolov (1990) has estimated that the three children he studied received an average of ten informative parental responses (both positive and negative) for every hour of mother–child interaction. Since mothers interact with their children for thousands of hours over the course of a single year, these numbers should accumulate quite substantially. Then it would be the cumulative effect of numerous presentations of potentially informative parental responses that lead to learning.

## 10    Functional readiness for learning

It is crucial to interpret the functioning of learning mechanisms develop-mentally – recognizing the changes that occur in children's ability to learn and their readiness to learn particular things as they develop. Nativist theories of language development claim that "recovery from overgener-alization is possible only if the learner is equipped with appropriate biases" (Morgan and Travis 1989, p. 534). This argument is based on the finding that there is no evidence for a direct and immediate connection between the presence of negative evidence and language learning. For example, Pinker (1989) argues that there is no evidence in which "parental feedback has led to persistent changes in children's language" (p. 13). The example he cites to suggest that feedback does not have an immediate effect on children's language is the much repeated case from McNeill (1966) in which a parent repeatedly attempts to convince a child to correct a grammatical error. However, there is no *a priori* reason to expect that, at any given time, a child is ready to acquire the element being modeled (Slobin 1973; Bohannon and Hirsh-Pasek 1984; Bates and MacWhinney 1987). If the child is not ready, then no amount of feedback or cajoling will lead to immediate acquisition. The competition model does not require such a direct and immediate connection. A more long-term effect is predicted *and* has been discovered in several studies of cue validity and cue strength (McDonald 1986; Sokolov 1988).

## 11    Benefits of a multiple factors framework

We are proposing that the learning mechanisms utilized by the child interact with the character of parental input. Although we know that children severely deprived of input do not fully learn language (Curtiss 1977) and that children do not learn language from mere exposure alone (e.g. hearing children of deaf parents who were exposed to television did not learn to speak; Sachs and Johnson 1972), there are indications that children do learn language in the relative absence of semantic contingency and implicit negative evidence. These data come not only from the individual differences between parent–child dyads reported in Sokolov (in press) and Post (1992) but also from reports that caregivers in the Samoan and Kaluli cultures do not provide their children with such input (Ochs and Schieffelin 1984; Lieven this volume). These findings suggest that semantic contingency and implicit negative evidence cannot be the only means through which children may learn language.

Snow *et al.* (1987) examined the evidence concerning the lack of semantic contingency in other cultures and argued that there are two ways that parents can build instructive *discourse frames* for their children. One route is by "being highly responsive to the child's actions, gestures, and vocalizations" (p. 79). This is the traditional form of semantically contingent input. The second is by "imposing predictable texts on the child often enough so that the child comes to recognize what the structure of the texts is" (p. 79). Given the repetitious nature of the second mode, the structure of these routines may be quite complex. Children eventually learn the routines and as they do so gradually analyze their components. One example of frequently occurring complex parental routines is joint book-reading or story-telling (Snow and Goldfield 1983). Another example is the complex routines used by the Kaluli when addressing their children. When the conversational input of the Kaluli is viewed in this manner, its richness as a source of information about the language system becomes clear. Although there appear to be multiple routes through which input may affect acquisition, input that "feeds" some learning mechanism is clearly critical for language acquisition to take place.

Within the multiple factors framework, we can contemplate learnability tradeoffs for particular parent–child dyads or even cultures. For example, if a particular culture prescribes parent–child interactions composed primarily of routinized language interactions, children in this culture have to effectively utilize learning mechanisms which help in analyzing routines, for example storage of large chunks, subsequent analysis and breakdown of the linguistic information in the chunks. Alternatively, we might hypothesize that, in children with language disorders, a deficit may be compensated for by the predominance of one factor over the others.

The multiple factors framework has a number of advantages in weaving together otherwise tangential facts about language development. We know that children follow rather divergent paths to language mastery; such individual differences are not an aberration within the proposed framework but simply the evidence of differential reliance on various learning mechanisms. The child need not be viewed as a passive learner driven either by innate constraints or by contingencies in the environment; every learning pattern is the product of a learner–environment interaction. The flexibility provided by considering different learning mechanisms emphasizes the role of the child as an active learner utilizing the information provided in the environment and making generalizations.

Finally, this theoretical framework does not preclude the presence of innate constraints or the search for them. The possibility that children have innate biases for acquiring word meanings or for bootstrapping into syntax has profound implications not only for theoretical argumentation but also for clinical and educational procedures. Though the findings that

children develop systems of communication in the absence of sophisticated input (Goldin-Meadow 1982; Bickerton 1984) and that developmental dysphasia has a familial basis (Gopnik 1991) are suggestive, until
evidence providing a more direct genetic relationship is available, we must
avoid positing innate constraints solely because of conclusions about the
availability of negative evidence.

# 3 Crosslinguistic and crosscultural aspects of language addressed to children

*Elena V. M. Lieven*

## 1 Introduction

Just as systematic individual differences between children learning the same language have to be accounted for by theories of language development, so differences between languages and between language-learning environments will condition the claims of any theory of language development to universality. Our theories of how children learn language are largely based on the acquisition of English by children from middle-class or upper-middle-class environments in the United States or the United Kingdom. These need to be tested against studies of language development in cultural settings other than those of the middle classes in advanced industrial societies and for languages other than English.

There are two "straw positions'" which can be used to characterize the extremes in approach to crosscultural studies of language development. First is the idea that child-centered "motherese" is universal and therefore, *ipso facto*, of central importance in children's learning of language. The second is that there are cultures in which speech is never addressed to language-learning children and that therefore it must be possible to learn to talk simply by listening to adults talking to each other. Even if the empirical parts of these two positions were true, the conclusions drawn from them need not be, and, as I shall show in this chapter, they are in fact false. Probably nobody subscribes fully to either position, but stated in this way they demonstrate why looking at language development in a very wide range of cultures is an essential constraint on theory building.

The following questions will be addressed in this chapter:
1 What is the range of environments within which children learn to talk?
2 Do adults from other cultures and subcultures see themselves as adjusting their language to children and, if so, to what purpose?
3 How, if at all, might these adjustments relate to the child's task of learning language structure?

By "environment," I mean the characteristics of the interpersonal surroundings within which young, language-learning children spend their time. Is it dyadic or polyadic, mainly alone with the mother, with other adults, with siblings, with a group of children? By "culture" and "subculture," I mean a community defining themselves or defined by others as having a coherence of both living style and ideology. In referring to "our culture" or "children from the type of background usually studied," I mean families from middle-class backgrounds in which one of both parents have post-school education, living in urban and technologically advanced settings. All these terms are approximations and all would give any self-respecting sociologist and anthropologist nightmares. Also, as already mentioned, children from the same backgrounds can be significantly different in their approaches to learning language (Lieven, Pine and Dresner Barnes 1992; Pine this volume). However, for the purpose of this chapter, I will be comparing across cultures and subcultures. I will therefore be interested in working-class and/or ethnic-minority groups learning English and other languages, in children learning language in non-industrially advanced, traditional cultures and in children learning languages other than English from the same type of middle- and upper-middle-class backgrounds as those most typically studied.

There are articles on language development and socialization scattered throughout the literature, but there are two relatively recent edited volumes that provide an invaluable start while also illustrating some of the methodological problems involved in this area. Slobin's edited volume (1985b) provides the main basis for the crosslinguistic study of language development but is very varied in how much the individual chapters say about the context of this development. However, the chapters on Japanese, Samoan, and Kaluli are notable exceptions to this and the authors of these chapters have also written more extensively in another edited volume (Schieffelin and Ochs 1986) about the environments in which language learning takes place in these societies.

Major methodological problems are involved in the comparison of language-learning studies crossculturally. Studies of children learning English (and, to some extent, other languages originating in Europe) tend to have larger numbers of subjects and to be conducted by developmental psychologists or psycholinguists. It is usually possible to get some idea of the relative quantities of various types of talk by both adults and children; but they are often almost completely unreflective about the culture within which the child is growing up, and this is particularly true of the studies of children learning English. Studies of children from non-industrialized cultures and/or learning non-Indo-European languages tend to pay much closer attention to the entire context in which children are learning to talk, but they rarely take a quantitative approach. This is often because the researcher is a native English-speaker observing the culture "from outside" and also because s/he is more likely to be an anthropologist or cultural linguist. In addition, there are all the dangers more generally associated with comparisons across cultures: for example, how can we be sure that what look like similar behaviors are actually fulfilling the same functional role in the two different cultures? These factors make it difficult to draw definitive conclusions, but they do generate material which can make an important contribution to current debates in the field.

## 2     The range of environments in which language is learned

Theories of environmental influences on language learning have tended to be built upon the study of the mother–infant dyad. In fact, of course, most children in the world grow up in polyadic situations. So while these children spend little time in dyadic conversation with one adult, they spend a lot of time in one of the following situations: with the mother and other siblings/children; with older children or others acting as caregivers; sitting around with a group of adults and children. This is not only true of children in non-industrialized cultures; in many economically advanced societies childcare arrangements may be less dependent on the mother staying at home with the children. Thus Berman (1985) reports that Israeli children spend a good deal of time with other children and with caregivers other than the mother. There are also subcultures within highly industrialized countries in which children spend the day surrounded by other adults and children, sometimes with their mothers and sometimes not (see Heath's 1983 study of the African-American "Trackton" community, one of two rural working-class groups she studied in the southern United States). More polyadic patterns of childcare are very typical of children raised in rural, economically traditional societies. The children in Schieffelin's (1985) study of the Kaluli of Papua New Guinea spend their time with their mothers and siblings, while Ochs (1985) reports that, among the Samoans, elder children are set to look after the young child but usually in sight of the mother. Nwokah (1987), in her study of a rural Nigerian village, reports that young children are looked after during the day by male or female "maids" (eight- to twelve-year-old children) while the mothers go to market or work in the house, and that these maids usually take the children to a communal space in the village, largely frequented by children. Bavin (1992) also says that the Warlpiri-speaking aboriginal children in her study spent their time in communal groups surrounded by other adults and children.

We know that all these children learn to talk and Slobin's edited volumes (1985b, forthcoming) describe the course of their development. But we know considerably less about how to characterize the speech that they hear and how they might make use of it. Studies of some of the cultures mentioned above state that there is little or no speech to infants until they themselves start to talk. In other cultures adults do talk to children, but in ways normally regarded as unhelpful by child language researchers (e.g. elicited imitation). Finally there are cultures in which, despite being very different from those of the standard studies, adults appear to use something very like child-sensitive speech.

## 2.1    The absence of Baby Talk to prelinguistic infants

A particular challenge as to how the child learns to talk is provided by studies which suggest that the children involved are simply eavesdroppers on the language around them at least until they can make a reasonable attempt at taking part in the ongoing conversation. Can children construct the utterance–meaning pairings which even the most committed nativist agrees have to be entered into the system without being involved in either talking themselves or being spoken to? Within our own culture, a study of Dutch children listening to German television suggests that the provision of sentences in a language with almost no information as to their meaning does not result in learning (Snow, Arlman-Rupp, Hassin, Jobse, Joosten, and Vorster 1976). The hearing child of deaf parents in a study by Sachs and Johnson (1972) also did not learn from the television although he did show signs of linguistic-type structuring in his gestures. This is complemented by work by Newport and Meier (1985) and Goldin-Meadow and Feldman (1977) on children learning American Sign Language (ASL) and by Bickerton (1981) of children learning a pidgin as a first language. These studies all suggest that young children either develop, or have innately, capacities for the symbolic representation and ordering of relatively abstract signs. So, on the one hand, children do not appear to learn just by hearing utterances in a language without any meaning attached to them. On the other, children obviously bring both knowledge and skills to the language learning situation. So how do children start talking in cultures in which speech is not addressed to them? Can we really compare their situation to that of having a television on?

   The reasons which people in different cultures and subcultures give for not talking to prelinguistic children vary. For those speaking Quiché Mayan (Pye 1986 and 1992), infants are regarded as especially physically and spiritually vulnerable and needing to be kept calm and quiet. Mothers may croon softly to the child but no attempt is made to treat it as a conversational partner. The Kaluli speak of infant babbling as "bird talk" and see this as part of nonspeaking infants' closeness to the animal and spirit world – something to be discouraged (Schieffelin 1985).

In Samoa relative status is central to all interaction including that between a child and its caregivers. People of lower status adjust their language when interacting with those of higher status and, given that age takes precedence over youth and parents over children, it would be unthinkable for a caregiver to adapt her/his speech to a prelinguistic infant (Ochs 1985). People from Trackton (Heath 1983) think that children cannot be taught and have to learn things for themselves.

In the research that was spurred by Chomsky's characterisation of speech to children as "rather restricted in scope ... and fairly degenerate in quality" (1965, p. 31), there was an initial tendency to view any evidence of speech adjustment to children as necessarily helpful to language learning. Evidence that Baby Talk occurred in many cultures was seen as further support for the idea that the child's environment was especially adapted to make language accessible to children. Early evidence was largely in terms of phonetic (reduplication, consonant reduction) and prosodic (mainly higher pitch and pitch range) changes. Cruttenden (this volume) has dealt with these in detail. It is clear that it is characteristic of many cultures that adults (and older children) alter prosodic features of the language when talking to prelinguistic and young language-learning children. Equally, even where speech to babies is adjusted, it is not always in the ways mentioned above: Pye (1986) reports that Quiché Mayan mothers talk to their babies using low, monotonic, "crooning" speech and Harkness (1971) says that Guatemalan mothers appear to use a low pitch "rapid fire" style when talking to their babies. In addition, as Cruttenden points out, there can be no speech adjustments in those cultures in which, typically, people do not talk to prelinguistic babies. Obviously if they are not present in all cultures, then these particular behaviors cannot be necessary for language learning. Two questions follow from this: when present, do they serve any useful function? If so, is this function accomplished by other sorts of behavior in cultures in which this particular style of speech to children is not found?

For instance, Cruttenden suggests that one important function of the raised $F_0$ and pitch range, at least from the point of view of the caregiver, is in maintaining the child's attention on the caregiver's voice and actions. Schieffelin (1985), who reports no speech to children prelinguistically in the Kaluli of Papua New Guinea, says that caregivers will sometimes hold the baby up facing away and "speak for them" in a high-pitched voice. Perhaps this is functionally equivalent? In general, it is important to ask whether the prelinguistic child who is not spoken to either needs and/or is given the opportunity to link voices and faces and thereby to start registering the structure of attention in conversational interaction. This in turn presents a challenge to our current theoretical assumptions about the importance of the prelinguistic structuring of attention for the learning of reference and conversational turntaking (Bruner 1975; Tomasello and Todd 1983). Unfortunately, resolving this issue is not going to be at all easy since it requires a study of infant attention in a culture in which infants are not spoken to prelinguistically.

There is no detailed evidence on this, but it is interesting that almost all studies which report an absence of speech to prelinguistic children also report that the baby is continually present in the social space: in a sling on the mother's back, on someone's lap, in another child's arms, etc. This is very unlike the most frequently studied language-learning environments which tend to be of middle-class or upper-middle-class families in advanced industrial societies. Here the mother spends most of her time looking after the child or children on her own; children will not be carried around all day and will typically be put down to play and sleep. We really have no information about whether or how the prelinguistic infant in the quite different cultures described above starts to make sense of what is going on around her/him and how this might feed into the process of learning language. However, Dunn and Munn (1985) demonstrate how children in the second year of life show understanding of what is going on in conflicts between their mothers and older siblings, despite the fact that they are not direct participants in these interactions. Many of the studies of cultures in which there is less talk to early language learners suggest that children may be picking up information from the pragmatics of the situations and routines around them. Thus Schieffelin (1985) reports that while there is no talk by adults to the baby, there is a lot of talk about it, and babies learn to attend to the verbal environment in which they live. Heath's (1983) study of Trackton children also shows clear evidence of this. She reports that when children start talking they do so by echoing the ends of utterances they overhear in the adult conversation, and many of the examples she gives show that the baby is at least attending enough to what s/he hears around her/him to be able to repeat it. Also a study by Dunn and Shatz (1989) of a group of English families shows that children aged 24–36 months pay attention to conversations between their mothers and older siblings and develop their abilities to intervene in them.

Another suggested function of Baby Talk to prelinguistic infants is that it helps the child to segment speech through stress patterns, which emphasize content words, longer pauses between clause boundaries, etc. (Peters 1983; Cruttenden this volume). In cultures which do not have Baby Talk to prelinguistic infants, this potential aid in segmenting will be absent; but children appear to solve this problem for themselves. As well as the phenomenon of echoing the speech that they hear, initially presumably without understanding, many studies of these cultures report that children start to produce unanalyzed, rote-learned segments which they have picked up in routinized situations (e.g. Warlpiri: Bavin 1992; Kaluli: Schieffelin 1985). This has also been noted in studies of individual differences between children learning language in the same culture (Lieven *et al.* 1992) and in many other cultures in which babytalk occurs (Turkish: Aksu-Koç and Slobin 1985; West Greenlandic: Fortescue and Olsen 1992). Watson-Gegeo and Gegeo (1986), Peters and Boggs (1986), and Lieven *et al.* (1992) all suggest that such frozen phrases may then be used to bootstrap the child into segmenting the utterances that s/he hears and can also be analyzed to provide the basis for slot-and-frame type productive utterances. This capacity of children to pick up the ends of utterances they overhear and to repeat frequently occurring and highly routinized utterances is clearly part of the repertoire of skills that the child brings to language learning (Lieven 1984) and it certainly ensures that the child is able to start talking – something which marks an important transition for both the child and her/his caregivers in many cultures.

Reports of cultures in which there is no talk to prelinguistic infants are not widespread and, of course, it is a matter of degree. But Bavin (1992), Heath (1983) and Pye (1986) do suggest that children are really spoken to very little by adults until they can produce at least multi-word utterances. And while Schieffelin (1985) and Ochs (1985) describe an explicit language-teaching style used by adults (discussed in section 3 below), they both make it clear that children spend much of their time listening to the conversations around them rather than directly taking part in them. There are three widely attested skills that children show in these and all other language situations which may partly help them construct utterance–meaning pairs in the absence of large numbers of more or less explicit examples: (1) the capacity for generative word play with echoic imitations; (2) quite remarkable memory for the relation between an utterance not fully understood and the pragmatics of the situation in which it was initially uttered (Snow 1983); and (3) a sensitivity to the frequency and routinization of utterances and events (Lieven 1987). Heath (1983) makes it clear that Trackton children, after an initial stage in which they simply imitate portions of what they overhear, subsequently start to "play around" with the imitation in a way very similar to the crib speech reported by Weir (1962) and Kuczaj (1983). Lieven and Pine (1992) suggest that this breaking down and rebuilding of rote-learned phrases can provide the basis for a form of early productivity, although work is still in progress to establish what happens to these structures as the child develops. Such behavior provides evidence of the child's sensitivity to distributional frequencies in what s/he hears, but does not necessarily imply that the child understands the utterance. However, children do not produce these utterances out of nowhere. They often seem to be triggered by the repetition of a routinized exchange and/or a word in the child's immediate environment, and they may be enough sometimes to generate a response from those around.

This research suggests that in addition to the symbol-making and ordering skills we noted at the beginning of this section, children also bring a number of other skills which depend on memory and the ability to identify patterns in their environment. However, it would be quite wrong to characterize this environment as a kind of meaningless backdrop in the child's life. Children in these cultures are immersed in a structure of meaning which may well need less articulation in terms of Baby Talk directed at them precisely because they are a much more integral part of it.

## 2.2    The role of siblings and older children

Many children growing up in polyadic situations are taking part in multi-party conversations from an early age and in many of these cultures adults have particular interactional techniques to help them do so, which are discussed in section 3 below. But these children also spend a great deal of their time in the company of other children, either alone or with other adults. There is not much evidence of the effects of the presence of siblings on children's language but Barton and Tomasello (this volume) review what there is. They report young children's language in conversations which include their mother and an older sibling as more complex than when alone with the mother. While, on the one hand, there is some suggestion that younger children may take slightly longer to learn to talk than singletons or first-borns, it may also be that a more genuine set of concerns about which the child wishes to communicate is generated with other siblings present than in what has to be in some senses the somewhat artificial "conversations" that take place within mother–infant dyads in our own culture. It is interesting that many of the examples of elicited imitation by mothers, reported by Schieffelin (1985) for the Kaluli, involve teaching the child specific language to deal with their older siblings.

Probably the best place to look for children's language learning in situations involving other children is the immersion learning of a second language by children in school. Wong Fillmore (1979) reports strategies which are very similar to those of the Trackton children discussed above (Heath 1983), with children identifying pieces of language relevant to pragmatically significant and highly routinized situations. Nwokah's (1987) study, referred to in section 2 above, compared the speech to young children of their child caregivers ("maids") and their mothers in a rural Nigerian village. She found that the maids tended to be much more directly controlling, producing short utterances mainly prohibiting the child from doing things. This is somewhat similar to the evidence that Barton and Tomasello (this volume) review on the language of children to their younger siblings in our culture, which also tends to be more controlling and monologic by contrast to the mothers' more dyadic approach. But, as Barnes, Gutfreund, Satterly, and Wells (1983) among others have argued, directive utterances which link the utterance directly to the child's behavior, usually with a highly pragmatically interpretable intonation pattern, may give very young children quite a lot of information about language, particularly if they involve a certain amount of rephrasing and repetition which directives, in an attempt to get the child's compliance, often do. This highly directive style of language may be less helpful as the child starts to talk more. For instance, Harkness (1977) reports that among the Kipsigis children of western Kenya, success in language at four years of age is predicted by the relative amount the children spoke to adults rather than to other children. It may well be that children exposed almost exclusively to the speech of other children learn to talk more slowly and in a more limited way. Bavin's (forthcoming) work on children learning Warlpiri suggests something of the sort in that she says that parents show no concern if the child is not speaking by three. But the evidence does not all go one way, even in our own culture.

## 3    Language socialization

Attitudes to whether language has to be explicitly taught to children vary greatly across cultures. Some cultures, like Trackton – the rural African-American community of the Piedmont Carolinas, studied by Heath (1983) – think that children cannot be taught and have to find out for themselves. Heath quotes the following as a typical way of thinking about development:

ANNIE MAE:    He gotta learn to know 'bout dis world, can't nobody tell 'im. Now just how crazy is dat?
    White folks uh hear dey kids say sump'n, dey say it back to 'em, dey aks 'em 'gain 'n 'gain 'bout things, like they 'posed to be born knowin'. You think I kin tell Teegie all he gotta know? Ain't no use me tellin' him: learn dis, learn dat. What's dis? What's dat? He just gotta learn, gotta know; he see one thing one place one time, he know how it go, see sump'n like it again, maybe it be de same, maybe it won't ... (Heath 1983, p. 84)

By contrast, the Kaluli say that once the child has used two critical words (mother and breast) s/he must then be "shown how to speak": "The entire process of a child's development, of which language acquisition plays a very important role, is thought of as a hardening process (*by adults*) and culminates in the child's use of 'hardwords', speech that is well-formed and situationally appropriate." (Schieffelin 1985, p. 533; my italics).

All the cultures studied show sensitivity to teaching the social uses of language and the ways that adults talk or do not talk to children reflect the ideologies of child rearing that characterize the particular culture. Conversation in Trackton is, to a considerable extent, a matter of floor holding, and one can see how children would have to learn to do this in order to get attention and be heard in a culture where adults do not initiate conversation-like interactions with young language-learning children. The way we talk to children in our own culture also reflects the ideological underpinnings of the child-centered approach. Ochs (1982) points out that a style which emphasizes the expansion of large numbers of utterances which originate with the child involves a sort of "putting-of-the-child" first, which would be unthinkable in Samoa, where people of lower status are the ones who make adjustments to those of higher status. By contrast, Clancy (1986) reports that middle-class Japanese mothers rarely directly refuse a child's requests but appeal to the child's feelings about others in attempting to divert their socially inappropriate behavior. They often speak "for" the other, who may not have said anything. This behavior foreshadows the strong social avoidance of direct requests and refusals that characterizes interaction outside the home in Japan. Mandarin-speaking parents in Erbaugh's (1992) study, while teaching kin terms of address explicitly, seem more like middle-class parents in Anglo-American cultures, allowing a kind of amnesty for young children in terms of both behavior and talk and using large numbers of expansions of the child's utterances to keep the conversation going. Explicit teaching of politeness forms of address and request is reported in many societies, including Samoa (Ochs 1985), Japan (Clancy 1985), Turkey (Aksu-Koç and Slobin 1985), and Nigeria (Nwokah 1987). It is also, of course, prevalent in western society, although rarely noted, perhaps because it is regarded as not very important, at least in the groups usually studied, and also because it is relatively simple. *Please* and *thank you* will usually suffice and one does not have to add a complex set of politeness markers as one does in Japanese or of addressee kinship terms as one does in Warlpiri (Bavin 1992).

Teaching children how to use language is not confined to forms of address and politeness, however. In many societies the child is explicitly taught how to interact with peers, report events, talk to their older siblings, etc. Thus Miller (1986) reports that working-class mothers in Baltimore, USA, try to teach children how to learn when they are being teased and when not, by teaching them the contextualization cues for teasing (mainly intonational). Schieffelin (1985) describes the Kaluli use of an elicited-imitation strategy (*elema* "say after me") to teach the social uses of assertive language – teasing, shaming, requesting, challenging, reporting (p. 531), usually in triadic interactions involving the mother, the language-learning child, and someone else. Watson-Gegeo and Gegeo (1986) also report the extensive use of elicited imitation among the Kwara'ae (of the Solomon Islands) to teach the child how to do a wide range of things with language, including reporting events. According to Ochs (1985), Samoan children are socialized starting at about the age of two into performance using Bible verses, hymns, the alphabet, etc., using the speech register used for Western-introduced situations (school, the Christian religion).

Another method of teaching socially appropriate language is the tutorial prompt in which the adult asks a question to which s/he already knows the answer. Many cultures use a mixture of elicited imitation and tutorial prompting. Thus Demuth (1986) reports the use of both strategies in Basotho during extensive practice sessions in which Sesotho-learning children are taught how to interact with others in terms of family names, recitations, and prayers; but she also makes clear that these techniques are used to prompt language in everyday interaction as well. Erbaugh (1992) notes that the Chinese children in her study were extensively prompted for the correct kin terms of address using *What do you call X?* This technique is also widely used among the Kwara'ae (Watson-Gegeo and Gegeo 1986). It is clear from Watson-Gegeo and Gegeo's examples that these prompting routines can be very extensive; for instance, they give an example of where tutorial prompting, backed up by providing the answers when the child does not reply, was used to take the child through the complex reporting of an event.

In our own culture, these tutorial questions are used to prompt both for politeness (e.g. *What do you say?*) and for labels (*What's this?*, *What's that called?*). As Pine (1992b) points out, tutorial prompts for labels are quite highly directive and not particularly "child-centered," yet there is evidence that they do encourage a growth in the child vocabulary of labels. Presumably the use of tutorial prompts for a rather more extensive set of functions may be equally successful. The subtlety and complexity of these issues is demonstrated by Fernald and Morikawa (1993) in a study which compares the speech of a group of middle-class Japanese and US mothers to their young, language-learning children. While the mothers from both cultures talked an equal amount about objects, the mothers from the United States showed a more extensive use of questions to prompt labeling while the Japanese mothers seemed to use the objects to emphasize the polite verbal routines surrounding exchanging the objects with their children. This indicates that even in two subcultures that, according to Fernald and Morikawa, show widespread similarities in the ways by which mothers talk to children, cultural specificities can be emphasized while superficially similar forms are used.

The use of a child-centered style which takes the child's utterances as a starting point and expands them in a conversation-like interchange has been regarded by students of child language acquisition as the optimal way of helping the child learn to talk by contrast with a more "directive" style. Many studies report the presence of a "child-topic expanding" style in other cultures (Japanese: Clancy 1985; Korean: Clancy 1989a; Israeli: Berman 1985; Mandarin Chinese: Erbaugh 1992). However, to my knowledge almost all these studies are of families from academic or middle-class backgrounds, which leaves open the question of whether other groups in these societies also use a relatively high level of expansions. Although Heath (1983) reports that one of the two working-class groups in her study did use a high level of expanding (Roadville), while the other did not (Trackton), Miller's (1986) study of three working-class families in Baltimore suggested a lower rate of expansions than has normally been found for middle-class families. This raises the question of whether we are dealing with the effects of higher education or of some ideological homogenization of the upper middle classes in advanced industrial societies. It might also lead us to be cautious about strong claims for the value of a topic-expanding style for children learning language since plenty of children learn to talk in the absence of such a style and in the presence of a style that looks rather "directive" by comparison. However, if we look at the supposed functions of the topic-expanding style, the same functions can often be identified in other, more commonly found, forms of speech to children.

The claims for the value of expansions are (1) that by following the child's preceding utterance, the caregiver ensures joint attentional focus, and (2) that providing an expanded (and extended) version of the child's utterance gives the child important syntactic and semantic information in the most useful form. As we have seen in Samoa, among the Kaluli, the Luo (Blount 1977), and in rural Nigeria, while children's own topics are rarely responded to in a conversation-like way, there are explicit attempts to teach the child what to say in interaction with others. While Schieffelin (1985) states that the utterances which the mother wants repeated are not adapted to the child, and often attempt to push the child into ongoing interactions that the child may not be interested in, she also says that the mother will spend a good deal of energy trying to get the child involved. In addition, it is clear from her examples that the speech to be imitated is located in the here-and-now and in the actions and speech of those around the child. Here the mother organizes the child's focus of attention rather than responding to it as with the expanding style. The child will almost certainly not initially understand what it is saying but these imitations evoke responses from those around which, in turn, lead the mother to provide another model to imitate. The child rapidly learns to imitate what the mother says and it is clear from the examples that the mother rephrases and repeats the utterance until the child says something and will often continue to encourage her/him to copy a succession of related utterances. This may well give the child the same sort of segmental and syntactic information which, it has been argued, sequences of child topics and their expansions by adults provide.

These studies do not quantify the proportion of interactions which take the form of elicited imitation or tutorial prompts. Nor is it possible, in the absence of within-culture comparisons between caregiver–child dyads which differ on the relative use of these styles of interaction, to get any idea of whether or how they are used by the child in language learning. But these attempts to elicit imitation are certainly child-directed (in terms of being focused on getting the child to speak) though they are not necessarily child-centered (in terms of the child's prior focus of attention). In terms of the two functions outlined above, namely organizing the child's talk around a joint focus of attention and providing her/him with a series of semantically and syntactically related utterances, they may have more in common with topic expansions than one might at first think.

One can, I think, conclude from the above that children being raised in polyadic situations and/or in cultures where the practices of child-rearing are very different from those of middle-class groups in advanced industrial societies, are hearing or actively being provided with a substantial number of utterances for which they can make some pairing with meaning. Whether the relative proportions of these are less or greater is impossible to say. This is partly because the studies cited above tend not to provide detailed quantitative data but also because we have not fully solved the theoretical problem of how we know when the child has made the link between utterance and meaning even for the most detailed studies in our own culture. Thus there seems little reason to think that these studies provide support for the idea that children can learn language in an infinite range of environments, including one in which they simply input a sufficient variety of sentences which are relatively meaningless to them into their "Language Acquisition Device" and grammar effortlessly emerges. The environment is made meaningful both by the child itself and by others. Language is used in a variety of highly routinized situations in which the child is often implicitly or explicitly involved. In addition to which, in many of these cultures, there are explicit attempts to train children in what to say in particular situations. On the other hand, there is good evidence that children bring a range of cognitive, social, and processing skills to the problem of learning to talk. While there are suggestions in the literature that amount of talk to the child and high levels of expansions may be associated with rate of language development, I have tried to show that environments with much lower levels of "child-centered speech" may provide all the ingredients required to make progressive sense of the language being heard and that these ingredients can be analyzed in functionally very similar terms to those suggested for the components of a highly child-centered style. Basically, if the differences between adult–adult talk and adult–child talk in the middle-class environments of industrialized societies are functional in simplifying the child's task in learning language, then one can find their equivalents in other, seemingly very different, settings.

In their chapter on the language of fathers and siblings (this volume), Barton and Tomasello draw attention to what they call the "Bridge Hypothesis," which suggests that fathers in traditional, Western-style, nuclear families may provide a bridge between the intimate language of the home and that of the outside world of adults, while siblings may do the same for relations with other peers. The dyadic, child-centered style of talking to children may well require this kind of a bridge as the child starts to talk to anyone other than the mother. It may also reflect a very different ideology and set of child-rearing practices from those of other societies. Perhaps, too, it prepares a child for some of the tasks that lie ahead in a world of school-based education and a more anonymous outside world. In the sorts of societies in which children grow up from the beginning in polyadic situations, such bridges will be of a different kind. It may be that explicitly training the child in how to speak for itself is one of these.

## 4    Issues and problems in studying input crosslinguistically

We have established in the first two sections of this chapter that while children learn to talk in a wide range of different environments, they do so in situations which are relatively routinized and in which, often but not always, adults make attempts to teach them what to say. We have also seen that children bring a range of skills to these situations and rapidly make themselves a talkative, if initially somewhat imitative, part of their verbal environment. In the final section of this chapter, I look briefly at some technical and methodological issues in the crosslinguistic study of language-learning situations. I can do little more than raise these here since the available data do not usually address the question directly and the complexities of the different languages are very great.

Any normal two-year-old can learn any of the world's languages. The devices used by these languages to express meaning are extremely varied. To name just a few almost at random: there are syntactic word order languages (English) and languages in which word order is exclusively used for pragmatic rather than syntactic ends (Turkish); there are languages with no inflectional morphology (Chinese) and languages with extensive morphology in which, for instance, there are inflections on the verb for both object and subject agreement (West Greenlandic); there are languages which use tone for syntactic purposes (Sesotho) and languages in which tone is a matter of pragmatics (English); there are languages in which words stand alone (Chinese) and agglutinative languages in which words can be almost infinitely extended in a cycle of nominalizers and verbalizers with all their attendant morphology (Warlpiri); there are languages in which the phonology changes for pragmatic purposes (Samoan) and languages in which phonology changes in complex harmonization patterns (Hebrew). All these languages are learned by children at roughly the same time and with roughly equal ease and difficulty (see Slobin 1985), though, as we have seen, under rather different environmental circumstances.

However, one important, but little emphasized, point about the study of the language that children hear is that it should indeed be what they do hear. Ochs (1985) makes this point in her study of Samoan acquisition. Grammars of Samoan report it to be an ergative language, while acquisition studies report the ergative marker to be absent from young children's speech. It turns out that this marker is also absent from informal domestic speech and is only used in speech-making situations by adult men. So the study of input should look at actual input rather than at a grammar of the adult language.

The emphasis on the child as an active constructor of language may have led to a tendency to ignore potentially relevant aspects of the input. For instance Budwig and Wiley (1991) in their study of children's special use of pronominal forms suggest that an account in terms of the child's cognitive predispositions may have to be modified since there are somewhat unexpectedly close similarities between aspects of the children's system and the adult input. While, in the end, children learn to talk like adults, if not like grammar books, we need to have a clear idea of the order in which they are faced with particular parts of the language in terms of both presence in the input and frequency of use.

Without careful attention to the actual language being used to children, it is difficult to know whether crosslinguistic differences in order of acquisition are due to the language *per se* or rather to different maternal styles of talk. Thus Gopnik and Choi (1990) in their comparative study of development of early labeling concluded that the fact that the Korean children in their study learned labeling later than the English-speaking children was due to a greater emphasis in the Korean language on verbs. However, Fernald and Morikawa (in press) suggest that it is more likely to be due to differences between the relative emphasis put by English and Korean mothers on the naming of objects as opposed to the social routines involved in playing with them.

Comparisons between children learning different languages can also be used to bear on the question of order in cognitive development. Thus Clancy (1989b), in her study of Korean acquisition, noted that *wh*-questions did not develop in the order predicted by the theory of their relative cognitive complexity. The children in her study used "how" much earlier than would be predicted on the grounds of cognitive complexity. A study of the input, however, showed that Korean mothers were using the word translated as *how* in English, in contexts which suggested that the word should actually be translated as *what*.

One has also to pay attention to the implications of different input styles for detailed aspects of the language-learning task. Thus, as Schieffelin notes for the Kaluli, the *elema* technique means that the complex system of shift of reference used in Kaluli is directly modeled rather than, as in English, the child having the problem of working out what *I* and *you* refer to. On the other hand, Demuth (1986) says that the elicited imitation technique is used for both direct and indirect speech ("Say *I'm going to hit you*" and "Say *you're going to hit him*") which may add to the complexity the Basotho child faces, although she does also say that most prompting is in triadic contexts and in direct reporting form. However, we cannot assume that all speech adjustments to children are necessarily helpful. An example from Bavin (1992) suggests that some of the consonant reductions used in Warlpiri Baby Talk may actually make it less easy to hear the morpheme breaks in this polysynthetic language. Bard and Anderson (1983) also report that words isolated from child-directed speech are less intelligible to adult subjects than words originally addressed to an adult. While there are a number of possible explanations for this result (e.g. Cruttenden this volume), it reinforces the point that theories of the relationship between input and language learning are likely to need to be sophisticated, multifaceted and complex (see Durkin 1987).

There is also the question of how much information about language structure children are being given relatively directly. The use of clarification requests is reported widely in all studies, but direct correction of language is less widespread. However Schieffelin reports that Kaluli adults correct "the phonological, morphological or lexical form of an utterance, or its pragmatic or semantic meaning" (1985, p. 533), which accords with the Kaluli view that children have to be taught to talk. It would be interesting to look at this in detail to see whether, in this very language-conscious society, adults adjust material they choose to correct to the child's developmental level. It is clear that the extensive use of elicited imitation results in a considerable amount of initial rote-learning of forms which are only subsequently analyzed. It is also the case that the prompting sequences which many of the authors above describe result in a lot of early grammatical parallelism, where most of the marking of forms in the adult's speech can be largely copied by the child in its own subsequent utterance with only minimal changes. Thus, in answering questions, West Greenlandic-speaking children can often copy the verbal aspect markers used in the adult's preceding questions (Fortescue and Olson forthcoming); Kaluli children often seem to follow the pragmatic word order patterns provided in the immediate context (Schieffelin 1985); a Polish-speaking boy is reported initially to use the feminine form in self-reference, presumably copied from the mother (Smoczyńska 1985).

However, while the first two sections of this chapter suggest that children are not hearing a random or arbitrary set of sentences of the language, there is little evidence to suggest that, in most cultures, parents are explicitly teaching grammar. Even in those cultures where they may see themselves as doing so (e.g. Kaluli) it is clear that children are bringing a fairly formidable range of interactive, processing, and generative skills to the problem of learning to talk. In this respect, the study of language acquisition crosslinguistically supports the findings for English.

## 5      Conclusions

In order to learn to speak the particular language of their community, children need to be able to (1) register distributional features of the language and (2) construct utterance–meaning pairs. The child-centered style of speaking to children may be one way of enabling them to do this but it is clearly not essential. Other ways of talking to and around children also seem well adapted to generate the kind of language from which the child can learn. In addition to any specifically syntactic skills that children bring to the language-learning task, they bring interactive skills like the ability to imitate what they hear. It is interesting that Trackton children spend such a lot of their early language development imitating, and that adults in so many cultures demand echoic imitation from their children.

The imitation itself will ensure some sort of passive registration of distribution within the language, while the elicitation of imitations within interactional contexts may help the child to register utterance–meaning pairs.

Children are clearly not having to learn language from something like a television set; but nor are they being presented with a graded set of syntax lessons. On the one hand, the study of child language development cross culturally supports the idea that children will only learn to talk in an environment of which they can make some sense and which has a structure of which the child is a part; on the other, children can clearly learn to talk in a much wider variety of environments than those largely studied to date. This, I suggest, is only partly because of the repertoire of skills that the child brings to the task of learning to talk. It is also because there are systematic ways in which the structure within which the child is growing up gives her/him access to ways of working out the language. Looking at child language learning in other cultures may refocus our attention on what is, to me, the central issue to be explained: how do children learn to talk from what they hear? This question sometimes tends to get lost in discussions of how a very small minority of the children in the world experience their early language environment and of why some children might learn language faster than others.

# 4    Child-directed speech and influences on language acquisition: methodology and interpretation

*Brian J. Richards*

## 1    Introduction

A survey of publications about language acquisition written from a variety of perspectives reveals how far a common body of research into environmental influences can be used to support opposing theoretical perspectives. A newcomer to the field would surely be bewildered by the proliferation of statements which seem directly to contradict each other. On the one hand we learn that "these results ... certainly suggest that 'motherese' is an effective teaching language" (Furrow and Nelson 1986, p. 175) and "Considerable evidence ... supports the view that particular aspects of adult·talk to children may affect how children learn to talk" (Lieven 1984, p. 15); on the other hand we read "It does not follow that it [motherese] is causally involved in the acquisition process itself, still less that motherese or any specifically modified form of input is necessary to language acquisition" (Smith 1989, p. 146), or, from a recent book on second language learning, "The effects of babytalk on children's first language development have been impossible to prove" (Cook 1991, p. 98).

Snow, Perlmann, and Nathan (1987) ask what features of interaction with the child facilitate, or are necessary for, language acquisition. They conclude that, "This recurrent question has become, as more and more research is directed to it, not easier but more difficult to answer. Results of different studies are often contradictory" (Snow *et al.* 1987, p. 65). Just how contradictory is illustrated by Hardy-Brown (1983, table 1, p. 618). In a comparison of results from two much-quoted studies of the effects of maternal language on children's language (Newport, Gleitman, and Gleitman 1977; Furrow, Nelson, and Benedict 1979) she points out that of twenty-four mother–child correlations they had in common, only *one* relationship was statistically significant and in the same direction in both. Of the remaining twenty-three, only half were even in the same direction, that is to say positively or negatively correlated in both investigations. Similarly, evidence of causal relationships between maternal *yes–no* ques-

tions and children's auxiliary verb growth, which is usually regarded as
one of the more robust environmental influences, is far less consistent
than is usually assumed (Richards 1990a). But the problem lies not just in
conflicting results but also in their interpretation. Thus one can find
Newport *et al.* (1977) quoted both in support of positive effects of
"motherese" (e.g. Weistuch and Byers Brown 1987) and to deny them
(e.g. Smith 1989).

The aim of this chapter is to clarify these issues by examining the
methodology and findings of research into effects of the linguistic
environment, particularly on the *rate* of children's language development.
Although many of the methodological points will also be relevant to
investigating influences on *style* of development (e.g. Furrow and Nelson
1984), readers are referred to Pine (this volume) for discussion of this
issue. In particular, I shall discuss the type of evidence required for
drawing conclusions about universal and facilitative processes, paying
particular attention to the notion of causation, and evaluate the methodology of previous studies in the light of such requirements.

## 2      Child-directed speech and individual differences: the universals fallacy

The fact that preschool children vary extensively in the rate at which they
develop language has long been recognized (Cross 1978). Wells (1986c,
p. 117) reported that for a sample of 128 children developing normally,
the difference between the least and most advanced at 42 months was the
equivalent of between 30 and 36 months. A closer look at the figures
(Wells 1985, p. 123) suggests that the least advanced performed at the
level of the average child aged between 24 and 30 months, while the most
advanced was beyond the level of the average five-year-old (Richards
1990c). It is not surprising therefore that researchers have been concerned
to explore the roots of these differences.

At the same time, the developing interest in the "motherese" register
during the 1970s, was seen as a possible counter to Chomsky's (1965)
claim that the child's linguistic environment was too complex, disor-
ganized, and deviant to allow acquisition to take place without innate
grammatical knowledge. This generated further attempts to discover
whether more motherese was better for the child (e.g. Furrow *et al.* 1979).
Paradoxically, however, claims that a simplified register would be an ideal
teaching language were themselves attacked on the grounds that simplification would provide an insufficiently rich database from which to induce
the structure of language (e.g. Hornstein and Lightfoot 1981). Besides, it
was claimed, simplification could actually be harmful because insufficient

exposure to the full range of syntactic structure would cause grammatical rules to be discovered more slowly (Gleitman, Newport, and Gleitman 1984). More seriously, there would be insufficient evidence to reveal erroneous rules (see Pinker 1988). The very existence of simplified characteristics of child-directed speech (CDS) was also called into question (Newport *et al.* 1977), and there followed a theoretical and methodological debate between the authors of Newport *et al.* (1977) and Furrow *et al.* (1979) about the interpretation of their respective findings (Gleitman *et al.* 1984; Furrow and Nelson 1986; see Pine this volume). Did maternal speech adjustments accelerate language growth (as claimed by Furrow *et al.* 1979) or did mothers who provided "a greater range of data from the language" (Gleitman *et al.* 1984, p. 69) provide a more useful database?

Thus, according to Bennett-Kastor (1988, p. 3) "the issue of 'motherese' and its facilitating effects (or non-effects) was in large part a response to a theoretical position – innateness." In addition, however, a substantial body of research into the predictors of language variation has entirely different motivations, for example, to evaluate day care provision (e.g. McCartney 1984), to inform styles of interaction with the hearing-impaired (Lyon 1985) and to replicate previous findings on linguistically handicapped populations (Yoder 1989). It is ironic, however, that investigating facilitative effects of CDS may actually throw little, if any, light on the question of innateness. Demonstrating a relationship between *variation* in features of the linguistic environment and *variation* in rate of development would not weaken the nativist position (Hardy-Brown 1983) any more than the absence of such relationships would strengthen it. As Hardy-Brown points out (p. 615), the idea that this kind of evidence could refute the nativist position mistakenly presupposes that influences on *individual differences* are also *universal* causes of language development. Unfortunately, this has not always been appreciated, something which has frequently clouded discussions about the relative contributions of innate linguistic competence and input. The confusion arises from a failure to recognize that both heredity *and* environment can contribute to universal phenomena as well as to individual differences, and that the causes of universals and individual differences are not necessarily related (Hardy-Brown 1983, p. 614).

The methodological problem of determining the contribution of heredity to individual differences will be considered below under "the genetic confound," but it is worth emphasizing that a correlation between, for example, the frequency of mothers' contingent responses and children's language development is *not* evidence that contingent responding is necessary for human language acquisition (Plomin and DeFries 1985, p. 4). Similarly, if auxiliaries in *yes–no* questions addressed to children rather than those in declaratives predict the rate of children's auxiliary verb learning (Newport *et al.* 1977), this should not be interpreted to mean that *yes–no* questions are more useful for learning auxiliaries than declaratives (e.g. Gleitman *et al.* 1984); it simply indicates that in the one case two sources of variation are related, while for the other variable no such relationship exists, maybe because its frequency exceeded a threshold beyond which it ceased to be advantageous (see Richards 1990a, pp. 228–9). Since all the children in the sample were developing auxiliaries, and all received at least some exemplars both from declaratives and from *yes–no* questions, we have the presence in each case of both the effect and the putative cause, and can therefore draw no conclusions as to whether these two variables are necessary or sufficient conditions.

If a condition associated with an effect is claimed to be *necessary*, we need to show that absence of the cause is always accompanied by absence of the effect. Evidence for the necessity of a certain type of input would be its universal distribution among the languages and cultural settings in which normal acquisition takes place (i.e. all known natural languages) and its absence from the input to children who fail to develop some feature of language. Despite the optimistic claim of a "recognition that children the world over are presented with a special language register" (Bohannon and Warren-Leubecker 1988, p. 90), the condition of universality may not be fulfilled for "motherese" (see Lieven this volume). Nor is there clear evidence that children whose language fails to thrive have been deprived of specific features of the register, rather than subjected to general linguistic deprivation, such as Genie (Curtiss 1977), or lack of conversational interaction, such as hearing children of deaf parents whose main source of linguistic data is television (Ervin-Tripp 1973).

For such a condition to be claimed as *sufficient* one would want to show that the presence of that condition was always accompanied by the presence of a specified effect. The problem here is to isolate the putative cause from other influences – to show that speech adjustments are sufficient we would need a sample of children deprived of access to the adult register, and, to quote Neil Smith, "not even mothers can speak motherese all the time" (Smith 1989, p. 50). Experimentation can, however, play a useful role in investigating sufficient conditions for language acquisition (e.g. Nelson 1977a), and while most existing experimental research can tell us little about necessary conditions (Furrow *et al.* 1979) because items modeled are already present in the child's linguistic environment, studies of the acquisition of novel forms or an artificial language (e.g. Morgan and Newport 1981; Goldstein 1984) can be more informative.

Observational studies which relate input and interaction to variation in children's development rates have differed considerably in how far their aim was to investigate specific features of CDS. In many cases the variables have included quantity of verbal stimulation, the frequency of specific grammatical features or form classes, or sentence types. Nevertheless, as Hardy-Brown (1983) points out, researching the causes of individual differences is potentially of great value in the areas of child-rearing, education, and therapy. Both experimental and observational work has made an impact on practice, as can be seen from titles in, for example, "Child Language Teaching and Therapy" such as "Motherese as therapy" (Weistuch and Byers Brown 1987), and "Clinical applications of recasting" (Watkins and Pemberton 1987). The same applies to second language teaching (e.g. Ellis 1984, 1985a; Krashen 1985). It has been suggested on the basis of Newport *et al.*'s (1977) findings that professionals working with preschool children should ask more questions in order to speed up children's acquisition of modal auxiliaries (Bliss 1988). However, given the contradictory statements quoted in the introduction to this chapter, it is all the more important that the findings of input studies are subjected to careful scrutiny to ascertain whether the variables manipulated or observed can be interpreted as having exerted a *causative* influence on the process of acquiring language.

## 3     Inferring causation

Textbooks and articles on statistics or research design usually make the point that correlation does not show causation, let alone the direction of effects. However, the problems of inferring causation are not confined to passive observational studies using correlational statistics. One difference between observational and experimental research is the degree of control the researcher has over the independent (putatively causative) variable, but its manipulation will not necessarily mean that causation will be unequivocal.

In a summary of the arguments surrounding the notion of causation, Cook and Campbell (1979, pp. 9–36) refer to the work of, amongst others, Bertrand Russell, David Hume, John Stuart Mill, and Karl Popper, from whom they derive a set of criteria for inferring causation. Those which bear most directly on the literature reviewed in this chapter are the following:
1 "covariation between the presumed cause and effect";
2 "temporal precedence of the cause";
3 manipulation of the independent variable to remove the confound with spurious causes;

4 the need for the concept of control to rule out alternative explanations.
(Cook and Campbell 1979, pp. 31–2)

In addition, they agree with Popper that it is necessary to proceed by
seeking to falsify predictions rather than confirming them, but with the
proviso that there should be a large number of replications before accepting that a proposed cause has or has not been falsified.

It is possible to regard the four criteria as a hierarchy. Depending on
how many of the conditions are fulfilled, they can be used to place
research into the effects of input on a continuum leading from concurrent
correlational research (e.g. Cross 1977), through lagged (T1, T2) correlational designs (Newport *et al.* 1977), single subject intervention designs
(Kearns and Salmon 1984), to the controlled experiment (Nelson 1977a).

However, the concept of "control" needs to be considered further. The
difference between the "classical" experiment and the quasi-experimental
approach lies in the random allocation of participants to treatment
groups and control groups (e.g. Nelson, Carskaddon, and Bonvillian
1973). Randomization seeks to ensure that groups do not already differ
on the dependent variable and that there are no systematic differences
between groups on unmeasured and unconsidered, but possibly confounding, variables (Ferguson 1981). As an additional safeguard against
placebo effects (positive changes resulting from nothing more than the
novelty of the treatment), the control group is usually exposed to some
novel but neutral condition. Typically in child language research, this
consists of extra play sessions. The aim is therefore to show that there are
changes in the experimental group beyond those occurring in the control
group.

In some studies two or more discrete relationships are investigated, in
which case the experimental groups can act as simultaneous controls. In
an investigation into the facilitation of early syntax through vertical
structures, for example (Schwartz, Chapman, Prelock, Terrell, and
Rowan 1985), an experimental group were engaged in conversation which
elicited and modeled noun–noun constructions while a control group
took part in an investigation into vocabulary acquisition. Similarly, an
intervention study by Keith Nelson (1977a) used recasts to introduce two
categories of syntactic structure to children who had shown no previous
evidence of using them. One group of six thirty-month-old children
received recasts containing "complex questions" (tag questions, *wh*-
negatives, and negative polar interrogatives), while a second group
received "complex verbs" (future or conditional forms, and two-verb
sentences). Intervention in the form of recasts, which took place during
five sessions over a period of five months, resulted in each group using the
target structures to a much greater degree than the nontargeted items.

Frequently, however, in a study which aspires to be experimental, the controls described above are simply impractical; in certain contexts, one wishes to study the effects of treatments (therapy, methods of instruction, linguistic interaction, or classroom organization) to which a school, teacher, or therapist is already committed. In these circumstances there may be organizational or ethical constraints on the random assignment of children and teachers to experimental and control groups. A quasi-experimental study by Speidel (1987) illustrates the enforced use of a non-equivalent control group design.

Speidel wished to establish whether small group conversations between a teacher and six Hawaiian first-graders would facilitate the students' acquisition of Standard English. The conversations formed a central part of a wider program to enhance reading skills. Based initially on natural-istic observation, Speidel's analysis systematically went through several stages. Firstly, she confirmed that the interaction *was* conversational rather than teacher-dominated: there was a high level of responsiveness and semantic contingency in the utterances of both student and teacher. Secondly, she demonstrated that there were instances of feedback and an appropriate level of tuning by the teacher which provided opportunities for learning. Thirdly, she showed that the students made use of such learning opportunities by inserting elements they heard into their own utterances. Finally, she asked the question whether the six children studied had made larger gains on standardized tests of grammatical production in Standard English than a comparison group of similar students who had not participated in the discussions. There was no classroom observation of the comparison group, but it was known that their medium of instruction was Standard English with no additional language teaching. It was also believed that they took no part in small group discussion work.

The results showed that the conversation group made significantly greater gains than the comparison group on the *Carrow Elicited Language Inventory*. This finding is consistent with the original hypothesis that the conversational nature of the small group reading lessons furthers the development of language skills. Nevertheless, Speidel urges caution in inferring causation, pointing out that the gains observed in the conver-sation group could have been brought about by other factors. The absence of a control group receiving a neutral treatment means that placebo effects cannot be ruled out; the fact that the "treatment" was part of a program to develop literacy raises the possibility that grammatical gains were mediated by advances in reading skills; and because the participants were the students of two teachers in two different schools, the contribution of school and teacher effectiveness is unknown. The latter point is particularly important because the teacher of the "experimental group" is praised for "her superior teaching skill, her patience, flexibility and openness to being taped, as well as her personal interest in the research" (Speidel 1987, p. 131). Nevertheless, Speidel's investigation progressed through a series of four logically sequenced stages, each of which contributed to a coherent set of findings supporting her hypothesis of facilitation through small group discussion.

In common with correlational research, some problems of attributing causation from non-equivalent control group designs arise from the possible existence of influences which are correlated with the independent variable (e.g. an association between the general skill of the teacher and the provision of the treatment) or with the dependent variable (e.g. an association between growth in reading skill and the development of the grammar of Standard English). Other problems are more specific to the latter type of research: in passive observation studies placebo effects may result from being subjected to observation, but this is a condition to which all participants are subjected equally, and would be regarded as a problem of sampling error, rather than an additional difficulty in attributing causation. Conversely, the difficulty of interpreting direction of effects, a pervasive issue for passive observation, is less likely to concern us where the independent variable is under greater control.

## 4    The nature of the evidence for environmental effects

While considerable evidence exists which is *consistent* with general or specific effects on rate of language, one has to look harder for evidence which unequivocally *supports* such influences. The fact that children acquiring Quiché in Guatemala appear to be linguistically behind English-speaking children of the same age (Ingram 1989, p. 131) and do not have mothers who engage them in interactional routines may be consistent with the hypothesis that the CDS register facilitates, but is probably not the most parsimonious explanation, given the comparative lack of speech addressed to learners of Quiché. It does, however, provide support for the influence of the linguistic environment. Nevertheless, claims about the effectiveness of CDS are frequently at the level of observations of this kind for which there are no controls for confounding factors such as overall quantity of linguistic interaction. Conclusions about the facilitative nature of input tend to be drawn from the following types of evidence:

1 In case studies looking at specific domains of development rather than input, an unexpected finding may encourage the researcher to undertake an analysis of input for an explanation, for example Bernstein-Ratner

(1990) on an unusual feature of phonological development, Budwig and Wiley (1991) on children's self-reference. This is a useful exploratory approach, but researchers usually urge caution. To assume a causal link without further verification would be an example of the *post hoc* fallacy – the assumption that because A precedes B, then A causes B. The value of showing that specific aspects of mothers' language subsequently emerge in children's speech (see Snow *et al.*1987, p. 75) depends on the uniqueness of that behavior – would it have developed at this point anyway?

An interesting example of a retrospective analysis of input which compared groups of children found to be developing differently is by Landau and Gleitman (1985). They studied the preschool language development of three blind children and found that in comparison with sighted children at a similar MLU, they were delayed on only one measure of internal syntactic structure, "the mean number of morphemes that appear in the verb + auxiliary" (p. 42). The authors interpret this as an index of auxiliary verb growth, which in previous research (Newport *et al.* 1977) had been correlated with the frequency of *yes–no* questions addressed to children. By comparing the frequency of such questions addressed to two of the blind children with Newport *et al.*'s sighted children at a comparable age and MLU, Landau and Gleitman confirm that the blind children were exposed to a relative scarcity of *yes–no* questions but an abundance of imperatives (Landau and Gleitman 1985, p. 48). The authors take this as further evidence for the role of *yes–no* questions in making the usually unstressed auxiliary more salient, one aspect of what I have called the Auxiliary Clarification Hypothesis (Richards 1990a). On its own this study provides rather a weak causal link between input and development, direction of influence being a particular problem. Nevertheless, it is consistent with a series of studies (Gleitman *et al.* 1984; Shatz, Hoff-Ginsberg, and MacIver 1989; Richards 1990a, 1990b) which suggest that the relationship between *yes–no* questions and children's verbal auxiliaries is a reliable one, even if the mechanisms underlying it are not fully understood (Richards and Gallaway 1993).

2 Causation may be inferred by linking two or more known phenomena, often from studies looking at quite separate areas. Snow (1981, p. 201), for example, reasons as follows: at-risk populations such as premature and small infants, and those who have suffered respiratory distress syndrome (a) may have disturbed patterns of interaction with their mothers, and (b) are over-represented among children with language and learning difficulties. Contingent responding is therefore facilitative. Such conclusions involve what Snow *et al.* (1987, p. 75) call an "inferential leap," given the existence of alternative explanations such as perinatal stress

(Snow 1981), or genetic and social factors. Here, however, the conclusion is supported by evidence that in such cases development is not hindered *unless* early mother–child interaction is disrupted.

Indirect evidence is not always strengthened in this way. Sometimes inferences are based on the assumption that one feature of interaction entails another: there is evidence that increased physical contact after birth (assumed to sensitize the mother to the child) and an increased quantity of interaction predict faster language development, but this does not demonstrate that contingent responding is responsible (e.g. Snow 1981, p. 200).

3 The third source of evidence is passive observation research using correlational statistics (e.g. Newport *et al.* 1977). Although these allow statistical controls and tests of significance, they may only fulfill the first of the criteria for inferring causation and pose many problems of interpretation. These will be considered in detail in section 5.

4 A fourth source is quasi-experimental research with *indirect* control over independent variables through the manipulation of parental behavior: this can be achieved by increasing the desired maternal behavior through positive feedback (see Bates, Bretherton, Beeghly-Smith, and McNew 1982, pp. 57–8) or by training programs. Weistuch and Byers Brown (1987), for example, educated mothers of children with expressive language delay on twenty aspects of language development and facilitation through motherese. Comparisons with a quasi-control group showed desired changes in both maternal language behavior and children's MLU and multi-word utterances.

5 Finally there is experimental or quasi-experimental research involving *direct* manipulation of the independent variable(s). Here the work of Keith Nelson on the use of "growth recasts" has been particularly influential (e.g. Watkins and Pemberton 1987). Although the definition of a recast varies slightly in the literature, with some commentators treating recasts and expansions as synonymous, they are essentially "replies that keep the basic meaning and reference of a child's prior utterance, but that build in a growth opportunity because there is a more complex language structure in the reply than in the child's prior utterance" (Nelson, Heimann, Abuelhaija, and Wroblewski 1989, p. 316). Nelson's contribution is particularly important in four respects. Firstly, a relatively low frequency of experimental recasts can accelerate syntax learning (Nelson *et al.* 1973; Nelson 1977a, 1977b; see also Nelson 1987, p. 315). Secondly, the use of later-acquired structures such as passives (Baker and Nelson 1984) and complex questions, complex verb meanings, and verb

combinations (Nelson 1977a) can be advanced. Thirdly, self-recasts by the adult can also be facilitative (Baker and Nelson 1984; see Nelson 1989, p. 293). Lastly, there is a correspondence between experimental findings on recasts and their relative complexity, and the results of observational studies (e.g. Nelson, Denninger, Bonvillian, Kaplan, and Baker 1984; Farrar 1990) which would otherwise be less secure, particularly because of doubts over direction of effects.

Bates, Bretherton, and Snyder (1988) point out that a great deal of research is implicitly, though not statistically, correlational. The first two sources of evidence fall into this category. They may or may not fulfill the criterion of temporal precedence, but even if they do, they provide only weak evidence of a causal link. The next section will deal with problems associated with passive observation research (as in paragraph 3 above) which is explicitly correlational.

## 5    Passive observation studies using correlational statistics

Research under this heading usually correlates naturally occurring differences in input frequencies (I) at a certain point in time (T1) with measures of children's language level (C). Correlations may be concurrent (I1 × C1) or lagged (I1 × C2). Details of such studies are provided in tables 4.1 and 4.2 (pp. 86 and 88). The problems associated with this design are of two types. Firstly, the results may be undermined by worries over attributing causation, particularly because of reciprocal effects between children and their interlocutors. Secondly, despite fairly strong evidence for the influence of semantic contingency on language development (Snow *et al.* 1987, pp. 76–7; Cazden 1988) and for the effects of CDS on vocabulary growth (Bohannon and Warren-Leubecker 1988), the number of statistically significant results from these studies is low compared with the number of statistical tests carried out (Bates *et al.* 1982; Bohannon and Warren-Leubecker 1988). On the one hand, this raises the specter that the significant findings may have occurred by chance, or that researchers have wrongly attributed the main direction of influence. On the other hand, some (e.g. Bohannon and Warren-Leubecker 1988) would attribute this lack of success to inadequacies in the design of many of the studies published to date. Both of these views are dealt with below under a series of headings which deal with aspects of correlational research design.

### 5.1    Direction of effects

Because of the reciprocal nature of conversation, passive observation studies have to address the issue of the direction of influence. Cross (1977) used a concurrent (I1 × C1) design which correlated features of maternal input with measures of sixteen children's productive and receptive language and their age. All subjects were middle-class fast developers with an older sibling judged to be linguistically advanced. From this it was assumed that the mothers "would be providing optimally appropriate linguistic inputs and thus were an ideal sample to observe the kinds of interactions which promote acquisition" (p. 155). Because there were significant correlations between 35 out of 62 maternal variables and child language, particularly comprehension, Cross's study is frequently quoted as evidence for the facilitative nature of CDS. However, as the author herself makes quite clear (p. 182), this interpretation is unwarranted. There is no evidence that the correlations result from anything other than the mother responding to the child. Many of the variables, particularly if tuned to the child's linguistic level, may have the *potential* to facilitate, but there is no indication that they do so. There is no evidence that tuning is finer, or that the maternal variables occur more frequently, than for children developing less fast.

In a follow-up analysis, Cross (1978) tried to overcome this problem using a concurrent matched pairs design. Eight pairs of children were matched for sex, family size, and three linguistic variables: MLU, upper bound, and comprehension of syntax. In each pair the younger child was assigned to an "accelerated group" and the older to a "normal group," the average age difference being 7;1 months. Sixty paired t-tests were performed to test for differences between the mothers' speech to the two groups. To assess whether significant differences had come about as a result of mothers' adjustments to children's age, correlations were computed between children's age and each maternal variable which had shown significant effects. Only three such correlations proved to be significant, leaving fourteen variables, mostly categories of contingent responses, associated with rate of development. Even though it lacks a longitudinal dimension (Ellis and Wells 1980, p. 47) from which we might infer a causal link between *previous* maternal behavior and current language level, this new design represents an advance on the previous study. The validity of its findings depends to a large extent on the adequacy of matching the pairs of children if we wish to rule out the possibility that measured or unmeasured differences between the groups elicited differential maternal styles.

Longitudinal (I1 × C2) designs are, of course, no guarantee that direction of effects is unequivocal. An *apparent* influence of input on children's later language can result from possibly unmeasured correlations between input at T1 and characteristics of the child at T1, and between child

Table 4.1. *Details (where available) of participants in correlational studies of input effects*

| Author(s) | Date | N | Sex | SES | Age(T1) | MLU(T1) | Population |
|---|---|---|---|---|---|---|---|
| Barnes et al. | 1983 | 32 | 16B,16G | mixed | 1;6–2;9 | 1.00–2.21 | normal |
| Bee et al. | 1982 | 193 | mixed | mixed | birth | | normal first born |
| Cross | 1977 | 16 | 6B,10G | MC | 1;7–2;8 | 1.49–3.44 | fast developers |
| Cross | 1978 | 16 | 6B,10G | MC | 1;7–2;9 | 1.5–3.5 | fast developers |
| Ellis and Wells | 1980 | 26 | mixed | mixed | from 1;6 | 1.5 | normal: early fast, late fast v. slow developers |
| Farrar | 1990 | 12 | 6B, 6G | MC | 1;10 | 2.17 | normal |
| Furrow et al. | 1979 | 7 | 4B, 3G | MC | 1;6 | 1.0–1.4 | normal |
| Gleitman et al. II | 1984 | 6 | 6G | MC | 1;6–1;9 | 1.05–3.32 | normal |
| Gleitman et al. III | 1984 | 6 | 6G | MC | 2;0–2;1 | 1.16–3.46 | normal |
| Hampson and Nelson I | 1990 | 36 | mixed | MC | 1;1 | | normal: early talkers v. late talkers |
| Hampson and Nelson II | 1990 | 45 | 24B,21G | MC | 1;1 | 23–118 words receptive vocabulary | referential v. expressive at 20 months |
| Hardy-Brown et al. | 1981 | 50 | 25B,25G | mixed | 1;0 | | normal, adopted |
| Harris et al. | 1986 | 10 | 5B, 5G | MC | 1;4 | | normal v. slow |
| Hoff-Ginsberg | 1985 | 22 | 11B,11G | MC | 2;0–2;6 | preverbal 2.05 | normal |
| Hoff-Ginsberg | 1986 | 22 | 11B,11G | MC | 2;0–2;6 | SD=0.43 2.05 SD=0.43 | normal |
| Lyon | 1985 | 7 | | | preschool | | hearing-impaired |
| McCartney | 1984 | 166 | mixed | mixed | > 3;0 | | children at 9 daycare centers |
| Murray et al. | 1990 | 14 | 5B, 9G | mixed | 0;9 | | medically low risk |
| Nelson et al. | 1984 | 25 | | | 1;10 | | normal |

| | | | | | T1 | | |
|---|---|---|---|---|---|---|---|
| Newport et al. | 1977 | 15 | 15G | MC | 1;0–2;3 | 1.00–3.46 | normal |
| Richards | 1990a | 32 | 16B,16G | mixed | 1;6–2;9 | 1.00–2.21 | normal |
| Richards | 1990b | 33 | 18B,15G | mixed | 1;9–2;0 | 1.30–2.05 | normal |
| Richards and Robinson | 1993 | 33 | 18B,15G | mixed | 1;9–2;0 | 1.30–2.05 | normal |
| Scarborough and Wyckoff | 1986 | 9 | 6B, 3G | MC | 2;0 | 1.30–1.42 | normal |
| Smith et al. | 1988 | 28 | 14B,14G | MC | 1:3 | 3–39 word vocabulary | normal |
| Tomasello and Todd | 1983 | 6 | 4B, 2G | MC | 1;0–1;1 | 2–7 word vocabulary | normal |
| Yoder | 1989 | 5 | 4B, 1G | MC | 2;10–4;4 | 1.72–2.72 | specific productive language disordered |
| Yoder and Kaiser | 1989 | 10 | | WC | 1;10 SD = 4 months | 1.13 SD = 0.11 | normal |

Key: B boys; G girls; MC middle class; SD standard deviation; T1 time 1; WC working class.

Table 4.2. *Design of correlational studies of input effects*

| Author(s) | Date | Waves of data collected | Intervals in months between data collection | Alpha level | Tail of test | Statistical analysis |
|---|---|---|---|---|---|---|
| Barnes et al. | 1983 | 2 | 9 | 0.05 | 2 | I1 × child RGS multiple regression |
| Bee et al. | 1982 | 5 | 8 and 12 | 0.05 | | I1 × C1 |
| Cross | 1977 | 1 | – | 0.05 | 2 | I1 × C2 partial correlation |
| Cross | 1978 | 1 | – | 0.05 | 2 | matched pairs, t-tests |
| Ellis and Wells | 1980 | 2 | no. of months required to gain 2 morphemes MLU | 0.05 | | t-tests comparing input to early fast developers, late fast developers and slow developers |
| Farrar | 1990 | 2 | 6 | 0.05 | 2 | I1 × C2 partial correlation |
| Furrow et al. | 1979 | 2 | 9 | 0.05 | 1 | I1 × C2 |
| Gleitman et al. II | 1984 | 2 | 6 | 0.10 | 2 | I1 × C2 partial correlation |
| Gleitman et al. III | 1984 | 2 | 6 | 0.10 | 2 | I1 × C2 partial correlation |
| Hampson and Nelson I | 1990 | 2 | 7 | 0.05 | 2 | (a) t-tests on I1 comparing mothers of early and late talkers (b) I1 × C2 partial correlation |
| Hampson and Nelson II | 1990 | 2 | 7 | 0.05 | 2 | I1 × C2 partial correlations performed for whole group and separately for referential and expressive groups |
| Hardy-Brown et al. | 1981 | 1 | – | 0.05 | 1 | I1 (adoptive mothers) × C1 |
| Harris et al. | 1986 | 2 | 8 | 0.05 | 1 | t-tests on I1 comparing normal and slow developers |
| Hoff-Ginsberg | 1985 | 4 | 2 | 0.05 | 1 | I1 × proportional child gains |

| | | | | | | |
|---|---|---|---|---|---|---|
| Hoff-Ginsberg | 1986 | 4 | 2 | 0.01 | 2 | I1 × child RGS |
| Lyon | 1985 | 2 | 12 | 0.05 | 1 | I1 × raw child gains |
| McCartney | 1984 | 1 | – | 0.10 | 2 | multiple regression to examine effects on children's language of variable quality in 9 daycare centers |
| Murray et al. | 1990 | 2 | 9 | | | multiple regression |
| Nelson et al. | 1984 | 2 | 5 | 0.10 | 2 | I1 × C2 and I1 × raw child gains and t-tests on input to children |
| Newport et al. | 1977 | 2 | 6 | 0.08 | 2 | Double partial correlations high and low on syntactic growth |
| Richards | 1990a | 2 | 9 | 0.05 | 2 | removing effect of age and MLU I1 × child RGS |
| Richards | 1990b | 4 | 3 | 0.10 | 2 | I1 × C2 partial correlations |
| Richards | 1993 | 4 | 3 | 0.10 | 2 | I1 × C2 partial correlations |
| Richards and Robinson | 1986 | 2 | 6 | 0.10 | 2 | I1 × C2 |
| Scarborough and Wyckoff | 1986 | 2 | 6 | 0.05 | 2 | I1 × C2 and multiple regression |
| Smith et al. | 1988 | 3 | 3 and 2 | 0.05 | 2 | Input data from T1 to T2 × C2 and cross-lagged correlations |
| Tomasello and Todd | 1983 | 2 | 5 | 0.05 | 1 | I1 × C2 or child RGS |
| Yoder | 1989 | 2 | 12 | 0.05 | 1 | I1 × C2 or child RGS |
| Yoder and Kaiser | 1989 | 2 | 5 | 0.05 | 2 | I1 × C2 or child RGS |

*Key:* RGS residual gain score; C1 child at T1; I1 input at time 1; T1 time 1.

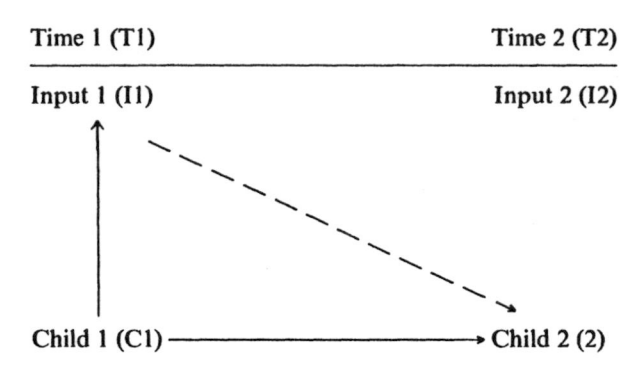

Figure 4.1 Longitudinal correlation design

characteristics at T1 and language level at T2 (figure 4.1). Child characteristics which might elicit differential input could be of many kinds, including variation in age, language level, physical behavior, or degrees of
handicap. In a study of seven hearing-impaired preschool children (see
tables 4.1 and 4.2), Lyon (1985) found measures of maternal control to be
negatively correlated with children's language gains twelve months later.
There were, however, no controls for language level, age, or hearing loss
at T1, all of which could have been powerful influences on input frequencies. As an example, maternal directives (I1) in Lyon's study negatively
predict children's gains (C2 minus C1) on the Reynell Expressive Scale
($rho = -0.90$). But mothers' directives at T1 are also *positively* correlated
with the children's hearing loss ($rho = 0.89$). This in turn is *negatively*
correlated with children's gains on Reynell ($rho = -0.90$). Magnitude of
hearing loss could therefore be the cause of both maternal directiveness
and slower language growth (see figure 4.2).

Variation in effects on children's interlocutors can be reduced by
ensuring that the children are as similar as possible at T1 with regard to
age and language indices. Furrow *et al.* (1979) and Scarborough and
Wyckoff (1986) used subjects who were assumed to be so well equated
that direction of effects would not be problematic (see table 4.2). Bohannon and Warren-Leubecker (1988), however, argue that if the child's level
of comprehension is the main determinant of fine-tuning, then it is this
variable above all else which should be controlled. Otherwise, if the use of
CDS is to some extent a measure of the child's failure to understand
(Bates *et al.* 1982), then the negative relationships between input frequency and child comprehension at T1 may mask causal (I1 × C2) influences on later language level.

While the maximum reduction in variation between children at T1 is

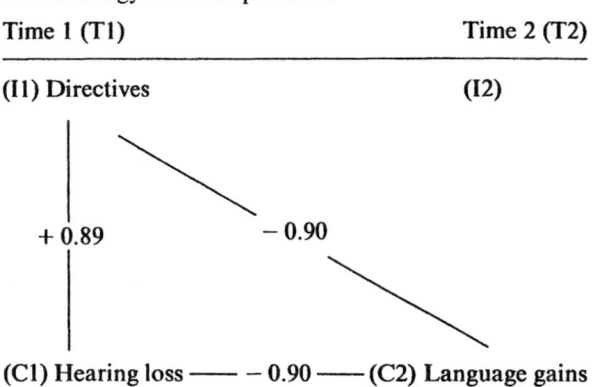

Figure 4.2  One pattern of correlations in Lyon (1985, pp. 124–5)

desirable, this aim may be impossible in respect of all the dependent variables being investigated, let alone other unmeasured factors to which adults respond. The usual answer has been to use statistical controls through regression procedures and partial correlation in order to remove the effect of the C1 variable(s). The problem here is that partialing out a general measure such as MLU (e.g. Newport *et al.* 1977) equates children on that particular measure only (Schwartz and Camarata 1985) and does not necessarily remove the correlation with the dependent variable. A more effective solution is to partial out each C1 variable separately (e.g. Farrar 1990; Hampson and Nelson 1990; Richards 1990b; Richards and Robinson 1993), but this still fails to remove the influence of other child characteristics which are correlated with the dependent variable.

A possible solution to bidirectional effects is cross-lagged panel correlations (Murray, Johnson, and Peters 1990). An application in the field of lexical development is by Tomasello and Todd (1983) who wished to confirm that the collaborative maintenance of interaction by mother and child influenced vocabulary size. Since the focus was on the reciprocal manipulation of attention and behavior by mother and child, interpreting direction of effects was particularly important. The thinking here is that in order to infer that input influences the child rather than *vice versa*, the I1 × C2 correlation should be larger than the C1 × I2 correlation as well as being larger than the synchronous (I1 × C1 and I2 × C2) correlations (figure 4.3). Nevertheless, in an extensive critique of this approach, Cook and Campbell (1979), pp. 309–21 draw attention to several difficulties. One assumption of the procedure is that of "stationarity," the condition that the synchronous correlations remain stable over time.

Unfortunately, data frequently fail to fulfill such assumptions. The reliability of developmental measures is likely to change over time, and

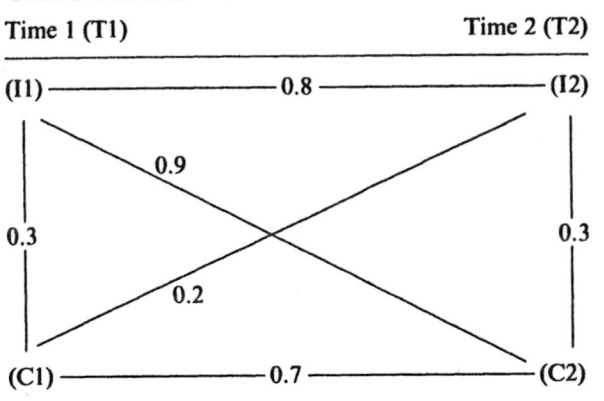

Figure 4.3  Cross-lagged panel correlations: an ideal case

indices of language development are no exception. For specific linguistic items such as auxiliaries per verb phrase, zero entries may be relatively common at the beginning of a study, and sampling error is likely to be greater until children produce an item with greater regularity. At T1, therefore, less reliable discrimination between children is likely to attenuate (I1 × C1) correlations causing the stationarity condition to be broken. Cook and Campbell point out that a variable whose reliability is increasing is likely to be mistakenly judged to be an effect rather than a cause.

Other difficulties with this procedure occur when positive and negative effects are confounded, causing I1 × C2 relationships to be masked, and when the study lacks sufficient power to show up a significant difference between the I1 × C2 and C1 × I2 correlations. Sample sizes in child language studies are rarely large enough to allow significant differences between correlations to be detected (Bates *et al.* 1982). Nevertheless, an inspection of a pattern of correlations corresponding to those in figure 4.3 is always informative and allows alternative explanations, such as the influence of I2 on C2 to be considered.

## 5.2    Gains

Elsewhere I have argued that in order to identify a causal influence on language growth, the dependent variable should be the *gain* in language since the input was sampled (Richards 1991). This seems to be a fairly common-sense observation. Nevertheless, some studies have simply correlated input at T1 with child scores at T2. In some cases (e.g. Scarborough and Wyckoff 1986) this was because children were so homogeneous at T1 that T2 scores were in fact equal to gains. In others (e.g. Yoder and Kaiser 1989), the researchers had found no significant correlation between C1 and C2 scores and therefore regarded them as independent. The problem with this latter approach is that the children who make the most progress are not necessarily those with the highest scores at T2. As demonstrated in a reanalysis of Yoder's (1989) data for five specific language-disordered children (Richards 1991), this can be sufficient to distort the results. Yoder reported a nonsignificant correlation of 0.58 ($df = 3$) between maternal requests for confirmation that the child's utterance had been understood and child auxiliaries per verb phrase at T2. The corresponding correlation with children's residual gain scores (see below) would be significant at 0.83 (Richards 1991).

Although some researchers (e.g. Nelson *et al.* 1984) have entered raw gains (T2 minus T1) into their analyses, this approach has been criticized on the grounds that gains, whether raw or proportional, tend to be negatively correlated with the child's initial status (Barnes, Gutfreund, Satterly, and Wells 1983). In other words, the higher the starting point, the more difficult it is to make further progress. This is what Gleitman *et al.* (1984) have referred to as the "effects by the child on the child" (p. 46). One common solution has been to use residual gain scores (see table 4.2 for examples). These are the differences between the scores obtained at T2 and the predicted scores for T2 calculated from the regression of T2 scores on T1 scores (see O'Connor 1972). By definition, residual gains have a zero correlation with initial status. They do not, however, remove what Gleitman *et al.* (1984) call the "effects of the child on the mother" (p. 46), and are therefore less effective than partialing out the influence of C1 on I1 and C2. In fact, the use of partial correlation and multiple regression makes gain scores, residual or otherwise, unnecessary (O'Connor 1972).

## 5.3    Statistical significance and sample size

One factor which makes the results difficult to compare is the variation in approaches to statistical significance – choice of alpha level, and of one- or two-tailed tests. Even if the reader consults statistical tables, it is not always clear whether tests are directional (one-tailed) or, if partial correlations have been used, how many degrees of freedom remain. Table 4.2 shows that a large proportion of studies use two-tailed tests with an alpha level of 0.05. However, even more use either two-tailed tests at the 0.10 level, or one-tailed tests at the 0.05 level. In terms of the magnitude of the correlation coefficient or value of *t* required to be statistically significant, the latter two procedures are identical.

A lower alpha level reduces the probability of type I error (the mistaken rejection of the null hypothesis), and this is of particular concern in exploratory work where a large number of statistical tests may result in significant correlations occurring by chance. Schwartz and Camarata (1985) suggest two solutions – the application of tests which adjust for multiple comparisons, and a reduction in the number of tests performed. This can be accomplished either on theoretical grounds, or by reducing the number of variables by factor analysis (e.g. Barnes *et al.* 1983). However, as Schwartz and Camarata point out, the answer is not to use split-half correlations – the insistence that each correlation should hold true for separate halves of the data (e.g. Newport *et al.* 1977; Gleitman *et al.* 1984; Hoff-Ginsberg 1985; Scarborough and Wyckoff 1986). A more detailed discussion of split-half correlations and the confusion between reliability and statistical significance can be found in Furrow and Nelson (1986).

A second concern is type II errors (the mistaken acceptance of the null hypothesis) in studies with small sample sizes. Table 4.1 shows one correlational study with a sample of five, and others with samples of six and seven children. The power of such studies to detect real correlations is small, and the probabilities of replication with a sample of similar size are equally small (Hardy-Brown 1983). Woods, Fletcher, and Hughes (1986, pp. 115–17) demonstrate the extent to which the probability of type II error would decrease in a hypothetical study of children's vocabulary as samples rise from 140 to 500 and 1,000 children.

Finally, whether to use directional (one-tailed) or nondirectional (two-tailed) tests is itself controversial, the latter being more conservative. Some advocate the greater use of one-tailed tests on the grounds that direction of differences or relationships is seldom irrelevant (Ferguson 1981). On the other hand, even if the direction of the effect has been predicted, one can seldom be confident that an unexpected result in the opposite direction has occurred entirely by chance. What is important is that authors provide sufficient information about statistical tests and procedures to allow comparisons with other studies.

## 5.4    *Intervals between samples*

It can be seen from table 4.2 that intervals between T1 and T2 vary from two months (Hoff-Ginsberg 1985) to twelve months (Yoder 1989). In designing a study, several factors need to be balanced. The first is temporal erosion of lagged correlations. This is the phenomenon of correlations becoming weaker over longer intervals, possibly resulting in the failure to detect real influences. Long intervals may also cause stage-related effects to be confounded and other nonlinear relationships to attenuate correlations. On the other hand, short intervals may be insufficient for effects to become apparent – the time lag between a cause and a measurable effect is likely to vary from domain to domain (Bohannon and Hirsh-Pasek 1984) and could be considerably delayed if one is measuring production rather than comprehension (Murray *et al.* 1990). In handicapped populations more time may be required for children's progress to be compared reliably.

Bohannon and Warren-Leubecker (1988) have suggested that more varied "causal lags" should be investigated. Hoff-Ginsberg (1985) took four samples at two-monthly intervals and computed all possible lagged correlations between maternal and child language measures. As well as the three sets of correlations involving an interval of two months (I1 × C2; I2 × C3; I3 × C4), there were also lags of four months (I1 × C3; I2 × C4) and six months (I1 × C4). There are two problems here: firstly, the large number of statistical tests carried out compared with the small number of significant results obtained make interpretation difficult; secondly, problems over direction of effects are exacerbated once the later input measures are entered into the analysis. This is because a sample of children which is relatively homogeneous at T1 will no longer be so by T2 and will be even less so by T3 and T4. A later analysis by Hoff-Ginsberg (1986) used input at T1 only and correlated this with the child at T2, T3, and T4, a procedure later followed by Richards (1990b) and Richards and Robinson (1993).

## 5.5    Frequency

Since no variable can correlate with another variable more strongly than it can correlate with itself, one reason for the lack of success in finding environmental correlates of language acquisition may be the unreliable sampling (Bates *et al.* 1982) of both dependent and independent variables, and the use of indices whose validity is questionable. It is possible that the greater number of significant correlations with vocabulary growth (e.g. Tomasello and Todd 1983; Tomasello, Mannle, and Kruger 1986; Smith, Adamson, and Bakeman 1988) reflects our ability to measure it more reliably and validly.

Correlational studies search for differential effects on the language of children resulting from variation in the frequency of features of the language they hear. It is usually assumed implicitly that there is a substantial relationship between the features of the utterances *addressed to* children and the smaller number of utterances which are actually heard, attended to, and encoded. Since we have no reliable way of comparing input with "take-up" (see Gallaway and Woll this volume) or of assessing the relative influence of utterances overheard rather than addressed to the child, assumptions of this nature, imperfect though they are, are necessary in order to proceed at all. On the other hand, it is too simplistic to suppose a linear relationship between quantity of input and child progress (e.g. Bohannon and Hirsh-Pasek 1984; Schwartz and Camarata 1985; Bohannon and Warren-Leubecker 1988). Such an assumption ignores curvilinear relationships – threshold and stage-related effects, and the possibility that sensitivity to frequency will vary between aspects which encode universal meanings and those which are language-specific (Newport *et al.* 1977; Bates *et al.* 1982). From the "rare event" perspective Nelson has also criticized the idea that amount of input causes progress, rather than its quality and timing, and the context in which it is embedded: "a little of the right kind of evidence for the child's current level is often all that is required to induce an advance to the next level" (Nelson *et al.* 1984, p. 48). On the other hand, a more positive view of frequency measures is also possible if the frequency of an item alters the probability of the simultaneous occurrence of conditions which constitute the "rare events" and trigger advances (Richards 1990a).

In most of the published research analyses are carried out expressing the frequency of each input variable as a proportion of the total number of utterances addressed to the child. This avoids confounding specific effects with overall quantity of speech, and reduces the intercorrelation between the independent variables. The influence of the overall quantity of speech addressed to children (e.g. Barnes *et al.* 1983; Murray *et al.* 1990) is one of the most consistent findings in the literature on environmental effects (Bates *et al.* 1982) and is something which needs to be controlled for.

One study which neglected to do this is Barnes *et al.* (1983). Three of their input variables were based on frequency of occurrence in 27 minutes of recording. These were "direct requests in context of control (directive)," "extending utterances," and "question–comment." Between them, the first two of these were significantly related to four measures of language gains, but reanalysis using percentages (Wells 1985, pp. 389–92) produced results which are very different. Some results become stronger: extending utterances are now more strongly and more consistently related to child gain scores – they now correlate with eight out of nine rather than three out of eight. Similarly, "adult utterances in joint activity" which was not reported in Barnes *et al.* but which produced no significant correlations, now predicts gains on four child measures. Directives, however, now only correlate with one measure rather than three.

The results of this reanalysis are interesting given the findings of Ellis and Wells (1980), who based their work on transcripts from twenty-six of the thirty-two children later used by Barnes *et al.* Ellis and Wells investigated the influence of adult speech variables by comparing the input to three groups of children: early fast developers, late fast developers, and slow developers. Groups were defined by the age range during which the children progressed from an MLU of 1.5 to 3.5 morphemes. Of the thirty-four variables, ten (all discourse functions and locus of reference) showed significant differences between the early fast developers and the slow group. These were, however, all variables which were expressed as absolute rather than proportional frequencies.

Pine (1990) has recently pointed out that measures of maternal semantic contingency are usually expressed as a proportion of the *mother's* utterances, whereas it is the proportion of *child* utterances to which there are semantically contingent responses which is a more valid measure of responsiveness. In similar vein, Hoff-Ginsberg (1990) compared interaction in working-class ($n = 30$) and upper-middle-class ($n = 33$) mother–child dyads. On one maternal variable (the number of topic-continuing replies) raw frequencies were higher for the upper-middle-class group, while proportional frequencies were higher for the working-class group. However, when expressed as a proportion of *child* utterances the upper-middle-class group came out higher.

Frequencies of linguistic items such as lexical verbs per child utterance (Barnes *et al.* 1983) or inflections per noun phrase (Newport *et al.* 1977) also require caution. Frequency measures do not differentiate between the first emergence of items or structures and their extension to a wider range of contexts (Bohannon and Hirsh-Pasek 1984), nor do they distinguish between the latter and stereotyped or partially analyzed usage (Richards 1990a). There is also the danger of a temporary increase in the frequency of items which are in the process of being acquired, which then falls as the child concentrates on other domains. In fact, compared with measures such as MLU, which has been subjected to considerable scrutiny in a variety of languages and populations (e.g. Hickey 1991; Scarborough, Rescorla, Tager-Flusberg, Fowler, and Sudhalter 1991), little is known about the reliability and validity of many of the dependent variables which are entered into statistical analyses, and it is usually impossible to translate the numbers quoted into any meaningful concept of performance. In the case of auxiliaries per verb phrase, for example, it is conceivable, that at a stage of development before auxiliaries cooccur with the copula (e.g. *It must be mine*), this measure underestimates auxiliary frequency in children who frequently use copulas, since the latter also enter into the verb phrase count.

Following Brown (1973), the proportion of filled obligatory contexts has also been used as a dependent variable (e.g. Yoder 1989). Nevertheless, the use of this approach for items such as the auxiliary and copula has been questioned on the grounds of coding reliability (Kuczaj 1979; Richards and Robinson 1993). There is also the possibility of U-shaped distributions where children progress from partially analyzed inclusion, through omission, to a stage of productive inclusion (Richards 1990a). At the same time there has been a recognition that even relatively low inclusion rates may conceal systematic semantically based preferences of children with regard to the contexts in which morphemes are included and excluded (see Slobin 1988).

Elsewhere (Barnes *et al.* 1983; Wells 1985; Richards 1990a, 1990b) researchers have complemented measures of frequency with an index of the diversity of linguistic items. Such measures include semantic range, range of auxiliary meanings, semantic complexity, and range of func-tions, all used by Barnes *et al.* (1983, p. 72), and range of auxiliary forms used by Richards (1990a). Here the problem is that such indices are confounded with sample size – the larger the sample of speech, the greater the probability of sampling a wider range of linguistic behavior. In studies which include measures of vocabulary growth (e.g. Bates *et al.* 1988) this problem has been addressed by calculating the ratio between the number of *types* and the number of *tokens*. However, it has been shown (Hess, Sefton, and Landry 1986; Richards 1987) that the resulting type–token ratio (TTR) is still a function of the number of tokens – the larger the sample the smaller the ratio. This is because, as the sample size increases and an ever-increasing proportion of the subject's repertoire of tokens has already been sampled, it becomes progressively more difficult to sample *new* forms. Richards (1990b) attempted to overcome this problem using linear regression analysis to control for the effect of sample size on the range of auxiliary forms. However, a better solution lies in the mathematical modeling procedures adapted by Malvern (1991). Although these are not yet fully available because of the labor-intensive nature of producing curves for each child which show the relationship between sample size and TTR, software is currently being developed which will automate this procedure and provide an index of range which is independent of sample size (Knott, Malvern, and Richards work in progress). It is worth noting that measures of range which are uncorrec-ted for sample size are likely to produce spurious correlations because they are confounded with the loquacity of the children, and loquacity itself is quite often positively correlated with a number of child language measures (Richards 1987). Type–token ratios, on the other hand, are more likely to cause effects to remain undetected because more talkative children obtain lower ratios.

nvironment confound

, p. 613) argues that correlations within the family are
...d by genetic factors. Parents of high verbal ability could
...inguistic environment for their children as well as passing
...ty genetically. This would bring about a correlation between
. children's language. Both twin and adoption studies allow
...s to be made of the relative contribution of heredity and environ-
, but in order to investigate variation in environmental influences
...nin the family without the genetic confound, an adoption design is
necessary. This can take two forms: a *partial* adoption design confined to
examining relationships between children and adoptive parents, or a *full*
adoption design which includes correlations between children and natural
parents. Here, one can have greater confidence in apparent environmental
influences if an aspect of child development is not predicted by features
(e.g. the intelligence) of the natural parents.

Nevertheless, quite apart from the logistics of obtaining participants,
adoption designs are not unproblematic. In particular, selective placement of children into families which are similar to their natural parents
can endanger validity.

As part of the Colorado Adoption Study (Plomin and DeFries 1985),
Hardy-Brown, Plomin, and DeFries (1981) used a full adoption design to
examine the contribution of home environment variables to the communicative competence of fifty one-year-olds (see tables 4.1 and 4.2). Maternal imitation and contingent vocal responding were both found to be
significantly correlated with child communicative competence (Hardy-
Brown *et al.* 1981). Nevertheless, the cognitive ability and memory ability
of natural mothers also predicted the children's language (p. 714). Therefore inherited language ability could have been eliciting differential input.
As the authors themselves point out, direction of effects is a problem, and
this is particularly true since the design is concurrent (I1 = C1) rather than
lagged.

The genetic confound can also be reduced by passive observation
outside the family setting (using environments such as nursery schools or
the homes of child minders) which are likely to make a substantial
contribution to the child's experience. One danger, though, is that results
could still be confounded with systematic patterns of parental choice.
McCartney (1984) investigated the effects of the quality of day care on
language development in a large sample of the children (see table 4.1) in
nine day-care centers. She controlled for parental selection of centers as
well as for the age, family background, and the amount of time children
spent at the centers, and found that quality of day care was equally

predictive of language ability as the family back[...]
guage level was predicted by the quantity of verba[...]
enced and the number of utterances with a represen[...]
while controlling utterances were a negative predictor.[...]
these findings rests on the assumption that direction of effect[...]
matic because the study looked at effects on groups of children[...]
centers. This is justified provided there are no between-group di[...]
which might elicit variation in linguistic stimulation. However, t[...]
here of a concurrent design (I1 × C1) again means that the results sh[...]
be interpreted with caution.

## 5.7     The holistic fallacy

The holistic fallacy, which is the assumption that effects are more widely
applicable or more uniform than may be the case, has taken numerous
forms in the child language literature. It can be an assumption about
populations, contexts, stages of development, or about the homogeneity
and internal consistency of variables investigated. A growing body of
research suggests that a higher degree of differentiation is required to
avoid confounding different effects. Snow *et al.* (1987), for example, show
how extensively processes can vary across situations. In more routinized
contexts such as bathtime, as compared with, for example, free play,
mothers show a higher degree of fine-tuning and there is greater complexity in the language of both mother and child. At the same time, the child
has less need to use scaffolded utterances than in less structured activities.

An example of the danger of confounding subvariables as a result of
undifferentiated coding schemes can be found in a study of environmental
predictors of copula verb development (Richards and Robinson 1993).
The overall frequency of copulas addressed to children failed to predict
children's development. However, subcategorizing the input showed
(albeit weak) positive effects of full copulas and a *negative* influence of
contracted copulas. A failure to differentiate between, for example,
simple and complex recasts (Nelson *et al.* 1984) is equally likely to cause
relationships to remain undetected.

With regard to populations, it is frequently taken for granted that what
is facilitative (or otherwise) for children developing normally will be
equally helpful or unhelpful to the language-delayed or language-
impaired child (see Conti-Ramsden; Gallaway and Woll this volume).
Nowhere is this more apparent than in discussions about "controlling"
styles of interaction. Similar assumptions are often implicit in work on
second language acquisition (e.g. Krashen 1985). Lyon (1985) makes the
point in the context of hearing impairment that: "The hearing-impaired

child may both elicit and need a different pattern of discourse in order to learn language optimally ... Comparisons between mothers and hearing and mothers and hearing-impaired children may not provide the answers ... It may be more useful to look at the strategies of mothers of hearing-impaired children who are developing language relatively successfully" (pp. 121–2). As yet few findings have been replicated in populations with special language needs. Exceptions are Yoder's (1989) study of children with specific productive language disorders and Lyon's (1985) investigation into interaction with the hearing-impaired. However, there are limitations to both studies which make their interpretation difficult (see sections 5.1 and 5.2 above).

On the other hand, even within a normal population, different processes within subgroups may also cancel each other out and cause effects to remain undetected. This may be the result of differences in age, stage of language development, or style of development. Early studies such as Newport et al. (1977) seemed to assume that features of input would be equally facilitative over a broad span of age and language level. In reality, heterogeneous samples may contain groups of children for whom quite different input features are effective. Children acquiring the auxiliary, for example, might exploit different sentence types (questions versus declaratives) depending on the extent to which they used analytic or holistic strategies (Richards 1990a, pp. 230–1). Computing correlations separately for subgroups can be informative (Schwartz and Camarata 1985) provided there are reliable and valid ways of identifying them. Techniques of cluster analysis (see Woods et al. 1986, pp. 249–72 for a readable introduction) can be of help here (Skehan 1989).

Two examples of different results in subgroups of normal populations follow. Firstly, Hoff-Ginsberg (1990) computed correlations separately for different social class groups and found that semantic contingency was a predictor of rate of children's language development in the working-class group only. Secondly, Hampson and Nelson (1990) looked for effects of maternal measures taken at 13 months on child MLU at 20 months in separate groups of early and late talkers, and in separate groups of referential and expressive children. In their first study, children were classified as early or late talkers on the basis of their productive vocabulary at 13 months (T1). Referential repetition and references to objects positively predicted MLU at 20 months for the early talkers only, although, as the authors indicate, this difference may have been the result of a truncated range in the slow group (Hampson and Nelson 1990, table 6). In their second study, however, correlations were computed between maternal measures at 13 months and MLU at 20 months, initially for the full sample of forty-five children. Although twelve significant relationships were found, all but two of these disappeared when children's vocabulary size at 13 months was partialed out, and these explained only a very small amount of the variance. On the other hand, separate analyses for the referential and expressive children uncovered a set of relatively powerful relationships for the referential group which were not present in the data from the expressive group. After partialing out initial vocabulary size it was found that the frequency of maternal references to objects, object nouns, and referential repetitions predicted MLU at 20 months for the referential group. There were no significant effects for the expressive group.

### 5.8    Summary

This section has identified factors which contribute to three types of problem in correlational research. Firstly, there are those which make results of different studies difficult to interpret and compare. These include heterogeneity of subjects at T1, differences in approaches to statistical significance, and the length of intervals between sampling. In addition, there is the problem of variation in the age and stage of the children studied and inconsistency in the definition of variables under investigation. Secondly, some factors contribute to the generation of invalid results – significant results occurring by chance, positive correlations between child and input variables at T1, the use of independent variables which are confounded with quantity of speech, and the genetic confound. Finally, other factors militate against the identification of real influences. These include small sample sizes, unreliable measurement, temporal erosion, confounding subvariables or stage-related effects, failure to use measures of the child's comprehension, insensitivity to threshold effects, and negative correlations between input and child language level at T1. However, we will now consider whether experimental designs offer benefits which can overcome some of these problems.

### 6    Experimental designs in language acquisition research

Several authors have called for a greater emphasis on experimental research into input and interaction to complement more exploratory correlational research (Bates *et al.* 1982; Schwartz and Camarata 1985; Yoder 1989). In addition to the fact that experimental designs can remove some of the threats to the validity of passive observation studies, they can also systematically vary frequency and rate of presentation, and look for generalizations beyond the items presented to related items (Ingram 1989, p. 224). In this way, Shatz *et al.* (1989) compared the effect on children's auxiliary growth of the contiguous and noncontiguous presentation of pairs of sentences containing the modal auxiliary *could*. The study also compared the contribution of pairs of sentences in which *could* was placed initially, medially, or in both positions. No effect was found for the spacing of sentences. However, of the three experimental conditions, pairs of sentences containing *could* in initial position were found to be most facilitative, although none of the groups differed significantly from the control group. Effects were generalized to other modals, but not to nonmodal auxiliaries. The design of this study had the additional merit of confirming long-term effects, taking speech samples three weeks, two months, and four months after enrichment.

In laboratory-based studies it is important to discover whether progress, and generalizations to related linguistic items, hold firm beyond the training items and whether they can be detected in spontaneous speech. Kearns and Salmon (1984), working with two aphasic patients, used a single subject (ABAB) reversal design, to examine the effect of training auxiliary third person singular *is* on auxiliary *is* in different contexts, and on copula *is*. The reversal design seeks, in the absence of a control group, to infer causation from increases in performance following both training and retraining. The four phases are: A baseline measurement; B training; A *reversal* training; B retraining. Reversal entails not just the removal of the treatment, which is often sufficient to bring about a drop in performance, but a deliberate retraining of the original baseline state of knowledge. Kearns and Salmon found some degree of generalization to take place and which was maintained in follow-up testing two and six weeks later. However, there was virtually no transfer to spontaneous speech.

## 6.1    Problems with experimental designs

A useful summary of threats to internal and external validity of experiments is provided by Cohen and Manion (1985, pp. 194–7). As the authors point out, these factors are usually an even greater problem in quasi-experimental approaches and as such, many are dealt with elsewhere in this chapter. Here, I shall focus on several specific points.

It has already been seen that effects found in the laboratory do not necessarily transfer to real life. It is also the case that putatively facilitative features of linguistic interaction which occur in real life may be difficult to replicate under controlled conditions. In a much discussed study, Cazden (1965) investigated the effect of expansions and modeling well-formed sentences on the language of twelve preschool children. Contrary to expectations, expansion was found to be less facilitative than modeling. Several problems with the methodology have been discussed, including the need for the adults who provide the enrichment to speak the same dialect as the children's parents (Nelson 1977a), but there were also difficulties in maintaining the required experimental condition without distorting the interaction in other ways. Expansions can fulfill a number of discourse functions, and Bates *et al.* (1982) observe that Cazden's expansions were more like corrections (therefore less helpful) than recasts, which are more likely to extend the child's topic and are found to be facilitative. At the same time tutors in the modeling condition, who had been told to avoid using expansions, found themselves increasing the frequency of extensions to maintain the natural flow of conversation (Cazden 1988). The apparent superiority of modeling could therefore be spurious. In Shatz *et al.*'s (1989) study there is also the possibility of unforeseen negative consequences of the three experimental treatments, which could account for their failure to be associated with progress beyond that of the control condition. They suggest that the experimental conditions introduced a degree of overcomplexity into the children's linguistic input which adversely affected them.

Obviously, experimental research into the influence of input and inter-action will be limited to those independent variables which are capable of identification, isolation, and manipulation, and which are free from ethical concerns (there would be serious reservations about increasing the frequency of features considered to be negatively correlated with pro-gress). In addition, the volume of enrichment has to be sufficient to overcome the influence of the home linguistic environment. Even so, experimentation may be less successful at detecting long-term effects, or synergistic effects where one independent variable is only effective in the company of others.

## 7     Conclusion

Bates *et al.* (1982) draw attention to the lack of social correlates of language acquisition, pointing out that the only really consistent finding was the contribution of the quantity of language input rather than specific inputs related to specific developments. Subsequent research has paid more attention to specific relationships and the processes by which they are mediated, for example between auxiliaries (Shatz *et al.* 1989; Richards 1990a, 1990b) or copulas (Richards and Robinson 1993) in various syntactic frames in the input and child auxiliary or copula growth. Similarly, Farrar (1990) looked for relationships between each of nine morphemes in recasts addressed to the child and the development of the *same* morpheme. Thus the presence of progressive and plural morphemes in recasts was found to predict rate of development of the progressive and plural in the child. In other respects, too, it is evident that progress has been made since the early correlational studies of the 1970s. Despite the reservations outlined in this chapter, and the continued use of relatively small samples, there is evidence of more sophistication in research design and greater caution in the interpretation of results. There is also evidence of a degree of theoretical cohesion in areas such as the influence of semantic contingency and children's vocabulary development which was not evident in the earliest studies, and of a convergence of observational and experimental research.

Nevertheless, there is less evidence as yet of the use of what Bohannon and Warren-Leubecker (1988, p. 100) call "newer statistical techniques" such as more sophisticated regression procedures and causal modeling for handling reciprocal effects and nonlinear relationships, and for exploring complex configurations of causal links. Causal modeling, or path analysis, using software such as LISREL (LInear Structural RELations: Jöreskog and Sörbom 1978) has been used more extensively in the field of second language learning (e.g. Gardner 1983; Gardner, Lalonde, and Pierson 1983), but has much to offer the first language field. The procedures allow models to be tested for goodness of fit, allowing alternative models to be compared. Methods are also available for systematic adjustment of a model in a way which avoids bias resulting from the personal preferences of the investigator (Gardner *et al.* 1983).

By its very nature, research is evolutionary and additive. It is important to remember, therefore, that the result of an early exploratory study can become so deeply rooted in the collective knowledge of researchers in a field that it is almost impossible to eradicate, even when it has been totally overtaken by developments in methodology, theory and subsequent (re)analyses. Thus, when drawing on the results of previous studies of the effects of input and interaction, authors, researchers, and practitioners frequently fail to differentiate between previous findings according to the strengths and weaknesses of the research design. Instead, writers go through the ritual of referring to published work regardless of published criticism of its validity. We need to be aware, therefore, of developments such as the following: the findings of Newport *et al.* (1977) have been superseded by Gleitman *et al.* (1984), and even these need to be interpreted with caution; the evidence for environmental effects on the child is stronger in Cross (1978) than in Cross (1977); in a succession of increasingly rigorous analyses of the same data base, the findings of Ellis and Wells (1980) were overtaken by Wells (1980), Barnes *et al.* (1983), and finally Wells (1985); at the same time, results relating to children's auxiliaries in these studies have to be reappraised as a result of a more finely grained analysis by Richards (1990a). In future, we need to continue the process of refining research methods and use a convergence of correlational, case-study, and experimental approaches, including single subject designs to focus on a single problem. In the meantime, statements about the weight of evidence for or against the influence of features of input on language development need to be evaluated carefully against their research history and the methodology of the studies concerned.

## NOTE

I would like to thank Viv Edwards, Clare Gallaway, Richard Ingham, Mair Richards, and Roger Straughan for their helpful comments on previous drafts of this chapter. Responsibility for remaining defects lies, of course, entirely with myself.

# Part II

# Specific aspects of input and interaction

# 5     The rest of the family: the role of fathers and siblings in early language development

*Michelle E. Barton and Michael Tomasello*

## 1     Introduction

At one time there was a simple picture of the role of the linguistic environment in child language acquisition. The classic motherese hypothesis – as embodied, for example, in many of the papers in the inaugural Snow and Ferguson (1977) volume – went something like this. Just as children cannot learn to ride a bicycle by simply being given one, they cannot learn to speak a language by simply being exposed to one. In both cases adults must provide some training wheels. In the case of language this means addressing children directly, in a high pitch, with child-friendly utterances – morphologically and semantically simple words put together into short and simple sentences – that are tuned in to the child's current focus of attention or conversational topic. In general, empirical research with Western middle-class mothers has confirmed that how well adults do these things is reliably associated with such outcomes as children's early vocabulary size and mean length of utterance (MLU); and there are even some experimental results that suggest a causal role for motherese (see Bohannon and Warren-Leubecker 1988 for an overall review).

The complications with this hypothesis that have emerged in recent years are twofold. First, mothers in some other cultures do not interact with their children in the same way that Western middle-class mothers do. Kaluli and Samoan mothers, for example, do not adapt themselves and the environment nearly so much to their children; they do not believe in training wheels for very young children, or at least not in training wheels of the same kind (Ochs 1982; Schieffelin and Ochs 1983). Although there has never been a direct quantitative comparison of such things as vocabulary size or MLU among same-aged children in these cultures, Ochs and Schieffelin report that Kaluli and Samoan children acquire language on much the same timetable as Western middle-class children. The implication is that what Western middle-class mothers are doing is not necessary for language acquisition, and moreover, that the variability being tapped within this group by studies of motherese is basically trivial, accounting for only a few months difference in the age at which children reach the linguistic milestones that they would have reached anyway without the training wheels.

Findings such as these are clearly important for our understanding of the role of the linguistic environment in child language acquisition. But these findings do *not* imply, as some researchers seem to believe, that there are *no* features of the linguistic environment that are necessary for language acquisition. The findings of Ochs and Schieffelin imply only that the most obvious adaptations of Western middle-class mothers are not necessary features (Snow in press). It is presumably the case that no children will learn language normally in the absence of a linguistic environment, for example, or in the presence of a tape recorder playing grammatical sentences, or in the presence of adults speaking to one another about philosophy. The challenge in crosscultural work is to find those features of children's linguistic environments that are present in all cultures and those that vary between cultures, and, what has yet to be done, to document any differences in language acquisition style or competence that may result. The challenge in the study of individual differences within a culture is basically the same: to identify those features of the linguistic environment that affect the child's language acquisition in specific ways, and thereby to determine basic parameters of the role of the linguistic environment in the acquisition process.

The second complication of the motherese hypothesis is a growing dissatisfaction among researchers with structural-linguistic measures of child language such as vocabulary size and MLU. These purely quantitative measures are increasingly being seen for what they are: only one aspect of children's communicative competence. A variety of other skills are necessary to become a competent user of language, especially skills falling into the categories of pragmatics and conversation. Many researchers are now asking: of what value is a large vocabulary if children do not know how to use their words in the appropriate contexts? Of what value is the ability to construct long sentences if children do not know how to use them in conversation or adapt them for the needs of different listeners with different knowledge of the conversational topic? Of what value is the ability to construct grammatically correct *wh*-questions if children do not know how to use these questions to ask an interlocutor to reformulate an unclear message when clarification is needed? The point is that children's structural-linguistic skills only make functional sense in the context of their pragmatic and conversational skills. Many, perhaps most, researchers interested in the role of the linguistic environment have thus turned their attention to communicative competence more broadly defined, which includes not only structural-linguistic skills but also pragmatic skills as displayed in ongoing communicative interactions in natural conversations. And in many cases it is these skills that seem to be more sensitive to environmental variations, as evidenced, for example, by the discovery of different "styles" of language acquisition and use by children within the Western middle-class population (e.g. K. Nelson 1981).

In these two ways, then, the study of motherese, or, as it is now more typically called, child-directed speech (CDS), has moved slowly away from studies aimed solely at Western middle-class culture and from those aimed solely at the structural-linguistic features of the CDS within that culture. More recently, a third direction of movement is taking place as well. Within Western middle-class culture, members of the family other than the mother are beginning to be investigated. Early research seemed to show that fathers and siblings from Western middle-class families adjust their speech to language-learning infants in many of the same ways as mothers in terms of higher vocal pitch, restricted vocabulary, and shortened sentence length – implying that what the child learns from them is similar as well. But more recently, as the focus has shifted to discourse and communication, important differences have emerged. Fathers and siblings do not adapt their conversational interactions for young children – either because they are not competent or because they are not motivated to do so – nearly as much or in as many ways as do mothers from the same families. In the traditional training wheels view, this might imply that as linguistic partners fathers and siblings are not as important to the child's language acquisition as are mothers.

But, once again, a focus on the child's communicative competence has broadened our view. From the point of view of discourse and communication, it might reasonably be supposed that requiring children to adapt their language to the needs of others – rather than having others always adapt to them – might have some beneficial effects on their developing communicative competence. Berko Gleason (1975) proposed just this with respect to secondary caregiver fathers. She proposed that because they are less knowledgeable than primary caregiver mothers about their child's experience, knowledge, and competencies, and about the idiosyncrasies of their child's sometimes childish language, fathers are more challenging communicative partners for young children. Fathers facilitate the development of their children's conversational skills by forcing them to take into account the point of view of a less knowledgeable, and perhaps less accommodating, listener. Berko Gleason pointed out in addition, however, that fathers are usually more knowledgeable and more accommodating, and closer affectively to the child, than almost all other adults excepting the primary caregiver mother. She thus further proposed that fathers serve as a kind of linguistic "bridge" to the wider community of adult speakers with whom children will eventually need to communicate effectively. Even more than fathers, adults in this wider community will require children to adapt their communicative attempts in ways that are considered conventional by the linguistic community as a whole.

Mannle and Tomasello (1987) reasoned that, like fathers, siblings might also present the language-learning child with particular challenges. Siblings are obviously different from fathers in many ways, but like fathers they would seem to accommodate to the child much less than do mothers. Continuing the analogy, Mannle and Tomasello hypothesized that siblings might also serve as a kind of linguistic bridge to a wider community of speakers, only in this case the community would be the community of peers. Mainly for reasons of age, peers share many characteristics with siblings as communicative partners – although they are in most cases younger and less familiar with the child than the sibling. It is also important that the presence of siblings leads to many more multi-party conversations for young children within the family setting (e.g. mother–child–sibling), which present their own communicative challenges, and which might also serve as a kind of bridge in the child's developing competence in multi-party conversations.

In this chapter, our aim is to relate what is known about the way fathers and siblings communicate with beginning language learners, and what effects this may have on their development of communicative competence. In particular, we are concerned with evaluating the status of both the Father Bridge and the Sibling Bridge Hypotheses in the five years since the Mannle and Tomasello (1987) review, and also in exploring, as that review did not, issues of multi-party conversations in the home. There are both new data and new theoretical orientations that would seem to justify the current update.

As in that previous review, however, we cannot begin without two caveats. First, we will focus on Western middle-class fathers and siblings only; this is quite simply because data on other cultures are almost totally lacking. Second, we will focus for the most part on prototypical, perhaps stereotypical, fathers and siblings. Again for reasons of the availability of data, fathers in this chapter are mostly secondary caregivers and siblings are mostly preschool-aged children. There are some exceptions to these stereotypes in the available data, however, and some theoretical arguments to be made about how variations in the stereotypes might affect linguistic interactions with language-learning children.

## 2     Fathers

The premise of Berko Gleason's (1975) Bridge Hypothesis is that fathers, because they are less familiar with the young child's communicative devices than are mothers, require the child to make communicative adjustments in order to convey her/his message to this less familiar partner. Thus the first step in evaluating the Father Bridge Hypothesis is to document in what ways, if any, fathers are less sensitive, and therefore more challenging, conversational partners for their language-learning children than are primary caregiver mothers.

## 2.1    Fathers' interactive style

In apparent conflict with the premise of the Father Bridge Hypothesis, much of the early research found that fathers' and mothers' speech to young children was very similar in terms of structural characteristics. For example, fathers and mothers are reported to be similar on measures of MLU (although cf. Rondal 1980; Malone and Guy 1982); number of verbs per utterance; proportional use of declaratives, interrogatives, and requests; and the use of modifiers, locatives, absent object references, and repetitions (Golinkoff and Ames 1979; Kavanaugh and Jen 1981; Kavanaugh and Jirkovsky 1982; Lewis and Gregory 1987; Lipscomb and Coon 1983). Taken together, these results indicate relatively few differences between mothers' and fathers' speech to young children, with a variety of characteristics of motherese being evident in paternal speech to young children as well.

It is important, however, that almost all of the reported similarities between mothers' and fathers' speech to very young children have revolved around structural-linguistic aspects of language. Because communication is posited to play the central role in the Bridge Hypothesis, these structural-linguistic characteristics do not pertain to the hypothesis in any direct way. It is not clear, for example, that longer or shorter sentences from parents affect communication directly. Rather, it is the pragmatic/conversational domain that is most relevant to the Bridge Hypothesis. It is in the area of pragmatics (the way language is integrated into the ongoing nonlinguistic and conversational contexts) that the fathers' reduced familiarity would be expected to have the greatest effects, leading to important differences between primary caregiver mothers' and secondary caregiver fathers' verbal interactions with young children. Indeed, it is when researchers have looked at pragmatic/conversational measures that important differences between mothers and fathers can be seen. For example, Killarney and McCluskey (1981) reported that the fathers in their sample had shorter dialogues with their children than did the mothers with their children. Similarly, Golinkoff and Ames (1979) and Rondal (1980) found that fathers took fewer turns in conversations with their children than did mothers with their children. In the same vein, Hladek and Edwards (1984) reported that the fathers of the two- to three-year-old children in their study responded less to their children's utterances than did the mothers. Moreover, in marked contrast to the mothers, the fathers were characterized as tending not to initiate inter-actions with their children, but rather waiting for the children to make the first overtures. These quantitative differences in mothers' and fathers' conversations with their children are consistent with the Bridge Hypo-thesis, indicating the fathers' lower level of support of their children's conversational attempts.

Other studies of pragmatics have identified particular qualitative aspects of fathers' speech style that call for adjustments or greater effort on the child's part. For example, several studies have suggested that fathers have a more demanding style in conversations with their children than do mothers. Malone and Guy (1982) found that fathers were more controlling of conversations with their children than were mothers. In their study of the conversations of ten parent–child dyads, fathers were found to use more imperatives and directives and fewer conversation-eliciting questions than did the mothers. Andrews and Bernstein Ratner (1987) reported similar results in their study of four families. Whereas the mothers' style was characterized by trying to involve the children in conversation (primarily by using more factual questions than the fathers), the fathers' style was mostly directive, using descriptions of objects and events to speak in monologues rather than to encourage the children's verbal participation. Both studies concluded by suggesting that fathers and mothers play complementary roles, with the fathers' directive style offering new communicative challenges for the children because it lacked the solicitous quality of maternal speech.

Other researchers have reported that fathers are also more lexically demanding because they tend to use a more varied vocabulary with their children than do mothers. Rondal (1980) studied five French-speaking couples interacting with their sons. Although fathers and mothers were found to make similar simplifications and adjustments for their children's levels of linguistic ability, the fathers were found to have higher lexical diversity, as measured by type–token ratio (TTR), with their sons than did the mothers. More recently, Bernstein Ratner (1988) conducted a study specifically comparing mothers' and fathers' vocabulary use in speech to their eighteen-month-old children during free play. Parents were given a set of toys intended to maximize the use of low frequency and superordinate labels. Results indicated that although there was not a statistically significant difference between fathers' and mothers' TTR as had been found by Rondal, the fathers' speech was more lexically demanding in that it contained a higher proportion of rarely observed (low-frequency) words and a lower proportion of highly common (extra-high-frequency) words than the mothers' speech to the children. Both Rondal and Bernstein Ratner concluded that their data indicate that fathers and mothers play complementary roles in the language acquisition process, such that the fathers' style leads children to have to exert themselves in an effort to communicate.

Along these same lines, Masur and Berko Gleason (1980) documented the ways mothers and fathers produced and elicited lexical information from their children within a play context. They observed fourteen pairs of parents playing individually with their $2\frac{1}{2}$ to five-year-old children. As found in Rondal (1980) and Bernstein Ratner (1988), the fathers used more varied labels with their children than did the mothers. In addition, however, they found that fathers produced more label and function requests (e.g. *What's this?* or *What's this for?*) than did the mothers. Similar findings are reported in McLaughlin, White, McDevitt and Raskin (1983). In their study of $1\frac{1}{2}$-, $2\frac{1}{2}$- and $3\frac{1}{2}$-year-old children's verbal interactions with their mothers and fathers, fathers were less able to adjust their speech to their children's linguistic levels than were the mothers. In addition, compared to the mothers, the fathers demanded more from their children in terms of a response by using fewer *yes–no* questions and more *wh*-questions relative to the total number of questions asked. These two studies thus suggest that fathers have a more demanding style of interaction, one that in turn calls for greater performance on the part of the children. This was particularly evident in the Masur and Berko Gleason study, where the immediate effect of the fathers' frequent demands of their children was that the children had a higher level of lexical production for their fathers than for their mothers.

Another line of research on mother–father differences has focused on parents' use of requests for clarification (e.g. *What?* or *You have a what?*). The request for clarification is of particular interest because it signals a lack of comprehension on the part of the adult and explicitly calls for the child to adjust her/his speech in order to repair the breakdown in conversation. Given the role familiarity is posited to play in the Bridge Hypothesis, it would be expected that if fathers are less familiar with their children's language and do not understand their children's speech as well as mothers (as was found by Weist and Stebbins 1972), there would be a higher percentage of requests for clarification in paternal speech to young children. Several studies have found that this is indeed the case (but cf. Andrews and Bernstein Ratner 1987). For example, Rondal (1980) found that fathers addressed proportionally more requests for clarification to their children than did the mothers. Rondal suggested that this difference may reflect less finely tuned comprehension skills on the part of the fathers (as Berko Gleason 1975 proposed) or that fathers demand more in terms of the child's verbal elaboration or provision of information. Moreover, Rondal argued that any of these explanations was compatible with his further finding that the children in his study produced longer MLUs for their fathers than for their mothers. Rondal interpreted his findings as being consistent with the Bridge Hypothesis, because the fathers' higher proportion of clarification requests led the children to adapt their language.

Mannle and Tomasello (1987) also examined differences in mothers' and fathers' use of requests for clarification, hypothesizing that fathers would have less comprehension of their children and thus produce more clarification requests than mothers. Their hypothesis was partially supported in their sample of 24 twelve- to eighteen-month-old children: 6 percent of the fathers' utterances were clarification requests compared to 1 percent for the mothers (because of low frequencies, however, this difference was not statistically reliable). Other potential sources of non-comprehension – topic changes and nonacknowledgments – were also compared between mothers and fathers. Again, fathers produced more of each of these, but the frequencies were too small to yield a statistically reliable difference.

Given that the mother–father differences reported in Mannle and Tomasello (1987) were in the expected direction, Tomasello, Conti-Ramsden, and Ewert (1990) did a more detailed analysis of parent–child conversational breakdowns and repairs. They conducted a reanalysis of the data from Mannle and Tomasello and a new analysis on follow-up data of the same children and their parents six months later. Again, their hypothesis was that fathers would show evidence of being less familiar with their children's language, as shown by more breakdowns and fewer repairs with their children than between mothers and their children.

Tomasello et al. (1990) found that fathers and their children experienced more conversational breakdowns than did the mothers and their children. Specifically, fathers used more requests for clarification, and more often used a nonspecific query to do so (e.g. What?) than did the mothers, who more often used specific queries (e.g., Put it where?) and multiple requests for clarification if the first repair was inadequate. Fathers also failed to acknowledge their children's utterances more often than did the mothers, and failed to return to the topic after the breakdown more often than did the mothers. Finally, when parental nonacknowledgments did occur, the children tended to repeat their original utterance more often for their fathers than for their mothers (for whom they elaborated the original utterance).

Tomasello *et al.* (1990) interpreted their results as support for the Bridge Hypothesis: their data indicated that the children's linguistic exchanges with their fathers were not as smooth as those with their mothers. The authors pointed out that both breakdown nonacknowledgments and requests for clarification signal to the child that some adjustment on the child's part is necessary before the conversation can continue. In the case of breakdown non-acknowledgments (i.e. the adult ignores the child's utterance) there is an implicit signal that there may have been a lack of comprehension and the repair attempt must be initiated by the child, whereas clarification requests explicitly signal the comprehension failure via the adult-initiated repair attempt. Despite these differences, however, both breakdown types required the *child* to make the repairing utterance. Tomasello *et al.* thus concluded that fathers were indeed challenging conversational partners, because their lower level of comprehension (more frequent breakdowns) placed the onus on the child to make adjustments in order to maintain the current linguistic interaction.

The data reviewed thus far, for the most part, suggest that along pragmatic lines secondary caregiver fathers' speech to their language-learning children is characterized by more demands and less comprehension than that of mothers. Goodz and her colleagues (Goodz, Bilodeau, Amsel, and White 1987; Goodz 1989; Goodz, Goodz, and Green 1991) have extended the study of mother–father speech to young children to bilingual families. Goodz hypothesized that being the primary transmitter of his language to his child would facilitate the father's fine-tuning of his speech to his child. To test this, Goodz has conducted several studies comparing father–child and mother–child conversations in French–English bilingual families in which each parent predominantly addresses their child in their respective native language.

Results of these studies have provided support for her proposal during the early stages of the language acquisition process. For example, in Goodz *et al.* (1987) fathers differed from mothers on only three out of twelve coding measures, with fathers using more *wh*-questions and indirect directives and doing less labeling than mothers. In Goodz *et al.* (1991) fathers were again found to be as skilled as mothers at maintaining conversations with their children and continuing their children's topics, as evidenced by the low occurrence of nonacknowledgments and topic shifts for both parents. Moreover, fathers did not differ from mothers in the proportion of requests for clarification they addressed to their children. That mothers and fathers modified their language to their children in similar ways, however, was found to hold primarily during the initial stages of language acquisition. That is, Goodz *et al.* (1987) found that as the children matured beyond the two- to three-word utterance stage, fathers in these bilingual families became somewhat less supportive of their children's communicative efforts (e.g. increased translation of non-native utterances addressed to them by the children compared to that of the mothers). Goodz (1989) reported a similar finding that fathers became less accepting of code switching in either themselves or their children as the children progressed linguistically. This was evident by the fathers' lower use of language switching themselves, and by their lower responsiveness to their children's code switching as they approached their third birthdays. Goodz and her associates concluded that these additional findings are consistent with the claim of the Bridge Hypothesis that fathers are less sensitive and more demanding of their children's linguistic attempts than are mothers, although in bilingual families this difference appears only after the child has progressed beyond the early stages of language development.

Goodz's data also offer a new type of support for the Bridge Hypothesis. Although it was found that during the early stages fathers' speech to their children appeared quite similar to that of mothers to their children (such that the mother–father differences reported in previous studies of monolingual families were virtually absent), this finding is also compatible with the Bridge Hypothesis when interpreted in terms of the role of familiarity. That is, at the early stages of the bilingual-to-be-child's language development, the father is the primary transmitter of his native language. Goodz and her associates argue that because it is necessary for the father to establish the basic foundation for that language, his ability to finely tune his speech to his child's is facilitated (Goodz *et al.* 1987). Thus the family's decision to maintain language separation between the parents necessitates the father's being familiar with the child's development of his language. In doing so, the father becomes as supportive a conversational partner as the mother – suggesting that familiarity, not gender, is at the root of mother–father differences typically observed in monolingual families.

Goodz's data (Goodz *et al.* 1987; Goodz 1989), however, also found that fathers in bilingual families resemble fathers in monolingual families after a certain point in their children's development. The question, then, is why do these bilingual fathers change their behavior? One possibility is that once the basics of his native language have been established, the father loses some motivation to remain involved in the learning process (perhaps because of time constraints if he is a secondary caregiver). Alternatively, if he is a secondary caregiver, perhaps the reduced time he has to spend with his child makes it harder to "keep up" with his child's linguistic progress, and his familiarity begins to wane. Whatever the case, however, the final implication is that the supportive characteristics of maternal speech are not gender-specific, but rather result from the particular social role the parent plays in the child's development. In the case of the secondary caregiver father, the role appears to complement that of the primary caregiver mother, such that fathers offer new communicative challenges to their children. To date, however, there have been no studies that have systematically varied caregiver status and gender in an effort to explicitly explore the issue of complementary parental roles.

## 2.2    *Effects on children's communicative competence*

Taken together, findings from studies of maternal and paternal speech to young children have repeatedly shown that secondary caregiver fathers' verbal interactions with their children are different from those of mothers. Moreover, as the Bridge Hypothesis posits, these differences are such that fathers tend to be more challenging partners in terms of pragmatic/ conversational measures. The next question, then, is what effects this style may have on the language-learning child. One possibility is that some aspects of a father's verbal style may engender immediate effects in his child's responses to paternal speech. For example, requests for clarification are a specific form of negative feedback (see e.g. Bohannon and Stanowicz 1988; Sokolov and Snow this volume, for a discussion of negative evidence) that indicate to the child that some aspect of her/his utterance is not well formed, and explicitly call for an immediate repair by the child. Because fathers have been found to pose more requests for clarification to their children than do mothers, the children have more opportunities to practice adjusting their speech for a less familiar partner when they converse with their fathers. Thus looking at children's repairs of requests for clarification would provide some evidence of the effects of fathers' conversational style.

Research examining child repairs has shown that young children are indeed able to make appropriate repairs (e.g. Gallagher 1981), and that two-year-old children tend to elaborate on their original utterance more often for an unfamiliar adult than for their mothers (Tomasello, Farrar, and Dines 1983). Tomasello *et al.* suggested that the children's differential responding reflects their differential assumptions about their partners: children assume that any lack of comprehension by their mothers is not due to their lack of familiarity with the linguistic forms being used, and hence a full or partial repetition is a sufficient repair; a stranger's lack of comprehension, on the other hand, may be due to their unfamiliarity with the child's language and hence a different linguistic formulation is needed. This finding suggests that these young children are sensitive to differences in their listeners' familiarity with their language and adjust their speech accordingly – a skill that can plausibly be extended to fathers. That is, based on this previous research and the assumption of the Bridge Hypothesis, one might predict that a father's reduced familiarity would lead his child to provide more elaborations for the father than for the mother. Unfortunately, no data exist to evaluate this hypothesis.

Other indications of immediate differential effects are also hinted at in the literature. For example, Tomasello *et al.* (1990) reported that when breakdown nonacknowledgments occurred, the children elaborated their original utterance more often for their mothers than for their fathers. Although this seems inconsistent with the Tomasello *et al.* (1983) data, this finding is based on a different kind of breakdown. In this case, the adults' nonacknowledgment is taken as a sign of lack of interest, not lack of comprehension (see Tomasello *et al.* 1990 for further discussion). The implication of this result is, once again, that children respond to mothers' and fathers' feedback differentially, presumably because of the different expectations they hold when interacting with each parent. Tomasello *et al.* (1990) speculated that with mothers, children provide new information in the face of nonacknowledgments because they are confident that their mothers will return to the conversation; with fathers, children do not have this expectation and therefore repeat their utterance so at least this one message will be received. This interpretation is bolstered by their additional finding that mothers returned to the conversation following a breakdown nonacknowledgment much more frequently than did fathers.

Masur and Berko Gleason (1980) also reported immediate differential effects of maternal and paternal speech. In their study, the children produced more diverse vocabulary for their fathers than for their mothers. Masur and Berko Gleason argued that this was in response to the fathers' higher proportion of "quizzing" utterances. Similarly, Rondal (1980) found that children's MLU was longer for their fathers than for their mothers, possibly resulting from the higher proportion of clarification requests in the fathers' speech than in the mothers'. In sum, there are several very substantial suggestions in the literature as to where we might find immediate effects of fathers' speech to young children. Virtually all are compatible with the Bridge Hypothesis, but further research is necessary to fully explore other predictions of this model.

The long-term effects of mother–father differences are also worthy of attention. Of central interest is whether fathers do indeed serve as bridges to the wider linguistic community, as originally proposed by Berko Gleason (1975). That is, does the father's pragmatic/conversational style with his child indeed pressure the child to broaden her/his communication skills to conform more specifically to the conventions of the general speaking community? To date, there are few data to answer this question, and as such the Bridge Hypothesis remains a proposal to be tested. Mannle and Tomasello's (1987) data, however, offer an indication of one potential effect of fathers' speech to their young children: lagged correlations found that the proportion of nominals in the children's vocabularies at twenty-one months were positively correlated with the fathers' minimal acknowledgements or off-topic replies when the children were fifteen months. This finding might be taken to indicate that young children's linguistic experiences with this type of paternal speech facilitate their development and use of conventional speech forms (i.e. nouns versus pronouns), and perhaps encourage the children towards a referential style. If this is found to be the case, the fathers will have prepared their language-learning children with skills that ease the transition to speaking to novel adults, whose even lower familiarity requires more conventional speech forms (e.g. general nominals rather than pronouns) for effective communication.

## 3       Siblings

By analogy with the Father Bridge Hypothesis, Mannle and Tomasello (1987) proposed that siblings also play the role of linguistic bridges. Because young children (preschoolers) are both limited by their own developmental level and are less familiar with the younger child's communicative devices than are mothers, it has been posited that preschool-age siblings also require language-learning children to make communicative adjustments in order to convey their messages. Thus, as with the Father Bridge Hypothesis, evaluation of the Sibling Bridge Hypothesis requires documenting in what ways, if any, preschool-age siblings are challenging conversational partners for their language-learning siblings and what effects this may have. Because siblings also present the language-learning infants with a multi-child speaking context (as in mother–infant–sibling triads), the unique challenges of this context and its potential effects will also be discussed.

### 3.1     Siblings' interactive style and its effects

As was the case with the first studies of fathers' CDS, the initial studies of siblings' CDS indicated that preschool-age children made the same systematic adjustments as mothers. Shatz and Gelman (1973) and Sachs and Devin (1976) both compared four-year-old children's speech to an adult with their speech to a two-year-old. In order to ensure that the children's speech was not affected by the feedback from the partner, Sachs and Devin also included a doll condition, in which the children were told to pretend the doll was a baby just learning to talk. Results from both studies indicated that the four-year-olds spontaneously modified their speech, even in the absence of listener feedback. As had been found with mothers in previous research, the children raised their speaking pitch, shortened their utterances, and simplified their sentences, and used more attentional devices and self-repetitions with the two-year-olds (and dolls) than with the adults. Thus, in terms of the structural-linguistic features of the CDS register, these two studies indicated that preschool-age children resemble adults as conversational partners with younger children.

Dunn and Kendrick (1982) investigated the speech adjustments of even younger children: 13 two- to three-year-old children were observed interacting with their fourteen-month-old siblings and their mothers. Again, the preschool-age children were found to make some modifications similar to the mothers in their speech to the younger siblings (e.g. shorter sentences and more attentional devices and repetitions). However, Dunn and Kendrick found that the preschoolers' use of attentional devices and self-repetitions occurred primarily in prohibitory and directive contexts, whereas mothers used these devices in primarily positive interactive situations. In addition, while all the mothers used a high proportion of questions when addressing their infants, only five of the thirteen children used any interrogatives at all. In sum, these data confirmed the earlier findings that preschoolers are capable of making some of the same kinds of structural modifications characteristic of the CDS register. But at the same time, the Dunn and Kendrick data also suggested that pragmatic differences may exist in how young children and adults use language when addressing infants: the preschool-age siblings did not use questions and nondirective utterances as a means of engaging the infant partner in conversation.

Taking the lead from the Dunn and Kendrick (1982) study, additional research on siblings' speech began to focus on pragmatics. Again, as with the research on fathers' speech, pragmatics has proved to be the area where the greatest adult-child differences can be seen. For example, Tomasello and Mannle (1985) compared three- to five-year-old children's conversations with their twelve- to eighteen-month-old infant siblings to those of their mothers with the infants. As they had hypothesized, Tomasello and Mannle reported that, compared to mothers, the preschoolers provided less nonlinguistic scaffolding (i.e. fewer object references and joint attentional episodes) and had fewer and shorter conversations with the infants. Moreover, when sibling–infant conversations did occur, the preschool siblings were highly directive and they did not use nearly as many topic-maintenance devices (i.e. questions, recasts, and topic continuations) as the mothers. Rather, the siblings' most frequent response to the infants' utterances was no response: fully 83 percent of the infants' utterances were ignored by the siblings as compared to only 21 percent by the mothers.

These results were replicated in a subsequent study using the same comparative methodology, but with older infants: 22- to 28-months old (Mannle, Barton, and Tomasello 1991). Compared to mothers with infants, siblings with infants had fewer and shorter conversations. In addition, the siblings were more unresponsive and directive in the few short conversations that did occur than were the mothers and infants. In addition, Mannle *et al.* found that siblings failed to repair breakdowns in their conversations with the infants almost twice as often as did the mothers. Finally, the infants' responses did not differ as a function of partner, thus ruling out the possibility that the observed mother-sibling differences could be attributed to differential behavior on the part of the infants. Together these two studies indicate clear differences between preschool-age siblings' and mothers' linguistic interactions with infants, such that the preschoolers are not as adept at making pragmatic adjustments that provide scaffolding for infants in their early conversational exchanges.

Martinez (1987) also examined conversations between four- and two-year-old children and between these children and their mothers. Although these children were not siblings, their ages make their data representative of the language skills of preschoolers. The conversations were coded as to the proportion of turnabouts (utterances that both respond to the previous utterance and require a further response), plain mands (turns that only require a further response), plain responses, and unlinked. He found that the mothers primarily used turnabouts (50 percent of the time) to maintain dialogue with their children, whereas the children used turnabouts only 10 percent of the time to sustain conversation with each other. When conversing with each other, the children relied mostly on unlinked turns (45 percent of the time) and plain responses (33 percent of the time), neither of which overtly set up (scaffolded) the next turn of the partner. Thus Martinez's data also demonstrated how preschool-age children do not use the kinds of topic-maintenance devices that mothers use to support their children's conversational participation.

Together, the results of these studies of sibling–infant conversational interaction indicate that although preschool-age children do use some features of motherese speech, they are not as adept as mothers at making pragmatic adjustments for younger children. Overall, siblings' speech to infants is unsolicitous: preschoolers tend to be unresponsive and directive, and they do not make use of topic-continuing devices such as questions and turnabouts.

Mannle *et al.* (1991) have suggested that the observed stylistic differences between mothers and siblings may derive from motivational and/or competency differences. That is, siblings may not be as motivated as mothers to converse with the infants, or siblings may lack some of the communication skills that make for effective conversation (e.g. being aware of the partner's background knowledge, ability level, or perspective). Whether these or other factors are at the root of the observed differences, they are not likely to be due to differential behavior on the part of the infants, as Mannle *et al.* found that infants behaved similarly with both maternal and sibling partners. Rather, the differences clearly reside in the different pragmatic skills of preschoolers and mothers, with the immediate consequence of these different interaction styles being that siblings and infants engage in fewer and shorter conversations than do mothers and infants. Moreover, the quantitative and qualitative differences between mothers' and siblings' conversations with language-learning children are consistent with the Sibling Bridge Hypothesis. That, is, the siblings' lack of support for the infants' early conversational attempts changes the nature of the interaction, such that the infant is left to her/his own devices for effective communication with a sibling to a greater extent than with a solicitous mother who provides scaffolding.

The next question, then, is what effects the siblings' behavior and interactions with the infants have on the infants' communicative development. Unfortunately, to date there are no data available to address the issue of whether sibling–infant interactions have any identifiable relation to the infants' process of language development. The predominant characteristics of sibling speech to infants – unresponsive, directive, and relatively devoid of conversation-eliciting questions and turnabouts – however, have all been found to be negatively correlated with early language development in studies of mother–infant interaction (e.g. Nelson 1973; Olson, Bayles, and Bates 1986; Tomasello and Farrar 1986). The effective implication is that laterborn children might be expected to develop language at a slower rate than firstborns because of the laterborns' greater time spent with an unresponsive partner (the sibling) and their corresponding reduced one-to-one time spent with a responsive adult partner (the primary caregiver) as compared to firstborns. There are suggestions in the literature that laterborn children may have a somewhat slower rate of vocabulary growth than firstborns (e.g. Nelson 1973; Jones and Adamson 1987) and that the amount of time language-learning children spend interacting with other children (siblings or peers) is negatively correlated with vocabulary acquisition (Nelson 1973; see Bates 1979 for a review). However, Bates noted that more time spent with other children correlates with less time spent with adults. Thus, it is not known if the effect derives from the experience with siblings, less time interacting with adults, or an interaction of the two.

Although further research is needed to identify what specific effects the sibling has on the infants' development of communicative competence, the data from sibling–infant interactions offer some support for the Sibling Bridge Hypothesis. Preschool-age siblings offer language-learning infants new communicative challenges *via* their unique conversational style in sibling–infant interaction. Whether these challenges serve the bridging function of pressuring the infant to develop new communication skills for communicating with the outside world, namely peers, is as yet unknown. One hint in this direction, however, is provided by Vandell and Wilson (1987), who found that infants' turn-taking skills with an unfamiliar peer were predicted by their early experience with their siblings. Other possible outcomes can be readily generated. For example, it is plausible that siblings' unresponsiveness could lead laterborn children to infer that they must make the conversational overtures for conversation, perhaps several times before getting the desired response from their partner. As such, laterborn children might be expected to initiate many conversations and to be persistent with their partners when a response is not forthcoming. Or another plausible outcome of engaging in interaction with an unresponsive partner might be the use of more obligatory speech forms (such as mands, questions and turnabouts, all of which require a response), or relatedly, to use more social-regulatory speech forms associated with a more expressive style (see e.g. Jones and Adamson 1987).

Whether these or other effects of sibling–infant interaction exist remains to be seen. Our laboratory is currently conducting a first study to test explicitly for these possible effects by comparing firstborn and secondborn children in their conversational interaction with a peer. It is our hypothesis that the secondborn children's experiences with their siblings will have prepared the secondborns with these kinds of communicative skills that will serve to prevent them from being easily thwarted by an unsolicitous, unresponsive peer partner. If this hypothesis is supported, it will be the first indication of how preschool-age siblings positively influence the communicative development of young language-learning children. Thus, while it may be the case that laterborn children exhibit slower development on some traditional measures of language development, such as vocabulary size, the implication of the Sibling Bridge Hypothesis is that if we look to other, more broadly defined measures of communicative competence, we may expect to find *positive* effects derived from sibling–infant experience. Clearly this is a promising area for future research.

## 3.2    The multi-child context and its effects

The sibling studies discussed thus far have focused on the preschooler as a dyadic conversational partner for the language-learning child, but this is not the only interactive role siblings play. The presence of a sibling also presents the opportunity for the formation of a multi-child speaking context – that of the mother–infant–sibling triad having received the most research attention. The importance of the multi-child context becomes clear when it is considered that (1) in many non-Western cultures it is the almost exclusive language-learning environment of young children (e.g. Schieffelin 1979; Ochs 1982; Schieffelin and Ochs 1983), and (2) in Western cultures it is typical of much of the interaction of laterborn children, and of an increasing number of firstborn and laterborn children in day-care or nursery school settings.

To date, most research of mother–infant-sibling triads has focused on the effects the presence of the sibling has on the mothers' language to the infant. Studies investigating the effects of the presence of a sibling (or another child) on adult–child interaction have produced converging lines of evidence that additional child participants lower both the quantity and quality of verbal input and joint attention an individual child may receive from the adult partner. For example, Schaffer and Liddell (1984) compared the language used by nursery school teachers when playing with a single child to that used when playing with a group of four children. Their results revealed that the group condition not only reduced the amount of speech the teachers directed to a given child, but altered the quality of their language as well. Compared to the dyadic condition in which the adult's language focused on the joint play activity the adult's language became much more controlling and directive in the group condition. Moreover, the adult's responsiveness to a given child was greatly reduced in the group condition as compared to the dyadic (51 percent versus 80 percent response rates for the group and dyadic conditions respectively).

Similar findings of divided adult attention have been reported in sibling studies. Jones and Adamson (1987) compared the language used during mother–infant dyadic exchanges to that used when a preschool-age older sibling was present as well (mother–infant–sibling triads). Like the Schaffer and Liddell (1984) study, the triadic situation reduced the amount of speech directed to the infant to less than half that observed in the dyadic setting. Moreover, the infant's own verbalizations decreased in the triadic as compared to dyadic setting. Comparable results were also found by Woollett (1986): when the older sibling was present the number of maternal utterances addressed to the infant decreased by 70 percent, and the number of infant utterances decreased by more than 50 percent.

It might be argued that the decrease in the quantity of maternal speech and maternal responsiveness to their infant is due to the older sibling's ability to monopolize the mother's attention more than the infant. Several studies of mothers with twins, however, have found the same effects as the sibling studies. For example, Tomasello, Mannle, and Kruger (1986) compared the linguistic interactions of mothers with twins to mothers with singleton children. As in the sibling studies, these mothers of twins also directed only half as many utterances to an individual twin child as did the mothers of singleton children, and the mothers had fewer and shorter conversations with the twin children than did the mothers and singleton children (see also Lytton, Conway and Sauve 1977; Bornstein and Ruddy 1984 for similar results). In addition, there was less than one-tenth of the time spent in adult–child dyadic joint attention in the twin setting than in the singleton setting. Finally, the mothers of the twins used proportionally twice as many directive utterances with their children than the mothers of the singletons. Thus, these data indicated that differences in maternal behavior are not due to the developmental level of the second child: the twins were at the same developmental level, and yet engendered the same effects on the mothers as did infant–sibling pairs. The inescapable conclusion is that these differences were a result of the pragmatic demands of the triadic conversational situation.

The implication of these "negative" influences on the adult in the multi-child context is that language-learning children who have to share access to their primary caregiver with their siblings, co-twins, or peers may experience a less than optimum language learning environment (Schaffer 1989). Given that both maternal directiveness and lower verbal stimulation are associated with slower vocabulary growth (see e.g. Nelson 1973; Olson et al. 1986; Tomasello and Farrar 1986), these second-order effects of additional children on maternal behavior may be a possible explanation for the slower rate of vocabulary growth found in twins (e.g. Tomasello et al. 1986) and to a lesser extent, in laterborn children (e.g. Jones and Adamson 1987; Nelson 1973). However, the fact that twins' vocabulary delay is generally recognized and robust (see Savic 1980 for a review), while the extent of laterborns' delay is debatable, suggests that there may be another factor involved in these effects. Tomasello, Mannle, and Barton (1989) have speculated that birth-spacing between the siblings may be a crucial variable in these triadic interactions, with twins representing the special case of zero-year spacing. It is their hypothesis that interacting with two young children of the same developmental level divides the adult's attention to a greater extent than does interacting with two children at different developmental levels, with the extent of the effect lessening as the age difference between children becomes larger.

(Moreover, this effect is posited to be greatest when the children are at the earliest stages of language acquisition.) The proposed explanation for this effect is that young children at the same developmental level require the same kind and amount of active linguistic and nonlinguistic support from the adult. In contrast, an older child in a pair presumably needs less support from the adult, thus making fewer demands on the adult's attention. This proposal remains to be tested.

The multi-child context typical of laterborn children's lives is not only important for its effects on maternal behavior. The multi-child context has other features that make it interesting in its own right, specifically because the multi-child context offers opportunities for linguistic inter-action that are not possible in dyadic settings. One opportunity the multi-speaker context provides is that of overhearing or monitoring the speech of others. Woollett (1986) specifically examined the language environment the mother–infant–sibling context provides a language-learning child. She observed the language environment of eighteen-month-to thirty-month-old children when alone with their mothers and when with their mothers and older siblings. She found that, compared to the mother–infant dyadic context, the presence of the sibling lessened the mother's sensitivity to the younger child (both in terms of the amount of language the mother used and her responsiveness to the child). At the same time, however, the sibling's presence also provided the young child with a more stimulating linguistic environment. For example, the mothers' and siblings' language models included more complex utterances, more questions and answers, less behavior-oriented speech, and more references to absent objects and events. Thus Woollett concluded that when the siblings were present, the infants were exposed to a variety of salient language models and communicative styles which were developmentally more complex than those observed in the mother–infant dyadic context.

Whether these more stimulating models provided in the mother–infant–sibling context are of developmental significance to the language-learning child, however, depends on whether the child is able to attend to and understand this ongoing speech. Being able to monitor and understand the speech occurring between two other speakers is necessary before one can attempt to join into that ongoing conversation. Forrester (1988) provided some initial evidence that 2½-year-old children do actively monitor speech occurring in multi-speaker interactions. In his study, Forrester investigated children's responses to hearing their names mentioned in a conversation between two other people. He reported that the 2½-year-olds were indeed monitoring these conversations, because when they heard their names mentioned, they demonstrated the response of looking at the addressee of that utterance, presumably in anticipation of the response.

Dunn and Shatz (1989) conducted the first study directly to examine two-year-olds' abilities to attend to and join in ongoing mother–sibling conversations, a further indication that young children are processing speech not addressed to them. Over the course of their third year, Dunn and Shatz found that the children were increasingly able to join into the mother–sibling conversations, and were increasingly able to do so by contributing new and relevant information to the conversation. In addition, the proportion of the children's statements that contributed new information was higher when they were intruding into the mother–sibling conversations than when they were responding to speech addressed directly to them. Dunn and Shatz concluded that two- and three-year-old children's intrusions indicated that they were very capable of attending to and processing speech not addressed to them. Moreover, these data suggested that the mother–infant–sibling triadic context may foster the infant's development and use of more sophisticated language skills (e.g. providing more new information) as they learn how and when to join in an ongoing conversation successfully.

Barton and Tomasello (1991) conducted a study to examine the dynamics of the mother–infant–sibling triadic context beyond that of simple intrusions. They observed nineteen- to 24-month-old infants interacting with their three- to five-year-old siblings and their mothers during free play. They found that even the youngest children were quite able to participate in triadic conversations, and that the proportional frequency of mother–infant–sibling conversations increased with age. Moreover, these triadic conversations were (quite unexpectedly) found to be nearly three times longer than mother–infant dyadic conversations at both ages. These longer triadic conversations were not due simply to the mothers and siblings increasing their contributions, as the triadic conversations elicited nearly twice as many *infant* turns as did mother–infant dyadic conversations. Finally, infants at both ages were clearly able to monitor and understand language not addressed to them, as they were just as likely to make an on-topic response to a comment or request addressed to another person as they were to one directed to themselves. Barton and Tomasello concluded that the mother–infant–sibling triadic context not only provided many opportunities and some practice at joining into ongoing conversations between other persons (something that is never possible in a dyadic context), but fostered increased and extended conversational interaction as well.

Barton and Tomasello (1991) suggested that these longer conversations may be a result of the change of dynamics in triadic as compared to dyadic interactions. That is, in triadic conversations there is somewhat less conversational pressure put on the infant; rather than taking half of all the conversational turns (as is required in mother–infant dyadic conversations), the infant can bide her/his time waiting for an interesting or comprehensible point in the discussion. Indeed, Barton and Tomasello found that in triadic conversations the infants took a quarter of the conversational turns (while mothers took a half and siblings took the remaining quarter of the turns). These three-way conversations also change the dynamics of interaction by focusing on a shared topic of interest. Because all three participants are actively involved, no one is left out trying to compete for attention on a different topic. Thus, mother–infant–sibling triadic conversations may be more easily sustained, with more infant participation, than dyadic conversations within the triadic context by virtue of a shared topic and a reduced conversational load for the infant.

Together these data on multi-speaker conversational experiences offer a new perspective on how siblings may function as linguistic bridges for language-learning infants. Given that mother–sibling conversations are more complex than mother–infant conversations (Woollett 1986), the opportunity to overhear these mother–sibling exchanges may facilitate the development of these more advanced devices. Some preliminary evidence that young children can learn new linguistic forms from overhearing others speak amongst themselves is provided by Oshima-Takane (1988), who found that children who overheard others using the deictic pronouns *me* and *you*, learned them more quickly than children who did not have such "eavesdropping" opportunities. It would be reasonable to expect that overhearing mother–sibling conversations could facilitate the development of similar language skills (e.g. the use of other deictic terms, third-party reference, and pragmatic skills) and, in turn, prompt the infant to use some of them in order to join in and participate in the ongoing conversation. Dunn and Shatz's (1989) data and Barton and Tomasello's (1991) data both suggest that this may indeed be happening when infants do make the effort to participate in a triadic conversation. Thus, by providing a context in which the infant must compete in order to join in, the sibling's presence in the mother–infant–sibling triadic context may facilitate the infant's development of language skills appropriate for multi-speaker interactions.

There are thus several reasons to believe that the unique context created by the sibling in mother–infant–sibling triads may have some beneficial effects on the infant's opportunities for learning a variety of pragmatic/conversational skills that are not available, or at least not to the same extent, in dyadic contexts. These include learning how to join in an ongoing conversation between other people, and, once having joined, how to maintain a topic and take turns in the more complex triadic conversation. Although it might be argued that these are effects of the triadic context in general rather than of the sibling–infant interaction, Barton and Tomasello (1991) have suggested that the sibling's role in mother–infant–sibling triads may be unique in its ability to facilitate infant participation. That is, they argue that mother–infant–sibling triadic conversations are more likely to concern topics that can be supported by a nonlinguistic joint attentional focus among all three interactants than are triads involving two adults and the infant. They also suggested that mother–infant–sibling triads may encourage longer conversations and more infant participation than triads including an adult and a same-age peer (including a twin), because in the latter case neither child can assume much of the conversational load on her/his own. Thus, it is the sibling's slightly advanced developmental level that is posited to facilitate these extended triadic conversations, which in turn encourage the infant's participation. The importance of these triadic experiences and the skills they may foster is obvious: the child's ability to converse in a multi-speaker context is essential for successful communication in all kinds of family, peer, and school settings.

## 4      The child's expanding social world

Most Western middle-class children have mothers as primary caregivers. Most of these mothers converse with their children in a particular way: they adapt their conversation to the child's competencies and needs, and they make frequent attempts to solicit the child's active participation in conversation from a very early age. They are able to do this well because they know so much about their individual child's knowledge, experiences, and language practices, and because they are highly motivated to engage their child in interaction and to show off her/his particular skills. This style has been shown to be conducive to the child's acquisition of a number of important linguistic skills. But by virtue of their high levels of knowledge and motivation, mothers are also likely on many occasions to anticipate their child's needs before they are linguistically expressed, to fill in gaps in incomplete or poorly expressed child utterances, and to preempt the child's participation in talking about a difficult topic. The maternal style may thus not be as conducive to the child's acquisition of some other types of communicative skills.

If mothers were the only people infants needed to communicate with, interaction with them alone would be sufficient for the child to become a communicatively competent member of her/his culture. There would develop a variety of idiosyncratic communicative devices that would subserve their communication needs quite well, and the need for devices more widely adapted socially would be minimal. But children do need to communicate with other people, even those with whom they share few or no common experiences – and this is the point of language.

Language is a set of social conventions designed to facilitate communication with other persons who have acquired the same linguistic conventions, whenever and wherever they may have done so. Natural languages are constructed so that they do not depend on an extensive amount of shared knowledge or experience of particular events. For example, what is expressed by a simple pointing may be expressed in other ways when the intended item, place, or activity is not physically present, and there are grammatical devices for indicating who-did-what-to-whom in the absence of a shared experience of the event as well. In a very interesting survey of several language groups and the social structures they evolved in, Parisi (1983) in fact argues that obligatory grammatical devices are associated precisely with those societies in which members must communicate with unknown interactants with unknown backgrounds and habits, and there are even some languages in which grammatical marking is obligatory only in those contexts in which it is clear that the listener could not reconstruct the intended who-did-what-to-whom relations on her/his own without marking. The problem for young children is that they are learning to communicate and acquiring language as a means of communication all at the same time. New communicative partners are constantly presenting them with new challenges that require them either to deploy their existing communicative skills in new ways, or else to acquire new skills that will help them to meet these challenges effectively.

To be a competent communicator, then, the child must learn to communicate in user-unfriendly as well as user-friendly environments, and this is where, on our hypothesis, fathers and siblings enter the picture. Fathers and siblings are not necessary features of the language acquisition process – or else single-parent children and only children would not acquire language normally, which they do. But if children are to communicate effectively with adults and children they have never before encountered, it would be very helpful if they had first had some practice with other adults and children with whom they have an affective bond and with whom they have a fair amount of previous social experience. The data we have reviewed in this chapter support the view that both secondary caregiver fathers and preschool-age siblings are less fluent conversational partners for young children than are primary caregiver mothers, and hence provide the children with opportunities to modify their speech for a less familiar partner. In particular, both fathers and siblings interact with nascent language learners such that, compared to mothers, they are:

1 less conversationally responsive, ignoring more often the child's linguistic overtures;
2 less conversationally supportive, providing the child with fewer conversation-maintaining devices such as questions and turnabouts;
3 less conversationally competent with the child in the sense that they experience more breakdowns, fewer successful repairs, and overall shorter conversations;
4 more directive of the topic of conversation and the child's behavior.

Thus, as their social worlds expand during their toddler and preschool years, children receive important feedback about their language skills from fathers and siblings who are familiar to them as interactants, but who on many occasions genuinely do not understand them. Clearly, the communicative styles of both fathers and siblings require the language-learning child to make adjustments and develop a variety of pragmatic skills. Although the outcomes of these experiences remain speculations at this time, it is plausible to expect that fathers and siblings play different roles in the infant's communicative development. Fathers may encourage the development of more linguistic means of communication (using language to serve a conventional referential function) *via* their lexically demanding style. Siblings, on the other hand, might conceivably lead to the development of more social and pragmatic skills for communication (using language to serve a social-regulatory or expressive function) *via* their directive style and the competition for the caregiver's attention they engender in the multi-child context. It is experiences such as these, then, that are proposed to serve as bridges, each in its own way, to the child's communication with other adults and peers with whom the child has not already established familiar routines of communication.

We have really just begun to document the different kinds of linguistic experiences that children have outside the mother–child context. There are as yet many unanswered questions, for example, possible differences between primary and secondary caregiver fathers as conversational partners, the role of birth spacing in sibling–child conversations, and the precise way that interactions with fathers and siblings might facilitate communication with other types of linguistic partners. These would be difficult questions to answer even with the full battery of experimental methods. But in the context of the real world, we must rely on the converging methods provided by naturalistic studies of children's linguistic interactions with different conversational partners, correlational studies that relate what happens in these interactions to the child's subsequent language skills or style, and experimental training studies that investigate the effects of particular kinds of interactions. Synthesizing information from all of these types of investigation will be necessary if we are to understand more thoroughly the various roles of the social-linguistic environment in the child's acquisition of communicative competence.

# 6 Phonetic and prosodic aspects of Baby Talk

*Alan Cruttenden*

## 1    Introduction

In an antecedent volume to this one, Ferguson (1977) produced a definitive survey of Baby Talk (BT), covering many languages, including both phonetic and prosodic aspects of the subject, and distinguishing three different functions of BT, simplifying, clarifying, and expressive. The simplifying function was associated with various segmental changes, while the clarifying and expressive functions were associated with prosodic aspects. In the same volume Garnica looked specifically at prosodic and paralinguistic characteristics of speech to English children aged two and five and to English adults, and found regular differences between speech to the two-year-olds and that to the adults, including wider pitch range and higher pitch (as realized by fundamental frequency ($F_0$), this being the acoustic correlate of perceived pitch), and more use of whisper and of rises. These two articles showed a wealth of evidence on the phonetic aspects of BT (e.g. a "canonical" syllable shape of CV), much of it crosslinguistic, but showed investigation of the prosodic aspects as only just beginning and wholly limited to English.

  In the present article it will become apparent that, while there has been little advance in our knowledge of the phonetics of BT (apart from some contradictory reports on the treatment of vowels), there has been a burgeoning interest in its prosodic aspects (much of this interest flowing from a series of important experiments by Fernald (e.g. Fernald and Simon 1984; Fernald 1985; Fernald and Kuhl 1987; and Fernald, Taeschner, Dunn, Papousek, De Boysson-Bardies, and Fukui 1989) and the putative facilitative effects associated with prosodic modification. In recent work the terms infant-directed speech (or A–I) and adult-directed speech (or A–A) have often been used. In this chapter I have preferred the older term BT (Baby Talk) as emphasizing the links with older work and being less cumbersome. I do, however, distinguish where necessary between BTPh (Baby Talk Phonetics) and BTPr (Baby Talk Prosody).

There is in general a methodological difference in the data-gathering between the two areas: BTPh is less amenable to experimentation and more dependent on naturalistic data (although this applies rather less to vowels than to consonants), while BTPr is rather more amenable to controlled data-gathering techniques. This difference probably reflects a different level of self-consciousness in the use of BTPh and BTPr; indeed, the more obvious processes of BTPh are often avoided by those who are unwittingly using BTPr. I survey firstly the characteristics of BTPh and BTPr; then possible facilitative effects and fine-tuning and finally cross-linguistic, crosscultural, variation.

## 2     Baby Talk phonetics

Many of the processes involved in children's phonological treatments of adult phonological systems (like regular substitutions and consonant harmony) are similarly represented in BTPh (see the crosslinguistic summary in Ferguson 1964). Of course the actual processes involved in any one language will often be different because the adult phonological system is different: if a language has no /r/, a process of "gliding" cannot be shown by a change from /r/ to [w]. But with this limitation child phonology and BTPh show similar changes both within and across different languages:

1 There are recurrent consonantal substitutions. For example, liquids are often replaced, either by a stop or by an approximant, e.g. *rabbit* → [wæbɪt], Hidatsa /mirapa/ "tea" → [bidapa] (Voegelin and Robinett 1954), and alveolars often replace velars. For example Ferguson (1964) found /t/ replacing /k/ in English, Spanish, Marathi, and Comanche.

2 Consonantal clusters are liable to be reduced to a single consonant (C). In English, for example, clusters of /s/ + C and clusters of C + approximant are commonly reduced to the C alone, e.g. *drink* → [dɪŋkɪ]. In Latvian BT, consonant clusters rarely occur (Rūķe-Draviņa 1977).

3 Consonant harmony may apply between consonants across an intervening vowel. For example, *dog* → [gɒgi], Japanese/nukwi/"warm" → [kukwi].

4 A simple consonant–vowel (CV) type of syllable structure predominates. Put together with consonant harmony, this will result in reduplicated structures like *horse* → [ʤiʤi] and *rice crispies* → [pipi], and Berber/aɣu/ → [ɣuɣu] "milk" (Bynon 1968). Additionally, English children have been shown to have a preference for trochaic rhythm (i.e. in a sequence of two syllables stress is preferentially on the first syllable) (Allen and Hawkins 1980), and this spreads into BTPh. The formation of BTPh diminutives in -*y* like *peggy* ( = "tooth") exemplifies a combin-

ation of a change from CVC to CVCV and the associated use of a trochaic rhythm.

It is not only in the area of consonantal substitutions and of syllable structure that BT is similar to child phonology but also in the area of phonetic amplification of particular types of segment. Thus Malsheen (1980) showed a reduction of overlap in voice onset time (VOT) between voiceless and voiced stops in the speech of adults to children at the first-words stage (this parallels the overaspiration of /p t k/ in child phonology, reported, for example, as category IIIA in Macken and Barton [1980]). Bernstein Ratner and Luberoff (1984) report that vowels before lenis consonants, which in the adult language are long compared with their counterparts before fortis consonants, are lengthened even more in speech to infants aged between 0;9 and 2;3. While the reports on segmental substitutions and syllable structure suggest simplification, these findings on the realizations of those segments used in speech to children suggest clarification; that is, the segments actually used are made more different from one another.

The general hypothesis that phonological structure is simplified in speech to children has been called in question by two articles in particular. Shockey and Bond (1980) compared adult-to-adult and adult-to-child speech on four measures: (i) the change of /t/ to [ʔ], word-finally, e.g. [aɪ laɪk ðæʔ]; (ii) ð-deletion in word-initial position in utterances like *in that* becoming /ɪnnæt/ or /ɪnæt/; (iii) the reduction of the sequence /ts/ to /s/ in utterances like *what's*; and (iv) the use of coalescent assimilation in sequences of /t/ + /j/ becoming /tʃ/ as in /wɒtʃu/ for *what you*. They actually found more reduction in categories (i)–(iii) in adults' speech to children than in adults' speech to other adults (category [iv] produced only a small number of contexts where the rule could potentially apply). Similar results were presented by Bard and Anderson (1983), who excised randomly selected words from parents' speech to their infants and from their speech to the experimenter, and, when the words were presented in isolation to other listeners, found those spoken to young children to be *less* intelligible than those spoken to the experimenter. An explanation suggested by the authors is that words in speech to children have greater predictability in context; that is, they are more redundant. But, as they point out, the surprising fact is that parents do not override the tendency for words to be less clear in redundant contexts.

Bernstein Ratner (1984a, 1984b) in turn produced evidence which did not sustain that of Shockey and Bond (1980) and of Bard and Anderson (1983). Bernstein Ratner (1984a) measured the clarification of vowels (in terms of $F_1$–$F_2$ spread) in mothers' speech to prelinguistic children (but all older than 0;9), to holophrastic children, to children with an MLU between 2.0 and 3.5, and to adults. She found little difference between speech to adults and to prelinguistic children; however, there was clarification of content words to holophrastic children, and clarification of both content and function words to telegraphic children. Furthermore, Bernstein Ratner (1984b) replicated the experiment of Shockey and Bond (1980) with the four phonological variables and found more reduction in mothers' speech to adults for final /t/ glottalization, initial /ð/ deletion, and /ts/ reduction (although the findings were contradictory for /t/ /d/ and /j/). All of which is very confusing until we consider the ages of the children involved in the various experiments:

> Shockey and Bond (1980): two- to four-year-olds (no more detail reported)
> Bard and Anderson (1983): 1;10–3;0
> Bernstein Ratner (1984a): Three groups:
> (a) pre-linguistic but over 0;9
> (b) holophrastic
> (c) MLU 2.0 to 3.5
> Bernstein Ratner (1984b): MLU 1.0–2.5

From this it is clear that those studies which found *more* reduction in speech to children (Shockey and Bond, Bard and Anderson) were principally involved with children *over* the age of two. On the other hand, Bernstein Ratner (1984a) found clarification of vowels to children at the holophrastic and telegraphic stages and it is likely that a large number of these children were *below* the age of two; similarly Bernstein Ratner (1984b) probably included a large majority of children below this age, given the reported MLUs. Thus the reports of less reduction were from children who were past that stage in linguistic development where adults feel the need to clarify (and so speech to children may then be less clear than speech to adults because it continues to involve words which are more predictable in context). I return to this later under the discussion of fine-tuning. Of course it nevertheless remains odd that even to children over two adults should reduce even more than they do to other adults. The explanation offered by Shockey and Bond (p. 272) is that "phonological reductions serve to set a tone of intimacy in a dialogue" and to further mother–child solidarity. Bard and Anderson, as already mentioned, point to the greater redundancy of mother–child speech, but still have to wonder how children ever learn full forms. This of course is not a problem in itself if they have learnt them at an earlier stage.

Table 6.1. *Mean fundamental frequency, narrowest pitch range, and widest pitch range in mothers of two-year-olds and five-year-olds (from Garnica 1977)*

|  | Mean fundamental frequency (Hz) | Narrowest pitch range (semitones) | Widest pitch range (semitones) |
|---|---|---|---|
| Group 1 |  |  |  |
| to 2-year-olds | 267.3 | 14 | 23 |
| to adults | 197.6 | 6 | 13 |
| (N = 12) |  |  |  |
| Group 2 |  |  |  |
| to 5-year-olds | 206.4 | 11 | 16 |
| to adults | 202.8 | 7 | 13 |
| (N = 12) |  |  |  |

## 3 Baby Talk prosody

### 3.1 Pitch height and pitch range

Some of the characteristics of BTPr are now well established, chief among which are the use of a higher pitch and a wider pitch range. Garnica (1977) was the first to experimentally confirm previously anecdotal evidence. Comparing twelve mothers' speech to their own two-year-old children with their speech to other adults (group 1), and twelve mothers' speech to their own five-year-olds with their speech to other adults (group 2), Garnica found clear use of higher pitch and wider range to the two-year-olds but much less evidence of this to five-year-olds. The relevant figures are given in table 6.1. Garnica also reported her mothers as using whispered speech quite frequently, as do Fernald and Simon (1984) for German mothers, and Pye (1986) for Quiché Mayan mothers. There are no other explicit mentions concerning other voice qualities in BT; similarly there is no talk of variation in loudness, and very little of tempo (i.e. speed of utterance), one exception again being Fernald and Simon (1984), who found the articulation rate much slower by mothers to their newborns than to adults.

### 3.2 Pitch contours

The evidence concerning mothers' use of particular intonational contours to infants is difficult to interpret. Garnica (1977) (for speech to two-year-olds) reports more use of terminal rises, particularly on imperatives. Ryan (1978) found frequent use of rises on declaratives. Reports on particular contours often concern the function to which the tune is put: Ryan suggests that rises encourage attention and interaction from the child; Stern, Spieker, and MacKain (1982) report the use of rises for attention and coaxing, and fall–rise for encouragement and maintaining attention; Fernald (in press) notes rise–fall for approval and low level for prohibition. (This is used by an English/German bilingual mother, speaking in German.) There are two problems with this sort of evidence. Firstly, when reports speak of rises or falls they are sometimes talking of the overall contour of the utterance, sometimes of the "terminal contour." This problem is most acute when rise–fall and fall–rise are discussed; usually descriptions of these contours in studies of Baby Talk appear to be referring to overall contours. Yet most descriptions of intonational meaning in adult English relate contours to stressed syllables: the most prominent and meaningful contour in any utterance is taken to be that which begins on the primary stressed syllable. Neither a description in terms of overall contours nor a description in terms of terminal contour (i.e. the final direction of pitch) relates pitch changes to stressed syllables. The result of this is that contours reported for motherese are often difficult to relate to adult intonational descriptions. The second problem with descriptions of contours in mothers' talk is that most of the meanings ascribed to contours, insofar as they can be compared with adult meanings (i.e. adult meanings to other adults) at all, are remarkably similar to those adult meanings; for example, Stern *et al.* (1982) report mothers' use of rises for getting attention and eye contact while O'Connor and Arnold (1961, p. 210) describe the meaning of high rise (which is the prototypical rise in English) on statements as "questioning, trying to elicit a repetition, but lacking any sense of disapproval or puzzlement." Indeed, intonational meanings are so nebulous that all the meanings reported for particular contours in BTPr can easily be accommodated within the general adult-to-adult meanings of those contours. So the only significant fact remaining relates to the increased frequency of particular tunes: and the only detailed reports on increased frequency refer to rises. Rises in general are socially more open, as they invite interaction. Mothers are doing a lot of this with their infants, and so the increased frequency of rises is not altogether surprising.

### 3.3    Boundary marking

Ryan (1978) noted that frequent use of (terminal) rises in speech to infants may also help in another way. They may help the child to segment the stream of speech; that is, if a terminal rise is heard, it signals the end of a grammatical "chunk." Other facts of prosody may also assist this function. Pauses, for example, in adult-to-adult interaction may be of two types, junctural pauses and hesitation pauses (for more detail, see Cruttenden 1986). The former are used as a marker of boundaries between grammatical constituents, almost always at clause boundaries, but sometimes at phrase boundaries when longer phrases are involved; the latter typically occur at points of uncertainty (e.g. where there is a word-finding or planning problem) and are as likely to be a filled (e.g. [əː]) as an unfilled pause. Evidence shows that pauses in BT are almost entirely junctural and, what is more, that pauses in BT are longer than in adult-to-adult interaction. For example, Broen (1972) found that pauses were a far more reliable cue to sentence boundaries in BT (children aged 1;6–2;2) than in adult-directed speech. This was confirmed by Fernald and Simon (1984), who also found such pauses to be longer than in adult speech. Another common clue to clause boundaries in human languages (probably universally – see Cruttenden 1986) is final syllable lengthening; Bernstein Ratner (1986) showed this occurring more regularly in BT than in adult-directed speech – indeed, mothers' speech to preverbal children involved lengthenings which were "almost 50 msecs longer than those observed in the mothers' speech to an adult listener" (p. 305).

## 3.4    Focus marking

The most important word within an intonation group (the "focus") in the adult language is regularly marked by making the stressed syllable of that word prominent in pitch and/or beginning one of a recurring set of pitch patterns at that point. But *high* pitch is not always present nor indeed is any sort of pitch prominence always present; it may be that listeners already know which syllable is normally stressed in a word and identify the word as particularly important in context because one of the recurring set of pitch patterns begins at that point. So in a sentence like *I think Peter did it*, the pitch peak (or, more correctly and acoustically, the peak in fundamental frequency ($F_0$)) may be on the first syllable of *Peter* with the syllables thereafter low (a "high fall"); or the pitch on *Pe-* may be mid and then the remainder syllables rise higher (a "high rise"); or *Pe-* may be mid, with a following peak on *-ter* and then the remainder syllables low (a "rise–fall"). Fernald and Mazzie (1991) performed an experiment to test the hypothesis that focused words in BT are more consistently associated with $F_0$ peaks than in adult-to-adult speech. For children (aged 1;2) mothers introduced new items of clothing on successive pages of a picture book; this was compared with students instructing other students on how to assemble the parts of a kitchen machine. Now the particular context in which the new items of clothing were introduced for children is, at first glance, one in which more affectively marked pitch contours (e.g. rise–fall beginning at a stressed syllable) might be used, compared with the intellectual task of assembling a machine. The findings of Fernald are therefore striking: the correspondence between $F_0$ peak and primary stress (= focus) (as judged subjectively by linguists) was greater in the speech to the children. A further interesting finding was that such $F_0$ peaks came more regularly at the ends of utterances of BTPr than in the student speech. There is certainly a tendency for focused words to come at the ends of utterances in adult-to-adult speech, but this tendency is apparently even stronger in BTPr. By both alignment of $F_0$ peak and in particular by end location children are being given a clear indication of focus in utterances.

There is, however, one difficult problem with the finding concerning $F_0$ peaks. If the $F_0$ peaks regularly occurred on focused words, then this would appear to mean that all following the peak was low; in other words the common pitch contour being used was evidently a "high fall." But if there was a preponderance of high falls, this would seem to contradict the reports previously mentioned under section 3.2 above which suggested that BTPr involves more rises. I have no special explanation for this apparent contradiction except to hypothesize that the context of introducing new items from a picture book is a rather special one in the life of an infant and very different from the interactive "conversations" from which the increased frequency of rises is usually reported.

## 4 Facilitation

It is clearly true that at least young infants prefer to listen to BT, and in an early study DeCaspar and Fifer (1980) found that infants three days old preferred their own mothers' voices (as opposed to other mothers'). Fernald (1985) played 48 four-month-old infants exemplars of previously recorded speech to infants and speech to adults and monitored their preferences as shown by head-turning. The infants showed an overwhelming preference for BT. Fernald and Kuhl (1987) in follow-up experiments played infants resynthesized versions of the speech samples used in the earlier work. The resyntheses were of three kinds: (i) a fundamental frequency envelope (i.e. the acoustic correlate of perceived pitch) with all the segmental effects removed; (ii) a similar signal showing an amplitude envelope (i.e. the acoustic correlate of perceived loudness), and (iii) a signal in which only durational effects remained. Infants now showed a preference for BTPr in condition (i) but not in conditions (ii) and (iii).

Werker and MacLeod (1989) repeated the experiment of Fernald (1985) for both four-month-old and seven-month-old infants, again finding more attentional and affective responsiveness to BTPr than to adult-directed speech. They added two further pieces of information: the four-month-old infants were more responsive than the seven-month-olds; and infant responses to BTPr were in turn more attractive to adults (which, of course, would aid mother–child interaction).

Obviously, then, young infants prefer BTPr, and it is the pitch pattern of motherese which is responsible for this preference. Such a preference aids language development at the very least in a general way; anything which encourages parent–child interaction and which involves spoken signals will also encourage language development. But such encouragement is only of a very general kind, and we must now ask whether the putative facilitative effects of BTPh and BTPr can be of a more specific sort. I divide such putative facilitative effects into five categories and ask to which category the various types of modification in BTPh and BTPr might belong.

*4.1     Solidarity*

Here belong those modifications which involve an imitation of the child's world, an enjoyment of the way the child is speaking, an indication to the child that an adult is on the same wavelength as the child. The adult speaks like the child to reinforce solidarity with the child. The principal manifestation of this effect lies in what I shall call BTPh1 (i.e. the first stage of Baby Talk Phonetics). BTPh1 mainly shows up in apparent "simplifications" of the adult language which do not occur in adult registers of the language (apart from registers which mimic BT like Pet Talk and Foreigner Talk; see Wesche this volume). These are many of the consonantal changes mentioned under section 2 above, like substitutions, cluster reduction, and consonant harmony, although BTPr high pitch may also be thought of as this type of accommodation. Adults name a dog as /gɒgi/ because this sort of sequence is familiar in children's babbling; they are showing solidarity with children by speaking like them and at the same time showing them that a child sequence can have a meaning. The consonantal and syllabic effects (in particular the preference for open syllables) which come under the heading of BTPh1 and which involve "simplifications" from the adult language have to be distinguished from those effects to be described as BTPh2, like the use of full forms of vowels, particularly in function words, and the use of unreduced alternants like those in the experiments of Shockey and Bond (1980) and Bernstein Ratner (1984b) mentioned in section 2, as well as those which involve phonetic amplification, like overaspiration. BTPh1 is often thought of as "cute," and can often produce arguments about the way parents should speak to children: many middle-class English parents will say that infants should not be spoken to in this way because it reinforces "wrong" pronunciations of words. BTPh1 is what the layman thinks of as Baby Talk, and would seem to be particularly characteristic of talk to pre-linguistic infants, although there is no firm evidence on this count. BTPh1 reinforces the solidarity between mother and infant.

## 4.2     Clarification

In section 2 the work of Bernstein Ratner (1984a, 1984b) was reported which showed less consonantal reduction in weak forms in BTPh between the ages of 1;0 and 2;5, and more differentiation between vowels in content words to holophrastic children and in both content and function words to telegraphic children. Superficially this would seem to contradict what takes place under 4.1. The apparent "simplification" in changing or losing consonants or vowels under 4.1 is in direct contrast to the mainte-nance of full forms or the keeping apart of vowels applying here. But this surely has to be explained as the use of different language at different ages. At the earlier age solidarity is the most important thing while at the later age learning the linguistic system is the most important. So clarifi-cation effects would be expected not to apply at the earlier age, nor for that matter can they be expected to apply at much later stages when the linguistic system is more advanced (and hence the findings of Bard and Anderson 1983). Use of carefully enunciated consonants and carefully differentiated vowels will of course increase the amount of redundancy in speech; it increases the "signal-to-noise ratio"; it increases the volume of cues to correct understanding. Some of the components of BTPr will also have clarificatory effects; in particular, a wider pitch range will widen the differentiation between pitch contours in much the same way as vowels are maximally differentiated.

## 4.3     Affect

As long ago as Lewis (1936) it was suggested that the communication of affect through intonation contours was central to the development of meaning. Fernald (1984) and Stern *et al.* (1982) emphasized the role which BTPr has in influencing infant emotion in the early months and concluded that wider pitch range and higher pitch level were correlated with positive emotion in the child. Stern, Spieker, Barnett, and MacKain (1983), who found a peak of sensitivity to prosody around 0;4, suggested that infants are at this stage learning to discriminate different emotions as they are expressed vocally. The idea is very credible and has been confirmed by a limited number of experiments but with respect to only a few emotions. Fernald (1989) found that adults can identify affective information (including approval, prohibition, and comfort) more easily in speech directed to infants than in speech directed to adults; the implication of course being that children can do this too. Fernald (1990) reported a number of experiments in which recordings were made of approval and disapproval in BT speech in languages other than English and played to English children aged between 0;5 and 0;9. The children correctly identified these emotions (they were most identifiable in Italian and least so in Japanese). Pitch contour must play a part in such identification of emotion (although there may also be voice quality differences) but the significant finding is that once again a controlled experiment showed infants more sensitive to such emotions in BT than in adult-to-adult speech; the most identifiable prosodic features of BT are wider range and higher pitch rather than pitch contour, and it is evidently these which lead to the preference for BT. What is being facilitated here is intonation itself. In other words, intonation is not being used to bootstrap into the linguistic system; rather, an intonation system with adjusted pitch range and pitch height is being used to introduce the child to some of the meanings of the adult intonation system.

## 4.4    Attention

At the beginning of section 4 it was claimed that infants prefer BT and that a major part of this preference was located in BTPr. This finding in itself shows infants *attending* to BT and this in itself will help language acquisition. The principal component of BTPr which increases infant attention is undoubtedly its high pitch. Wolff (1963) reported that, in the first three weeks of life, a high-pitched human voice was more effective in eliciting smiling, that is, in producing positive affect, than a bird whistle or a bell. Fernald and Mazzie (1983, 1991) found peaks of high pitch to be particularly associated with calling infants' attention to new objects and events. There are dissociable factors here: (i) the use of an overall high pitch (as exemplified statistically by measurements of higher mean $F_0$), and (ii) extra-high pitch peaks (which one reflected statistically by wider pitch range). Fernald (1984) hypothesized different functions for the two factors: (i) the use of higher mean pitch "move[s] pitch up into a frequency region well above that of normal adult conversation and thus not easily masked by background noises" (pp. 12–13), thereby enhancing the audibility of speech; whereas (ii) the use of particularly high peaks is an example of the figure/ground effect familiar in Gestalt psychology, whereby high and low tones are segregated. A third component of BTPr, apparently unrelated to high pitch, has also been suggested as being used for attention-getting: the use of rising tones (e.g. Stern *et al.* 1982). However it appears that Stern *et al.* are referring particularly to the use of a rise from mid to high, so a high pitch is still involved. Moreover, high rise is often used to get attention in adult-to-adult exchanges in English, so the only factor which is relevant to its inclusion as part of BTPr is how frequently it occurs since neither the contour nor its meaning are unique to BTPr.

## 4.5    *Segmentation*

The ways in which BTPr assists in segmenting the stream of speech follows directly from section 3.3 above. The boundaries between intonation groups or intonational "chunks" (which in turn correspond most frequently with clause boundaries – a sentence boundary is of course also a clause boundary – and less frequently with phrase boundaries) are in adult-to-adult intonation associated with various markers, two major ones of which are pause and final-syllable lengthening. Both these markers are more systematically used in BTPr. Thus infants are receiving clearer indications of the major constituents of the grammatical structure of the adult language.

What can we conclude about the facilitative effects of BT? We have clear evidence that at least young infants prefer BT, and we have set out five hypotheses about how BTPh and BTPr *might* facilitate language acquisition. Some are more direct (e.g. segmentation); some are more indirect (e.g. solidarity). It is difficult to see how we could ever have absolute proof of such facilitation and even more difficult to see how we will ever be able to measure (or even estimate) the extent of such facilitation. However, the final two sections of this article clearly bear on these issues: if BT is fine-tuned (i.e. produced with age appropriateness), then it is clearly the case that mothers in some way (conscious or unconscious) *think* BT is facilitative. If it is universal, then clearly mothers worldwide think it is facilitative.

## 5    Fine-tuning

In this section I will look at some of the variation in BTPh and BTPr which is clearly associated with different ages. I examine BTPr, BTPh1, and BTPh2 in turn to see if there is evidence for fine-tuning; I consider BTPr first because its effects apply even to the youngest infants.

Stern *et al.* (1983) compared the speech of six mothers to their children longitudinally at four different ages: (a) two to six days, (b) 0;4, (c) 1;0, and (d) 2;0 on a number of measures including four of fundamental frequency: (i) terminal pitch change (i.e. the degree of pitch change at the ends of utterances); (ii) transitional pitch change (i.e. the interval of pitch change between the end of one utterance and the beginning of another); (iii) pitch range; (iv) absolute high (i.e. the highest $F_0$ for each utterance). The highly significant results showed a higher mean on all measures at age 0;4. For example, for pitch range all mothers were higher at 0;4 than 0;0 (i.e. the two to six days group), all mothers were higher at 0;4 than 1;0 and five out of six mothers were higher at 0;4 than 2;0 (and very similar results were found for the other measures). These results argue that the period when BTPr is used for attention and affect is in the first half of the first year. This was confirmed by Werker and MacLeod (1989), who looked at two groups of infants aged 0;4 and 0;7 and monitored the attention time and affective responsiveness produced by BT. The younger group were more attentive and more responsive.

The measure of terminal pitch change in Stern *et al.* (1983) obviously includes final rises, although there is rather less firm evidence about the fine-tuning of pitch contours. Stern *et al.* (1982) suggested that mothers use rises in addition to higher pitch to get infants' (0;2–0;6) attention but, as already pointed out, to be significant this would really depend on the overall frequency of rises in BT compared with adult-to-adult speech and with speech to older children. Such a higher frequency was of course found in Garnica (1977), but this was for two-year-olds compared with five-year-olds and with adults. One piece of suggestive evidence, which is nonetheless difficult to interpret, comes from Larson, Ferrier, Chesnick, Liebergott, and Schultz (1982, reported in Ferrier 1985), who studied rises on directives addressed to children by their mothers at 1;0 and 1;10 and related the frequency of rises to the children's comprehension as measured by their "comprehension of two-term relations" (I presume this means two-word sentences). The mothers of children with good comprehension used a greater incidence of rises than the mothers of poor comprehenders at 1;0, whereas at 1;10 the incidence of rises for both groups was the same and equivalent to that for the poor comprehenders at the earlier stage. The evidence at 1;0 suggests either a causative relationship or a fine-tuning relationship or both; but the evidence at 1;10 is uninterpretable. Overall there is a reasonable suggestion that rises are used with greater frequency to children up to the age of 2;6 (some of Garnica's two-year-olds were this age) but no clear indication of fine-tuning during this age span. This is not to say it is not there; merely that the work has not yet been done.

As reported in section 3.3 above, a number of studies (e.g. Broen 1972; Fernald and Simon 1984) report that pauses are longer in BT and a better cue to constituent boundaries than in adult-to-adult speech. Moreover, children prefer to listen to motherese with pauses at clause boundaries (Kemler-Nelson, Hirsh-Pasek, Jusczyk, and Wright Cassidy 1989). It might be expected that pausing would therefore be at its peak when children were on the threshold of grammar. The only study which compares pauses at various ages (Stern *et al.*, 1983) does not provide entirely clear supporting evidence. Pauses of over 3 seconds were taken to indicate the end of an utterance and were therefore excluded, while breaks of less than 0.3 seconds were not considered as pauses at all. The average lengths of the remaining, utterance-medial, pauses in speech to children and adults were: neonate, 1.63; four months, 0.95; twelve months, 1.45; twenty-four months, 1.38; adults 0.68. This does appear to indicate some sort of peak at twelve months, although there is an even greater, unexplained, peak for neonates. We have no evidence concerning any change in the regularity with which pauses cue constituent boundaries over time. A different kind of cue which is used for boundary marking is that of final syllable lengthening, which is reported by Bernstein Ratner (1986) as more common in speech to her children (prelinguistic, holophrastic, and telegraphic) than to adults. But in this case we lack a study of very young children. Again, then, the case for fine-tuning of boundary markers remains unproven.

Turning back now to BTPh, I deal first with BTPh1 (i.e. segmental modifications which are not used in adult-to-adult speech). These are the various phonetic processes, like substitution, assimilation, and consonant harmony, which make BTPh1 similar to child phonology. There is no remotely comparative study of the use of such features at various ages; most of the reports of processes like these come from diary studies or are anecdotal, and ages are not always noted. The overall impression received from such reports is that these phonetic processes are essentially things of the prelinguistic (and possibly holophrastic) periods. They were noted in section 4.1 as being facilitative only in the somewhat indirect way of solidarity, whereby speaking like a child reinforces the intimacy between parent and child. If this is true, such effects would be governed by the child's own phonetic processes and would disappear as the child loses them.

Phonetic adjustments in BTPh2 often take the form of amplifications, such as overaspiration of voiceless plosives (Malsheen 1980), and over-lengthening of vowels before lenis consonants (Bernstein Ratner and Luberoff 1984). Both these modifications are designed to increase contrastivity between phonemes. Such overaspiration was found in speech to children at the holophrastic stage but not at the prelinguistic stage (see

Baran, Laufer and Daniloff 1977, who found VOT values for voiceless and voiced plosives not significantly different between mothers' speech to adults and to prelinguistic infants) or telegraphic stages. The overlengthening of vowels applied to nine children between 0;9 and 2;3; in this case results are not presented for individuals, so no age relation can be extracted. It looks as if there is some fine-tuning but, again, more data are required.

The problem of age and the interpretation of BTPh2 was previously discussed in section 2 with reference to the use of weak forms and maximally differentiated vowels, the problem being that experiments with children at a later age (1;10–4;0) found *more* distortion, while those with children almost certainly younger (judging by their MLU) found less distortion. Children at the prelinguistic stage were *not* judged to have less distortion. BTPh2 seems to be clearly fine-tuned for children in the holophrastic stage.

All-in-all, it can be concluded that we possess a limited amount of evidence that BTPh and BTPr are fine-tuned, adding strength to the conclusion at the end of the previous section that mothers intuitively believe that they are facilitating language acquisition. Fine-tuning for solidarity, for affect and for attention (as shown by BTPh1 and most of the BTPr effects) is at its peak in the prelinguistic stage; fine-tuning for clarification and possibly for segmentation (as shown by BTPh2 and some of the BTPr effects) is at its peak in the holophrastic stage.

## 6    Crosslinguistic variation

Ferguson (1977) opens with the following sentence: "In all speech communities there are probably special ways of talking to young children which differ more or less systematically from the more 'normal' form of the language used in ordinary conversation among adults." Ferguson goes on to marshal the evidence for this special way of talking from diary studies in a large number of languages, including Arabic, Comanche, Gilyak, Greek, Japanese, Kannada, Latvian, and Marathi. The putative universal features of such BT involve aspects of prosody, phonology, lexicon, syntax, and discourse. The features of BTPr mentioned involve higher pitch, wider pitch range, and special pitch contours, while those for BTPh involve favorite syllable shapes, substitution of simpler for more difficult sounds, and assimilation.

The universality of at least some aspects of BTPr has been confirmed by a large amount of data. Blount and Padgug (1977) found a high degree of similarity in Spanish-speaking and English-speaking mothers talking to children in the holophrastic stage. Fernald and Simon (1984) found that

German mothers' speech to their newborns has higher pitch, wider pitch range, longer pauses (almost invariably corresponding with sentence boundaries), and more use of whisper. Grieser and Kuhl (1988) reported almost exactly similarly for Mandarin Chinese. Finally, in the widest sample of all, Fernald *et al.* (1989) compared prosodic modifications in mothers' and fathers' speech to preverbal infants in French, Italian, German, Japanese, British English, and American English between the ages of 0;10 and 1;2. The measures again included pitch height, pitch range, pitch variability, and pause duration. With one or two insignificant exceptions, both mothers' and fathers' speech show "greater prosody" to children than to adults. There was some interlanguage variation, for example American English was most "exaggerated." This was in part confirmed by Shute and Wheldall (1989), who found a higher pitch in American BTPr than in British BTPr.

There have been some dissenting voices, chiefly among anthropologists/ethnologists, to this presumption of universality. Heath (1983), in her in-depth study of a black working-class community in North Carolina, reported that "everyone talks *about* the baby, but rarely *to* the baby" (p. 75); BT is not used and this includes not using special pitch or intonation patterns. Ochs (1982) and Schieffelin (1979) make similar claims for child-rearing in Samoa and among the Kaluli of Papua New Guinea (although Schieffelin notes that mothers "speak for the child in a special high very nasal voice register" [p. 86]). Of course, if parents do not talk directly to their children, then the characteristics of BTPr cannot show up. These reports of not talking directly to children would seem to apply in particular to children in the prelinguistic stage, and perhaps the claim for this stage should therefore be modified to: if parents talk to their infants in the prelinguistic stage, then features of BT including BTPr will be present. A similar sort of evidence is presented in Bernstein Ratner and Pye (1984) and Pye (1986). In this case the utterance involved was Quiché (K'iche') Mayan (Guatemala), and three mother–child dyads were studied (although there was only a very limited amount of data) where the children involved were 1;10, 2;0, and 2;9. Mothers' speech to their children and to other adults was compared acoustically for (among other things) pitch height, pitch range, and special contours. None of the predicted universals was found. Pitch height was actually found to be *lower* to the children. Two points need to be made, however: (i) the ages of the children were in fact not those where the maximum effect of prosodic modification might be expected; and (ii) Bernstein Ratner and Pye point out that pitch height is a highly utilized variable in adult-to-adult variation in Quiché, high pitch being used to high-status people. Children are of low status and so a potential conflict would occur if high pitch were thought appropriate for young infants. We would need more information on younger children for it to be fully concluded that high pitch to children is ruled out for this reason. On the other hand, anthropologists point out that all the evidence for BTPr comes from industrially advanced societies and usually from middle-class parents within such societies (see Lieven, this volume, for further evaluation of this discussion). We need more specialized studies (the Quiché Mayan data was originally collected for other purposes) from more traditional societies before we can be certain whether BTPr is or is not universal.

As for BTPh, the position on universals is different for BTPh1 and BTPh2. The evidence for universals for BTPh1 was thoroughly surveyed in Ferguson (1977). But the more recent evidence (mainly anthropological) mentioned above for BTPr has also thrown doubt on the universality of BTPh1. Pye (1986) found only limited phonological modification in Quiché Mayan and such modification did not concern the more common types like substitution and cluster reduction, but other, elsewhere unreported, modifications. Initial-syllable deletion, for example, was reported as occurring extensively in nouns and verbs, in mothers speaking to their children below the age of two. In section 2 above it was pointed out that BTPh1 involved modifications which reflected processes common in child language itself. Deletion of initial unstressed syllables is a feature of child phonology itself (Ingram 1989, pp. 372 and 378) and it is hence not surprising to find it in BTPh1. What is surprising in Pye's reports of Quiché is that the root syllable following the unstressed syllable remains whereas in child productions themselves in Quiché the root syllable is often dropped in addition to the unstressed syllable preceding it, leaving the final (stressed) suffix and/or termination to stand alone (Pye 1983, 1986). So *tʃatets'anoq* "play" (*tʃ-at-ets'-an-oq*, aspect-subject-root-intransitive suffix-termination) was reduced to *tets'anoq* rather than *ts'anoq* or *noq* (phonemic transcription, based on Spanish orthography). This is important as illustrating an area where BT does not exactly follow child phonology (evidently the lexical nature of a root has an effect in BT which it does not have in Quiché child phonology). As usual, we need more data! Heath (1983), Ochs (1982), and Schieffelin (1979) all also report, as mentioned above, that adults do not talk directly to their young infants (particularly under one year), and no talk obviously means no BTPh1. Some communities ignore babbling and do not "reinforce" into the first words; they evidently do not feel the need to show solidarity with their infants in this way or to impose meanings on the child's babble (but again, see Lieven this volume). As for BTPh2, we have no evidence at all concerning its crosslinguistic validity.

## 7     Summary and conclusion

In sections 2 and 3 of this chapter I surveyed the evidence for the existence of BTPh and BTPr. BTPh occurs in the form of phonemic changes (e.g. cluster reduction) and of phonetic amplification (e.g. overaspiration of voiceless plosives and maximally distinct vowels). BTPr occurs in the form of higher pitch and wider pitch range (and possibly more rises), longer pauses, and longer final-syllable lengthening at constituent boundaries, and a greater tendency to place prosodic focus at the ends of constituents (together with a more straightforward correlation between focus and higher pitch).

In section 4 six putative facilitative effects of BT were posited: (i) general (experiments show that children prefer to listen to BT); (ii) solidarity (BTPh1 involves adults speaking like children); (iii) clarification (BTPh2 widens the difference between sounds and wider pitch range maximally differentiates pitches); (iv) affect (affective information is more identifiable in BTPr); (v) attention (high pitch is more piercing); and (vi) segmentation (longer pauses and final-syllable lengthening delimit constituents). It was noted that we are a long way from proving such facilitative effects, but clearly mothers' use of BT suggests that they feel it is facilitative. Sections 5 and 6 show that the case for facilitation is strengthened by some evidence for fine-tuning and considerable evidence for at least BTPr as a near-universal.

Overall the balance of evidence comes down in favor of the existence of phonetic and prosodic adjustments in adults' speech to young children, in favor of the fine-tuning and near-universality of such adjustments, and in favor of their facilitative effects on language acquisition.

# 7    Language learning at home and school

*Peter Geekie and Bridie Raban*

## 1    The structure of classroom discourse

It has often been observed that going to school presents young children with a range of problems. Not least of these is the change in their relationship with adults from intimate individual contact with parents to relatively impersonal contact with a teacher who is responsible for the care, control, and education of a large group of children. This is a matter of great consequence since the quality of the interpersonal relations in the classroom inevitably influences the patterns of discourse which, in turn, have an impact upon the children's learning. Research over the last twenty-five years has exposed patterns of classroom talk which have been criticized as allowing few opportunities for children to be active participants in the educational process. Typically, classroom talk has been shown to be not only rigidly structured but also teacher-dominated.

One of the early studies of classroom talk was conducted by Sinclair and Coulthard (1975) at the University of Birmingham. However, this was not educational research. As linguists, their objective was to develop an initial model for the systematic study of discourse. They chose to analyze classroom talk as a starting point for their project because it seemed simpler than casual conversation: the classroom offered a highly structured situation in which meanings were likely to be relatively unambiguous and one participant was responsible for the allocation of turns and the direction taken by the discussion. It was, consequently, from talk in lessons conducted by teachers working with small groups of ten- to eleven-year-old children that their initial analytical system was developed. Their identification of an Initiate–Respond–Feedback (IRF) exchange as a characteristic feature of classroom discourse was of particular interest to educational researchers. This IRF exchange is made up of combinations of moves, beginning with an initiating move often in the form of a question, such as *Who won the Rugby Union World Cup in 1991?*; followed by a response *Australia*; and then by feedback, perhaps in the form of an evaluative comment *That's right*. In the majority of these exchanges, the teacher both initiated the interaction and provided feedback, while pupils were almost always expected only to be respondents. Given the fact that Sinclair and Coulthard deliberately chose lesson types in which the teacher would be exercising a maximum amount of control over the discourse structure, these outcomes are not surprising. Nevertheless, the basic structure of the exchange suggests that teachers are responsible for two-thirds of the talk in classrooms. This is consistent with other research findings.

In a later study, using methods based on those of Sinclair and Coulthard, Willes (1983) found similar patterns of talk in infant classrooms. Children going to school for the first time have to extend the language they have brought to school with them to include the language of the learner in an institutional setting; in other words, they have to discover what the rules of classroom participation are. She had anticipated that this would take some time and that the children would vary in the rate at which they learned these patterns of discourse. To her surprise, she found that even from the children's earliest days in the nursery, where teachers were conducting what they viewed as educationally significant activity with their children, the resulting discourse could be analyzed according to the Birmingham model (Willes 1983).

The children were not, however, expected to respond explicitly, but learnt through participation. They were treated from the beginning as "players" in the game of school. Their approximations of standard responses were accepted by the teachers until they learned to provide more conventional ones. Willes observes that, in doing this, the teachers behaved in much the same way as the mothers in Snow's study of the development of conversation between mothers and their babies (Snow 1972). Just as the mothers always behaved as if their infant children were already full conversational partners, so did the teachers behave as if the children had already become participating pupils. Willes remarks that the children learnt to become competent participants in classroom discourse in the same way that they learnt other games played according to rules outside the classroom, that is, with minimal explanation. A major difference, however, is that the teacher always remains the dominant player in the classroom, while the children are left few choices and little room to exercise their initiative (Willes 1981).

Willes says that the dominance of teachers over classroom talk is an unavoidable outcome of their obligations to control and care for the children in their classrooms. There were other types of talk as well. When the teachers assumed control of the class for instruction, formal discourse structures were seen, but at other times children used language amongst themselves for such diverse purposes as teasing, bragging, quarreling, plotting, imagining, and simply chattering. She found that in these situations, their utterances were more complex, and that they initiated frequently. Nevertheless, teacher-dominated discourse was observed to be the norm and Willes observes that "Insofar as it imposes on the pupil, most of the time, passivity and brevity, it does not commend itself as more than a limited and inflexible medium for learning" (Willes 1983, p. 147).

Mehan (1979) brought a sociological perspective to the study of classroom interaction. As an ethnomethodologist, he regarded the lesson as a "social act" which is an orderly entity arising out of the observable interactional "work" done by the participants, who assemble "initiation, reply and evaluative acts into interaction sequences" (Corsaro 1981, p. 45). Mehan's objective was to describe both the structure of the lessons and the structuring work of the individuals who brought them into existence (Mehan 1979).

Although his was not a linguistic analysis of classroom talk, Mehan acknowledged his debt to Sinclair and Coulthard (1975), whose work had led him to recognize that classroom discourse was best characterized as a sequence of ordered triples (i.e. as IRF groupings) rather than as the adjacency pairs which conversational analysts had identified as the basic organizational units of everyday conversation. He is insistent, however, that Sinclair and Coulthard's categories could not be applied to his data to determine what was happening between the teacher and pupils he observed (Mehan 1979). Instead, he identified the functions of speech in classroom discourse reflexively, using as his unit of analysis "interactionally accomplished sequences of action" rather than autonomous speech acts. Any act in a speech event like a lesson, he said, has a range of potential meanings. The actual meaning of a specific act could not be known until the entire sequence was completed, since the meaning is determined pragmatically by the participants (Mehan 1979).

Like Willes, Mehan produced data which suggested that there is a form of communicative competence specific to schools, which has to be learnt but is not explicitly taught. Instead, the children learnt to infer how to engage appropriately in classroom discourse by making use of information provided by the context. Operating mainly on the cues provided by the teacher, the children had to learn classroom rules for participating in the openings and closings of lessons, for turn taking, for producing acceptably ordered utterances and making coherent topical ties (Mehan 1979). The development of communicative competence in this setting did not, however, suggest simply a mastery of appropriate forms of talk. Mehan says that, in order to arrive at an understanding of interactional competence in the classroom, it is necessary to take account of what students know (i.e. the academic subject matter) as well as how they display that knowledge (i.e. acceptable forms of interaction). The separation of form and content by pupils led to what he termed inappropriate displays in the classroom.

## 2    Classroom discourse and the development of meaning

Barnes (1976) shared with Mehan an interest in the meaning of classroom talk. His research has often been criticized because he dealt only with those aspects of classroom talk which he felt were particularly important, rather than attempting to account for all his data. He has, nevertheless, exercised a substantial influence on educational research designed to answer questions about the relationship between language and learning. In one of his studies of classroom talk, he draws a distinction between exploratory and presentational talk. Exploratory talk helps children to discover the ways in which new knowledge or experience might modify what they already know. It involves the tentative exploration of possibilities and the group solution of problems. By contrast, presentational talk is essentially concerned with getting the right answers and satisfying the teacher's criteria. He claimed that in small group discussions without adult supervision, children and adolescents frequently engaged in exploratory talk. On the other hand, in lessons conducted by teachers it was presentational talk which was the norm (Barnes, Britton, and Torbe 1986). These lessons revealed familiar patterns, with pupils rarely initiating sequences of talk and seeming mostly to be engaged in trying to interpret signals about what might constitute acceptable answers to the teacher's questions. Such patterns arise out of the teachers' need to control both the content of lessons and the direction followed by classroom discussions (Barnes 1976); teachers leave little room for pupil participation in the negotiation of meaning in the classroom.

Rosen and Rosen (1973) were similarly interested in the role played by language in the development of knowledge at school. They were emphatic that teachers and pupils must share a background of knowledge and experience if classroom talk is to lead to effective learning. Children seem to have more linguistic ability, they say, than normally finds its way into their speech, especially at school. It is the job of teachers, therefore, to create situations which will cause children to use all their language resources in their learning (Rosen and Rosen 1973). In order that this might happen, the classroom must be a place in which "speakers must share a past, must share meanings, must have knowledge in common, must be able to make assumptions about each other and must have built their own network of conventions within which there is room for all those negotiations which language makes possible, facilitates and fosters" (Rosen and Rosen 1973, p. 39).

Edwards and Mercer (1987) hold similar views. According to them, education is a communicative process through which shared understandings are developed. Their analysis of three sets of three related lessons taught to small groups of primary school children led them to conclude that "classroom discourse functions to establish joint understandings between teacher and pupils, shared frames of reference and conception, in which the basic process ... is one of introducing pupils into the conceptual world of the teacher and, through her, of the educational community" (Edwards and Mercer 1987, p. 157). It is a perspective on learning which owes a great deal to Vygotsky and Bruner, aspects of whose work will be discussed in the following sections of this chapter. It implies that there will always be an asymmetry of knowledge and power in the context of learning. Teachers will necessarily exercise control and offer guidance because they are the more knowledgeable partners in the process of introducing children into what Edwards and Mercer describe as a pre-existing culture of thought and language. Successful learning, however, depends on the hand-over of control from teacher to pupil so that the child can eventually become self-regulating and self-correcting in the application of what has been learnt.

Edwards and Mercer are, of course, arguing against what they believe is an unhelpful Piagetian influence in British schools. They believe that pupil-centered inductive learning has often left children confused because teachers have failed to explain the goals and purposes of the lessons they have taught. But they are also emphatically making the point that the teacher-dominated discourse of formal education seems to be designed to prevent the transfer of competence from teachers to children from happening.

## 3    Language and learning at school and home

We have already pointed out that some researchers have remarked that inflexible teacher-centered patterns of talk might be a consequence of teachers' obligations to control and protect classes of thirty or more pupils (Willes 1983; Wells 1986a). But it has also been suggested that classroom talk is, in fact, not really very different from adult–child talk outside school. Indeed, MacLure and French (1981) and Wells and Montgomery (1981) make the point that there are no sharp discontinuities between the language of the school and the language of the home. Data collected with radio-microphones (that is, without an observer present) during the Bristol Language Development Study showed that the same types of interactional structures found in the educational setting (including questions requiring children to display knowledge) are also used by parents at home and are, therefore, not unfamiliar to children when they begin school.

Using the same data, however, Wells (1981, 1986a, 1986b) found that, although the styles of discourse at school and at home were not markedly different, the relative frequency of certain patterns were. For example, he found that children at school initiate fewer conversations with adults, get fewer turns, ask fewer questions, make fewer requests, and express a narrower range of meanings than they do in their conversations with adults at home. Furthermore, at school the teacher produces three utterances for every one by the child, while at home the conversations with adults are much more evenly balanced. It was also true that the syntactic complexity of children's utterances was greater at home, suggesting that they use their full linguistic resources less frequently when talking to their teachers. The picture that emerges, once again, is of children in school answering teachers' questions and complying with their requests, and of teachers choosing topics and allocating conversational turns.

Tizard and Hughes (1984) also used data collected with radio-microphones to compare children's conversations with adults at home and at nursery school. Their findings are very similar to those cited above. They discovered that adult–child exchanges at home were more frequent, of longer duration, and covered a much wider range of topics than similar exchanges at nursery school. To measure who controlled the talk in each setting, they categorized conversational turns in terms of whether or not they served to sustain the conversation. For example, asking a question or making a relevant comment on the other person's contribution was judged to sustain the conversation while simply answering a question or acknowledging a remark was not. It was discovered that children made 47 percent of the sustaining contributions at home, but only 19 percent at school. As before, the evidence suggests that talk in educational settings is dominated by adults and leaves little room for the child to do such things as initiating conversations, asking questions or making comments.

Such findings might not be significant in educational terms. If, however, psychologists like Vygotsky and Bruner are correct in asserting the essentially social nature of learning, then the teacher-dominated patterns of talk which have been so often revealed by researchers from a number of disciplines are unlikely to be creating an intellectually and linguistically stimulating environment for children in schools. It is to a consideration of aspects of Vygotsky's and Bruner's theories that we now turn.

## 4      Vygotsky: sign operations and cognitive development

Vygotsky's psychological studies have helped to bring a social emphasis into psychological research in the last twenty years and to give social interaction a central place in studies of cognitive development. According to Vygotsky (1978), it is sign production and use which permit us to control psychological processes like perception, attention, and memory. Instead of responding immediately to the dominant stimuli in the perceptual field, we are able to introduce links between stimuli and responses which inhibit direct impulses and allow complex psychological processes to develop in their place. These links, voluntarily introduced into a situation to replace natural stimuli as the causes of behavior, are "signs" according to Vygotsky's use of the term. To use one of his own examples, tying a knot in a piece of string as a reminder that something must be done extends the biological limitations of memory. Remembering is transformed into an activity which is controlled externally by a voluntarily generated sign – the knot. Through the deliberate production of such signs human beings are able to remember in a controlled and goal-oriented manner.

This restructuring of mental processes and behavior through the use of signs leads development "away from biological development and creates new forms of a culturally-based psychological process" (Vygotsky 1978, p. 40). It is possible, of course, for people to create and use idiosyncratic signs like the knot in the string, but it is the acquisition of social and cultural sign systems, like spoken and written language, which is most important. It is primarily through the use of language that children come to take part in the intellectual life of the surrounding community (Vygotsky 1978) and lay the foundations for the development of the distinctively human forms of mental functioning.

In fact, it is the acquisition of language, Vygotsky says, which provides a paradigm for the problem of the relationship between learning and development. It illustrates the ways in which external operations, which occur first on the social level, are gradually internalized. Language is a sign system which is first learnt by children in order to communicate in culturally appropriate ways with the people in their immediate environment. Then, over time, their language is reconstructed until it becomes a mental process in its own right which serves to organize their thought. According to Vygotsky, every one of the higher psychological processes develops in this way, as sign operations are transformed from interpersonal processes into intrapersonal ones.

During this process of cognitive growth "zones of proximal development" occur. Vygotsky (1978) defines the zone of proximal development as the distance between the level of development indicated by the child's capacity to solve problems independently and the level of potential development indicated by their capacity to solve problems with the guidance and collaboration of other people. As children encounter problems they cannot solve for themselves, they turn to others for help. Collaboration with another person leads to the development of "voluntary behavior": conscious control of one's mental processes and self-regulation of one's problem-solving behavior. It is such acts of learning that cause types of development which would not otherwise occur. The development of literacy is a good example of this process. Literacy does not simply consist of the mastery of a set of skills; it leads to the development of forms of thought specific to literate people (see Goody 1977; Olson 1977; Eisenstein 1979; Garton and Pratt 1989, for discussions of the cognitive consequences of literacy). According to Vygotsky, learning occurs first, and draws cognitive development along in its wake.

## 5    Bruner and the Language Acquisition Support System

Bruner is one of many psychologists influenced by Vygotsky's theories. His research into language development in children is part of what he has called a "quiet revolution" in developmental psychology which has taken place in the last fifteen years. It involves the recognition of children as social beings who, through social interaction, "acquire a framework for interpreting experience, and learn how to negotiate meaning in a manner congruent with the requirements of the culture" (Bruner and Haste 1987, p. 1). There are specific types of cognitive endowment which are necessary preconditions for language development; these endowments do not, however, generate language development of themselves (Bruner 1983a). Language growth requires innate qualities of mind that make us sensitive to language, but without social interaction development would not occur. It is social interaction, he says, which not only activates the children's genetic predispositions to learn language, but also provides frameworks within which they can discover the ways language can be used to get things done. Bruner proposes that there is a Language Acquisition Support System which adults use to structure the child's language input.

The principal feature of the Language Acquisition Support System is a routinized and repeated interaction between an adult and at least one child. It consists of a series of "moves" that define the context and make it predictable, providing a framework within which the meanings applicable to a specific situation can be negotiated. This standardization of structure further helps children to make sense of the context by distributing their attention over a series of ordered steps. It also permits them to make functionally appropriate responses even if they do not fully understand what the situation requires of them. What is involved is a division of labor and initiative which begins with the adult doing most of the work and providing most of the impetus which is needed to sustain the interaction. Then, as the children's competence grows, control is handed over to and taken by them. In fact, Bruner says that the mother of an infant behaves as a "communicative ratchet" who works to resist any regressive tendencies. Instead, she constantly "ups the ante" by raising her expectations in accordance with her child's developing knowledge and skills. A very important part of what the child is learning, in such contexts, is to master the patterns of discourse themselves. The child learns how to function within the format, but as s/he does so, the format itself changes, through a series of transformations, from a restricted and highly structured interaction pattern to a more flexible one which can be detached from its original context and used to solve other problems in new situations. This capacity to impose structure on a unfamiliar situation becomes an important aspect of communicative and cognitive growth.

The way formats function as a child learns to speak can be seen in Bruner's description of the development of reference. Ninio and Bruner (1978) observed a mother engaged in "book-reading" sessions with her son, Richard, over a period of two years. During these sessions the mother produced only four key utterance types:

1 an attentional vocative (*Look!*);
2 a query (*What's that?*);
3 a label (*It's a horse*);
4 feedback (*Yes*).

The mother tried first to establish joint attention. She then tried to make the child aware that there is a standard vocalization which "stands for" the referent, and then provided feedback that told him whether he had provided an appropriate response.

This was not a static interactive pattern. The mother constantly adapted her expectations to her son's current capacities. As soon as he could produce phonetically consistent babbles, she no longer accepted incoherent babbles. Once he began to produce recognizable words, phonetically consistent babbles were rejected. Then, when naming was being achieved routinely, the mother moved into a new zone of proximal development in which the child learnt that naming the referent is simply prerequisite to commenting upon it. The mother was not only always sensitive to what the child was capable of doing, but also raised her expectations in accordance with her assessment of the child's growing abilities so that she "remains forever on the growing edge of the child's competence" (Bruner 1983a, p. 77).

**6      Comprehension and learning in young children**

Comprehension is inseparable from social interaction. If people cannot discern the meanings with them, then the interaction fails. When children are involved, the likelihood of breakdown in communication is much greater because the child's deficits in knowledge and experience make it much harder to establish the necessary foundation of shared meanings. In a normal conversation, successful communication is not the sole responsibility of the listener. The speaker is also expected to aid the listener by presenting the message appropriately, following Grice's Cooperative Principle (Grice 1975), which can be briefly stated as follows: "speakers try to be informative, truthful, relevant and clear" (Clark and Clark 1977, p. 122). Young children, in particular, have limitations as conversational partners which adults usually try to overcome by such means as simplifying or rephrasing what they have said, or by giving additional information or further cues to their intended meaning (Bridges, Sinha, and Walkerdine 1981).

Bridges (1979, 1980) investigated the nature of the adjustments in message content made by thirty-two mothers engaged in an object-retrieval task with their 24- to 30-month-old children. Video recordings were made as the mothers directed their children to fetch specific objects in different parts of a room. The search sequences usually began when the mother attempted to draw attention to the object to be retrieved. Since the target objects were unfamiliar to the children, their identification, instead of being subsidiary to the main retrieval task, became an explicit and talked-about aspect of the activity. When the object to be retrieved had been identified, a request followed. In most cases this took the form of an embedded imperative (e.g. *Can you fetch the puppet for mummy?*), a question directive (e.g. *Where's the puppet?*), or an imperative (e.g. *Fetch the puppet*). Once the request had been made the mothers frequently provided additional information, in the form of clues, to guide the children in their search for the object. These clues included pointing, directed gaze, nonspecific verbal indicators (e.g. *over there*) and locative terms like *in the box*. As the search progressed, the mothers continued to make concentrated efforts to ensure that the children knew exactly what they were looking for. When a breakdown in the search occurred the mothers usually either repeated the same type of cue that had been given immediately before the breakdown, or offered assistance of a more explicit kind. The mothers reacted to feedback from their children by altering the sophistication of the clues they offered to assist the children in their efforts to understand.

Wood's investigations of the dynamics of adult–child dialogue also focused on the ways in which adults adapt their responses in communicative situations to help their children to understand what is being said to them. His studies, however, involved older children (three to five years old) and instructional situations. For example, Wood and Middleton (1975) asked mothers to teach their children to build a pyramid out of interlocking wooden blocks. Later, the children were tested to assess the effectiveness of the instruction. After matching the mothers' instructional strategies with the success of the children's learning, Wood concluded that successful instruction was dependent upon the ways in which the adults regulated their instructional behavior (that is, demonstrations, descriptions, and evaluations) to the current attention and ability of their children. The adults provided just enough support to help the children to overcome their current difficulties, and withdrew to a less direct level of intervention when children showed that they could manage a particular part of the task for themselves. Wood has described adult intervention as contingent upon the child's activity, and has further claimed that this contingency is based upon the adult's interpretation of the child's errors and what has happened as a result of earlier interventions (Wood 1980). The successful teacher also progressively relaxes control over the planning and execution of problem solving as the child shows that both the task and the strategies needed to complete it are understood.

In a similar study (Wood, Bruner, and Ross 1976), small children were taught to build a pyramid out of interlocking wooden blocks by one of the researchers. During the tutoring sessions it was the adult who took responsibility for controlling the focus of attention and keeping the ultimate goal in mind. She demonstrated that the demands of the task were not impossible and reduced it to subtasks which were appropriate to the children's current capacities. She did the things the child could not do, and she changed the structure of the context so that the children could, with her assistance, do the things they could not do by themselves. In Bruner's words, she allowed the children to "borrow" her knowledge and consciousness in order that they might eventually be able to solve independently the problems involved in the task (Bruner 1986).

In the study by Geekie described in this chapter, a teacher was seen to adapt the way she behaved in much the same way as did the mothers in the studies described above. This teacher adapted the content of her messages to the children to ensure that they understood the directives and clues that she was providing to help them to retrieve, either from memory or the immediate physical context, the information required to solve the problems involved in translating a spoken text into a written one.

## 7    The nature of Geekie's study

It has been stated that the "necessity for early language development of establishing communication frames between parent and child, and the importance of examining acquisition in its functional and pragmatic contexts, are repeated in the study of classroom discourse and knowledge" (Edwards and Mercer 1987, p. 202). Geekie's study was an attempt to investigate the early stages of the acquisition of written language in a functional and pragmatic context by examining classroom dialogue during periods of writing instruction in the first year of formal schooling. It had three distinctive features: first, it examined development in a specific curriculum area making it easier to examine the growth of shared meanings and forms of discourse; second, it focused on sessions in which the teacher was engaged in dialogue with individual children rather than groups of children; third, it extended over a period long enough to allow development in writing skills to take place. We were, therefore, able to see the changes in discourse which accompanied the growth both in knowledge and skill.

The study involved observations of a small group of five-year-olds. The data upon which this study is based were collected in a kindergarten class in a state school in a prosperous area of Wollongong, New South Wales. The five children in the study came from middle-class families.

From the beginning of the year, two types of lessons were observed and often recorded on videotape. The first was the "blackboard story" session which was a regular part of the literacy activities of the classroom. The second was the daily writing session during which children wrote "stories" of their own. At first the "writing" done by the children consisted of such things as copying words and sentences displayed around the room, writing individual letters or known words (e.g. *dad, mum,* their own and sibling's names) and even drawing pictures without any associated text. During these sessions the teacher moved around the classroom checking on the children's attempts at writing and providing individual assistance to children where it was called for. These periods of individual assistance sometimes went on for several minutes. Our decision to focus on individual children arose from the fact that we had noticed this happening during the previous year when we were engaging in preliminary observations.

The video recording of writing sessions in this classroom was done under conditions that were as close to normal as possible. The lessons were recorded at their usual time and the classroom was not isolated in any way for the purposes of recording. There were the normal interruptions to classroom routine (e.g. messages from other teachers and visits from the principal). Although the teacher's attention during each video-taped session was focused, at our request, on one of the selected children, she continued to give assistance to other children and generally to exercise control over the conduct of the activity in the classroom.

The data which are the basis for the discussion in this chapter consist of:

1 transcripts of five sessions recorded in the first three weeks of the school year (one session with each of the selected children);

2 transcripts of a second recorded session for each child selected on the basis that, during the session, they demonstrated an improved ability to write their chosen "story" but were still not yet independent of the teacher's assistance;

3 transcripts of three blackboard story sessions from the first six months of the school year;

4 field notes of the above sessions which were not captured by the camera but which were necessary in order to understand what was happening.

For the purposes of this chapter, we selected and analyzed sequences from the data involving searches for words and phonemes. The early sequence for each child was then compared with the later one, and each child's sequences were compared with those of the other children. We also identified search sequences in the blackboard story sessions and compared them with the sequences identified in the individual sessions.

## 8      Becoming competent participants in the writing session

The involvement of the children in the literacy activities of the classroom varied: some hardly participated, while others waited until other children responded and followed their example. Their participation helped them to respond appropriately when their teacher used the same types of prompts and asked the same types of questions during her exchanges with them during individual writing sessions. Like the pupils in Mehan's study, these children were learning not only how to gain access to the type of information they needed to solve the problems associated with producing a written text, but also the forms of response that were considered to be appropriate during this type of activity with this teacher. They were learning a type of discourse which was not just subject-specific but also teacher-specific.

To make sure that the children were aware of the sources of information in the classroom the teacher regularly drew the children's attention to signs around the room (e.g. "This is the door"; "Here is the piano"; "Mrs. Fisher sits here"; "When is your birthday?"; "Do you know the days of the week?"), and asked the children to read them. She also asked them to find and read familiar poems displayed on sheets of cardboard, and copies of their own "stories" attached to class notice boards. Words included in the *Breakthrough to literacy* program were taught and displayed in the teacher's *Sentence maker* at the front of the room after they had been formally treated in class. The activity of central importance, however, was the daily blackboard story.

The blackboard story session was controlled by the teacher; she selected the topic, asked all the questions, made all the requests, and provided evaluative feedback. She also allocated turns to the children and decided which responses, amongst the chorus of bids, were to count as acceptable contributions to the activity. The children acted exclusively as respondents and their answers to the questions (all of which were display questions) were brief. The teacher was, however, engaged in establishing a framework which would guide the children in their construction of their own texts. The various subsections of the framework, each of which needed to be learnt by the children in order to become competent participants in the writing activities of this classroom, are listed below:

1 A clear statement of the text to be written: e.g. "That's my story for today. Friday is my favourite day because tomorrow we have a holiday."
2 Clear identification of each unit of the message before it is written: e.g. "So the first word in my story is *Friday*."
3 Development of an awareness of the words in the print environment of the classroom: e.g. "Just a minute. What I want you to do is think about Friday, and think about if I've ever written Friday anywhere in our room. Or if you've ever seen the word Friday." One of the sentences on the blackboard is "Today is Friday." Also, above the blackboard is a display of eight cards: on the first card is written, "Do you know the days of the week?" and on the others are the days of the week.
4 Word search sequences, often initiated by a question: e.g. the teacher says, "Can anyone see the word 'my' in our room somewhere?" It is printed on a card in a sentence displayed in a stand on a table in front of the children. She looks towards the sentence and the children follow her gaze. One child is called upon to identify the word.
5 A phonemic analysis sequence within which the teacher identifies the phonemes and the children suggest letters which match the phonemes: e.g. The teacher says "Now I want the word 'is'" and makes the sound of the initial phoneme in the word twice. One or two children call out "i" and others follow their example. The teacher writes the letter on the blackboard and then says "Ssss." Some of the children say "s." The teacher writes it on the blackboard, completing the word.

6 Regular rereading of the sentence to keep it in memory and to help to identify each successive word: e.g. "Right. Let's read what we've got." The teacher points at the words as she reads "Friday is ... " Some of the children read with her.

The interactional routine which the teacher was establishing also resembled the "formats" which are a basic part of Bruner's Language Acquisition Support System (Bruner 1983a). Like the format, it consisted of a series of moves which distributed the children's attention over a series of ordered steps, making the task of translating a spoken message into a written text more manageable and predictable. The children were learning how to become competent players in this game by participating in it under the guidance of an adult who was prepared to fill in the gaps in the interactive sequence for them until they could enact the full routine for themselves.

## 9      Learning to write

Successfully taking part in a conversation depends upon being able to understand what the other participants mean and intend. Successful comprehension in such contexts depends upon the "cooperative orientation of conversational partners to shared meaning, and upon their negotiation of a shared framework of relations between utterance and context" (Bridges, Sinha, and Walkerdine 1981, pp. 120–1). This was also true of the dialogues that we recorded between the teacher and her pupils, although they were instructional sessions rather than normal conversations.

At the beginning of the year, most of the problems that occurred in these sessions were attributable to the limited foundation of shared meanings upon which the interactions were built. As the year went on, the body of knowledge and experience which the children shared with their teacher grew significantly, making reference to relevant aspects of not only the physical context but also information stored in memory more accessible for use in the writing sessions. In the discussions that follow, it will be seen that the children become better participants in the sessions with their teacher, not just because they have mastered the structures of classroom talk, but because the body of knowledge and experience which they shared with their teacher grew significantly, and because they became much more adept at presuppositional implication. That is, they improved in their ability to draw inferences from clues about which body of contextual assumptions was appropriate to the solution of immediate comprehension problems.

In sequence 1 below, the teacher is helping Emma (5;2) to write

"Stirling is having a birthday today." Emma has only been at school for two weeks and has had limited exposure to the routine activities of the classroom; however, she can recognize and name most of the letters of the alphabet and is aware of the basic conventions of written language (e.g. left-to-right progression). Although she can write some words (e.g. her own name and *mum*) she is not yet able to write a sentence independently. She has, however, framed her own "story" for this writing session. When the sequence begins, Emma has written, with the teacher's assistance, "Stirling es hav ... " Stirling has volunteered his name card to help Emma to write the first word and she has copied from it. Subsequently the teacher has broken "is hav ... " into phonemic segments and has helped Emma to locate letters to represent them. Each phoneme has been represented by a single letter. Charles, the boy sitting next to Emma, is taking a great interest in what is going on.

*Sequence 1* (TE Teacher, CH Charles, EM Emma)

| | | |
|---|---|---|
| TE: | we've got the v | |
| | now we want the -ing | |
| EM: | (no response) | (looks blankly into the middle distance) |
| TE: | -ing | (makes eye contact with Charles) |
| | can you remember this morning | |
| | in our story what said -ing? | |
| CH: | -ing | (breaks eye contact) |
| TE: | -ing | |
| | you remember ... | (notices Stirling's name card on the table) |
| | Stirling | (makes eye contact with Charles again) |
| | like the -ing on the end of | |
| | Stirling | |
| EM: | | (looks at what she has written) |
| CH: | -ing | |
| | -ing for England yes | |
| TE: | no | |
| | like an -ing | |
| EM: | | (points to where she has written "Stirling" in her story) |
| TE: | | (does not notice because she has been talking to Charles; turns back to Emma) |
| | -ing | |

EM: oh

(Stirling's name card is partly hidden by papers on the desk. The teacher picks it up and places it on the desk in front of Emma)

TE: which bit would say -ing?
EM: this bit            (points at the beginning of the word)
TE: no that's the "Stirl"       (runs her finger under "Stirl")
    -ing                    (runs her finger under the -ing)
EM: oh yeah            (points at the end of the word with her pencil, runs her pencil across the -ing and back again)

    those three letters
TE:                              (nods)
    those three letters
    that's right

As in Bridges' study (1979, 1980), the adult in this sequence first has to establish joint attention on the target item, and she uses common experience as a basis for the management of attention. When Emma fails to respond to her initial prompt to action ("Now we want the -ing"), the teacher refers to the blackboard story constructed less than an hour before. When that fails, she directs Emma's attention towards something closer which has also been part of the current conversation: Stirling's name card. Emma is not asked to recall the needed item from memory.

The object of the search is a physical part of the setting, and the teacher offers further clues, as Bridges' mothers did, by directing her gaze towards Stirling's name card on the desk and referring to its attributes ("Like -ing on the end of 'Stirling'"). Emma responds by pointing to where she has written "Stirling" in her text. She understands that her teacher wants her to refer to this word. Orientation to a shared meaning has been established, but the teacher does not notice and assumes that Emma has failed to respond again. As a result, she picks up Stirling's name card and places it on the table in front of Emma, clarifying the relationship between her subsequent utterances and the context to which they refer. Now, when she asks "Which bit says -ing?" it is clear that she is referring to the word on the card and wants an answer that refers specifically to it. The fact that Emma responds indicates that she now understands enough about what is expected of her to become a participant in the dialogue again. She points at the wrong part of the word but because joint attention is still fixed on the card, the teacher is able to repair the interaction by pointing at the relevant group of letters and naming it. This is an act of reference which the teacher has achieved not only by simplifying and rearranging the context to make the deictic demands manageable for the child, but also by providing the needed label.

From a structural perspective, it is clear that the teacher controls the interaction in this sequence. She allocates turns, asks all the questions, and evaluates the children's responses. This is consistent with the patterns of teacher talk identified in most research studies, but despite the control she is exercising, the teacher is adjusting her responses in accordance with what the child does at each point in the sequence. When a general verbal prompt to activity fails to produce an appropriate response from Emma, the teacher refers explicitly to Stirling's name card. When that also fails, she selects the material to be used in the solution of the problem by moving the card in front of Emma. Finally, she points to the relevant part of the word and names it. All that is left for the child to do is to perform the act of copying the identified unit. Like the successful tutors in Wood's studies (Wood 1980), the teacher has responded to each of Emma's failures by exercising a progressively greater degree of control over the interaction. Her level of intervention at each stage has depended upon what the child did immediately before (see Wood 1980).

The discussion above was about the management of joint attention and the achievement of understanding, but we also need to consider what Emma has learnt. When the teacher points to the letters and names them, Emma does not immediately copy them onto her page. Instead she says, "Oh yeah. Those three letters." It seems that she has only just realized that this group of letters stands for -*ing*. It is only at this point that the teacher realizes that Emma did not have this basic understanding. Mehan (1979) has observed that the meaning of an act initiated by a teacher is realized retrospectively when the pupil's act is evaluated by the teacher, and this sequence illustrates the point. When the teacher says, "Those three letters. That's right," she both verifies that Emma has understood the relationship between the phoneme and its written form and also shows that she understands what the child has learnt. Emma now has a more explicit understanding of the alphabetic system of writing, and the teacher has a better understanding of what Emma knows about writing. A basis for their discourse about writing, both immediately and in later sessions, has been established.

Sequence 2 involves the teacher assisting Emily (5;1), who has been at school for six weeks. Emily is trying to write, "I have some lizard eggs. I found them under the steps at home." So far, with the teacher's assistance, she has written, "I hav sm lezs egs at home. I fond um rndr . . . " and the teacher is about to help her to write "the steps."

*Sequence 2* (EM Emily)

| | |
|---|---|
| TE:  let's see | |
| let's read it together | (points at the beginning of the second sentence) |
| I found them under. . . | (pointing as she reads; Emily reads with her, then looks up at her and makes eye contact). |
| the<br>the | |
| | (Emily makes an indeterminate sound in response, and breaks eye contact) |
| the<br>the<br>like in. . . | (teacher looks towards the sentence on the window; Emily follows her gaze) |
| this is *the* window | (looks back at Emily and then back towards the window again) |
| and<br>and . . . uh | (looks around, towards the piano behind Emily, who follows her gaze) |
| here is *the* piano | (looks still further towards the piano; Emily stays focused on the sign on the piano) |
| and this is *the* door<br>can you see "the"? | (Emily stays fixed on the piano and makes a soft sound; teacher shifts her attention back to the sign on the piano.) |
| /ðə/ or /ðɪ/<br>the word /ðɪ/ or /ðə/<br>can you see which one that is?<br>here-is-the-piano | (teacher and Emily are both focused on the sign on the piano) <br>(slowly and deliberately) |

EM:  here-is-*the*...                    (pointing at the words as she
                                          reads them)
                                          (turns back to her page and
                                          starts to write, then hesitates
                                          and looks up at teacher)
TE:  will it fit in there?               (nodding towards the end of
                                          the line)
                                          (Emily raises her pencil and
                                          traces the shape of the letter
                                          "T")
TE:  T                                    (nods)
                                          (Emily starts to write)

In this sequence, the teacher makes a series of assumptions about what
Emily knows. She assumes that Emily will understand what she is doing
when she turns to read the signs in the room, and that she will know that
she should attend to those signs. She assumes that Emily knows what
words are, and that the signs consist of written words that refer to the
objects to which they are attached. The achievement of joint attention
still requires considerable effort, but this time the teacher achieves it
simply by looking at the signs and reading them. She does not need to
move the signs closer to Emily or even to point at them. Emily follows
the teacher's gaze and locates the signs because she understands the
presuppositional implications of her utterances and actions. She knows
that an invitation has been issued to her to participate in a search
strategy which has often been part of the literacy activities of the
classroom. She can locate the word she seeks because the activity consists
of a familiar series of moves.

The sequence also shows how language has come to be an instrument
for controlling attention. The teacher reads "Here is the piano" slowly
and deliberately, segmenting it into words so that Emily will find it easier
to match the spoken text to the written one. When Emily reads the
sentence herself and stops at the target word, she shows that she has
understood what she was being shown. She also uses language to control
her attention and locate the target word in the sign on the piano, although
she still needs her teacher to verify that she has actually located the target
item.

In sequence 3, Hannelore (5;9) is being assisted by the teacher as she
tries to write the sentence "We are having the cross country today." She
has just completed the word "cross" and the teacher is drawing her
attention to the next word. It is eleven weeks since the beginning of the
school year.

*Sequence 3* (HA Hannelore)

TE:   cross ... *country*

now where's country?               (Hannelore looks towards the
                                             blackboard; the teacher follows
                                             her gaze, then looks back at
                                             Hannelore, who continues
                                             looking intently at the
                                             blackboard)

you remember
I said it was a really hard word
country

HA:                                 (continuing to look towards the
                                               blackboard)

C-O-U-N-T-R-C-
Y                                     (corrects herself)

TE:   that's right

Establishing joint attention, which occupied so much time earlier in the year, is now quickly achieved. No rearrangement of the context is necessary; the teacher does not have to point or look towards the target unit. Hannelore knows that her teacher's question means that the word is part of the immediate context. Furthermore, she remembers that "country" was part of that morning's jointly constructed story. The blackboard story was available before, but it only became part of the context when the teacher prompted Hannelore's memory of it with her question.

Hannelore looks towards the writing on the blackboard. This situation, like the first two sequences, now resembles Bridges' object retrieval sequences (Bridges 1979, 1980), and the teacher, like the mothers in that study, offers a clue to the location of the required item. This time, however, she does not use pointing, directed gaze or locative terms to assist the child. The explicit deictic clues offered to less competent children are omitted. The teacher is adapting her contribution to the dialogue in accordance with her assessment of the child's capabilities. Bridges found that the mothers of the 24-month-old infants, in attempting to guide the children towards the object to be retrieved, referred mainly to its location in their clarifying comments. By contrast, the mothers of the 30-month-old children refrained from directly indicating the location of the object, but referred instead to the people, places, and events associated with similar objects in the child's previous experience. This is precisely what the teacher does in this sequence. She simply refers to a comment made about the target word while the blackboard story was being constructed earlier that morning. The sequence is focused more on the control of memory and less on the management of attention than the earlier sequences. Hannelore's immediate and appropriate response vindicates the teacher's assumptions.

In this next sequence, the teacher has withdrawn from direct control of the instructional situation. She still identifies the unit to be written but she simply helps the child to recall something that might otherwise have been overlooked. Her question is really a memory cue. By acting as an external aid to the child's memory, the teacher is, in Bruner's terms, allowing the child to "borrow" her consciousness.

Sequence 4 was recorded eighteen weeks after the beginning of the school year. Amy (5;8) has told the teacher what she intends to write ("My birthday is in October") and does not wait for her assistance.

*Sequence 4* (AM Amy)
While the teacher is speaking to other children Amy writes "My" in the top left-hand section of her sheet of paper. When she has completed the word she looks up and mouths "birthday" and then looks towards the *Breakthrough to Literacy Sentence Maker* at the front of the room. Among the words displayed is "birthday." While she continues to look intently at the folder, she mouths the word twice.

| TE: | my | (looking at what Amy has written)<br>(makes brief eye contact with Amy) |
| AM: | is that birthday? | (points towards the *Sentence Maker*) |
| TE: | well you<br>well what does it start with? | |
| AM: | B | |
| TE: |  | (makes eye contact and nods) |
|  | B | (Amy writes "birthday" looking up and down at the word card. She copies one letter each time she looks at the card) |

Amy has reached a point in her development when she needs little help from the teacher. She recalls "my" from memory and then identifies "birthday" as the next word. Then she looks towards the teacher's *Breakthrough to Literacy Sentence Maker* at the front of the room. "Birthday" is one of a number of words displayed in this folder but she is not certain that she has located the correct one so she points at it and asks for confirmation. It is now the child who is taking the initiative and controlling the interaction. The teacher follows Amy's point and asks her to identify the initial letter of the word. The word cards in the *Sentence Maker* are small and are ten feet from where the teacher and Amy are sitting. There are twenty cards on display, one of which has "boy" printed on it. The teacher is confident that Amy will not confuse "boy" with "birthday," and knows that the demands of her question are within Amy's capacities. Amy nominates the correct letter but waits for the teacher to confirm the accuracy of her response before she starts to copy it. She looks to the card for each letter, naming each one softly to hold it in memory while she writes it. The teacher watches but does not intervene in any way.

Amy seems now to understand the goals and intentions of the writing activity. Learning to write is one of those tasks Wood (1980) refers to as having goals which are distant and often ill-defined and, therefore, is a task which requires adult intervention. The children in our study had come to school expecting to learn to read and write but it was, of course, the teacher who decided on the nature, purposes, and goals of the classroom literacy activities. As Wood has observed, the child's entry into such activities depends on the child's trust in and desire to please the adult. Ultimately, however, to become writers, children have to establish their own purposes and goals for writing. Amy seems to have reached this stage in her development as a writer. She now does for herself most of the things the teacher previously did for her. For example, she can now hold her full text in her memory without assistance. She can identify each successive word in the text, and has strategies for writing them. She can cue the recall of items from memory by saying the word or the name of the letter she needs. She can remember the location of commonly used words around the classroom and find them for herself. Although she is not yet completely independent, she is using the strategies for the creation of a written text that she has learnt in interaction with her teacher in both group and individual writing sessions to regulate her writing behavior and make her capable of independently producing written texts.

The most significant feature of this sequence, however, is the fact that the teacher is now reactive rather than controlling in her behavior. She waits until Amy turns to her before she offers help. She is content to allow the child to proceed independently. She is, in fact, in the process of handing over control of the writing situation to the child, just as the mothers in Bruner's studies passed control to their infant children as their capacity to use communicative formats developed.

In the final sequence presented here, Amy no longer needs the teacher at all. She has decided to write a story beginning "Yesterday the twins came to play." Damien is sitting facing her on the other side of the table. She sits and thinks for several moments before looking at her page apparently ready to commence writing.

*Sequence 5* (AM Amy, DA Damien)

Amy looks down at her page and prepares to write. She says "yesterday"
  softly, hesitates, and then looks up and leans towards Damien.

AM:  Damien
     how do you spell "yesterday"?

DA:  look behind you                     (pointing at a chart on the wall
                                         behind AM)
                                         (Amy looks round)

DA:  I'm spelling it                     (means that he is also writing
                                         the word; looks at his page and
                                         then up)

     Y-E-S...
                                         (Amy continues to look)

AM:  Y... oh I found it

                                         (Damien is still watching Amy
                                         as she turns back to her page
                                         and prepares to write)

DA:  Y-E-S...

                                         (Amy glances briefly up at
                                         Damien)

AM:  I found it                          (writes "yes" and then turns to
                                         check as she writes the
                                         remaining letters; repeats the
                                         letters she has already written
                                         as she looks at the chart to find
                                         the letters she wants and then
                                         turns to write them)

Amy is now in full control of her writing. She is aware of what she needs
to know and she is no longer dependent on her teacher for guidance in
finding it. When she encounters a problem she asks another child for help.
Damien's reply is patterned on the routines the teacher has developed. He
first uses deictic reference to establish the general location of the word.
Because she shared Damien's knowledge of the classroom, Amy looks
towards the chart entitled "Words We Know." Damien adds clues by
naming the first three letters. This is sufficient to permit Amy to identify
it. When he starts to spell the word again, Amy silences him. He is
violating a maxim of conversation by offering more information than is
needed.

The patterns of exchange formerly used by the teacher have now
become the property of the children. Damien could have simply spelled
the word but he engages in an act of reference instead, and in a skilled and

systematic way. Both children are using language to regulate behavior. Amy is using her question to enlist Damien's help and Damien is using language to control and direct Amy's search for the word. The classroom has become a place in which children ask real questions of each other, and use both their knowledge of the specific discourse patterns of their classroom and their knowledge of how conversations work in the world outside the school to achieve the goals of a task they now thoroughly understand.

## 10    Conclusions

Most studies of classroom discourse have confirmed that it is dominated by adults. In formal educational settings, it is usually teachers who decide on the topics for discussion, ask most of the questions, and allocate turns at speaking. This has been a source of concern to many educational researchers who believe that such patterns of talk provide few opportunities for children to exploit their language resources.

Our study of language and learning amongst five-year-olds learning to write suggests, however, that there are different types of classroom talk which are complementary to each other, and that if individual exchanges between teacher and child are examined as well as formal group lessons, then developments similar to those found in dialogue between mothers and their children can also be seen in the classroom. The key points emerging from our study are summarized and discussed below.

As Mehan (1979) and Willes (1981, 1983) have suggested, children do need to learn to take part in classroom discourse by participating in it, but it seems that this might mean more than learning, in a general sense, how to interpret what teachers say, how to make appropriate responses and how to contribute to lessons in an acceptable way. All of these things no doubt need to be learned, but the children in our study were also engaged in learning specific forms of discourse appropriate to the particular aspect of the curriculum we had chosen to examine: learning to write. In the daily blackboard story sessions, the children learnt a standard way of approaching translating a spoken text into a written one. As they became familiar with the blackboard story routine, they were better able to infer from contextual cues which types of knowledge and strategies were to be taken as given in their conversations with their teacher during writing sessions. For example, when the teacher asked a question like "Where can we find Friday?" the children knew that this meant that the word was available in the classroom and that they should search for it. In the case of "Friday" they would also know where the days of the week were displayed and were very likely to locate it easily. In order to understand the teacher's intention in asking the question, the child had to be able to establish a presuppositional framework which permitted appropriate relationships between utterance and context to be established. The question was a cue which prompted the child's recall of both the location of needed items of information in the room and strategies for finding and using them. Later in the year they no longer needed their teacher to prompt their memories, but in the early stages, explicit back-references to the shared experience of formal literacy lessons seemed to be essential to the successful completion of the writing task.

The blackboard story was very similar to the "formats" which were the central feature of Bruner's Language Acquisition Support System (Bruner 1983a). Like formats, the blackboard story was a rule-governed game played over and over until the children were thoroughly familiar with its steps and strategies. It served to simplify the writing task because it provided a highly structured and predictable framework for action which distributed the child's attention over a sequence of steps. Eventually the children were able to use the framework independently of the teacher to produce their own written texts.

Adults constantly adapt their message form and content when speaking to small children to ensure that they are understood and this is what the teacher in this study did as she helped children with their writing. Instructional sessions, like all other social interactions, cannot proceed successfully unless the participants understand each other. Although the teacher exercised tight control over the individual sessions early in the year, she also adapted her responses to the capacities of the individual child even in her earliest contacts with them. Her responses were "contingent," in Wood's (1980) sense of the term, always being made in terms of her interpretation of the success or failure of the child's last move. If the children responded incorrectly or failed to respond at all, she intervened by exercising more control (for example, by selecting and arranging materials for use). If they succeeded, she withdrew and allowed them to take the initiative in solving their own problems.

Edwards and Mercer (1986, 1987) have expressed concern that the structures of formal classroom discourse seemed almost designed to prevent the transfer of competence from teacher to children. What we saw, however, was that the teacher did hand over control of the writing sessions to the children as soon as they seemed able to take it. The children learnt self-regulation as writers through social interaction. While the teacher acted initially as an external aid to memory and attention (i.e. as a "borrowed consciousness") for the children, they gradually took control of the functions she had performed in the early stages of the year: holding the place in the story, identifying the next word, remembering where to find a needed letter or word in the classroom, and so on. As Vygotsky would have predicted, the regulation of the mental processes they used in the construction of their written texts had its origin in social interaction, their experience of the joint construction of the blackboard story, and their individual exchanges with the teacher. Mastery of the written language seemed to depend upon being able to use spoken language to control mental processes, to cue recall and control attention as they had first learnt to do in their exchanges with their teacher.

Tizard and Hughes (1984) claimed that the environment of the nursery school provided a less stimulating linguistic and intellectual environment than the home and they attributed that in large part to the teachers' lack of familiarity with the children they taught. They have written that, although it is the school which is supposed to be extending the child's intellectual horizons, it was the mothers in their study who were responsible for linking the child's present to her/his past and future, and also to the world beyond the child's experience. Because teachers know little about the child's existence outside school, they cannot integrate the child's experience in the ways that are available to a parent (Tizard and Hughes 1984). Our examination of our data, however, shows that a type of familiarity did develop between the teacher and the children, specific to their developing relationship at school, and, even more specifically, to their joint experiences of learning to write. Because the teacher quickly became aware of what the children knew about literacy, she was able to relate their current writing experiences to relevant past writing experience and thus develop a body of shared knowledge and experience with them.

Our interests are those of the educator. We are engaged in trying to understand how children acquire the knowledge and skills associated with learning to be literate. Like Edwards and Mercer (1986, 1987) we believe that this type of development can be studied through the examination of discourse. We are also convinced that continuing investigations of children learning to read and write in the early stages of formal schooling will reveal continuities between discourse at school and at home, as long as the focus of study is on exchanges between teachers and individual children. Even in the most rigidly structured and teacher-centered classrooms such talk must occur, and whenever it does, teachers must surely engage in the adaptation of message content and form to ensure that they are understood. It might not be easy to collect examples of such dialogue, but the ways in which mutual understanding is reached in such situations will tell us a great deal about the regularities in learning both inside and outside the classroom. It seems to us that it will be through the analysis of naturally occurring dialogue, which is concerned with specific problems in particular subject areas, that a better understanding of classroom talk and the ways in which it contributes to the development of knowledge can be reached.

## NOTE

The authors wish to acknowledge the cooperation of the children in the kindergarten classes at Pleasant Heights Public School in New South Wales and the principal at that time, Mr. Owen Davies. Most of all we would like to thank Mrs. Rhonda Fisher for her tolerance and cooperation during the entire project. Her intelligence, common sense, and good nature made it a pleasure to be in her classroom. Her outstanding teaching abilities helped not only the children but also the researchers to arrive at a better understanding of how children learn to be literate. This chapter had its origins in a series of discussions between the authors while Peter Geekie was a Visiting Fellow at the University of Reading (UK) in 1989. It was those discussions which provided the framework for the chapter and which provided the stimulus for writing it.

# Part III

# Types of language learner

# 8    Language interaction with atypical language learners

*Gina Conti-Ramsden*

## 1    Introduction

Throughout this book, the notion that environmental input and social interaction are key ingredients to language learning is discussed from different points of view. In this chapter, this notion will be examined with atypical language learners in mind. It is well known that research with impaired populations has typically lagged behind that of normal populations and language acquisition has not been an exception. Thus, the state of the art in this field is quite dependent on advances made in research with normal language learners. Nonetheless, it is thought that examining the issues involved with special populations not only provides information which has clinical relevance for the assessment and remediation of atypical language learners but also has broader implications for the nature of normally developing processes and language systems in general. This chapter is divided into seven further sections. The next section describes what is meant by atypical language learners. Then follows a review of the research on parent–child interaction with atypical language learners. This review is general, while the two continuing sections specifically address the issues of semantic contingency and directiveness. In section 6, the issue of intervention is discussed. Then follows a section presenting areas that appear under-researched with atypical language learners. Finally, the chapter ends with some concluding remarks and suggestions for future research.

## 2    Atypical language learners

For the purposes of this chapter, atypical language learners will include specifically language-impaired (SLI) children and learning-disabled (LD) children. Although the literature on interaction has frequently treated these children separately, common threads in the results and methodological approaches make it possible to talk about them as a whole (Price 1989).

183

The population of SLI children is a heterogeneous one, generally described as having a linguistic system which, in certain significant aspects, is different from that of their normal language-learning peers. The clinical entity of language impairment in children is most often defined by exclusion: that is, language impairment is a developmental disorder characterized by the late appearance and/or slow development of comprehension and/or expression of spoken language in a group of children who are otherwise cognitively, emotionally, and physiologically intact (Leonard 1979; Stark and Tallal 1981). LD children, on the other hand, are children whose abilities are more like those of younger children than those of their peers (Reid 1988). LD children frequently fail to develop effective strategies for learning and also may fail to use the knowledge they have when it is required (Keogh and Hall 1983). Severity of LD is recognized as a continuum from mild to severe, the latter being more commonly referred to as "mental handicap."

## 3    Parent–child interaction

Differences between child-directed speech and adult-adult speech are so well known and well documented in the literature that the terms "motherese," and more recently, "parentese," have been coined to refer to them as a cluster of cooccurring behaviors. One of the most prevalent questions in the area of interaction with atypical language learners has been whether these children receive input which is similar to that received by normal language learners. That is, do parents of atypical language learners provide parentese to their children like parents of young, normally developing children do? The results of these investigations have been both limited and somewhat controversial. Nonetheless, it is evident that, if results are placed in a historical perspective, one can note an increasing awareness on the part of all researchers that the answer to this question may well be more complicated than was originally thought.

On the one hand, some investigators have argued that parental speech to atypical language learners is different from that of normally developing children (Buium, Rynders, and Turnure 1973; Marshall, Hegrenes, and Goldstein 1973; Wulbert, Inglis, Kriegsmann, and Mills 1975; Bondurant, Romeo, and Kretschmer 1983; Stoneman, Brody, and Abbot 1983), while on the other hand, other researchers have suggested that parental speech to atypical language learners is similar to that of normally developing children (Rondal 1977; MacPherson and Weber-Olsen 1980; Conti-Ramsden and Friel-Patti 1983; Fischer 1987).

What can account for such conflicting results? First, the clinical populations studied have not been comparable from study to study. The specification of groups of children who are atypical language learners is difficult and can act as a double-edged sword. Studies with relatively loose subject criteria include children with a variety of characteristics, for example, children with speech and/or learning difficulties. Studies such as these with a variety of subjects included may allow for more generalizability of their results; that is, their findings are likely to apply to a greater number of atypical language learners. On the other hand, such studies may present problems with the interpretation of data. With a variety of subjects included, it may be difficult to know which characteristics of the subjects are responsible for the results. For example, were the results due to the children's language problem, their cognitive learning problem, or their speech difficulty? Thus, investigations with loose subject criteria have problems disentangling subject variables. Conversely, studies with strictly defined subject criteria may yield results that are not easily generalizable to the population of atypical language learners but may well be quite relevant to the group under study. A second problem is that the groups used to compare atypical language learners have been different across studies. The earlier studies tended to use chronologically age-matched comparison groups, while later studies used groups matched either for language stage using mean length of utterance (MLU) or matched for mental age. More recent considerations of these different control procedures acknowledge the fact that each of these comparisons is useful and can shed different light on the same problem (Conti-Ramsden 1989). Third, the research with atypical language learners has seen a switch from more syntactic analyses of parental input to more pragmatic analyses; thus, it is not surprising that different results have been obtained. It appears that the social-communicative skills of atypical language learners are not a homogeneous, interrelated set of skills (Kamhi and Masterson 1989). Therefore, differences in the type of analyses used in research with atypical language learners may well have yielded differences in the results obtained for this group of children.

At this stage in our understanding of parent–child interaction with atypical language learners, it is clear that parents do use parentese when addressing their atypical language learners (Conti-Ramsden 1985). The parentese they use appears to be similar, although not identical, to that used by parents of normally developing children of the same language state. However, there may be variations in specific aspects of parentese which are significantly different from those received by normally developing children. These variations are usually related to the characteristics of the atypical language learner. Parents of SLI children may use simpler language when addressing their children; for example, mothers of SLI children use a smaller number of utterances per conversational turn than mothers of non-SLI children do (see Cross 1984 for a review).

Interestingly, in the research, one particular design had predominated, that is the comparison between a group of atypical language learners (be it SLI or LD children) and a group of normally developing children. Although the importance of such studies cannot be overemphasized, we need to be aware that such studies only provide a partial view of the relationship between parental speech and children's language-learning problems. This research assumes that normal and atypical language-learning parent–child dyads function similarly, and thus any differences found are likely to predict or exacerbate the child's language-learning problem in some way, and should be decreased through intervention. This may indeed by the case, but we cannot simply assume it. Instead, we need to demonstrate it. In other words, the exact relationship between particular aspects of parental language and child language problems needs to be specified.

A notable exception in this respect is the work of Lasky and Klopp (1982). These investigators examined seven SLI children aged between 2;2 and 3;9 years who had ten to thirty-two months delay in expressive/receptive language as measured by the *Receptive–Expressive–Emergent Language Scale* (REEL) (Bzoch and League 1970). These children and a comparison group of normal language-learning children matched for language stage were videorecorded with their mothers in a university playroom. Lasky and Klopp compared mother–child interaction in two main areas: verbal strategies and nonverbal strategies. Verbal strategies included questions, answers, commands, and imitations, while non-verbal strategies involved facial expressions, body posture, and gesture. Lasky and Klopp found that mothers of SLI children did not differ from mothers of non-SLI children in the frequency of their verbal and nonverbal interactions. Thus, mothers of SLI children used parentese in their interactions much as the mothers of normal language learners do. Then Lasky and Klopp studied the associations between measures of the children's linguistic maturity and their mothers' parentese interaction patterns. Interestingly, they found that, for the normal language-learning children, frequency of mothers' verbalizations, expansions, answers, questions, acknowledgments, providing information, and nonverbal behaviors were all positively and significantly correlated to their children's language development in terms of mean length of utterance and their combined language age (CLA, measured by averaging the receptive and expressive ages obtained in the REEL). This was not the case for the SLI group, for whom the only relationships found were between maternal use of acknowledgments and MLU and between maternal use of exact imitations and CLA. Thus, the same input may have different consequences depending on the characteristics of the adult–child dyad. More intensive research with SLI and other atypical language learners across time and in different contexts is very much needed.

## 4 Semantically contingent responses

Given the robustness of the findings that there are positive effects of semantic contingency on normal language-learning children's communicative development (Snow, Perlmann, and Nathan 1987; Pine this volume), it is natural that investigators interested in atypical language learners have asked similar questions of this population. Once again, the research design has been one of comparison with the normal, and the researchers have not been unanimous in their conclusions. Some investigators have found that mothers of atypical language learners use fewer semantically contingent utterances than mothers of normal language learners (Newhoff, Silverman, and Millet 1980; Cross 1981; Petersen and Sherrod 1982; Koenig and Mervis 1984; Horsborough, Cross, and Ball 1985), while other researchers have found that the linguistic environment of atypical language learners is similar, in terms of semantic contingency, to that of normally developing children (MacPherson and Weber-Olsen 1980; Lasky and Klopp 1982; Bondurant, Romeo, and Kretschmer 1983). Apart from the methodological considerations outlined in the section on parent–child interaction, there are other variables which may account for this discrepant picture. For example, researchers are increasingly aware of the role of individual differences in their results. It is well known that parents of language-impaired children vary as individuals with respect to their use of semantically contingent speech (Conti-Ramsden 1990). Thus, although group data may reveal certain differences or similarities, a closer look at the individual reveals heterogeneity: some parents behave very much like parents of normal language learners while others do not.

Conti-Ramsden and Dykins (1991) in their study of five language-impaired families began to explore the issues of heterogeneity and individual differences in SLI. They investigated families who had SLI children and who were at the same language stage as their younger non-SLI siblings. All children were matched for MLU and fell within Brown's stage I/early stage II (Brown 1973). The SLI group ranged in age between 3;0 and 5;10 while the younger siblings fell within 1;9 and 2;5. Conti-Ramsden and Dykins found two contrasting styles of conversational interaction among five families. One family was a somewhat reticent family who nevertheless used more utterances per turn than any other family. Their use of nonverbal information as part of dialogue was very limited. Their topic shifts were few and easily established, which allowed them to engage in lengthy interactions on a particular topic. The frequency of initiations was low, but a high proportion of these turns functioned not only as initiations but also as responses. Another family, on the other hand, showed the opposite pattern. This family was somewhat more talkative, but nevertheless used a smaller number of utterances per turn than four out of the five dyads. Their use of nonverbal information to engage in dialogue was high. This family engaged in frequent topic changes which were not easily established and resulted in very short conversations. The frequency of initiations used was high and a low proportions of turns functioned as both initiations and responses. These results point to the grave problem in generalizing from significant group results to individual families. There is no doubt that more research is needed on individual differences to find out whether certain characteristics of communicative interaction persist in a particular speaker; for example, are some people more frequent initiators, more frequent topic shifters and less frequent givers of feedback? Does a change in a specific aspect of interaction, for example, initiation patterns, have direct effects on other aspects of interaction for a particular dyad? How can we foster change in individual styles of interaction? Answers to these questions may go some way towards a deeper understanding of the role of individual differences in interaction.

Another problem to consider involves the issue of the comprehension status and age difference between atypical language learners and control groups (Bishop 1982; Rogoff, Ellis, and Gardner 1984; Ellis Weisemer 1985; Van der Lely and Harris 1990). If researchers match for chronological age, there will be a language difference between the atypical language learner and the comparison group. If the investigators match for expressive language stage, then there will be an age gap and there may also be a gap as to the comprehension abilities of the atypical versus comparison group of children. There is no easy solution to the difficulty of comparing atypical and normal language-learning dyads. Research which compares atypical language learners with some sort of norm needs to continue, controlling for as many relevant variables as possible. Nonetheless, it is necessary to acknowledge that comparability between dyads involving atypical and normal language learners may be impossible in communicative interaction. The reciprocal nature of interaction (that is, the mutual regulation of behaviors of the interactants) determines that interaction between atypical language learners and their parents will differ from that between normal language learners and their parents. Thus, the interpretation of results in this area should always remain cautious.

Finally, the effect that the child has on the parent has continued to be investigated by researchers interested in language-impaired children (Cross, Nienhuys, and Kirkman 1985; Horsborough Cross and Ball 1985). In the area of semantic contingency, a recent study by Conti-Ramsden (1990) has shed some interesting light on this area. Conti-Ramsden studied fourteen mother–child dyads with SLI children and fourteen normal language-learning dyads of the same language stage. She concentrated on the use of recasts by mothers, that is, a reply which structurally changes one or more components of the child's previous utterance but repeats the rest. For example:

C:   me hungry
M:   you are hungry?

C:   Ben car
M:   Ben has a car

Recasts have been thought to be semantically contingent replies *par excellence* in that they take the child's thought or focus of attention and they incorporate it into the parents' next utterance in the conversation, but this time, the utterance provides the adult form for the child to hear. The presence of such sequentially contingent speech has been thought to trigger a procedure of comparison between the child's version and the adult's version and in this way, help the child to learn language (Nelson 1977a, 1981; Nelson, Denninger, Bonvillian, Kaplan, and Baker 1984). Conti-Ramsden (1990) found that there was a significant positive correlation between maternal use of recasts and SLI children's level of intelligibility. Intelligibility was examined using an intelligibility index which represented the percentage of intelligible child utterances. It was found that the more intelligible the SLI child was, the more her/his mother was able to use recasts. Thus, intelligibility in SLI children helped their mothers to formulate recasts. This finding makes sense, as any person interacting with children needs to be able to understand what they intend to communicate in order to be able to take the linguistic form of their thoughts and put them in the adult version. Thus, fully unintelligible and partially unintelligible child utterances can hinder the ability of parents to be responsive and to reply contingently to the communicative attempts of their atypical language-learning child. This explanation recognizes the influence of the children's difficulties on the parent. Nonetheless, the influence of the parent on the child is also present. No matter how hard parents of atypical language learners try to be responsive, sometimes they cannot be because of their children's problems. Thus, parental language to atypical language learners may fail to reinforce their children's small steps towards acquiring the language system. In this sense, parental speech and more generally adult–child–directed speech to atypical language learners may have the potential for exacerbating the children's problem.

## 5    Directiveness and control

One of the most consistent themes in the literature on parent–child interaction with atypical language learners has been parents' directive style. This has been measured in different ways by different researchers, be it increased used of imperatives (Buium, Rynders, and Turnure 1973), mands, that is, demands, commands, and requests (Marshall, Hegrenes, and Goldstein 1973), or initiations in dialogue (Conti-Ramsden and Friel-Patti 1983, 1984; Conti-Ramsden, 1990). A highly directive parent tends to use language primarily to control the child's attention and behavior, rather than using language as a reciprocal, communicative, and informational exchange.

Possible reasons for these findings emerge from both partners involved in the dyads. From the point of view of parental involvement, Newhoff and Browning (1983) have suggested that parents' knowledge that their child is atypical may affect their interaction in various ways. For example, the parents may no longer be able to gauge the linguistic level and needs of their children, as the normal pattern of development has been disrupted and can no longer be used as a model. From the angle of the child's characteristics, there appear to be two possible explanations for the increased directiveness and control of parents of atypical language learners. First, the literature has consistently shown that atypical language learners are more passive in conversational interaction than their normal language-learning counterparts (Conti-Ramsden and Friel-Patti 1983, 1984; Bryan 1986). That is, they do not actively engage in conversational turn-taking nor do they initiate as often as normal language learners of the same language stage. Thus, it may be the case that in order to maintain a conversation with their atypical language-learning child, parents have to adjust their conversational style to be more directive and controlling and thus initiate more. A second possible explanation comes from the attentional abilities of atypical language learners. Parents of atypical language learners may have to consciously direct their children's attention to their own as well as to their parents' activities in order to achieve some level of involvement in the interaction (Conti-Ramsden and Friel-Patti 1983, 1984). Fortunately, these possible explanations are testable and researchers no doubt will be looking to investigate them more thoroughly.

What is of particular interest is the negative interpretation that directiveness and control has had in the literature. A variety of studies with young, normal language learners have suggested that parental speech that is used primarily to direct or control the child's behavior has been associated with a slower rate of language acquisition. Newport, Gleitman, and Gleitman (1977) and Furrow, Nelson, and Benedict (1979) both found in their longitudinal studies of one-year-olds that frequency of maternal imperatives (*Look here! Push it this way!*) was negatively correlated with children's gains in syntactic development. Cross (1978) and Demos (1982) also found this trend. Nonetheless, the way that directiveness is defined by the researchers is very important. Thus, Wells and his colleagues (Barnes, Gutfreund, Satterly, and Wells 1983) defined directives functionally, that is according to the role they played in discourse. For example, the question *Can you pass me the train?* can, in the context of a father talking to his child and extending his hand, function as an indirect request for the child to give the train to daddy and not to answer the question with a *yes* or *no*. With this definition, they found a positive correlation between parental speech and children's language growth. Such refinements in analysis need to be applied to the study of atypical language learners in interaction with their parents in order to be able to identify characteristics of parental speech which may help or hinder the communicative development of atypical language learners.

## 6        Intervention and parent–child interaction

Elsewhere in this volume (see particularly Pine, Sokolov and Snow, and Richards) it has been shown that the relationship between parent–child conversational interaction and language development is far from clear for normal language-learning children, let alone for atypical language learners. These areas are not only marred by methodological difficulties but are also controversial. Nonetheless, the impetus for using parent–child conversational interaction as therapy has remained, based on the more robust findings of the literature in this area.

The ideas behind the parentese approach consist of taking the normal, natural environment for language learning and helping parents of atypical language learners to replicate it. Specifically, researchers have looked in particular at parent–child conversational interaction with atypical language learners in the hope of finding something lacking or different from that of normal interaction, in order to be able to remediate these differences and produce changes in the parent–child dyads. In this vein and as discussed in the two previous sections, parents of atypical language learners have been thought to be more directive and controlling and less semantically contingent than parents of normal language-learning children, and naturally parentese therapy has concentrated on making parents less directive and controlling and more semantically contingent (Cross 1984; Watkins and Pemberton 1987; Weistuch and Byers Brown 1987).

The effectiveness of parentese therapy has been documented in a variety of studies where researchers argue that parental behavior can be modified in order to provide more opportunities for atypical language learners to acquire language. Thus parental conversational behaviors to their atypical language-learning children has been found to be amenable to change in terms of increased responsiveness and decreased directiveness (Cheseldine and McConkey 1979; Mahoney and Powell 1986), more equal balance in turn-taking (Seitz 1975; Mahoney and Powell 1986) and more child-centered speech (McConkey and O'Connor 1982; Giralometto 1988). In all cases, the studies report favorable outcomes to their programs. In addition, most of the above studies argue that changes in parental behavior produce concomitant changes in the children's language development. Thus, parentese therapy has been thought to affect children's MLU (Price 1984), to increase the number of verbal utterances (Seitz 1975; Giralometto 1988), to increase their lexicon (McConkey and O'Connor 1982), to improve scores on standardized tests of language development (Mahoney and Powell 1986), and to improve social–conversational skills (Giralometto 1988).

Unfortunately, it is difficult to separate the effects of children's maturation and other sampling variables from the treatment variables used in the above studies. Those studies which use control groups have found varied results, with a great deal of individual differences between parent–child dyads in response to intervention (Giralometto 1988). Thus, so far, the task of finding a true and unequivocal treatment effect of parental changes in language on their communicatively impaired children's language development has proved elusive.

Interestingly, some investigators have argued, particularly with respect to parentese intervention, that normal, adequate linguistic interaction may not be enough to help language learners to acquire language more successfully. That is, to apply the normal model may be insufficient, and indeed Cheseldine and McConkey (1979) and McConachie and Mitchell (1985) advocate non-normal modes of intervention with atypical language-learning children and their parents. That is, the normal model is not only used but enriched to maximize the chances of children learning language. This use of parentese as a "super-normal" model carries with it implications for research. It is necessary, for example, not only to have comparative studies with communicatively impaired and non-impaired children, but investigations which remain within the populations of atypical language learners, identifying and comparing different interactional styles in parent–child dyads, deriving histories of interaction after following a variety of communicatively impaired parent–child dyads over time, identifying successful *versus* unsuccessful dyads in terms of communicative interaction and planning shared successes and failures in communication, and research has yet to tap this source of information more fully, especially with respect to intervention.

Another consideration which applies particularly to parentese therapy is the psychological effect of such approaches on the parents involved. Attempts to monitor and change parental conversational behaviors imply that parents have somehow failed to provide what their children need, and, even worse, that they may have exacerbated their children's problems in some way. Thus, it is essential that parents are told clearly that their conversational interactions are in no way "wrong" or "poor" nor are they the cause of their children's problems. Instead, the non-normal rationale discussed above can be applied; one can argue that special children have special needs, and therefore that changes are necessary in order to improve language acquisition. This is very important and not always understood by parents participating in this type of intervention (Conti-Ramsden 1985).

Finally, although parentese as therapy has been shown to be effective in a number of studies, there is also evidence which suggests that parental conversational styles are difficult to change. For example, Tiegermann and Siperstein (1984) found in their intervention study with SLI children that individual maternal patterns of interaction were not amenable to change. Although all mothers in their study broadened their use of communicative behaviors and became more responsive, mothers who used a great deal of initiations and guided the interaction continued to do so, while mothers who took more of a listener–responder role also maintained their interactive style. This information emphasizes the need for more studies, more evaluation, and more use of experimental designs in the area of intervention using parentese.

## 7    Under-researched areas

Various areas addressed in the literature with normal language learners have not been directly investigated with respect to the population of atypical language learners. For example, one such area is the work on early prelinguistic interactions of mothers and their young infants engaging in proto-conversations (Bruner 1978, 1983b). This is not surprising as atypical language learners are rarely identified at this stage of the child's development. Similarly, the work on timing of parental contingent speech

(Harris, Jones, Brookes, and Grant 1986; Roth 1987) has mainly focused on young infants around twelve months of age, which once again has limited its applicability as a model for research with atypical language learners. To know how early parent–child interaction works with atypical language learners is desirable, and it is particularly desirable for SLI children with conversational and interactional disorders as well as for children with autism. As conversation appears to have its roots in early prelinguistic interaction, it is important that we try to assess in some way how this system works for the conversationally disabled child. Unfortunately, at present, our ability to identify children with conversational disorders in the presence of otherwise normal language is very limited. The earliest report has been of a three-year-old (Conti-Ramsden and Gunn 1986) although, more commonly, research with these children has been understandably limited to school-age subjects (McTear 1985; Adams and Bishop 1989; Bishop and Adams 1989). A possible starting point could be to interview parents of conversationally disabled children in order to ascertain the flavor of their earlier interactions.

Another point of departure has been correlational work on facilitative effects. This research with normal language-learning children had proved inconclusive and the correlational methodology used has been marred with difficulties (see Gleitman, Newport, and Gleitman 1984; Pine this volume; Richards this volume). Thus, a strong parallel line of thought with respect to atypical language learners has not been in evidence. Similarly, the issue of maternal rejection identified by Nelson (1973) has not been followed up in the way it was originally conceived, that is, for the very beginnings of expressive language (the first fifty words) and with respect to children's overextensions (for example, a mother not accepting the overextended use of *mouse* by her child to refer to squirrels). Instead, this idea had been translated into the use of disapproval, null-responses, or rejecting utterances by parents of atypical language learners. Some researchers have found that mothers of SLI produce fewer acknowledgments and more generally negative responses but these have usually been related to these children's decreased ability to communicate effectively and have not always been replicated by other investigators (see Cross 1984 for a review). In the same vein, the notion of routines having a special role in language learning (Snow *et al.* 1987) has been investigated more with respect to models of intervention than with respect to natural parent–child interactions with atypical language learners (Constable 1983, 1986). Thus this issue needs to be addressed by future research.

Finally, within the population of atypical language learners there are certain groups of children for which research has focused mainly on the children's linguistic characteristics and not on the characteristics of parent–child interaction. Specifically, research on parent–child communicative interaction for children with autism (Horsborough *et al.* 1985; Frith 1989) and for children with visual impairments (Mills 1983; Andersen, Dunlea, and Kekelis 1984) needs to emphasized. Parent–child interaction for children with hearing impairments has received a great deal of attention, however, and this literature is discussed by Gallaway and Woll (this volume).

## 8      Concluding remarks

The current state of our knowledge affords little guidance for parents of atypical language learners. Cumulative evidence suggests that normal language-learning children are exposed to a variety of interactive environments; that parent–child conversations with their normal language-learning children are quite different in character from culture to culture; and that different characteristics of parental language are likely to change depending on what aspects of the child the parent focuses on, what situation the parent–child dyad is engaged in, and what language stage the child is at. These facts taken together may bewilder us at first and push us to conclude that no language environment is better than any other for language learning.

Snow and her colleagues (Snow *et al.* 1987; Snow this volume) have suggested that the highly buffered nature of language learning, that is, its resistance to failure and the wide variety of successful language-learning environments available to the normal child, need not lead us to the conclusion that input language to the child is immaterial, but, instead, should lead us to recognize that it can work in different ways. The key common ingredient in the variety of parent–child environments available to the normal language-learning child is the fact that adults create context around the child's speech. Children then actively extract from the input language information which is useful to the development of their own communicative system.

Research with atypical language learners has pointed to various complicating factors when we deal with this type of population. First, atypical language learners may not be as skilled as normal language learners in their ability to extract, filter, organize, and use linguistic information and this in turn appears to affect parental input language. Second, features which have been thought of as possibly hindering language growth, such as rejection, directiveness, and ill-timing, may all be circumvented by the normal language-learning child, but the atypical language learner may not be able to do so. In this sense, parental language style may be a factor in the atypical language learner's rate of language development and this possibility needs to be investigated more thoroughly. Finally, we have seen throughout the discussion that features of parental language appear to be highly dependent on the language stage and other characteristics of the child. By definition, atypical language learners present a mismatch of characteristics to their parents in terms of their physical and cognitive maturity, age, and language ability which may have stronger effects than we have so far contemplated. Future research needs to address this array of important variables.

# 9 Interaction and childhood deafness

*Clare Gallaway and Bencie Woll*

## 1 Introduction

The study of language acquisition in deaf children is one in which questions of input take on a unique importance. Deaf children should not be viewed as exclusively of a monolingual background and as potential learners of the spoken language only. Between 5 and 10 percent are born to deaf parents, and if sign language is used in the home, such children may then acquire it as their first language. The majority of children with a prelingual hearing loss, however, are born to hearing parents. These parents may be using only spoken language with their children, or they may be learning and using a sign language or perhaps a spoken language in conjunction with some manual support system such as Cued Speech or Signed English. In other families, deaf children of deaf parents and deaf children of hearing parents may be learning language in a bilingual setting. Finally, other sociolinguistic situations exist, for example, when deaf children are members of a minority linguistic community.

A major theme of this chapter is the necessity of drawing a distinction between input by adults, intake received by deaf children, and their own consequent output. Specifying features of parents' language does not define what language or languages the child may be able to perceive or ultimately to develop. The general issue of what the child might be attending to and extracting from the input has been raised elsewhere in this volume (see Pine this volume; Richards this volume). In the case of deaf children, the possible relationship between input and output is particularly complex, since different languages (signed and spoken) may be involved. In this chapter, we shall first look at deaf children of hearing parents acquiring spoken language in a monolingual setting where spoken language is the only language to which the child is exposed, and then at deaf children in other language settings.

Acquiring a first language effectively is a task which often proves elusive for deaf children when that language is the spoken one. The conditions in which deaf children of hearing parents strive to acquire the

197

spoken language of their parents are substantially different from – and more difficult than – the situation where either parents and children are all deaf, or where they are all hearing. For children with a severe to profound hearing loss, the use of hearing aids cannot restore normal perception of speech. Therefore much less language is available through speech directed at the child and, in addition, incidentally perceived language is far less accessible to deaf children. In other words, the existence of a hearing loss leads to definably difficult conditions for the acquisition of spoken language: language experience is likely to be qualitatively and quantitatively inferior to that of the hearing child (see Swisher 1989). Nevertheless, even under these difficult circumstances, a substantial number of prelingually deaf children do acquire spoken language with enough competence to function efficiently in a hearing world. Some do not, but detecting such children early in life is still difficult; providing effective help towards developing spoken language is arguably even more so. Even though the question of language acquisition for the prelingually deaf has been the center of controversy for several hundred years, little consensus has been reached.

Much of the controversy concerns the issue of whether to introduce spoken or signed language or both in the first instance, or various eclectic systems. A substantial amount of research concerns comparative evaluation of these methods in the acquisition context (see e.g. Greenberg 1980; Meadow, Greenberg, Erting, and Carmichael 1981; Musselman, Lindsay, and Wilson 1988). This work will not be discussed here, since its aims are rather different from those of classical input/interaction studies. However, over the last decade a number of studies have been concerned with the linguistic context of language acquisition in young deaf children and are directly comparable with acquisition studies carried out with hearing children. Investigating the relationships between maternal language characteristics and language advance seemed to offer great promise to those concerned with spoken language acquisition in the prelingually deaf. If certain types of variation in the input were clearly related to accelerated language learning, and hence facilitative, then this would be valuable knowledge indeed. Not only could we perhaps show that some of the variation in success rate could be explained by differences in the linguistic input – it would also mean that the linguistic environment of deaf children could be as facilitative as possible, by informing intervention techniques. However, we are still far from understanding the relationship between linguistic environment and the normal acquisition process, as other chapters in this volume attest; in the atypical case, there are yet more factors clouding the issue. Indeed, the research on deaf children has come up with few answers to either theoretical or practical questions.

## 2    Interaction and the acquisition of spoken language by deaf children

Early studies of maternal speech addressed to deaf children predated even some of the earliest CDS studies. Goss (1970), comparing maternal language to deaf and hearing preschool children, found that the mothers of deaf children used less verbal praise and more verbal antagonism. Even more negative findings were reported by Schlesinger and Meadow, who characterized maternal language as "inflexible, controlling, didactic, intrusive and disapproving" (1972, p. 107). In a similar study with five- and six-year-olds, Brinich (1980) found an emphasis on maternal control with the deaf children and suggested that control takes over where reciprocal interaction breaks down. Wedell-Monnig and Lumley (1980) compared six hearing mother–deaf child dyads with six hearing child– hearing mother dyads on two occasions two months apart. Although these authors found that the mothers and their deaf children were in fact highly responsive to one another, they also noted that the mothers were dominant. Findings from these studies, which were concerned with general interactive features rather than specifically linguistic ones, gave rise to the notion that deaf children might be suffering the secondary handicap of controlling, discouraging, and negative interactions with their mothers which would provide a less facilitative environment for language acquisition and for social and cognitive development.

Some early studies were concerned with linguistic characteristics, however. Gregory, Mogford, and Bishop (1979) examined mothers' speech to the same deaf and hearing children at 18 and 24 months in a spontaneous play situation. On the second occasion, the language used to the hearing children was more complex, whereas the language addressed to the deaf children was less complex. Also, deaf children's mothers used more imperatives and fewer declaratives and commented less often on the child's vocalizations. Mogford, Gregory, and Keay (1979) reports picture-book reading with the same groups of children at 18 and 24 months. Again, deaf children's mothers did not use more complex language on the second occasion, and the deaf children's language had not developed. Cheskin (1981, 1982) looked at three hearing mothers of deaf children aged from 1;6 to 2;10 on one occasion: they used short sentences, repetitious and "restrictive" vocabulary and repeated their own utterances frequently, using language primarily to control and describe. However, particular features of this study (such as the fact that one child was not wearing hearing aids) render its interpretation problematic.

These findings have been too easily accepted as evidence for the unfacilitative nature of such interactions, and of mothers of deaf children's failure to adjust upwards in terms of language complexity, using either an actual or an implied comparison with mothers of hearing children. However, both the basis for and the significance of such comparisons have been questioned. While most would agree that interaction between hearing mothers and their deaf children is likely to proceed less smoothly than in the hearing situation, the stronger negative claim – that it is so unfacilitative as to constitute a secondary handicap – has not been satisfactorily proven. Similar trends can be seen in the literature concerning other atypical language learners (see Conti-Ramsden this volume). We continue with a more detailed investigation of these issues, drawing on more recent research.

### 2.1    *Maternal speech characteristics: determinants and possible effects*

Subsequent questioning of chronological age as an appropriate basis for comparing deaf and hearing children was a major step forward. If the chief determinant of CDS is the child's linguistic competence, then comparisons involving same-age deaf and hearing subjects are inappropriate. Interaction with a less competent speaker determines the level of adjustment and the simpler, apparently more directive nature of maternal language to deaf children is a feature of this. Several studies indicate that the child's language level is the major determinant of CDS. Cross, Johnson-Morris, and Nienhuys (1980) studied three groups of six children: hearing two-year-olds, deaf two-year-olds, and deaf five-year-olds who were similar in expressive language level to the hearing two-year-olds. The receptive language scores of the hearing-impaired groups were lower, with the deaf five-year-olds having similar scores to the hearing two-year-olds in Cross and Morris (1980) and the deaf-two-year-olds not scoring at all on the receptive tests. Language to the two-year-old hearing children differed from that to the other groups. Cross *et al.* concluded that children's receptive linguistic ability is the major determinant of CDS features. Using similar methodology, Nienhuys, Cross, and Horsborough (1984) took five groups of eight: hearing one-year-olds, hearing two-year-olds, hearing five-year-olds, deaf two-year-olds, and deaf five-year-olds, with the hearing one-year-olds and the deaf two-year-olds closely comparable in linguistic level. Maternal language was similar to groups with similar language levels.

This finding was supported by Hughes (1983), who compared thirty deaf child–hearing mother dyads with twenty-six hearing child–mother dyads with similar *receptive* language levels. Coding for various grammatical and conversational features showed no significant difference on most variables. Child cognitive level, which has also been considered a potential determinant of adjustments, was ruled out by Matey and Kret-schmer (1985), who took comparison groups of mothers and their Down's syndrome, hearing and deaf children aged 1;6 and 3;0; child's productive language level, not age or cognitive level, determined mothers' speech characteristics. A large-scale study of maternal language to seventy-four children ranging from mild to profoundly deaf (Gallaway, Hostler, and Reeves 1990) indicated that a hearing-impaired child's language level was also the most important factor in determining quantitative and syntactic characteristics.

Much of this research assumed maternal adjustment to be desirable but did not address the question of what kind of adjustment might best be suited to deaf children's needs. It may be neither possible nor appropriate for mothers of deaf children to adapt their speech in the same ways that mothers of hearing children do (Lyon 1985). It may not be possible because lack of skill in a conversational partner restricts the possible level of interaction; for example, responses to the child's utterances are obvi-ously limited by the quantity and quality of those utterances. It may not be appropriate because the atypical acquisition situation may require different types of adjustment (Lasky and Klopp 1982; Conti-Ramsden this volume). For example, increased incidence of attention-getters, such as vocatives, has been reported in speech to deaf children (Brinich 1980; Cross, Nienhuys, and Kirkman 1985; Mohay 1986). There is no *a priori* reason to view this as negative; it is more likely to be facilitative. After all, there is no point in speaking to children without first commanding their attention, and, as will be discussed later in this chapter, evidence is now emerging from studies of sign language acquisition that this issue is a relevant one.

It is difficult to assess this research objectively, since negative terms are used and unfounded assumptions of negative effects have been made. For example, the word "restrictive" or "restricted" is often used in describing maternal vocabulary or conversational style rather than the preferable neutral term "simple." Claims that particular CDS characteristics have negative effects on the language acquisition of deaf children are vacuous without empirical longitudinal evidence to support them, and, in addi-tion, the literature often fails to distinguish determinants from effects. For example, Nienhuys *et al.* (1984) concerns determinants but the authors then discuss the "possible effects" of the CDS characteristics, concluding "Perhaps maternal speech adjustments are so extreme ... that they no longer provide a language environment that is helpful to the child's linguistic development" (Neinhuys *et al.* 1984, p. 204). No empirical support, however, is provided by their study. Similarly, Cheskin (1981) claimed that self-answering of maternal questions deprived the children in her study of interactive opportunity; however, a certain amount of this may simply be a useful modeling exercise.

Power, Wood, Wood, and MacDougall (1990) have reanalyzed the data reported in Cross *et al.* (1980) and Cross *et al.* (1985), and added data from the deaf children (groups D2 and D5) collected three years later. Power *et al.* examined in particular the features "control" and "conversational repair" by mothers. However, in spite of its longitudinal appearance, this study is – like the previous ones – primarily concerned with reciprocal effects within interaction. The authors confirm that children's linguistic skill is the primary determinant of maternal speech characteristics, and claim that correlations between measures of maternal control and repair, and child language level seem to indicate that these features are helpful at the preverbal level but less so when children begin to speak. However, these correlations refer to simultaneous effects and therefore it is difficult to see why the authors interpret this as an effect arising from maternal conversational behavior rather than the other way round, that is, high levels of control and repair resulting from some children's continuing low level of conversational skill.

Mohay (1986) studied two pairs of hearing/deaf twins from the age of 16 months up to two years. Both mothers addressed more and shorter utterances, and more attention-getters, to the deaf twin; they did not appear to adjust their language to either hearing or deaf twins as they got older. However, the two mothers adopted very different communication tactics from each other with their deaf twins, and Mohay warns that such important details are obscured when group means are reported.

To sum up, mothers of deaf children can be observed making the same sorts of adjustment as mothers of hearing children, if children with similar language levels are compared. There is no strong evidence that continuing simplified speech provides an unfacilitative linguistic environment; it could in fact be supportive and reduce the processing load for a still incompetent speaker. A weaker claim has been made that mothers may have difficulty in finding an appropriate level of adaptation to cater for the child's changing skills (Hughes 1983; Mohay 1986; Gallaway *et al.* 1990). However, as has already been stated, the issue of what sort of input *is* appropriate for deaf children has not yet been settled.

Considering other members of the family, little work has been done. Tucker, Hughes, and Glover (1983) examined speech addressed to ten profoundly deaf children: mothers' and fathers' speech was predominantly similar. Bodner-Johnson (1985) analyzed dinner-table interactions in families, each having a deaf child aged between ten and twelve years; mothers tended to dominate the interaction and on the whole the deaf child was the center of attention.

## 2.2     Control and responsiveness

A central theme in the research is that certain verbal and/or nonverbal adjustments are said to characterize maternal language as controlling. The first question is whether such a characterization is justified. We have already commented that language which appears controlling may in fact be supportive: one finding from studies of normally developing children which would be consistent with the latter view is that of Barnes, Gutfreund, Satterly, and Wells (1983) that directives addressed to learners had a positive correlation with language gain. Directives, therefore, may be helpful to language development at some stage (see also Conti-Ramsden this volume; Pine this volume).

Likely positive aspects of structured and "controlling" language were described by Henggeler, Watson, and Cooper (1984) who investigated "verbal and non-verbal controls" in hearing mother–deaf child and hearing dyads. They rightly stress that understanding the interplay of verbal and nonverbal behavior is important for the correct interpretation of interaction (as does Kenworthy 1986), and suggest reasons for "controlling" behavior. Deaf children's mothers did exercise more control, but this varied across tasks, and this might simply reflect appropriate attempts to provide structure for a child with limited communicative ability. Henggeler and Cooper (1983) further report that the interactions were quantitatively similar but qualitatively different. The deaf children were less responsive to their mothers' requests. However, as the authors emphasize, this may be simply due to auditory problems, not necessarily a problematic mother–child relationship, as some have suggested. Deaf children's mothers used fewer indirect commands than the others: this is consistent with the notion that language containing a lot of simple imperatives gives way to language containing more indirect requests, formulated as questions, but still functioning as directives, as the child's language skills improve (Bellinger 1979, with hearing children; Gallaway et al. 1990, with deaf and partially hearing children). The complex relationship between linguistic form and language function has frequently been overlooked. Equating a high proportion of imperatives with intrusive behavior is false: White and White (1984, p. 45) point out "First, the heightened use of imperatives is an adaptive and appropriate behaviour in many cases. Second, intrusiveness is relative: the same set of words can be encouraging in one context . . . but invasive in another."

It is, therefore, an oversimplification to regard even imperatives as controlling. Furthermore, whether heavy use of them has detrimental effects on deaf children's language development will only be established on the basis of reliable longitudinal evidence. White and White (1984) found no clear connection between maternal language and later child spoken language. Lyon (1985) studied seven deaf children and their mothers on two occasions, twelve months apart: measures of maternal control and dominance of the conversation had negative correlations with child language gain by the second occasion. However, both measures were correlated with hearing loss (see Richards this volume); in other words, a mother trying to communicate with a very deaf child would initiate more as the child would initiate less.

One source of confusion is that "control" and "responsivity" are not always well defined and may variously relate to conversation, behavior, or both. These distinctions are crucial for interpretation and implications: claiming that mothers control their children's behavior (for example, by telling them what to do frequently) is different from claiming they control the conversational interaction (for example, by initiating exchanges frequently and thus dominating the conversation). This lack of clarity in the literature means that specifically linguistic insights are few. Studies restricted to conversational analyses are easier to interpret. Anderson (1979) found that the conversational strategies of three mothers with their deaf children were comparable to mothers of hearing children in the use of various turn-ceding and conversational repair strategies, but they tended to respond less rather than more as the children got older. Nienhuys, Horsborough, and Cross (1985) concluded that deaf children were involved in more "restricted" and mother-dominated interaction than hearing children but this study was cross-sectional and not controlled for direction of effects.

Control of the conversation does not necessarily imply lack of responsiveness to child initiations, as Wedell-Monnig and Lumley (1980) found; their mothers, though dominant in the interaction, were highly responsive to their children's initiating moves. Chadderton, Tucker, and Hostler (1985) and Lyon (1985) found that only a small proportion of child initiations went unanswered. However, a number of studies have reported hearing mothers of deaf children being less responsive than hearing mothers with hearing children. Mothers were less likely to respond to their deaf children's vocalizations (Gregory *et al.* 1979) likely to misinterpret them (Cheskin 1981), less likely to expand their children's utterances (Nienhuys *et al.* 1984), and less likely to be semantically contingent (Kenworthy 1986). However, some of the variation may stem from the quantity and type of parent guidance offered.

## 2.3    Quantitative and syntactic measures

Some studies found that mothers directed less speech to deaf children (Gregory *et al.* 1979; Nienhuys *et al.* 1984); Mohay (1986), on the other hand, found both her mothers directed much more towards the deaf twin. In the normal acquisition situation, there is wide variation: some mothers address ten times as much language to their children as do others (Wells 1986a). The seventy-four mothers studied by Gallaway *et al.* (1990) addressed between 266 and 1,394 words to their children in ten minutes. The children receiving more speech were younger and in higher social classes; their linguistic ability did not appear to be relevant. In the normal situation, quantity of speech has a positive correlation with language gain (Ellis and Wells 1980), but we cannot assume this is the case for deaf children; indeed, as we discuss later in the chapter, this may be another area where differences are to be expected.

In the normal situation, mothers' MLU is said to remain at approximately two morphemes ahead of the child's MLU throughout early language development (Cross and Morris 1980). In the cross-sectional study of seventy-four mothers with their hearing-impaired children, who were aged between three and seven, Gallaway *et al.* (1990) found a high correlation between child's and mother's utterance length. Mohay (1986), however, studying two deaf twins from the age of 1;4 to 3;4, found that her mothers' utterance length did not increase as the two deaf children advanced. Again, more work is needed.

Syntactic characteristics have already been discussed to some extent. A higher proportion of questions and imperatives is known to be a characteristic of CDS (see Pine this volume). In the area of speech to deaf children, however, this issue has been used to address functional issues such as control (maternal imperatives) and involvement in the interaction (maternal questions); investigation of specifically linguistic hypotheses, however, such as the relationship between maternal questions and advance in the child's auxiliary system (see Richards this volume) is so far absent from the field. Gallaway *et al.* (1990) described the distribution of syntactic structures in the speech of seventy-four mothers with their deaf and partially hearing children. There were indeed more questions and imperatives than in speech to adults, but there was enormous variation between mothers, some of whom used as few as six questions and some as many as sixty in the first 100 utterances. This is a caveat against generalizing from small-scale studies, since so much individual variation exists.

## 2.4    Interaction during the preverbal period

Successful early interaction is now generally regarded as a prerequisite for language acquisition. Even in the earliest stages, differences in interactive behavior will be expected when the infant is deaf due to the unavailability of the auditory channel (Kenworthy 1986). Meadow, Erting, Bridges-Cline, and Prezioso (1985), finding that deaf infants of three, five, and eight months had more physical contact with their mothers than hearing infants, suggested that mothers of deaf children exploit the tactile kinesthetic channel for gaining and holding attention rather than well-known CDS features such as shorter utterances. Nienhuys and Tikotin (1983) analyzed the expressive behavior of one hearing and one profoundly deaf infant each with their mothers on five occasions, between the ages of eight and eleven months. The fact that the deaf child spent longer in "Avert and attend" phases was taken to support Wood's suggestion on reference (Wood 1982, p. 87). One prerequisite for the acquisition of a linguistic system is the recognition that words refer, that is to say, that recurring clusters of sounds relate to objects and events in the world. According to Wood, arriving at this awareness is harder for the deaf child because s/he cannot easily visually inspect the world while simultaneously experiencing the language that refers to it. Gregory and Mogford (1981) found young deaf children acquiring nominals at a slower rate than hearing counterparts and took this also to support Wood's thesis. Further studies on preverbal interaction in signing children are reported in section 3 of this chapter.

## 2.5    *Phonetic and prosodic characteristics*

Although no research to date has systematically investigated this aspect of CDS with deaf children, professionals (probably correctly) continue to stress the importance of using "well-intonated speech" to them. In fact, abnormality might be expected in this area, since hearing people sometimes adapt to deaf people by using distorted speech which is actually more difficult to understand than normal speech: intonation may be altered and information from second-formant modification may be lost (Huntington and Watton 1986, p. 16). One interesting study exists: Hughes and Huntington (1983) played tapes of mothers talking to their children and sought listeners' judgments as to whether the children were hearing or deaf. The whole range of possibilities occurred: some mothers were easily recognized as addressing deaf or hearing children, whilst others were occasionally or systematically misallocated. Features which played a role in the judgments included formal, conversational, and phonetic/prosodic characteristics. More research is needed in this area.

## 2.6    *Teacher talk*

When children enter school, much of their day is spent interacting with teacher(s) rather than parent(s); the classroom linguistic environment, therefore, has come under scrutiny (see, for example, Tizard and Hughes 1984; Geekie and Raban this volume). For profoundly deaf children, whose language may be very delayed, the question is whether the classroom is facilitative not just for language *development* but also for language *acquisition*. Educational practice with deaf children must also be considered; intervention strategies focusing on teaching rather than interaction may have unintended residual effects on the type of language used (Kenworthy 1986). Proposals for intervention proliferate, some offering a middle course: graded and structured input designed by reference to notions of "typical" acquisition order. Assessment of these methods is beyond the scope of this chapter, though it must be stressed that no such system has been agreed to foster universal success.

Even if language is not being taught, the nature of "teacherese" must be considered. Recent research suggests that conversations at school are more adult-dominated, fostering shorter contributions and less initiative in children than those with mothers (Tizard and Hughes 1984). Wood, Wood, Griffiths, Howarth, and Howarth (1982) observed teachers with six- to ten-year-old deaf children, and found that extensive teacher questioning led to little elaboration from children, who adopted a rather passive role, using few clarification questions. Convincing experimental support was further provided in Wood and Wood (1984), where three teachers were asked to vary their conversational style systematically along a "more–less control" dimension; the same children were shown to say more when the teachers adopted less controlling conversational moves, such as comments rather than questions. The general notion that "teacherese" tends to be more controlling than "motherese" is also confirmed by Bishop and Gregory (1985) looking at a book-reading session (they did also find, however, that teachers elaborated more on a topic than did mothers) and by Power, Wood, and Wood (1990). Huntington and Watton (1986) also found that teacher questions had a negative relationship with child utterance length overall, but open questions at least encouraged multi- rather than single-word answers.

Unfortunately, it is sometimes overlooked that the use of questions in the classroom may not be primarily designed to stimulate language but to lead children through logical thought processes by presenting choices in question format, that is, to facilitate reasoning rather than language. If there is a direct conflict between these two aims, then this issue has to be carefully considered with respect to deaf children's classroom environment.

Recent studies of the deaf child's classroom linguistic environment have frequently been designed to consider the characteristics of auditory-oral, signing and Total Communication classrooms. For example, Wood and his colleagues have carried out extensive investigations of signed English in the classroom, of which Wood and Wood (1992) is the most recently published report. This research raises issues which fall largely outside the scope of this volume and therefore will not be dealt with here, but it clearly represents an important step forward in the area.

## 3    Sign-language development

It is only in the past fifteen to twenty years that systematic studies of sign language development have been reported in any quantity – either in deaf children or hearing parents, or in deaf children of deaf parents. This can be partly explained by the general increase in child language research from the 1970s onward. Research on sign language development in deaf children has been strongly influenced by the trends in research in the spoken language field, although it has always lagged behind developments in child language research generally. More recently, researchers undertaking work in sign language development have switched from studies which aim to replicate findings for spoken language acquisition, to recognizing that there are unique contributions of great theoretical importance available from studying language in a different modality.

We might expect that the use of a visual modality of interaction would create very different interaction patterns, because eye gaze is a prerequisite for receiving communication. The different modality of sign language might result in a different pattern of development compared to spoken language. Sign language research thus provides a unique means of examining if language involves domain-specific or general cognitive capacities.

### 3.1    *Early interaction: child-adjusted signing*

An early study of prelinguistic interaction (Maestas y Moores 1980) deals mainly with features of American Sign Language used by deaf parents to their children aged 0 to 16 months, which appear designed to increase the salience of signing. Features included signing onto the child's body, manipulating the child's hands to articulate signs and signing with the child held on the lap (and facing away from the mother) to provide some kinesthetic input to the child of sign movements. Signs vary greatly in form from their use in adult–adult interaction as a result of such modifications. Erting (1987), in a more recent study, has described the precise modifications in the form of signs found in child-directed signing when compared with signing to other adults. Woll, Kyle, and Ackerman (1988) and Woll and Kyle (1989) report similar observations for British Sign Language-using parents.

The role of parental input and interpretation in the prelingual stage has been investigated by Petitto (1988), who has provided evidence that sign babbling occurs in deaf children exposed to sign language in the home, in a parallel way to babbling in hearing children. However, the responses of hearing and deaf parents to their child's early communications can be usefully compared and contrasted. Hearing parents are unlikely to interpret the sounds uttered by their hearing children as potential words unless they hear some phonetic resemblance to the words they represent, and are also unlikely to assign meaning to a large range of gestures produced by their hearing child. In contrast, deaf parents seek meaning in gesture rather than in vocalization but are likely to attribute linguistic status to prelinguistic gestures, and thus may offer over-rich interpretations of the child's behavior. Petitto (1988) reports on a number of studies exploring whether deaf children's prelinguistic gestures are similar to sign language naming, whether the deaf child can differentiate nonlinguistic gestures from signs, and on the general question of whether signed languages are easier to learn. Gesture types and their frequency and use are reported to be similar for deaf and hearing children, but in an informal study, a deaf researcher viewing recordings of a hearing child aged ten to eleven months not exposed to sign language, described over 100 "sign" utterances, including combinations of sign. In the light of such recent studies, we can assess early studies which claimed cognitive and linguistic advantages for deaf children acquiring a sign language (for example, Brill 1969). These findings are related to the claims that first signs appear earlier than do first words and that sign combinations occur earlier than word combinations (Schlesinger and Meadow 1972; Bonvillian, Orlansky, and Novak 1983); these claims, however, have been criticized on various theoretical grounds (Caselli 1983; Petitto 1988).

Clearly, an accurate understanding of the linguistic nature of early communications as gestures or sign is necessary to assess the role of parent–child interaction correctly at this early stage. This issue will be returned to later in looking at the reported acquisition of signed language in the total absence of adult input.

## 3.2    Deaf mothers and early interaction

Communication in a visual modality can only take place when both participants can see each others' signing as well as the context for that signing. The mother is faced with the task of gaining attention to give information, while at the same time maintaining a link between that information and the referent. In contrast, mothers and children communicating through hearing can simultaneously attend to a referent and to the message about it.

Harris, Clibbens, Chasin, and Tibbitts (1989) specifically explored the communication strategies of deaf mothers in relation to children's ability to perceive the signs addressed to them and their nonverbal contexts. Mothers articulated a high proportion of signs in a location in which the child could see them, although individual differences were noted in the strategies they used to relate signs to the nonverbal context. Tapping on the child's body as an attention-getting device in the first year was relatively unsuccessful, the most successful strategy being to sign within the child's existing focus of attention. For hearing children of hearing parents, of course, tapping as an attention-getting device occurs rarely, the most usual strategy for gaining a child's attention being the use of vocatives.

The deaf mothers in a Dutch study (Mills and Coerts 1990) used a range of strategies to ensure that children were paying visual attention before beginning to communicate. The dominant strategy to ensure visual attention in the Dutch study was passive; mothers waited for the child to look at them and then signed in normal signing space, or shifted signing space into the child's visual field.

### 3.3     Deaf and hearing mothers contrasted in the prelinguistic stage

In an extensive longitudinal study of early interaction and language development in children with deaf parents, Kyle and colleagues (Kyle, Ackerman, and Woll 1987; Woll and Kyle 1989) studied eleven deaf families with deaf and hearing children and a control group of hearing families with hearing children. Deaf mothers consistently produced less language (either speaking or signing) in interacting with their infants during the first year of life, when compared to a hearing control group. Utterance function also showed striking differences. Hearing mothers asked many more questions than did the deaf mothers, whose most frequent utterance function was naming.

Since interaction in sign language requires visual attention to the speaker, for a child learning sign language both the adult language and the social context for that language must be visually attended to, requiring the child to learn to divide attention between language and the relevant context. In the "star" experiment (Kyle 1990) mothers were asked to get their child to look at painted stars on poles placed in the corners of the room. There were striking differences between deaf and hearing mothers. Hearing mothers varied in strategy but generally began to point to the star and to speak about it simultaneously. Deaf mothers had a consistent but contrasting approach. Firstly they got the child to attend to their face. They then signed and/or said "star." This was immediately followed by turning their gaze towards the star and at the same time sweeping their arm in a point towards the star. Fourthly, while maintaining the point, they glanced back at the child to check that the child's eye gaze was directed at the star. Finally they drew the pointing hand back towards their body and returned their own gaze to the child's face. This task was viewed by deaf mothers as a normal type of prelinguistic interaction game.

Gregory and Barlow (1989) studied a group of nine hearing and seven deaf mothers, all with deaf infants, from the time of diagnosis of deafness until the infants were twelve months old. They found qualitative differences in the interactions of deaf and hearing mothers with their infants. While deaf mothers succeeded in establishing patterns of interaction, joint activity, and mutual play, hearing mothers had much more difficulty with interaction. Much of their time was taken in getting the attention of the child, and even where attention was established, they found it difficult to sustain communication. Children with deaf mothers attended to their mothers more than did deaf children with hearing mothers (94 percent compared to 75 percent). Fifty-nine percent of acts by deaf mothers of deaf children were followed by contingent acts of the child, whereas for deaf children of hearing mothers it was only 23 percent. Conversely, of those acts which were completely unrelated to the preceding act of the mother, 41 percent of the total were in deaf–hearing dyads, while only 19 percent were in deaf–deaf dyads. Deaf mothers attended to the child's focus of attention virtually all the time (99 percent as opposed to 86 percent for hearing mother–deaf child dyads). The deaf mothers' acts were significantly more likely to be contingent upon the acts of the child, and acts by the deaf mothers unrelated to the child's activity were rare (7 percent) as opposed to 41 percent of unrelated acts by the group of hearing mothers with deaf children.

In the hearing mother–deaf child group, there is neither a high level of contingency, nor a well-established joint function of attention. Gregory and Barlow conclude that differences are not just attributable to differences in mode of communication among deaf and hearing mothers; rather, that deaf mothers are generally better at establishing the mutually contingent activities that are prerequisites of language development.

## 3.4    The form of input: deaf mothers in the first year

Newport and Meier (1985), Kyle, Ackerman, and Woll (1987), and Mills and Coerts (1990) have all observed that deaf mothers vary in the proportion of sign, speech, or sign and speech mixed which they offer to children.

Mills and Coerts (1990) deal with the issue of spoken language input to deaf children of deaf parents. They point out that apart from minimal exposure, it is not clear what features of input are crucial for language development. They consider whether there are quantitative and/or qualitative differences in the function and form of input in the spoken and signed languages. As they point out, because it is possible to produce at least some elements from a sign language and spoken language simultaneously, any analysis needs to include use of either or both languages. This is not the same as stating that these deaf mothers are using a signed system representing the spoken language. They observe, as do Kyle and colleagues, that the proportion of communications in sign is relatively low in the first year of life, with the child receiving less exposure to sign language than to spoken language. They also point out (and this relates to the research on spoken language input by deaf mothers to hearing children) that there needs to be a distinction between input and intake, in view of the varying degree of intelligibility of deaf mothers' spoken language.

Moores and Moores (1982) describe a functional difference in the use of signed and spoken language by deaf mothers in the period 0–6 months, reporting that emotional and affective content is associated with spoken language, but is rarely found in the mothers' signing. These findings are supported by Mills and Coerts, with object orientation (praxic function) associated with the use of signing by the mother.

It appears that deaf mothers are highly successful in making sign communication visible, even to young children. However, they appear more passive than hearing mothers in turn-taking during the first year of life, waiting for the child to give visual attention before communicating. All deaf mothers appear to use a mix of spoken and signed language with their children, with an early bias to spoken language, gradually shifting to sign language during the second half of the first year. There is a strong relationship between function of language communication and language modality: as children become more oriented towards objects, so does the language of the mother, and this increase in object orientation is linked to the use of sign language.

### 3.5    Hearing and deaf mothers in the second and third years

Gregory and Barlow (1989) compared reading activities in three contrasting dyads, hearing mother–hearing child, hearing mother–deaf child, and deaf mother–deaf child at 24, 30, and 36 months, to measure the degree of participation of the child in the setting. This was achieved by counting the proportion of dialogues with active contributions by the child and actual number of communicative acts. Gregory and Barlow identified features of the interactions both deriving from the child's hearing status and from the mother's. In deaf mother–deaf child and hearing mother–hearing child dyads, the children made significantly more contributions to the interaction than did deaf children with hearing mothers. At thirty months, for example, 93 percent of dialogues in deaf mother–deaf child dyads had active turns by the child; in hearing mother–hearing child dyads it was 84 percent, but only 60 percent in hearing mother–deaf child dyads. However, all hearing mothers behaved in similar ways, regardless of whether their children were deaf or hearing. Deaf mothers signed or spoke far less than hearing mothers, their MLU was much shorter, and they repeated themselves much more. Gregory and Barlow suggest that this is because deaf mothers do not use book-reading as a decontextualized, extending, elaborating activity as hearing mothers do. Rather, they focus the attention of the child exclusively on the book. Nevertheless, deaf children with deaf mothers do not necessarily benefit less from the situation, despite hearing mothers' more complex speech, than deaf children of hearing mothers. They point out that it is in the actual structuring of the situation that deaf mothers show particular competence, not in the use of sign language *per se*. Both of these studies demonstrate that problems of deaf children with hearing parents may arise not only from the limited input of language, but also with respect to the difficulty that they have in establishing necessary prelinguistic skills for interaction.

## 3.6     Exploiting the modality

The extensive use of naming functions by deaf mothers was described above. In the second year of life, this naming is expanded into a tutorial type of play session, where mothers teach their children the signs for objects (Woll and Kyle 1989; Kyle 1990). This is largely accomplished by the mother pointing to an object or picture of an object, and providing a model sign for the child. Model utterances, usually consisting of a single sign, varied in significant ways from the articulation of the same sign in other contexts. They were characterized by extensive reduplication of a sign's movement, often at slow speed, and with movement across a large area. Attempts by children to articulate these signs were followed by acknowledgments using a more normal form of the sign. Mothers thus provided models of signs for children that were spatially and temporally expanded only when they wanted the child to attend to and copy the form. Such devices are not available in spoken languages, which instead make use of other types of child-adjusted language. It is therefore important to appreciate the role of modality in understanding how the child-directed adjustments may operate.

## 3.7     Signing systems and input

As we mentioned earlier, a number of systems for encoding spoken language into a visual form have been developed for use with deaf children. Although it is beyond the scope of this chapter to discuss these in detail, two important observations must be made. Firstly, it is impossible to create an identical copy of a language when changing modality. This can be seen clearly enough in the differences between spoken and written language. The notion that manually coded English somehow models the speech code by allowing the child to perceive English word order visually, and thereby internalize it, is not tenable. One would not suggest that in order to learn French we should first practice such sentences as *He makes of the sun* in order to prepare for the sentence *Il fait du soleil*. The point raised in the introduction to this chapter, that input and intake are not identical, must also be reiterated. From the hearing person's point of view, simultaneous communication appears to be a mixture of modes: the oral/aural, the nonverbal, and the manual. From the deaf child's point of view, what is experienced is unimodal, being primarily visual.

Secondly, manually coded English cannot be performed consistently or accurately enough to provide effective language input. Teachers using simultaneous communication have been shown to present deficient models of English in their signing (Marmor and Petitto 1979). In the majority of sentences produced by experienced teachers using speech accompanied by signing, major sentence constituents were missing from either the spoken or signed channels, or both.

Swisher and Christie (1989) raise other concerns with the use of signing systems by hearing parents, in their study of the use of manually coded English (a sign system designed to represent spoken English) by hearing mothers with deaf children. They point out that manually coded English, unlike either spoken English or a sign language, has no community of adult users, nor established conventions for turn-taking. Parents must work out for themselves how to use a visual code with a deaf child. In addition, they receive no specific training in how the allocation of attention to message and referent might be made sequential for the child and how this, in turn, will change the timing and rhythm of discourse. Learning to use a visual form of communication requires the parents to develop a new set of awareness and interactional sensitivities, changing communicative habits.

Hearing mothers using sign systems appear not to have access to the strategies employed by deaf mothers. Swisher (1990) found that deaf children aged four to six years were seeing only about two-thirds of their mothers' utterances in their entirety from beginning to end. Factors which affected the child's view of an entire utterance included whether the mother made an explicit bid for the child's attention, such as tapping the child on the body or moving into the child's line of vision, and whether the mother could deal with the mechanics of turn-taking.

All the mother–child dyads described by Swisher and Christie (1989) had communicative routines marked by periodic communication breakdowns caused by lack of comprehension and overt communication clashes. In contrast with these hearing mother–deaf child dyads, they studied a hard-of-hearing mother (who had normal spoken language) who was herself the daughter of deaf parents and who had a deaf child. She exhibited sensitivity to the child's visual needs in the handling of discourse and in managing the required switches in attention between referents (in a book) and herself.

### 3.8    Development of discourse strategies: middle to late stages

Deaf children of deaf parents of course learn attention-getting and -sustaining strategies from their parents. Prinz and Prinz (1985) explored the acquisition of discourse strategies in deaf children of hearing parents in later stages of language development (3;10 to 11;5). These strategies include the use of eye contact to signal the intention to communicate and sustain conversation turns; the use of other attention-getting devices such as body positioning, tapping the addressee, and waving; the negotiating of turn-taking; topic initiation, maintenance, and change; and the repair of discourse structure after interruption. Deaf children of hearing parents and deaf children of deaf parents used similar discourse strategies, suggesting that deaf children of hearing parents could acquire these from deaf peers and from older deaf children.

### 4    Acquiring language in the absence of input

While most studies in sign language acquisition processes have focused on deaf children of deaf parents (the archetypal native signers), deaf children of hearing parents without a sign language model form the majority of the deaf population. As we have already pointed out, these children may not be exposed to a sign language but may nevertheless acquire some form of signing. In some cases this is through exposure to a sign language by contact with deaf children of deaf parents at school, or to some signed system used by teachers or parents. A general acquisition principle is, of course, that the later one has access to a sign language, the less likely the child is to acquire all features of the grammatical system.

Goldin-Meadow and her colleagues have stressed the ability of deaf children not exposed to any form of signing (neither a sign language nor a sign system) to exploit the visual–gestural modality in a way which is strikingly similar to sign language, and indeed, to natural language generally (Feldman, Goldin-Meadow, and Gleitman 1978; Goldin-Meadow 1979; Goldin-Meadow and Mylander 1985). Mohay (1982) has presented similar findings for deaf children of hearing parents in Australia.

The children develop a communication system consisting primarily of gestures, the properties of which bear a close resemblance to those of early conventional language. This system is claimed not to arise from the parent's gestural communication. Among the features they describe are the tendency to convey information by concatenating discrete units into strings, utterances with a limited range of predictable surface patterns, and recursion. Goldin-Meadow and her colleagues conclude that children can learn the "resilient" properties of language under a wide range of environmental conditions. Those features which can be acquired despite reduced or absent adult input are contrasted with those which can only be learned in the presence of adult input.

However, this work has been criticized, for example, by de Villiers (1985), who doubts Goldin-Meadow's claim that these deaf children make no use of oral input, and suggests that she under-represents the role of mothers in modeling gestures. Bates and Volterra (Volterra 1983; Bates and Volterra 1985) raise the same objections, and further suggest that such research should include other possible sources of gestural input to children (such as the gesturing of other children and teachers in the schools which the subjects attend).

Volterra (1983) and Volterra and Caselli (1985) propose common criteria for evaluating gestures and vocalizations in the early stages of symbolic development for hearing children and for deaf children with and without sign language input. All children studied by Volterra developed referential and deictic gestures, and all children progressed to combinations of *deictic + deictic* gesture and *deictic + referential* gesture. However, only children exposed to adult models of sign language developed utterances consisting of *referential + referential* gesture. She reanalyzes Goldin-Meadow's data and finds that none of the children in these studies show combinations of two referential gestures. Only a child exposed to a sign language input takes this essential step towards development of language. Since children both exposed and not exposed to adult models of sign can use symbolic gestures and combinations of gestures to communicate, these do not depend on exposure to a linguistic model. What does depend on exposure is the ability to combine symbols (referential gestures) with each other. This indicates that the symbolic capacity (meaning) and combinatorial capacity (syntax) are separate, that both are necessary to the development of language, and that the ability to use the two together depends on adult input.

Loncke, Quertinmont, and Ferreyra (1990) raise the question of the use of the terms "native" and "non-native" signers. The use of these terms suggests important differences between those children with relatively early, rather than late, exposure and acquisition. Where children are exposed to a sign system which is structured to parallel the spoken language, and thus omits many grammatical features of sign languages such as simultaneity in morphology, visually based sign order, the grammatical use of space, etc., deaf children nevertheless go beyond the limitation of this input and exploit the visual gestural modality in the same way as sign languages do (Livingston 1983), although they differ throughout their lives from children with deaf parents. Newport (1984) found evidence that native and non-native users differ in their ability to master features of morphosyntactical operations which persists throughout life. Loncke *et al.* (1990) report differences in mastery of specific features of the sign language grammar. While all children, regardless of age or extent of exposure to sign language, were able to master the use of spatial loci as reference points in sentences or discourse, and could use appropriate hand configurations in verbs of motion, non-native signers demonstrated a lack of mastery of directionality and sign order.

## 5    Conclusions

A striking feature of the research presented in this chapter is its wide diversity, partly stemming from different aims and methodology in the two areas of signing and oral acquisition. We now consider whether any individual areas have progressed significantly, and also whether any fundamental general insights have emerged.

Studies of oral language have proceeded in a paradigm largely based on early input studies, but little of significance has emerged. The majority of studies preceded the constructive debates on methodology, facilitative effects, and the interpretation of cause and effect which are now continuing in the normal acquisition area, and many did not take account of the complex reciprocal nature of interaction. Most studies, therefore, present what we now know to be an oversimplified picture. In addition, the essential question of what may or may not be facilitative in this atypical acquisition context of childhood deafness has barely been considered. Longitudinal studies which might shed light on this aspect are absent. Studies benefiting from recent debate are also largely lacking, although one exploratory study involving intervention and promising new directions has been described recently (Dromi and Ringwald-Frimerman 1990).

Recent work on sign acquisition offers useful insights from a different modality, and furthermore, has begun to provide information on how the behavior of deaf mothers diverges from that of hearing mothers. This can serve as a starting point for the assessment of what features of CDS and child-directed behavior may be facilitative specifically for deaf children. Still, this research is in its early stages and findings are based on small numbers, so conclusions remain tentative. Some areas where differences have been observed are in gaining and maintaining child attention in the early stages of communicative development, in the structuring of conversational interaction and in the quantity and functions of mothers' language to their children.

We should also consider how far studying language acquisition in a different modality can shed light on our understanding of child-oriented adjustments in speech. The fact that child-adjusted signing exists supports the notion that some such adjustment may be universal, and can even be observed operating in another modality. In addition, the acquisition and reconstruction of sign language by children not receiving it from their parents raises essential issues about minimal input requirements and about acquisition and the universal characteristics of the linguistic system.

As a postscript to this chapter: input studies can also derive insights from studies of hearing children of deaf parents who do not provide a model of spoken language. This issue will be dealt with in Richards and Gallaway (this volume).

NOTE

We should like to thank John Bamford, Wendy Lynas, and Fatima Costa Janjua for their comments on earlier drafts of this chapter.

# 10 Input and interaction in second language acquisition

*Marjorie Bingham Wesche*

## 1 Introduction

The nature of the linguistic environment available to learners of a second/ foreign language and its role in the learning process have been important issues for second language acquisition (SLA) researchers and language educators over the past two decades.[1] Inspired by work in first language acquisition suggesting that oral language input tuned to the language development level of learners might play a causal role in language acquisition (see Richards and Gallaway 1993) and the early second language research on "foreigner talk" (Clyne 1968, 1977, 1978; Ferguson 1971, 1975), a few SLA researchers began to investigate these issues in classroom situations – notably Henzl (1973, 1979), Hatch (1974, 1978a, 1978b) and her students (Wagner-Gough and Hatch 1975; Long 1981a), and in natural communicative settings (the Heidelberger Forschungsprojekt 1975; Meisel 1975). Of particular interest have been the modifications to language and, more recently, to conversational interaction patterns made by native speakers when addressing less proficient non-native speakers – both in and out of classrooms. Several hundred studies now exist which document the nature of these modifications, the conditions under which they occur, and their possible purposes, and recent research has attempted to link learning contexts and input/interaction features with SLA outcomes.

Research on the linguistic environment of the language learner has in the main followed a "research-then-theory" strategy (Long 1985). Initially cross-sectional and quantitative in approach, yielding descriptions and taxonomies, research now includes longitudinal case studies and classroom ethnography, as well as quasi-experimental and experimental studies. The expanding view of what is to be acquired by the second language (L2) learner has also brought a shift in focus in these studies from phonological, morphosyntactic, and lexical features to a more "ecological" perspective, including discourse features and genres, pragmatics and the learner's "socialisation through language and socialisation

219

to use language" (Ochs 1986, p. 2). As Heath (1986, pp. 145–6) argues, "all language learning is cultural learning" or "learning that enables a member of the family and community to behave appropriately within that group," and Wong Fillmore (1989) emphasizes that it is in the presence of social bonds ensuring ongoing relationships that language development progresses.

A few models and theoretical formulations in SLA have explicitly taken into account the nature of the learner's linguistic environment and its influences on acquisition outcomes, most notably Krashen's Input Hypothesis (1980, 1985), the Learnability/Teachability Hypothesis (Pienemann 1984, 1989, 1992), and formulations based on a universal grammar (UG) perspective (cf. Cook 1985, 1988; White 1989). While Krashen's hypotheses have stimulated empirical research on input comprehensibility, related recent work has focused on the nature of input processing by learners and its relationship to the acquisition of different language features (see Chaudron 1988; VanPatten 1990; Ellis 1992; Issidorides and Hulstijn 1992). Some researchers have begun to look at learners' capacity to acquire given target language (TL) grammatical knowledge within the framework of theoretically specified internal constraints (see White 1985, 1989, 1990; Pienemann 1984, 1989, 1992; Morgan 1986; Pankhurst, Sharwood-Smith, and Van Buren 1988; Braidi 1990, 1991; White *et al.* 1991). Over the course of the above work, classroom researchers have consistently attempted to sort out the implications of these studies for more effective second language instruction, and some are currently investigating the effects of pedagogical "input enhancement" activities within a communicative paradigm in controlled classroom experiments (Harley 1987; Lightbown 1987, 1992; Lightbown and Spada 1990; Carroll, Roberge, and Swain 1991; Day and Shapson 1991; White 1991; White, Spada, Lightbown, and Ranta 1991; Spada and Lightbown forthcoming).

This chapter is divided into six further sections. Sections 2, 3, and 4 overview research on language addressed to second/foreign learners in naturalistic and classroom contexts, characterizing input varieties in terms of linguistic and interactional modifications: *Foreigner Talk*, *Foreigner Discourse*, *Language Teacher Talk* and *Interlanguage Talk*. Contexts in which modifications are made, and factors which appear to account for their occurrence and variability will be discussed, including their role in SLA.

The fifth section presents theoretical perspectives on the role of the linguistic environment in SLA, ranging from the view that "comprehensible input" plays a primary causative role (Krashen 1980) to the view that input characteristics serve mainly to "trigger" internally determined syntactic restructuring. Claims about the role of modified input/interactional features in SLA as well as shortcomings of current theoretical models in dealing with input selection by learners, its internal processing and integration into interlanguage grammars will be discussed, together with more inclusive recent frameworks for SLA study.

The sixth section will provide an overview of current research relating the linguistic environment of the language learner to SLA outcomes. It will focus on: (1) the socialization of L2 learners through language and to use the new language; (2) how ambient linguistic data are selected, processed and may lead to restructuring of the L2 learner's internal grammar, and (3) experiments with "input enhancement" (fine-tuning of input, increasing salience of input features and relations, and task manipulation or feedback to require in-depth learner processing of the data).

## 2        Typology of modified codes

The evolution of terms used to refer to the special language varieties associated with language learners reflects the shift in concern of SLA researchers from modified speech addressed to and used by foreigners as a linguistic phenomenon – presumably associated with the development of pidgins – to an interest in the role of learner-directed speech in SLA. Ferguson proposed the term "Foreigner Talk" (FT) in 1971 for the "simplified" speech used by a native speaker (NS) with a non-native speaker (non-NS) who lacked full understanding of the target language, attributing the concept "at least as far back as Schuchardt ... 1909" (Ferguson and DeBose 1976, p. 103). While similar in some ways to other special varieties – notably Baby Talk and speech addressed to deaf persons – FT was seen to merit special attention for its apparent relevance to the pidginization process (Ferguson 1971). Ferguson (1975), interpreting an elicitation study in which university students were asked to rewrite sentences as they would say them if addressing illiterate, low-proficiency second language speakers of English, hypothesized the existence of an FT register as part of the competence of native speakers of American English. As a register, it was seen to have both specific uses and defining structural features, the latter including nonstandard features (e.g. omission of function words and inflections) and hyperstandard forms (e.g. use of full lexical forms instead of contractions, avoidance of slang; Ferguson 1975, 1977; Ferguson and DeBose 1976). Both "simplifying" (omission, expansion, and rearrangement) and "nonsimplifying" (elaborating, regularizing, and attitude-expressing) features were thought to cooccur in FT. Ferguson (1975) also noted the negative attitudes towards such speech expressed by many of the students, even though most reported they would probably use it in the proposed situations. Valdman (1981) would later hypothesize social functions for this type of FT, that is, to maintain distance between NSs and non-NSs who were considered inferior, even while providing linguistic accommodation to allow the non-NSs to function in the society.

At about the same time as Ferguson was carrying out his initial studies of FT, the Heidelberg research group was collecting data on guestworker German and Australian "industrial immigrant talk" (Clyne 1968; Heidelberger Forschungsprojekt 1975), then subsequently on speech addressed by factory foremen and others to German and Australian workers (Meisel 1975, 1977; Clyne 1977, 1978). Both the non-NS and NS varieties exhibited many nonstandard features. Other studies of this period also reported ungrammatical speech to non-NSs in other contexts, for example in speech by sales clerks in American department stores (Ramamurti, cited in Larsen-Freeman and Long 1991), that of young NS children interacting with non-NS age peers in school settings (Wong Fillmore 1976; Katz 1977) and in office window interactions of Dutch municipal employees (Snow, van Eeden, and Muysken 1981). These studies and later work clearly distinguished between learners' "interlanguage talk" (IL) as a simplified code and the language addressed by NSs to learners. While research has focused on the characteristics of the latter, IL remains of interest because it is a major source of target language data for many learners (Krashen 1980; Porter 1983; Long and Porter 1985; Chaudron 1988).

Henzl was the first researcher to gather empirical data on, as she named it, the Foreign Language Classroom Register (1973, p. 207). This was for her a subvariety of FT, involving "talking up" to students in language classes as opposed to "talking down" to factory workers. Henzl compared the features of texts recorded by Czech NSs for adult NSs with those recorded by the same NSs for non-NS university learners of Czech. The recordings for the students were characterized by well-formed utterances, showing systematic modifications from the NS-directed tapes in aspects of phonology, syntax, lexicon, and delivery "in accordance with [speakers'] judgement of what is easy, simple and clear for the listener to hear, perceive and comprehend" (1973, p. 218). A subsequent study involving professional L2 teachers addressing second language students in Czech, German, and English classrooms revealed similar modifications and exaggerated gestures (Henzl 1979). Henzl's work indicated that FT in the classroom environment is grammatically well formed. Such classroom speech has subsequently come to be referred to as Language Teacher Talk ("the classroom language that accompanies exercises, the language of explanations ... and the language of classroom management" [Krashen

1981, p. 121]). As Chaudron (1983b, 1988) makes clear, based on reviews of classroom input studies, Teacher Talk to non-NSs in classrooms can be considered a subset of normative FT which also shares features with teacher talk in *first* language classrooms; it is not systematically or qualitatively different enough from either to posit a sociolinguistically distinct register.

In the mid 1970s, Hatch called attention to the need to study language input to learners and its possible role in SLA, and subsequently, to the importance of discourse and interactional characteristics of NS–non-NS conversations and extended texts, or "Foreigner Talk Discourse" (see Wagner-Gough and Hatch 1975; Hatch 1978a, 1978b; Hatch, Shapira, and Wagner-Gough 1978). Hatch and her associates noted that even in cases where modifications to the linguistic code appeared to be minimal, NSs often took on much of the "work" of conversation with non-NSs, thus facilitating their continuing participation. For Hatch, the role of input features in the acquisition process might involve "incorporation" of NS speech elements by the learner (Wagner-Gough and Hatch 1975; see also Wong Fillmore 1976 for examples from playground language in early SLA). Hatch also proposed the far-reaching possibility, based on first language acquisition research, that out of learning to interact verbally, learners may internalize "horizontal" (sentence level) syntactic knowledge from the "vertical" discourse constructions they jointly build with their more proficient interlocutors (Hatch 1978b, p. 404). These proposals were influential in stimulating a number of data-based studies of FT (including Language Teacher Talk) in SLA contexts, early ones including Gaies (1977, 1981, 1982), Freed (1978), Hatch (1978a), Hatch *et al.* (1978), and Peck (1978). This body of work subsequently led to a number of studies of interactional structures in NS–non-NS conversations and of NS–NS conversations in pedagogical contexts (see below).

In 1980, Arthur, Weiner, Culver, Ja Lee, and Thomas proposed that two types of FT be distinguished. In their view, subsequently accepted by researchers, "Foreigner Register" should be used to refer to the speech variety used in learner contexts such as classrooms which, while exhibiting systematic variation in the frequency and range of application of certain phonological, morphological, syntactic, or semantic options, maintains standard rules. Foreigner Talk in other contexts, characterized by non-standard rules, would be recognized as a separate, reduced code. Long (1983a) summarized the empirical support for the distinction in a review of studies of ungrammatical FT by NSs, concluding that ungrammatical FT occurred in the presence of certain situational factors, including:

1 non-NS with zero or low proficiency;
2 NS perception of own higher social status;

3 prior NS experience with non-NSs but only those at low proficiency
levels;
4 spontaneous occurrence of NS–non-NS conversation (e.g. task-related
on factory floor).

In Long's view (reiterated in Larsen-Freeman and Long 1991), factors
1, 2, and 4 are necessary conditions for ungrammatical FT, and no single
factor is sufficient. Several other studies, while largely in accord with these
findings, suggest the need for a more refined, possibly interactive model to
explain nonstandard features in FT. Terrell (1990) studied working-class
male Spanish-speakers in casual encounters with a higher status learner of
Spanish. While these NSs produced some ungrammatical FT, their
general lack of linguistic and interactive accommodation to the learner –
perhaps due to lack of interest in pursuing the interaction – was even more
notable. The Dutch study reported in Snow *et al.* (1981) found high
intersubject variability in NS-generated ungrammatical features. While
partly related to L2 interactants' error frequency and type, such features
were further seen by the researchers as a relatively precise accommodation to learner norms by certain individuals, experienced in dealing
with non-NSs, who apparently wished to provide affective support as well
as to ease communication. The other type of situation described in the
literature in which ungrammatical FT sometimes occurs, appears to
violate all of the above conditions. These are the rare individual cases of
extreme speech convergence by NSs to the speech of their non-NS interlocutors in ongoing relationships with a high level of positive affect and
familiarity. Two such cases are described by Hatch *et al.* (1978): firstly,
informal conversations between an NS and her close non-NS friend; and
secondly an experienced NS teacher addressing adult learners of English
as a second language (ESL) in a relatively informal classroom environment. Clyne (1978) describes similar speech used by bilingual NS children
in Australia speaking English to their low-proficiency immigrant parents.
McCormack (1984) documents the use of non-English intonational contours by a Canadian woman of Lithuanian extraction and receptive
Lithuanian ability when interacting with non-NS relatives who respond
to her in Lithuanian and broken English. He views the intonation patterns as a demonstration of involvement and solidarity with the interlocutors. Such accommodations may in fact be fairly frequent among
bilingual interlocutors in situations such as those described, who have at
their disposal a large repertoire of potentially accommodating speech
features. It appears that, in addition to the FT-evoking factors identified
by Long, affective concerns may in certain cases outweigh considerations
of efficient communication, the use of normative speech, or provision of
an appropriate model.

The following discussion of NS language addressed to learners will be limited to the cases in the literature – the vast majority – in which discourse addressed to language learners conforms to standard use and can be characterized as a (highly variable) register shift. This will be referred to as Foreigner Discourse (FD) to capture the importance given in more recent research to discourse and interactional features, and to distinguish it from ungrammatical FT.

## 3       The nature of linguistic and interactional modifications in Foreigner Discourse

Several hundred studies describing and comparing NS–non-NS, NS–NS, and non-NS–non-NS discourse in a variety of situations have consistently revealed both impressionistic and quantifiable differences between the language addressed to learners (FD) and that addressed to NSs. These occur in the suprasegmental, phonological, morphosyntactic, semantic, and discourse subsystems, as well as in interactional patterns and in nonverbal behavior accompanying speech. A series of excellent published reviews (Hatch 1983a, 1983b; Long 1983a; Ellis 1985a, pp. 127–63; Chaudron 1988; Larsen-Freeman and Long 1991) and two collections of papers (Gass and Madden 1985, including a résumé by Larsen-Freeman 1985; Day 1986) have tracked this expanding literature on the linguistic environment of the non-NS language learner through the late 1980s. Ethnographic research outcomes furthermore suggest that not only language behavior is involved; rather, where proficient TL users and cultural members take responsibility for helping non-NS learners not only with language but also in understanding the ways language is used in the new culture, one finds them juggling a complex set of organizational, extralinguistic, cognitive, and social elements to provide "scaffolding" assistance to help the learner perform at a higher level than s/he could do without support (Hawkins 1987). Individual learner characteristics in evoking such support should not be underestimated (Wong Fillmore 1976).

It is important to emphasize the variability in NS modifications to learners, which appears to depend upon individual factors such as speech style, as well as upon the discourse, social, and cultural contexts, and interactions among them. Thus while even young children make such modifications (Wong Fillmore 1976, 1989; Hirvonen 1985, 1986, 1988; Cathcart-Strong 1986) and linguistic and/or interactional modifications are claimed to be present in all successful L1 and L2 acquisition (Long 1983a; Krashen 1985), the complexity of the factors at work makes it impossible to predict the occurrence of modifications in any given situation.

Research on what "triggers" FD in casual encounters between strangers indicates that it results from NSs' assessment that non-NSs cannot comprehend normal NS speech (Varonis and Gass 1985). This assessment may initially be based on such factors as a non-NS's appearance, age, nonverbal behavior or accent, then it may be revised by the NS, together with FD modification, through feedback from the learner as the interaction progress.

Most researchers agree that NSs use FD primarily to facilitate comprehension of meaning by learners. Hatch (1978a, 1978b) furthermore suggests that FD modifications may also serve to establish positive affect and as an implicit language-teaching mode. Krashen (1980) proposes that FD and its subset, *Language Teacher Talk*, as well as *Interlanguage Talk*, all have instructional value for learners.

Linguistic modifications frequently found in FD are summarized below. For more detailed discussions of particular issues, see Hatch (1983a, 1983b), Chaudron (1988), and Larsen-Freeman and Long (1991).

### 3.1    Specific features of Foreigner Discourse

Modifications by native speakers from the norms of speech addressing other NSs have been described by researchers at all levels of the human communication system. This research is briefly summarized below.

*Speech rate, phonology and prosody:* The speech rate in FD tends to be slower than NS–NS discourse, to be slower when addressed to lower-proficiency non-NS, and pauses tend to be more frequent and longer (Henzl 1973, 1979; Hatch 1983a, 1983b; Wesche and Ready 1985; Håkansson 1986; Mannon 1986; Chaudron 1988; Derwing 1990). Slower delivery results in more careful articulation, provision of full underlying vowel forms and consonant clusters, and avoidance of contractions, so that word boundaries tend to be more clearly delineated. Pauses provide processing time and mark clausal and sentential boundaries, although longer pauses may also reflect greater planning time by speakers (Chaudron 1988). Exaggerated intonation, including frequent stress on topic nouns, is also often found in FD, particularly in that addressed to lower-proficiency learners (Lynch 1988). This may help to direct learner attention to important content words and aid in identifying major constituents.

*Morphology and syntax:* As previously noted, FD utterances are in general grammatically well formed. A minor exception, sentence fragments in some teachers' speech to non-NSs – in some ways resembling the meaningful fragments found in problem-solving NS–non-NS conversations (Bygate 1988) – has been attributed to didactic functions such as elicitation and repetition (Hyltenstam 1983). In neither case are these fragments like the deviant forms in FT.

Individual FD utterances tend to be shorter than NS–NS discourse (in words per T-unit or words per utterance),[2] and syntactically less complex (in sentence nodes or clauses per T-unit, amount of preverb modification, or number of subordinate adverb, adjective, and noun clauses per 100 T-units; Gaies 1977; Freed 1980; Long 1981a; Scarcella and Higa 1981). They tend to be propositionally more transparent, use canonical word order more frequently, retain optional grammatical forms (e.g. relative pronouns), and overtly to mark optional grammatical relations (see Larsen-Freeman and Long 1991). There is a tendency to rely more on present tense verbs and adverbial time markers and to avoid certain tenses or the conditional (Wesche and Ready 1985; Sato 1986; Swain and Lapkin 1986; Harley 1992a). There is also a tendency to move topics to the beginning of utterances. These features may enhance topic salience and highlight new information at the end of utterances (Hatch 1983a, 1983b).

One other tendency noted in various studies is for NSs to use given sentence frames in a formulaic way – for example to mark definitions (*This means...*; *It is a kind of...*; Hatch 1983a, 1983b; Wesche and Ready 1985). This redundancy may increase the salience of the formal structure and its function to the learner.

These adjustments to morphology and syntax, like those at the phonological level, again appear to make utterances easier for learners to process through more apparent constituent boundaries, reduced syntactic complexity, and clearer signaling of form–meaning relationships.

*Vocabulary:* Many examples are given in the FD literature of the use of more frequent, neutral, and concrete vocabulary items, as well as of the avoidance of idioms and slang. Studies have shown FD to have less varied vocabulary than NS talk (measured in type-token ratios),[3] particularly with lower-proficiency learners. Other tendencies include use of a higher percentage of copulas to total verbs, and of full noun phrases or proper names instead of pronouns. Such modifications could ease processing demands on learners through a reduced set of more familiar forms, and more explicit forms resulting in clearer referents.

The tendency of NS interlocutors to restate information using other – often related – words or synonyms, is another important feature reflected in vocabulary modifications. This not only calls attention to the initial word and allows more processing time for meaning, but it provides information on derivationally and collocationally related words, form-class relationships and semantic features (Hatch 1983b). Chaudron's (1982) study, however, demonstrates that teacher vocabulary elaboration may in some cases lead to learner confusion about what is an alternative and what is additional information. Not all NSs may be equally able to provide clarifying modifications, and learners at different levels may differentially benefit from given modifications.

*Discourse:* Discourse-level features have been less studied than sentence-level phenomena; also, procedures and measures for classifying and quantifying them – and even the utility of such an approach – are less agreed upon (see van Lier 1984). Discourse features have nonetheless been identified for both extended one-way (information transmission) and two-way (interactional) discourse between NSs and non-NSs, and for interactions between non-NSs in and out of classrooms. One-way FD in university lectures compared with parallel NS–NS lectures by the same professors revealed more consistent and explicit rhetorical patterns for introducing, defining, and illustrating new topics (Vanniarajan 1988). Studies of the distribution of sentence types have revealed a tendency for teachers – particularly more experienced teachers – to use more questions with non-NSs and more declaratives with NS learners (Pica and Long 1986). Questions are used more often in FD as topic-initiating moves (Long 1981b), marking new topics and requiring a response from the non-NS. However, the fact that a high proportion of questions may also reflect clarification requests, comprehension checks, confirmation checks (Hatch 1978a, see below), and rhetorical questions (Wesche and Ready 1985) reveals the oversimplification inherent in this type of analysis. For examples of more finely grained analyses see Sato (1986) and Hawkins (1987).

The tendency of NSs to repeat or paraphrase utterances they address to non-NSs (exact repetition or semantically equivalent repetition) is another widely reported characteristic of FD (Long 1981a; Early 1985; Wesche and Ready 1985). This feature may be subtle; for example, Mannon (1986) found significantly more self-repetition in Language Teacher Talk than in NS talk after intervening discourse even though the number of repetitions immediately after the initial statement was the same. Self-repetition appears to be particularly important for teachers – who, concerned with communicating given content, recycle it, particularly with lower-proficiency non-NSs (Ellis 1985b). Both exact repetition and paraphrase may aid learner comprehension, but their differential effects in SLA remain unexplored. Intuitively, it would seem that paraphrase provides richer lexical and structural data (Wesche and Ready 1985).

Foreigner Discourse contexts involving NS–non-NS conversational interaction have been singled out by some researchers as of particular importance for SLA. Hatch (1978a) proposed a taxonomy of interactional moves, later refined and elaborated by Long (1981a) and others, most notably Pica and her colleagues. This included "comprehension checks" (to see if the listener has understood), "clarification requests" (for more information or explanation), "exact self-repetitions," "exact other-repetitions," "restatement" (or semantic self-repetition) by the speaker, "other restatement" (semantic other-repetition), "expansion" (of non-NS statement), and "topic switches." A considerable body of recent work has described interactional moves and compared inter- actional structures of NS–non-NS and non-NS–non-NS conversations in different situations, and their possible role in SLA (see the review and bibliography in Young 1988; also see Sato 1986; Bygate 1988; Pica 1991a, 1991b, 1992). Long's (1981b) study comparing experimental NS–non-NS and NS–NS conversational dyads indicated that most types of linguistic modification in one-way FD were not differentially present for the two groups (the exception, T-unit length, being shorter for NS–non-NS inter- action). This was confirmed in later studies (see Long 1983a, 1983b; Long and Sato 1983; Pica and Long 1986). On the other hand, many inter- actional differences were apparent (e.g. stress on key words, utterance- initial topics, more questions and self-repetitions), which could provide greater transparency of semantic/syntactic relationships for learners. This led Long to propose that interactional modifications may be the crucial factor in facilitating TL comprehension by non-NSs (Long 1981a, 1981b; Pica, Young, and Doughty 1987). Features differentiating NS–non-NS from NS–NS interactions probably have several causes, one being the difficulty of sustaining conversations with low-proficiency non-NSs, another being attempts by NSs to provide scaffolding to learners to avoid conversational trouble, and a third to repair conversations when they break down (Gaies 1982). Conversation-sustaining strategies used by NS interlocutors with non-NS include selection of "here and now" topics, use of extralinguistic contextual information, and acceptance of non-NS topic control – often resulting in relatively brief topic treatment and abrupt topic shifts (Arthur et al. 1980; Long 1981a; Scarcella 1983). Another device is the use of stress or pauses before topic words (Hatch 1978b; Long 1981b) to introduce or call attention to topics.

As in teacher talk to non-NS, questions appear to be particularly important in NS–non-NS conversations (Freed 1980; Long 1981b; Scar- cella and Higa 1982; Varonis and Gass 1982). The preference in FD interaction for *yes–no* questions requiring only a one-word answer, and "*or*-choice" questions (e.g. *Are you going to the party or the movies?*) are examples of scaffolding, which, unlike *wh*-questions, embed the answer in the question, and provide additional processing time and an easier task to help the learner remain in the conversation (Hatch 1983b). "Display" questions (to which the questioner knows the answer), which reflect an explicit didactic intent, characterize language teacher interaction (as they do one-way teacher FD), but are infrequent in other NS–non-NS interaction (Long and Sato 1983). Other supportive moves characteristic of FD interaction include expansions by NSs of non-NS statements (which provide well-formed models for what non-NSs presumably wished to say).

Negotiation strategies used by NSs to repair conversations when they break down also characterize both the interactional structure of non-NS–non-NS discourse and one-way FD. These include comprehension and confirmation checks, clarification requests, repetition, and restatements. Long (1981a) describes "decomposition" as a further NS strategy to avoid or to deal with conversation breakdown. For example, if the non-NS misunderstands an initial question (e.g. *What time shall I pick you up tomorrow night?*), the NS may then "decompose" the task into a more manageable *yes–no* question (e.g. *Shall I pick you up tomorrow night?*) or uninverted question (*I'm picking you up tomorrow night, right?*), or with topic left dislocation (*Tomorrow night I'm picking you up, right?*) followed (after non-NS acknowledgment) by the initial "new" comment (*What time shall I come?*). Bygate (1988) carries this analysis further, proposing that oral interaction which includes meaningful sentence fragments provides learners with the opportunity to deal with subclause constituents as building blocks for clausal structures and joint conversations.

Interactional research on FD has been largely limited to quantitative analyses, surface features, and temporary interactions. Careful studies are needed of possible multiple functions of given moves (e.g. correcting as well as explaining), multiple realizations of given functions, and longer sequences of discourse within continuing relationships, in different contexts. Particularly valuable are the ethnographic studies which follow learners over days, weeks, or months to capture more precisely their interactional patterns and meanings, and SLA outcomes (e.g. Sato 1986; Hawkins 1987; Weber and Tardif 1991).

The research so far on interactional modifications, although limited, allows a few tentative generalizations. Interactional contexts tend to provide L2 learners with more varied and complex language data than does one-way FD. Its enhanced comprehensibility, appropriateness to the learner's level, its timing, and learner involvement in the interaction may explain facilitative effects on SLA. Krashen (1985) emphasizes the importance of input comprehensibility, while Ellis (1991) argues that it is the nature and quality of interactional modifications which facilitate SLA by bringing specific linguistic information to the learner's attention. Braidi emphasizes timing: "It is entirely possible that well-timed linguistic modifications (i.e. when the non-NS is having difficulty processing the input) are the necessary condition, and it is the interaction which allows the interlocutor to alter the input at the right moment" (1990, p. 94). Pica (1992) underlines the importance of socially supportive relationships between learners and TL speakers in providing nonthreatening opportunities for learners to negotiate meaning, and to benefit from interactional modification.

Many studies mention the use of nonlinguistic support to the meanings being communicated in FD by both NSs and non-NSs. Visual cues which can help clarify form–meaning relationships include seemingly exaggerated or more explicit use by NSs of gestures, objects, graphics, and drawings to reinforce referential meaning. For example, NS university professors were observed to make more detailed blackboard diagrams, to write out full words instead of abbreviations, and to use exaggerated iconic gestures when lecturing to non-NS students, in contrast with parallel lectures to NS (Wesche and Ready 1985). Native speaker children interacting with non-NS children may use drawings, gestures, and reference to nearby objects to help communication (Wong Fillmore 1989).

## 3.2   Principles underlying Foreigner Discourse modifications

Both simplifying (restrictive) and elaborative modifications in FD have been repeatedly noted in the literature. The notion of "regularization" of surface forms seems to account for many of the features noted, such as provision of full underlying phonological, grammatical, and rhetorical forms, greater use of canonical word order, and a reduced repertoire of nonetheless well-formed constituents (Chaudron 1983a; Long 1985; Larsen-Freeman and Long 1991). However, other FD features such as longer pauses, fillers, vocabulary elaboration, a greater proportion of questions or more familiar style are not explained by regularization. Wesche and Ready (1985) have proposed redundancy (formal, semantic, and across levels of the communication system) as a more inclusive characterization. This, however, also fails to capture certain systematic features of FD (e.g. longer pauses, more familiar style). More recently the distinction between "syntactic simplicity" (achieved through regularization and more limited sets) and "semantic simplicity" or greater transparency of meaning (achieved through familiar vocabulary, reference to the "here and now," but also at times through more elaborative speech) has been proposed as helpful in characterizing FD features and in considering their role in SLA (Braidi 1990). Semantic simplicity is not a guarantee of syntactic simplicity; Braidi (1990, p. 85) discusses cases in which elaborative speech or other scaffolding moves may actually interfere with syntactic parsing by complicating phrase structure, for example through the use of multiple tokens of the same constituent. She cites an example from Kelch (1985): "And the magma, the melted rock, moves toward the ocean. If the mountain maintains, keeps up the flow of lava. ... "

The question again arises as to which kinds of adjustments increase comprehensibility, which may facilitate SLA, and whether these are necessarily the same. Faerch and Kasper (1986) and Sharwood-Smith (1986) propose that comprehended input is an overlapping but not identical set with input which leads to acquisition. Relevant evidence from French immersion classrooms and discipline-based L2 at the university level showing the partial independence of language and content learning supports this view (Swain 1988; Wesche 1989; Ready and Wesche 1992).

### 3.3    *Variability*

In FD, as with FT, considerable individual variation has been found among NS interlocutors in similar situations in the type, range, and amount of adjustments they provide (see Henzl 1973, 1979; Hatch *et al.* 1978; McCormack 1982; Gass and Varonis 1985; Wesche and Ready 1985; Brulhart 1986; Sato 1986). This variability apparently relates to such aspects of individual speech style as the experience of NS interlocutors with non-NSs, their sensitivity to affective considerations, and their motivation to communicate successfully with non-NSs (Wong Fillmore 1989; Terrell 1990).

Systematic differences in the kind and amount of modification have likewise been found to relate to contextual variables, presumably bearing upon comprehensibility. These include learner characteristics such as accent and apparent TL proficiency (Snow *et al.* 1981; Snow and Hoefnagel-Höhle 1982; Varonis and Gass 1985), age (Freed 1980; Krashen 1980, 1985; McCormack 1982; Scarcella and Higa 1981; Hatch 1984), gender (Gass and Varonis 1985), and personality (Wong Fillmore 1976, 1989; Gaies 1982; Hirvonen 1986; Derwing 1990). Other contextual variables isolated in the research include the nature of the communication task, for example, one-way or two-way, or clarification-seeking *versus* evaluative question prompts (Long 1981a; Doughty and Pica 1986; Pica 1992); the perceived importance and conceptual difficulty of the information to be conveyed (Wesche and Ready 1985); the relationship between the interlocutors (social and situational status, familiarity; see Larsen-Freeman and Long 1991). Evidence of "rough-tuning" of FD to learner proficiency levels has also been noted in both cross-sectional and developmental studies. Whether more sophisticated input leads or follows learner L2 development is still far from clear, however.

The frequency and choice of modifications has also been found to vary through the course of a given interaction or extended one-way discourse, indicating that NSs tune their adjustments at many levels depending upon their evolving perception of the comprehensibility of the discourse to non-NSs. This in turn appears to depend upon the propositional clarity of the discourse (as in more planned discourse *v.* spontaneous digressions), and the familiarity or novelty of each element being presented, as well as upon both involuntary and solicited feedback that NSs receive from learners about their comprehension (Wesche and Ready 1985; Vanniarajan 1988; Ehrlich, Avery and Yorio 1989).

## 3.4    Comprehensibility

The relative comprehensibility of FD *versus* NS talk for L2 learners is an important issue in input research, since the theoretical position that FD input facilitates L2 acquisition rests largely upon the claim that acquisition-promoting language input must be comprehended by learners (Krashen 1980, 1985; see 5.2 below).

How might FD modifications aid discourse comprehensibility? As suggested above, learners need to segment incoming speech into constituent parts – sounds, words, clauses, utterances, and sequences of utterances related to a particular topic. They also need access to the referential, grammatical, social, and other meaning of these formal constituents. And they need time to process the incoming information and to identify form–function–meaning relationships. Foreigner Discourse generally provides a well-formed, simpler, more regular, more explicit, and more redundant model than NS discourse. It also tends to be delivered more slowly and to be punctuated by pauses, thus allowing the non-NS interlocutor more processing time. All of these features might be expected to increase the comprehensibility of the input to learners.

A number of studies have linked FD modifications with increased text comprehension and recall by non-NS (see Chaudron 1985b, 1985c and Chaudron, Lubin, Sasaki, and Grigg 1986) for a discussion of research methodology). Long (1985) found global facilitating effects of FD on measured non-NS comprehension of oral input, using two versions of propositionally equivalent lecturettes. Ghahremani Ghajar (1989) reported on an experiment in which parallel NS and FD psychology lecture excerpts were administered to equivalent groups of advanced ESL students. Students who heard the FD text had significantly higher cloze summary scores, showing greater retention of content. This study extended the previous findings to naturally occurring FD and non-FD texts, but again it was impossible to determine differential effects of given FD modifications.

In a review of twelve studies comparing non-NS comprehension of modified and unmodified lecturettes or reading passages, Parker and Chaudron (1987) concluded that elaborative modifications consistently led to improved comprehension. In Kelch's (1985) study of such modifications, improved comprehension was related to slower delivery, while the effect of linguistic modifications was less consistent. As might be expected, the effects of modification were greater at lower proficiency levels.

Pica *et al.* (1987) found improved comprehension by non-NSs of NS directions in an interactional *versus* an input context. The interactional context provided syntactically more complex language and longer texts with more repetition of content words. They concluded that semantic redundancy was the most important aid to comprehensibility in this situation. Chaudron and Richards (1986) found some evidence of greater comprehensibility of lectures containing more discourse "macromarkers," which indicated major information, sequencing, and hierarchical relationships. In this study "micromarkers," or sentence-linking and pause-filling words, did not have this facilitative effect and may even have impeded content comprehension and recall. Issidorides (cited in Issidorides and Hulstijn 1992) indicated that suprasegmental cues were important to the comprehensibility of Dutch by non-NS learners. Such results are presumably related to findings on the facilitative effects of familiarity with textual and cultural schemata in written texts on reading comprehension (Johnson 1981).

### 3.5    Foreigner Discourse as an implicit teaching mode

As previously discussed, FD modifications may facilitate SLA in several ways. Increased input comprehensibility may indirectly aid SLA by freeing learner attention to concentrate more on formal structures and form–function–meaning relationships than on meaning alone. Positive affect communicated by the NS to the non-NS might have a similar effect, lessening anxiety and negative distraction. Successful comprehension helps learners stay in interactions longer, thus gaining more exposure to target language data. Foreigner Discourse may help SLA through its provision of redundant (generally easier-to-process) models at all levels of the communicative hierarchy, which tend to make constituent boundaries more salient and form-meaning relationships more accessible (Cook 1988). On the other hand, as mentioned above, FD modifications which aid comprehension and lexical L2 development (e.g. vocabulary elaboration through restatements, use of time adverbials) may in fact reduce the need for syntactic parsing and thus not necessarily aid syntactic development (Sato 1986; Braidi 1990).

# 4       Other kinds of language input to learners

## 4.1     Nonmodified talk

In addition to more or less tailored FD addressed to them, most L2 learners are exposed to large quantities of nonmodified discourse addressed to NSs, in schools, through the media, and in written documents. The features of unmodified NS talk are not at issue here; they represent the norms which most non-NS are trying to acquire. The main question has to do with the role of such input in SLA, including whether acquisition can proceed without modified input, particularly at beginning stages, and at what point in the acquisition process unmodified input is necessary or useful. As noted above, it has been claimed that linguistically or interactionally modified FD is present in all successful language acquisition (see Larsen-Freeman and Long 1991). There are also indications that attention to, and processing of, unmodified (i.e. NS-directed) input is vital to continued L2 development of advanced learners towards the formal complexity and the full semantic and pragmatic meanings that characterize native speakers (see White 1985; Krashen 1989; Tudor and Hafiz 1989; van Lier 1991).

## 4.2     Interlanguage talk

Most non-NS are exposed to large quantities of interlanguage discourse in their families, communities, and language classrooms, in addition to FD and nonmodified speech. The effect of IL input on SLA is an important issue, with psycholinguistic and pedagogical implications. While exposure limited to restricted and nonstandard linguistic data of IL speakers is recognized as inhibiting L2 development towards NS norms, the question in the L2 classroom, where teacher NS models and standard language teaching materials are also available, is, how much and what proportion of IL data to learners can be tolerated? Will learners attend to IL speech as a model in preference to the NS teacher's speech (Beebe 1985)? Are the pedagogical advantages of learner–learner interaction in the target language outweighed by the negative aspects of being exposed to more IL data, or *vice versa*? As Braidi (1990) points out, there are no research data relating well-formed *versus* deviant input to rate of SLA. Nor is very much known about specific effects of IL data on the learner's developing L2 system. Some evidence of long-term effects comes from classroom studies of the language output of children in Canadian immersion programs who learn a large part of their school curriculum through the medium of their L2 (Selinker, Swain, and Dumas 1975; Lapkin 1984;

Lyster 1990; Vignola and Wesche 1991; Harley 1992b). A classroom variety has been described which is formally simplified (e.g. over-use of periphrastic future, generic *v.* specific verbs, avoidance of certain tenses), and errors persist in areas of French grammar which are incongruent with English, as well as in communicatively noncritical areas (e.g. gender of inanimate nouns). This classroom variety is also functionally restricted (e.g. *tu* and *vous* are distinguished for number but not relative status; lack of sensitivity to register shifts). Certain characteristics of the register can be traced to English, and IL input may indeed be more likely to have such an outcome in settings where all L2 learners share the same L1 (Harley 1992b). However, it is not fully clear whether such features of the immersion classroom variety result from deviant IL data, from the lexically and functionally restricted data of the classroom, from other factors such as learner selection of peer over teacher models, or from a combination of factors. Cross-sectional studies of older immersion learners show continuing, if slow, progress towards NS norms (Harley 1984, 1992a, 1992b). Nonetheless, comparative studies of immersion learners at different grade levels and follow-up studies of the written language of immersion graduates at university indicate that syntactic errors and simplification, lexical and functional restriction are quite persistent (see Lapkin, Hart, and Swain 1991; Vignola and Wesche 1991; Wesche 1992; Harley forthcoming). Recent studies by Genesee, Holobow, Lambert, and Chartrand (1989) and Baetens-Beardsmore (1990) present evidence that the presence of NS peers in "super-immersion" school programs leads to more nativelike TL production by non-NS students.

It is pedagogically as well as theoretically important to understand the effects of IL input in SLA, because small group interaction among learners in L2 classes can increase students' opportunities for oral language use. Carefully chosen small group tasks can provide practice in extended, negotiated, varied conversation, which moves beyond the "display" question–answer sequences that often characterize teacher-fronted oral activity. Because such practice takes place between equals in a supportive atmosphere, the resulting discourse can be better tailored to individual needs and interests than whole-group activities (see Kramsch 1986a, 1986b, 1987; Pica 1987, 1991b).

Several studies have attempted to describe the language produced by non-NS learners carrying out small group tasks in their L2. Porter (1983), studying adult Hispanic ESL learners, discovered that non-NSs produced more talk with other non-NSs than with NS partners, particularly with advanced non-NS partners (because these conversations lasted longer). Porter also found that non-NSs negotiated repairs to conversational breakdown with other Spanish-speaking non-NSs similarly to the way

NSs did this (e.g. using such strategies as clarification requests, confirmation and comprehension checks, repetition and reformulations), thus gaining practice in conversation management. Learners did *not* make more errors when interacting with peers than with NSs. There was little correction of conversation partners either by NSs or by other non-NS, and likewise, only rare requests for conversational help to either type of partner. Porter concluded that while NSs offer more accurate TL input, non-NS learners can gain genuine communicative practice by working together, without increased performance errors – at least in the limited time period of the experiment. Several research teams have investigated non-NS–non-NS classroom interactions to gather information on the kinds of learner characteristics and tasks which might provide the most useful language practice. Varonis and Gass (1982, 1985) found that paired non-NS interlocutors with different L1 backgrounds and different proficiency levels generated more repair negotiations than did interlocutors of the same L1 background and proficiency level. Pica and Doughty (1985) compared the discourse produced by low–intermediate ESL students in both teacher-fronted and small group (four students) discussions, using one-way tasks. While students were equally grammatical in both contexts, there was significantly more (even if not very much) student talk in the group condition than in the teacher-fronted condition. In a similar study comparing teacher and small group discussion using two-way and one-way tasks, they found more interactional activity in the group condition with two-way tasks, but no difference in the teacher-fronted condition (Doughty and Pica 1986). Varonis and Gass (1985) in their study of intermediate level ESL students reported that both one-way and two-way tasks led to similar amounts of conversation breakdown and negotiation, although this activity decreased in both conditions with task familiarity when the pair switched roles. Recent work summarized by Pica (1992) underlines the influence of tasks on resulting language activity. She points out that "socially provocative tasks" such as debates and problem solving may lead to little negotiation, since one learner often dominates, whereas tasks whose completion depends on the pooling or exchanging of individually held information evoke more equal participation, and require that learners take each others' needs into account.

These classroom experiments suggest that certain kinds of learner–learner interactions can be very useful in providing increased and more varied language practice, and with experience in negotiating for shared meaning, outcomes which are more difficult to achieve in NS–non-NS interaction. While performance errors in these interactions have not been found to be greater than those with NSs, the long-term effects of frequent

IL input from such activities, particularly when there is a shared L1, are not known.

## 5    Theoretical perspectives on the role of the linguistic environment in second language acquisition

Current theoretical perspectives in SLA which attempt to take explicit account of the role of the linguistic environment in SLA vary considerably in the relative importance attributed to learner-internal factors and to linguistic environment features. The most ambitious theoretical formulations to date have dealt with the acquisition of L2 syntax. They vary in perspective from a view of language input as the essential causal factor which determines the rate and ultimate shape of SLA, to that of a limited role for input features as potential triggers to internally programmed restructuring of the IL grammar. These triggers are activated only when the learner is ready to receive positive evidence to confirm specific syntactic properties of the target language from among highly constrained possibilities. Some researchers, noting both the extreme variability in SLA rate and ultimate attainment, and the need to explain not only syntactic development but rather the more inclusive ability to use the L2 effectively in varied contexts, suggest that a more complete model will incorporate elements from both of the above views as well as give greater attention to the social context in which SLA occurs (Gass 1988; Wong Fillmore 1989; Ellis 1991).

### 5.1    *Universal grammar*

There is wide acceptance in first language acquisition theory that humans possess innate knowledge specific to language – known as universal grammar (UG) – which constrains the linguistic knowledge the organism needs to acquire from the environment, and thus the amount and kinds of linguistic data required in language acquisition. There is, however, far less agreement among researchers and theoreticians about the continued existence and possible role of such predispositions in second language acquisition. Still, a UG framework is increasingly being applied to research on the acquisition of second language syntax (see Liceras 1985; Zobl 1985; Schachter 1986; White 1987, 1989, 1990, 1991; Cook 1988, 1989; Braidi 1990). The main factor cited to support the hypothesis of a universal basis to linguistic knowledge is that input data is too deficient to account for the species-universal fact of language acquisition (Chomsky 1965). It has been argued that ambient input data may provide too degenerate a model due to performance errors. It has also been claimed that ambient data does not provide adequate and reliable negative data (on what is *not* possible in a language) so that certain innate knowledge must be assumed (see Sokolov and Snow this volume). Most important, however, is the claim that adult NS grammars are *underdetermined* by the input data available, since learners acquire certain rarely occurring constructions, and do not make certain kinds of errors that one would expect in the absence of innate knowledge. Similar arguments and evidence are invoked with respect to the operation of UG in SLA, although this is far more controversial (see White 1989).

Universal grammar proposes that learners possess a set of abstract linguistic principles (e.g. syntactic movement, phrase structure) which can vary in certain ways and which restrict what is possible in human language. For some of these principles, languages vary along universally shared "parameters" which govern sets of properties. These parameters are thought to have initial "unmarked" settings which will emerge in learners' grammars in the absence of contrary evidence from TL data. There also exist more "marked" possible settings which can be triggered when the learner hears positive evidence in the given language. That part of the grammar which is governed by innate principles and constraining parameters is known as the "core" grammar. The "peripheral" grammar consists of elements which are not part of innate knowledge and must presumably be acquired through the use of general cognitive abilities. With respect to the acquisition of grammar, the role of the linguistic environment is seen as limited to providing data containing evidence to confirm for the learner any marked parameter settings for the core grammar of the language. The theory deals only with a restricted, if crucial, set of phenomena – those aspects of linguistic competence which are deemed universal.

The relevance and usefulness of a UG approach to SLA remains controversial. The theory is neutral with respect to much of what must be acquired, for example the lexicon (words, meanings, and syntactic properties; grammar which is not part of the core; discourse organization and markers; anything which might be considered part of a theory of performance). A strict UG view, while it may – if indeed UG remains accessible in SLA – provide an explanation for the shape of some parts of the eventual interlanguage grammar, is not helpful in explaining the dramatic individual differences found in the rate and ultimate mastery of the second language. The theory itself is still challenged with respect to first language acquisition, although most L1 researchers accept the position that adult L1 competence is intricate and complex in ways that go beyond the input available to learners. Even if input is not degenerate, as the child-directed speech literature suggests, and even if L1 learners do not require negative feedback, there remains the problem of underdetermination.

Second language researchers within a UG framework have additional questions. If UG exists in L1, does it remain fully or partially accessible in SLA? If it does, how is it mediated by the presence of the already acquired L1? Is it in fact possible for a second language learner to acquire a competence equivalent to that of a native speaker (Braidi 1990)? Can UG be reactivated in SLA at initial (i.e. unmarked) settings, or is the acquisition of the second language filtered through existing L1 settings, which may themselves be differentiated in their influence – for example, according to whether the feature being learned is part of the core or peripheral grammar in either or both languages? Are the input requirements for confirming specific L2 parameters indeed freely available in even limited amounts of TL input, as Cook (1989) suggests, or is it important to distinguish between parameters for which evidence is readily accessible (e.g. the "pro-drop," or "null subject," parameter) and those involving optional rules, for which positive evidence may be available, but not evidence on usage constraints? Braidi (1991) suggests that finely tuned input may be required in the latter case. For White (1990), very specific negative evidence may be required for a change to a more restrictive L2 parameter setting from a more inclusive one transferred from the L1. (This problem may not arise in L1 acquisition, where in the face of ambiguous data, children are thought to opt initially for the more restrictive parameter setting, allowing a subsequent move to a more inclusive setting from positive evidence only). Finally, as noted above, it must be remembered that UG is concerned with grammar rather than with language and its use, and makes no claims about the importance of input evidence which may be required in the development of many aspects of communicative competence in either L1 or L2.

## 5.2    The Input Hypothesis

Krashen's Input Hypothesis, which largely predated UG approaches to SLA research, continues to make the strongest claim about the role of the linguistic environment in SLA (Krashen 1985, 1992). In Krashen's view, evolved from his earlier formulations of Monitor Theory (e.g. 1978, 1981), a second language is acquired by processing "comprehensible input" – language which is heard or read, and understood, and which contains novel formal elements. If meaning is not understood, the input is processed as noise. For Krashen (1980, 1985), modifications in speech addressed to learners are important insofar as they increase input comprehensibility. However, Krashen is careful to point out that novel input does not have to be simplified or modified in order to be comprehensible. Extralinguistic information may, for example, provide the needed clues to meaning. To lead to acquisition, TL samples must contain structures (lexis, sounds, morphology, syntax) just beyond the learner's current competence, whose meaning is understood with the help of the linguistic and extralinguistic context. The learner must also be receptive to the input, that is, have a low "affective filter." Thus if the learner's current competence may be characterized as $i$, next-to-be acquired rules in the data according to a natural sequence of acquisition, or $i + 1$, could be acquired by the learner. While noting a significant role for an "internal language processor" which follows the common acquisition sequences noted by researchers (1985, pp. 2–3), Krashen does not speculate on the psycholinguistic process by which input becomes "intake" for internalization into the IL grammar.

Krashen presents considerable evidence from empirical studies which accords with his position. However, the impossibility of operationalizing and testing basic constructs such as $i + 1$ in the absence of a theory of grammar (Gregg 1984), and the resulting impossibility of finding direct, indisputable evidence for it (see Ellis 1991) is a severe shortcoming to its usefulness in SLA theory building. White (1987) furthermore argues that input which is *incomprehensible* is, in some cases at least, necessary for acquisition of new knowledge. In her view, IL development will not necessarily progress when meaning is successfully understood. For IL restructuring, the learner must become aware at some level that her/his current IL rule system is inadequate before growth can occur, so incomprehensible input may be required.

## 5.3   The Multidimensional Model

An "interactionist" or "multidimensional" view, which aims to specify the relationship between internal language readiness and usable input information about the TL, is found in the work by Pienemann and his associates (see Pienemann 1984, 1989, 1992). In this evolving theoretical model, "learnability" refers to the logical possibility of acquiring the grammar and the inferential mechanisms for achieving this; "teachability" refers to whether a given structure can be processed by a learner at a particular point in time (Pienemann 1992). Using cross-sectional and longitudinal data from naturalistic adult language learning, Pienemann and others formulated a sequence of word order rules in German as a second language which account for most possible positions of verbal elements in German main clauses. Each sequentially acquired rule incorporates and elaborates upon the preceding ones, constituting an implicational scale. Canonical word order is thus acquired before initialization and finalization strategies for moving sentence elements, which must in turn be acquired before the strategy for avoiding changes to elements in subordinate clauses. A similar sequence has been worked out for English (Pienemann 1992). In this model, structural complexity is determined by the difficulty of the cognitive operations involved in producing the rules at each stage for mapping underlying meaning onto syntactic form. The underlying speech-processing "strategies" mastered by the learner at each stage constrain what is teachable to that learner at that point in time. Ambient language input (including instruction) can lead to further acquisition only if it respects the currently mastered rule (or processing constraints); stages cannot be skipped. Empirical studies of child and adult learners of German and English from typologically different languages provide support for this theory, and indicate that first language background does not affect developmental sequences (Pienemann 1984, 1989, 1992; Ellis 1989; Lightbown and Spada 1990; Spada and Lightbown forthcoming).

According to current learnability theory, not all structures are constrained by developmental processing limitations. Some, known as "variational features," can be acquired at any time. Individual differences in learner motivation and orientation towards accuracy or communicative effectiveness (varying over time and contexts) influence which variational features are acquired.

Pienemann's Teachability Hypothesis (1992) is part of a causal process model which can make predictions about what will happen next, and which attempts to link various factors (e.g., affect, input) to precise outcomes. It differs in kind from other models in that it is formulated in terms of what cannot be learned at a given point in time; that is, what TL data is not usable at a given stage, rather than what can be learned. As yet, however, it deals with very limited areas of German and English syntax, and relatively little empirical research is available on it.

While each of the above models has engendered research insights into some aspects of the relationship between the linguistic environment and SLA, it is evident that the eventual theoretical characterization of this relationship will be both more comprehensive and more specific than any of them, and will accommodate both data-driven and model-building research approaches (see Schachter 1986; Braidi 1990). None of the three deals systematically with external factors having to do with the initial perception of ambient linguistic data, or with how these data are internally processed and selectively integrated into the learner's knowledge system once they have been noticed. A psycholinguistic processing model is required as part of an eventual SLA theory, such as that proposed by McLaughlin (McLaughlin, Rossman, and McLeod 1983; McLaughlin 1990). In addition, the phenomena to be explained must extend beyond syntactic development to contextualized language use in culturally appropriate ways. Wong Fillmore (1989) and Gass (1988) have recently proposed frameworks for SLA studies which, while skeletal, suggest what an eventual theory of the environmental/acquisition relationship will need to explain.

## 5.4    Teachability

Wong Fillmore in her investigation of L2 "teachability" emphasizes the variability in SLA outcomes "even among young learners ... even when children have the same need, motivation and opportunity to learn the language" (1989, p. 313). In three large-scale studies of ESL children in California schools, she has traced this variability, noting the influence of individual learner differences, group membership, and factors in the learning context. Her framework for SLA includes three elements, social, linguistic, and cognitive processes, which are seen to function interactively in a compensatory way. Essential social processes for SLA include continuing contact between TL speakers and learners. This not only provides vital TL linguistic data and access to meaning, but also "the motivation needed to keep both parties talking despite the difficulties that come from not sharing a common language" (p. 321). Teachability involves going beyond providing learners with what might be "learnable" at their current stage to include the social, linguistic, and cognitive support system which will give them access to the language. Linguistic processes include how TL speakers are predisposed to "select, modify and support the linguistic data they produce for learners" (p. 323). The linguistic processes at work for learners have to do with the prior L1 and L2 linguistic knowledge and experience which determines how they will interpret the TL data available to them. Both language-specialized and general cognitive processes are also seen as essential to learners' figuring out how the language works; for example, segmenting linguistic data into constituents, assigning meanings, noting functional equivalents with L1, and recognizing patterns. Since all these factors interact in any given learning situation, a linguistically rich and supportive learning environment can sometimes compensate where other factors would predict poor learning outcomes.

While Wong Fillmore's framework is still far from the precision necessary to generate testable hypotheses for theory building, it identifies the various factors to be considered in an eventual SLA theory.

## 5.5    An integrated framework

Gass (1988) proposes an overall framework to account for the conversion of ambient speech data converted into learner grammatical development, evidenced in output. She proposes five levels of activity plus a number of factors mediating between levels. The first level is *input apperception*, the process by which the learner perceives some part of the available TL data and relates it at some level to existing knowledge. Mediating factors which filter what is apperceived may include frequency, affective influences (e.g. motivation, model selection), prior L1, L2 and world knowledge, and selective attention, which "allows a learner to notice a mismatch between what he or she produces/knows and what is produced by speakers of the second language" (p. 203). Level 2 is *comprehension*, which varies in completeness, from a range of possible semantic information to structural analysis. This is followed by level 3, *intake* or attempted integration of a subset of what is comprehended (the rest serving only for momentary communication requirements); then level 4, *integration* of elements of the mental representation into the IL grammar. Integration into IL occurs either through grammatical restructuring or through long-term unanalyzed storage for eventual use. The fifth and final level is *output*, which is both an imperfect reflection of learner competence, and, possibly, a further stage in acquisition, requiring deeper syntactic analysis and processing by the learner (cf. Swain 1985, 1988; Burger 1989 for contrasting views). For Gass, an adequate model of SLA must be interactive rather than linear (see Edmondson 1986), and must include all the variables known to play a significant role in acquisition, while accounting for the fact that not all input is converted into the learner's grammar, as well as that parts of a learner's grammar go beyond the actual input (Gass 1988, pp. 199–200). Gass's framework indicates the complexity of the interacting factors and mechanisms which intervene between the occurrence of ambient speech data and development of learner grammars, and suggests the kinds of research questions which must be addressed in the development of adequate explanatory models for various aspects of SLA.

It should be reiterated here that most research on the linguistic environment of L2 learners has been essentially atheoretical, and that in spite of the large body of factual information which now describes this input, there is as yet little specific evidence as to whether or how its various features influence SLA. Research continues within several different traditions, with increasing recognition of the need for more inclusive models.

## 6     Current research

The main current research lines dealing with input/acquisition relationships include *language socialization* studies which attempt to link the social/cultural environment of language learners – including the L2 classroom – with SLA and sociocultural outcomes, experimental studies of *input processing* which attempt to isolate mechanisms involved in input comprehension and integration, and classroom experiments involving *input enhancement* of various kinds to make particular input features more salient to learners and to promote deeper analysis.

## 6.1    Language socialization

In language socialization research, the learner is viewed in the role of cultural member, learning to use the L2 to accomplish social and cognitive goals in the new cultural context – often on the limited basis of classroom experience. One of the main methodologies for this type of research is ethnography, "long-term studies of the daily habits of a particular social group in which researchers both observe and participate in the lives of those they are studying" (Heath 1986, p. 153). The emphasis is on description, process, and meaning structures in a natural setting, using data from observation and field notes by researchers and other participants (teachers and students), analysis of video and audio recordings, semi-structured and open-ended interviews with parents and children, and indirect elicitation techniques (e.g. puppets, story completion). The unit of analysis may involve long stretches of discourse spread over days (Hawkins 1987). Such an approach can help differentiate the SLA/ integration experience of, for example, language-majority children in French immersion kindergarten (see Weber and Tardif 1991), already equipped with the North American culture of childhood and knowledge of the ways language is used in school, from that of ESL children in California from varied and distant cultural backgrounds, who must learn "not only the vocabulary and grammar of English but also the ways of using English the school expects" (Heath 1986, p. 144). In Heath's view, it is crucial to understand these children's patterns of language learning and use if one is to understand language socialization across cultures, including second language acquisition. Her research indicates that schooling, to promote integration for academic and vocational success, must provide experience in the greatest possible range of oral and written language uses. Related research by Hawkins (1987) on the development of both English knowledge and higher-order cognitive skills by such students presents evidence that it is through "scaffolding" of language interactions by teachers and more proficient peers that learners can perform communicatively beyond their current level of competence. With such support L2 students use new language forms to accomplish tasks, for example, they recognize cause and effect or understand the significance of event sequence, and gradually become able to do this independently. Mohan's theoretical constructs help explain some of the findings of the ethnographers (Mohan 1986, 1991). He sees the analysis of the "knowledge structures" as well as the "linguistic structures" which underlie language use as essential in understanding how language is acquired, and furthermore advocates their systematic linking in school curricula. While the concept of scaffolding provides "an account of how language is used to 'do a task'" by language learners with the help of more expert speakers, it is not an adequate account of how language is used to interpret or reflect on a task or to discuss knowledge.[4] For Mohan, any given text can only be understood in the cultural context of a given discourse community and the immediate communicative context with its attendant communicative purposes. Thus the linguistic and discourse knowledge required for understanding a science textbook is of limited use without accompanying knowledge structures about how science is done, and of cultural features such as the role of a text in the academic subculture of school science and in the particular science class.

## 6.2     Input processing

Another current research approach is the experimental investigation of input processing. This research presumes an information processing model of speech and reading processes. It attempts to specify the nature and sequence of events by which certain features of input are experienced as salient by learners through such means as innate universals and expectancies, frequency of occurrence, perceptual salience, learner attention, and task demands (see Schmidt 1990), thus becoming candidates for further processing and eventual modification of the IL grammar. Researchers active in this paradigm include Chaudron, who initially provided a framework for isolating and studying "intake" (Corder 1967) as distinct from input and comprehension (see also Gallaway and Woll this volume), and who has continued to work on the development of theory and methodology for exploring intake (Chaudron 1985b, 1991; Chaudron *et al.* 1986). He and his colleagues have inventoried elicitation tasks for use in input-processing research differing in the type of learner responses required, the amount of encoding or recoding required, and the time allowed (e.g. nonverbal pattern matching, elicited imitation, written recall, grammatical accuracy judgments; Chaudron 1985a). Hulstijn (1982, 1989a, 1989b, 1990); Hulstijn and Hulstijn 1984) and VanPatten (1987, 1988, 1990); VanPatten and Cadierno (1992) are other currently active researchers who have responded to Chaudron's call for more rigorous methods. They have addressed themselves to the relationship

een learner attention to the meaning of utterances and to the formal
~tures of the language input. Their experiments have attempted to
.anipulate learner attention to assess outcomes while controlling for
such factors as current L2 knowledge, linguistic characteristics of the
input, and salience of particular features in the input. Hulstijn (1989a,
1989b) has used artificial as well as "real" Dutch target sentences to take
account of prior L2 knowledge, in isolation and in running texts, under
highly controlled conditions. He reports evidence that learner attention to
form (i.e. grammatical morphemes, lexical items) at the moment of input
encoding is a sufficient condition for incidental learning of structural
elements. Less clear is whether exclusive attention to meaning inhibits the
acquisition of formal elements. In future research he intends to deal with a
wider variety of linguistic features, and take into account L1 and verbal
aptitude differences as well as previous L2 knowledge, input tasks, and
features.

VanPatten's research concerns the strategies and mechanisms involved
in processing form–meaning connections during comprehension. He and
Cadierno present evidence that when learners attend to the precise
meaning of sentences signaled by the grammatical features of interest (e.g.
through matching pictures with sentences), they retain the grammatical
information and can use it in subsequent interpretation tasks better than
those who are presented with models and rules, followed by practice
examples (VanPatten and Cadierno 1992, 1993). In another experiment
with L2 learners of Spanish, VanPatten found that comprehension
decreases markedly when both meaning and morphology (functors) must
be attended to, while attending both to a lexical item and its general
meaning does not interfere with comprehension (1990). Like Hulstijn's
work, VanPatten's experiments suggest that learners normally interpret
L2 input initially for meaning, using content vocabulary. Only if this fails,
or if the task they are faced with induces them to do otherwise (as may
happen in the language classroom) do they carry out grammatical analysis. Still, Hulstijn, Ellis (1992), and others note considerable individual
differences in the way subjects approach these tasks.

## 6.3    Input enhancement

The third current approach to input research involved pedagogical intervention. In these classroom experiments, L2 learners' attention is directed
to specific formal features of language within meaning-oriented activities,
with the goal of developing increased grammatical accuracy. Some of this
work has been carried out in immersion programs (Harley 1987; Day and
Shapson 1991), and some in intensive ESL programs in Quebec schools

(Lightbown and Spada 1990; White *et al.* 1991; Spada and Lightbc
forthcoming). Results to date suggest that when varied input enhanc
ment activities focusing on the same grammatical principle (e.g. increas
ing salience through frequency or other means, providing feedback, and
setting tasks such as pattern recognition which require analysis of different language features) are pursued in the context of meaningful language
use over an extended period, they can lead to changes in learners'
interlanguage system.

The current attention to more complete and integrated models, and the
complementary research approaches that have replaced the earlier
descriptive studies of the linguistic environment of the language learner
are promising developments, and should lead to significant progress in
our understanding of the relationships between ambient linguistic data,
attendant factors, and SLA.

## 7     Conclusions

From all the above, it is clear that much of the target language input
directed to learners is modified in various ways to take account of their
lower proficiency. The resulting Foreigner Discourse is dynamic and
extremely variable, involving selection by NSs from a repertoire of strategies available at different levels of the human communication system.
These include interactional as well as linguistic adjustments of various
kinds. The occurrence of FD modifications is influenced both by relatively stable factors (e.g. type of discourse, the ages, personalities, and
relationship of the interlocutors, the proficiency of the learner) and by
changing factors as the discourse unfolds (e.g. newness or complexity of
content, communicative objective, learner feedback, and environmental
distractions). Their main purpose appears to be more effective communication, including better comprehension by non-NS interlocutors;
however, such modified input is also thought to facilitate learner development of different aspects of their L2 knowledge. How TL linguistic input
– modified or not – influences SLA is not well understood  nor do
researchers agree on its importance. The developing picture from multi-
perspective research activity suggests that input–SL A relationships are
multiple and complex, and that to understand them researchers must take
account of learners as active participants in generating, filtering, and
processing the available TL and contextual data. They must also take
account of the sociocultural context of SLA as well as of the cognitive and
psycholinguistic processes by which target language data help to build
learner grammars.

## NOTES

1 I wish to acknowledge the help I received in this project from many fellow researchers who shared their work, including unpublished materials, with me: Hugo Baetens-Beardsmore, Susan Braidi, Susanne Carroll, Elaine Day, Willis Edmondson, Rod Ellis, Barbara Freed, Susan Gass, Barbara Hawkins, Tuula Hirvonen, Juliane House, Jan Hulstijn, Claire Kramsch, Sharon Lapkin, Diane Larsen-Freeman, Patsy Lightbown, William McCormack, Jürgen Meisel, Bernie Mohan, Teresa Pica, Manfred Pienemann, Catherine Snow, Nina Spada, Merrill Swain, Tracy Terrell, Leo van Lier, Bill VanPatten and Lydia White. Particular thanks are due Craig Chaudron, Steve Krashen, Mike Long, Birgit Harley, and Brian Richards for their insights, articles and encouragement, and to Evelyn Hatch for her inspiring pioneering work in this area. I also wish to express my gratitude to Beatrice Magyar for her word-processing and bibliographic expertise, to Junhong Zang for editorial help, and to my family and the editors for their patience.

2 A T-unit is any syntactic main clause and its associated subordinate clauses (Hunt 1966; Chaudron 1988).

3 A type–token ratio applied to vocabulary analysis is the number of different words ("types") divided by total number of words produced ("tokens"). However, as noted by Richards (1987), the resulting ratio is a function of the length of the text analyzed (i.e. the more words the smaller the ratio).

4 The framework developed by Mohan and his colleagues for teaching/learning ESL and school content systematically relates thinking skills and appropriate language to knowledge structures, and is currently under large-scale experimentation in schools in the Vancouver area.

# Conclusion

# Conclusions and directions

*Brian J. Richards and Clare Gallaway*

## 1    Introduction

In her Introduction to this volume, Snow[1] has commented on the huge volume of research carried out in the area of input and interaction in recent years. In each of our chapters, the facts and implications of a particular area of this vast body of research have been drawn together. It remains to consider how our current understanding of the issues has been increased by the contributions.

A common criticism leveled against studies of children's language acquisition is that theoretical frameworks proposed for individual areas may shed light on those areas but may be less enlightening for others; for example, an explanatory theory for certain phonological facts may bear no relation to any sort of theory devised to explain semantic phenomena. The chapters collected in this book cover a number of aspects of input and interaction, and the question of what is, or is not, viewed as significant varied according to the area studied. In her Introduction, Snow has drawn attention to the fractionation of the research field. We need, therefore, to seek consensus amongst researchers to make some general statements, and this volume, we hope, has served as a forum for drawing together differing perspectives.

In this chapter, we hope to summarize what we find are the salient points to emerge from the collection as a whole. However, we would not wish this to be viewed as a definitive statement about the content of the book. The quantity and detail of the material presented in each chapter provides much more of interest and relevance than we can possibly deal with in this short chapter, and we expect and hope that readers will be able to focus on themes of interest to their own research and find connections other than those included here.

In commissioning chapters our aim was to relate the features of input and interaction in a variety of social contexts and cultures to the development of those acquiring language both normally and atypically. The contexts are those of the family, the classroom, and different cultural and

253

linguistic settings, including the acquisition of both first and second languages. In addition, three chapters deal with specific domains of language, or theoretical and methodological issues: Cruttenden (ch. 6) examines the features and functions of phonetic and prosodic modifications, Sokolov and Snow (ch. 2) look at negative evidence and the question of learnability, and Richards (ch. 4) evaluates the strength of evidence for relationships between child-directed speech and the development of language and its relationship with research methodology.

With regard to the family, Pine (ch. 1) considers the mother's child-directed speech adjustments and their possible relationships with language development and individual differences, while Barton and Tomasello (ch. 5) look at the wider context of fathers and siblings in an examination of the "Bridge Hypothesis" – the view that the child's communicative skill (as opposed to language acquisition) is further developed through interaction with a less familiar partner with fewer shared meanings. The family context is also an important factor in Gallaway and Woll's chapter on interaction and childhood deafness (ch. 9), with its contrast between deaf and hearing mothers and between the development of sign and spoken language; and in chapter 8, Conti-Ramsden surveys the literature on parent–child interaction with atypical learners and considers the implications for intervention.

The cultural setting and the important theoretical question about the necessity of making the linguistic code more accessible is addressed by Lieven (ch. 3) in a consideration of the universality of speech adjustments with regard to different languages and cultures. However, this theme has become an important threat running through a number of chapters including Barton and Tomasello (ch. 5) and Cruttenden (ch. 6), and makes an important contribution to Sokolov and Snow's multiple factors framework in chapter 2. Two chapters, Geekie and Raban's contribution on language and literacy at home and at school (ch. 7) and Wesche's chapter on second language acquisition (ch. 10), focus on the classroom and provide the most direct link with educational issues.

## 2    Describing child-directed speech

### 2.1    *The range of linguistic environments in normal populations*

One of our stated aims has been to bring together and survey in some detail the extent of variations in the nature of language addressed to learners, and the contexts in which these differences can be observed. With respect to children acquiring language normally, it is still the case that by far the largest quantity of research has concerned interaction within a particularly narrow setting – that is, between mothers and their infants in a literate, Western, child-centered society. This fact has been commented on frequently throughout this volume. Clearly, there has been a need to expand our understanding of what constitutes a "normal" linguistic environment in other societies and other family settings. It is evident from the chapters by Lieven, Cruttenden, and Barton and Tomasello, that this area is now being addressed in some detail – though these authors make the point that much more investigation is still needed within the areas they have described. In addition, while much has been made of variation in the interactional style of mothers in Britain and the United States (Pine,[1] Richards) and while comparisons have been made *between* different languages and cultures (e.g. Grimm, Shatz, Niemeier-Wind, and Wilcox 1990), we know far less about the degree of variation *within* other cultures.

Before we move on to a discussion of the significance of these findings, let us consider briefly some important basic facts to emerge from the chapters. The description of child-directed speech may be simpler than its interpretation, but providing an accurate description is still a far from straightforward task, as is witnessed by the continuing debate about intelligibility (e.g. Bard and Anderson 1983; Cruttenden). It has, of course, long been accepted that speech modifications to learners do not add up to a unitary phenomenon called "motherese"; rather, different features cluster together in different combinations, which makes description a complex matter. Still, our knowledge has been extended by the relatively recent addition of work on language used by adults other than mothers and siblings (Barton and Tomasello) and by the crosscultural investigations referred to above.

The research described by Barton and Tomasello provides evidence that fathers and siblings modify their speech differently from mothers when addressing younger children. Fathers' speech to their children appears to be structurally similar to that of mothers, but rather different in pragmatic functions; on the whole, fathers are less comprehending and more demanding. Siblings, likewise, appear to have some ability to adapt their speech but in general are less accommodating to younger children than adults are. Barton and Tomasello go on to discuss the possible effects that these differences may have. They also point out that, at least during the early stages of language development, the role rather than the gender of the parent may be responsible for these differences. This is indicated by research into bilingual families where each parent speaks a different language with the child and where differences in interaction style are reduced, suggesting that in monolingual environments whether one is or is not the primary caregiver, may be the determining factor for differences between mothers and fathers. This is an area where research into fathers as primary caregivers would provide a useful comparison.

A vital point to note here is that it has been all too easy to work from an oversimplified view of any individual child's linguistic experience. Varying proportions of input from father, mother, and siblings (and indeed, grandparents) must be taken into account when assessing the nature of a child's early linguistic environment. This point is taken up again by Lieven in her chapter on crosscultural and crosslinguistic aspects when she addresses the question of the range of environments in which children learn to speak. The mother–child dyad around which so much research has centered is hardly the predominant situation for child-rearing worldwide. Further, a wide range of beliefs and customs concerning the nature of language addressed to children can be identified.

Even though our knowledge of crosscultural and crosslinguistic context may still be limited, it is quite clear that we should not now generalize about facilitative effects of particular aspects of the linguistic environment, nor for their necessity, from studies of one particular setting. An understanding of the known variations between these different settings must now be considered a starting point for further investigations rather than an optional extra. Lieven points out that in some societies, adult talk to children shows characteristics which contrast with those considered by many to be facilitative. Yet those children do, of course, learn to speak. Information about the presence or absence of particular features in various communities is essential. However, Lieven also reminds us that the absence of a particular feature from any culture's adult–child register may simply mean that its function is achieved by some other type of behavior, even possibly nonlinguistic behavior – or it may not serve a useful purpose at all.

With respect to the available range of CDS characteristics, it might be thought that some of the phonetic speech modifications offer a unique chance for investigation. The absence or presence of some items of phonetic modification such as substitution is a relatively clear-cut issue, unlike, for example, relative proportions of interrogatives or imperatives, which operate on a continuum. However, this area has attracted little research and, as Cruttenden remarks, our knowledge of phonetic modifications has barely advanced since the early work by Ferguson (1964, 1977). Certain general observations have been made, that is, that the same sorts of modifications seem to occur in different languages, but systematic observations of a wide range of languages for crosslinguistic comparison are lacking. This means that we have too little knowledge of how widespread a particular feature may be in the world's languages and cultures, nor do we have detailed data on the distribution and extent of such modifications within particular languages. Prosodic modifications, however, have attracted a good deal of recent research interest. The work by Pye (1986) on Quiché suggests that detailed investigations of other languages would uncover different ranges of modifications. In summary, much more descriptive work is needed in this area, particularly from a crosslinguistic perspective.

We shall not attempt here to reproduce well-known facts about maternal language addressed to children from the classical studies (see Snow 1986; Richards and Gallaway 1993, which both include summaries of features). It is now well documented that stage-related variations in input arise as any individual child becomes more competent; studies of individual differences between mothers have also made significant contributions since the pioneering studies of the 1970s (e.g. Nelson 1973; Lieven 1978a). However, the point is made by Conti-Ramsden that there is still insufficient understanding in many areas of what constitutes the range of normal variation to serve as a yardstick for atypical studies. In a study of conversational interaction in families with a language-impaired child, Conti-Ramsden and Dykins (1991) report divergent conversational strategies, and Conti-Ramsden points out that we need to know about the extent of characteristics of interactive style within individuals (for example, whether some people are more frequent topic shifters, or less frequent givers of feedback). The validity of this observation holds, of course, for normal as well as atypical situations. A recent study by Petersen and McCabe (1992) illustrates an instance of differing parental styles which appear to influence development: one child, whose mother's supporting questions focused on context (who, where, when, etc.) showed contextual orientation in her narratives, but less sophisticated plot structure than a child whose mother emphasized event elaboration. It is likely that our knowledge of such variation will continue to increase.

## 2.2    Atypical populations

Research into speech addressed to atypical children has generally been designed to answer questions related to facilitating acquisition. Even though the motivation, therefore, is often with the ultimate aim of informing intervention, basic descriptive facts are still needed. The simplest of these has been whether the linguistic environment of atypical children is the same as, or different from, that of normally developing children. The chapters by Conti-Ramsden and Gallaway and Woll explain how far this question can be answered, but perhaps more importantly, they also discuss whether it is still an appropriate question to ask.

In both these chapters, it emerges that much of the research to date on language-impaired and language-disordered children and on spoken language development in hearing-impaired children has been simplistic in nature and methodologically crude. Although it has been shown that there are both similarities to, and differences from, the interaction of adults with normally developing children, the significance and possible outcomes of these similarities and differences with atypical children need sensitive reevaluation in the light of current views. Both chapters deal with the problem of interpreting the differences, some of which arise from the obvious difficulties of conversing with a speaker with a rather low level of linguistic competence. For example, whether a predominance of imperatives can have an unequivocally negative effect on the language acquisition process of any particular child or group is still far from clear.

In the chapters by Snow, and Sokolov and Snow, a perspective is presented which may eventually suggest new approaches to research in this area. The robustness of the language acquisition process – the fact that all normal children learn to speak successfully – is now generally accepted as evidence that it is "well-buffered against variation" (Snow). In other words, normal first language acquisition can take place under widely differing circumstances because the nature and quantity of linguistic input is so far beyond minimum requirements that the process is protected. Although there are clearly some situations where the amount and quality of the input *does* drop below what is required in normally developing children (cases of extreme deprivation, and some cases of hearing children with deaf parents: see Bishop and Mogford 1988), features with apparently negative effects in the input rarely occur in large enough quantities to upset the whole balance of the process.

While the process is indeed well buffered against variation in normally developing children, there is probably a reduction of the buffering in atypical children, such as those with language disorder or hearing loss, and, as indicated by Wesche, some second language learners. Such children, therefore, are much more dependent on optimal input. Establishing what the optimal input might consist of, however, has been difficult for reasons which have been thoroughly charted in this volume.

However, in the multi-factor account offered by Sokolov and Snow, it is suggested that learnability tradeoffs between one area and another may work to the learner's advantage; a weakness or difficulty in one area may be compensated for by a stronger influence or factor which is suited to different learning mechanisms. This appears to be a promising direction to pursue further investigations, but much needs yet to be established; empirical evidence of what the tradeoffs are and how they operate will certainly be difficult to come by. A first step in this direction is to disentangle the various functions of language addressed to learners, and to establish which features achieve which functions.

## 2.3    *Language addressed to second language learners and young writers*

Two chapters in this book are concerned not with children acquiring their first language, but with second language learners (Wesche) and children developing literacy in the classroom (Geekie and Raban).

Wesche notes two fundamental strands of influence on research into input and interaction in second language acquisition: interest in the "Foreigner Talk register," and research into first language acquisition suggesting a causative role for finely tuned input. The result is a burgeoning literature on the language used both in classrooms and in informal interaction between native speakers and non-native speakers of a lower level of proficiency.

In detailing modifications in interactions with second language learners, Wesche initially makes a distinction between "Foreigner Talk" and its subvariety, the "foreign language classroom register." Both are regarded as a simplified register which potentially makes the target language more accessible through greater comprehensibility and ease of perception, and both contain discourse features which maximize the learners' participation in conversation. However, while the classroom variety consists almost exclusively of well-formed utterances, Foreigner Talk in other contexts frequently contains nonstandard features which appear to be triggered mainly by a combination of low proficiency in the non-native speaker, a perception of superior status on the part of the native speaker, and a high degree of spontaneity of the conversations. Additional influences are the existence and type of previous experience with non-native speakers, and affective factors and informality. In other respects, the classroom variety is not qualitatively different from varieties in other contexts except for those aspects which are features of classrooms in general. The key distinctions made by Wesche, therefore, are between "Foreigner Discourse" (the language addressed to language learners which is in the standard form), ungrammatical "Foreigner Talk," "interlanguage talk" (the simplified and frequently nonstandard form used by other learners and second language speakers in the environment), and "non-modified" input (the language of the media and documents to which the learner is exposed in educational and other settings). Foreigner Discourse is shown to involve modifications in speech rate, phonology and prosody, syntax and morphology, vocabulary, and discourse features, involving processes of both simplification and elaboration, such as the restating of information and using synonyms.

At first sight, the existence of ungrammatical forms in Foreigner Talk would appear to contrast with all we know about child-directed speech in first language acquisition. This is described almost exclusively as well formed and as consistently supplying functors in obligatory contexts. On the other hand, a recent publication by Chafetz, Feldman, and Wareham (1992) suggests that this is not always the case. They claim that ungrammatical parentese, predominantly the omission of closed-class items, occurs if parents' theory of language development leads them to adopt teaching strategies which omit "difficult" words in order to facilitate the acquisition of open-class items. The authors regard parents of children with handicaps to be more prone to using such strategies. On the question of whether ungrammatical input matters, Wesche's account of the long-term effects of immersion programs may be relevant; while acknowledging the lack of evidence concerning the influence of interlanguage input, she does quote research showing the development of a simplified, more restricted classroom variety of language, with persistent grammatical errors. Nevertheless, there are other possible explanations for this, and it is not yet possible to demonstrate a causal link between specific features of interlanguage and learning outcomes. What may be crucial in both settings is the proportion of nonstandard to standard forms, the situational and linguistic contexts in which they are embedded, and the developmental stage of the learners.

Geekie and Raban deal with the notion of language addressed to learners within the classroom context, and more particularly they consider a research study concerned with the conversational interaction between young writers and their teacher. Their starting point is the widely held view that patterns of classroom interaction may be too rigidly structured and teacher-dominated, and lacking in shared context for productive learning to take place. However, in their study, they show that certain aspects of the classroom context may be more closely comparable to interaction in the home than many educationalists have previously acknowledged. In many respects, the structure of routines in the classroom they describe closely resembles the formats analyzed by Bruner (1983a).

## 3    Functions of child-directed speech

A contributory factor to our increased understanding of the CDS register has been the separation of various functions which may be achieved by its features. Some of the most recent research has been aimed at examining possible relationships between particular features and corresponding aspects of child language (Pine). Investigating such relationships rather than following the type of earlier "scattershot" approach (Snow) is now generally accepted as the way forward. In order to discuss these relationships, let us first establish a classification of the various functions which can be identified within child-directed speech. It should be noted in passing that we are not suggesting that conscious intent underlies speech modifications; if adults are using shorter sentences and thus maintaining children's attention, there is no suggestion that this activity is conscious. The only functions which are obviously achieved through conscious effort are the teaching of politeness routines and certain other attempts at socialization through language, overt corrective feedback, and routinized language games.

The earliest attempt to separate out functions within CDS was by Ferguson (1977); *simplifying*, *clarifying*, and *expressive* functions were attributed to various phonetic and prosodic features. This categorization has been superseded by attempts to schedule functions in a way which is both more detailed and more generally applicable to structural and interactive features of CDS as well as phonetic and prosodic ones. Still, Ferguson's original terms have generated a good deal of debate and we have used them here as a starting point for a more complete classification of functions.

First, the notion of *simplification* has been one of the most controversial, and Pine gives a critique of the debate between Newport, Gleitman, and Gleitman (1977) and Furrow, Nelson, and Benedict (1979) about the contribution of simple and complex factors to children's language acquisition. Simplification should now be seen as of limited usefulness as a global explanatory concept for two major reasons. Firstly, what constitutes simplicity with reference to language acquisition and particularly children's language acquisition during the early stages, is not a straightforward matter. In addition, there is the now well-known learnability argument concerning the need for exemplars of at least moderately complex as well as simple structures if the full linguistic system is to be acquired (see Gleitman, Newport, and Gleitman 1984 for discussion). Newport *et al.* (1977) made the distinction between processing simplicity and syntactic simplicity. They regarded child-directed speech as being syntactically complex through factors such as the large proportion of questions, while features like reduced utterance length facilitated processing. The problem is that language can be simple or complex on several dimensions simultaneously including, for example, perceptual salience and phonological structure (see Cruttenden), and notions of complexity or simplicity may simply depend on one's theoretical orientation. Thus, the view that "motherese" was more syntactically complex because of "deletions" relies partly on the assumption that a yes–no question containing an auxiliary verb (*Do you like it?*) is simpler than a yes–no question without an auxiliary (*Like it?*). Global measures such as MLU and proportions of sentence types can tell us little about the overall impact of simplicity or complexity and nothing about the features attended to and processed by the child (i.e. input *versus* intake). What are more informative are the utterance-by-utterance relationships both within and between participants in conversation, and the role of these relationships in directing attention towards currently sensitive areas of development. These are what Nelson describes as "selective focus points of 'hot spots' of engagement and analysis that lead to a heavy concentration of available processing capacity on highly relevant exemplars for stage-relevant acquisition" (Nelson, Heimann, Abuelhaija, and Wroblewski 1989, p. 310).

However, it is now widely accepted that one helpful form of simplification is the reduction of processing demands on the learner. This may be achieved by features such as repetition, routine, memory priming, provision of scaffolding, transparency of meaning, pauses and rate of delivery, "decomposition" of task (see Wesche).

Secondly, the notion of *clarification* has always seemed intuitively appealing, but has generated a certain amount of controversy. Cruttenden comes down in favor of a clarification function for child-directed speech. However, the role of child-directed speech in clarifying phonological structure has been disputed (e.g. Fletcher 1985). This is based on research by Shockey and Bond (1980) showing *increased* phonological reduction in speech addressed to children, and by Bard and Anderson (1983) showing that isolated words have a *lower* level of intelligibility. Cruttenden explains the discrepancies in the literature by reference to children's stage of development and a degree of fine-tuning. Specific forms of clarification can be subsumed under the general heading of intelligibility; for example, increasing the salience of features which would be otherwise unstressed, contracted, or phonologically reduced (see Pine, Richards on auxiliary verb clarification). Other features facilitate form–function mapping or clarify by aiding segmentation. Modifications of timing and intonation, for example, may assist with the identification of word, sentence, and major constituent boundaries (Cruttenden, Wesche). Using repeated sentence frames and recasts can also achieve this function.

Thirdly, *expressive* features have been considered much less, probably because it is more difficult to relate them to general theories of acquisition, and indeed some features which may be determined by the need to express affection or solidarity with the child may look counterproductive in terms of language acquisition (e.g. the use of proper nouns rather than pronouns to refer to the addressee). Similarly, Wesche's chapter suggests that one of the triggers of ungrammatical Foreigner Talk is a high degree of affect and informality. Nevertheless, language which expresses affection and solidarity with the young speaker is frequently assumed to encourage participation in conversation by making it a more rewarding experience. Hence Cruttenden regards as facilitative those features of Baby Talk Phonetics and Baby Talk Prosody which are associated with positive emotion in the child, and which show solidarity by imitating the child's own speech. The nonstandard features noted by Wesche can also be regarded as accommodation as a marker of solidarity, and standard features of Foreigner Discourse which promote positive affect are seen as potentially useful for the second language learner, in particular for their potential role in reducing anxiety. It is in the area of second language learning that factors such as motivation, interest, attitudes to learning and other speakers, and prior experience have been more fully explored, for example in Gardner's "socio-educational model" (Gardner 1983; Gardner, Lalonde, and Pierson 1983).

As well as the three broad categories identified by Ferguson, we would like to include a number of additional functions: *attention factors, feedback, modeling, conversational participation, the teaching of routines.*

Concerning *attention*, focusing the child's attention on the interaction (whether or not the child is an active participant – see Lieven) *and* on relevant aspects of the context is a necessary condition for the acquisition of a language and for successful communication. Here we will briefly mention gaining attention and directing attention to appropriate aspects of the interaction. With respect to gaining attention, Cruttenden notes young children's preference for "Baby Talk" and highlights the potentially facilitative role of prosody in gaining their attention, particular its overall higher pitch and extra-high pitch peaks. In the context of speaking and signing mothers, Gallaway and Woll discuss attention-getters (the use of the child's name, interjections such as *Look!*) and indicate how much caution is required in interpreting this area. Research carried out by Woll and her colleagues indicates that deaf signing mothers expend more energy and use different strategies in creating shared attention in early interaction than do hearing mothers. Directing attention is the third aspect to be considered, and Wesche, for example, discusses the role of prosody and nonlinguistic support (e.g. gesture) in Foreign Discourse in directing attention to aspects of both the situational and the linguistic contexts. Lieven discusses ways in which the child's attention might be directed towards form–meaning pairings in less child-centered cultures, while Conti-Ramsden also points out that atypical language learners may need their attention directing more than normal children do, which might result in an apparently more directive interaction.

The issues of *providing feedback*, that is, giving feedback about the acceptability of utterances, has been discussed by Sokolov and Snow. They point out that even in the absence of overt negative and positive feedback there is now evidence for differential implicit feedback depending on the well-formedness of the child's utterance. Such feedback seems to occur most often when the utterance is at the upper limits of a child's ability and contains only one error. According to Sokolov and Snow, probabilistic models of learning can overcome the absence of totally consistent data.

A related issue, since it can provide information about acceptability and provide the data required for making advances, is that of *modeling*, which can be defined as providing examples of correct utterances and correct conversational structure, either in its own right or as part of the feedback process. The work of Farrar (1990) quoted by Pine and Richards would seem to indicate that the well-substantiated effects of recasts are brought about by their ability to provide data rather than their other conversational functions.

*Facilitating conversational participation* is a function which is achieved by various conversation-sustaining and scaffolding strategies such as contingent responding, giving encouraging feedback, and using turn-eliciting and turn-ceding devices. These include clarification questions and comprehension checks, and repairs.

*Explicit teaching of social routines* (such as *Say Bye-bye*, *Say thank you*) can also be observed; this feature may be less directly connected with the acquisition of the linguistic system, but it provides a way in to the appropriate use of language. It could also be seen as providing an alternative route exploiting different processing mechanisms through the acquisition of formulae which can be segmented and analyzed more fully at a later stage (see Richards 1990a; Lieven; Sokolov and Snow).

The *potentially* facilitative functions of child-directed speech identified and discussed above is summarized below. These categories correspond approximately with the classification in Richards and Gallaway (1993):

> managing attention
> promoting positive affect
> improving intelligibility
> facilitating segmentation
> providing feedback
> provision of correct models
> reducing processing load
> encouraging conversational participation
> explicit teaching of social routines

It is important to remember that almost all of these functions occur as part of normal conversational behavior amongst adults. What is crucial therefore is the way in which they mesh with the structure of discourse and with the child's current linguistic systems. It should also be noted that the functions described are not independent. Features which are described as semantically contingent frequently may act to keep the conversation going, aid segmentation through partial or expanded repetition, promote positive affect, clarify, and provide negative feedback and correct models. It is the multifunctional nature of child-directed utterances which makes unequivocal statements about facilitation so difficult. As Pine points out, far too few specific links have been made between carefully delineated aspects of input and linguistic advances. It may seem reasonable that the above functions would make a difference, and there is much evidence that semantic contingency, for example, is facilitative, but the final causal link (Richards) is frequently lacking. Nevertheless, there has been at least partial success in relating the functions of input variables such as recasts (Farrar 1990) and *yes–no* questions (Richards and Robinson 1993) to specific areas of linguistic development in the child.

## 4        Implications for professionals

### 4.1      *Education*

There can be no doubt that work on input and interaction has influenced the work of teachers at nursery, infants, and junior level. In the United Kingdom volumes such as *Learning through interaction* (Wells 1981) and *The meaning makers* (Wells 1986a) have become standard textbooks in teacher education, particularly for courses in language and literacy. As one might suspect from Wesche's chapter in this volume, the influence of research into first language interaction can also be seen on the training of second language teachers (e.g. Ellis 1984). Too little is known about teachers' understanding of the theoretical underpinnings underlying their practice, but research is currently being carried out (Drever work in progress) into the nature of teachers' personal theories of the language acquisition process and the origins of these. What is already becoming clear is that specialist language teachers and those concerned with the general language development of their pupils and students do have strongly held views on how language is acquired and the types of input which will be beneficial. What is equally clear is that such beliefs can have a dramatic effect on classroom practice, whether they are derived from courses of training or based on nothing more than personal intuitions.

Regrettably, perhaps inevitably, even the models offered by institutions of teacher education are frequently oversimplified. There is often a lack of awareness of the controversies in the field, and an expectation that a review of the research will unequivocally provide guidance to the practitioner. The chapter by Richards in this volume gives an indication of how such oversimplification of the issues might come about. A good example is a profile sheet used in one British university for recording the progress of prospective teachers of foreign languages. This requires somewhat overoptimistically an "Understanding of the processes of language acquisition and their implications for FL classrooms" and "Understanding of the factors which affect the learning of FLs" (*Profiling and partnership* 1991, p. 9). It appears that ticks against these items are a prerequisite for passing the course. The circulation of such a document to all teacher-training institutions in the United Kingdom can only make life more difficult for those who wish to take a more differentiated approach in seeking to inform practice through research.

Personal theories of language acquisition and a lack of understanding of issues such as the possible role of feedback can be used as a justification of classroom practice. This is particularly evident in discussions of highly controversial and politicized areas such as error correction and the formal teaching of grammar where terms such as "correction," "error," and "teaching" are themselves not clearly defined. An example is provided by a recent letter from a headteacher to the *Times Educational Supplement* (Taylor 1992) which attacks the structured teaching of language and the correction of errors even for older children, on the grounds that "If we were 'taught' to use language in the first place – taught to speak – the chances are we would never learn" (p. 24). Ironically, Lieven's chapter indicates that, in at least one culture, language is taught, and that development proceeds normally. Similarly, because of the range of meanings subsumed under "correction," the extent to which current views on the correction of language is influenced, directly or indirectly, by Brown and Hanlon's (1970) finding of a lack of overt correction of grammar, and to what extent this is to do with politicized issues to do with Standard English, is difficult to gauge. The unconsidered application of assumptions about early development to entirely different settings and developmental stages (in this case to teenagers) is far from uncommon in education and is an example of what Richards refers to as the "holistic fallacy." What seems to be lacking is a clearer view of the different forms and functions of feedback in the classroom. Although this is apparent among some researchers and academics (e.g. Tomasello and Herron 1989 on foreign language classrooms) it appears lacking among practitioners. Sokolov and Snow initially draw attention to the distinction between the conditioning and information-providing views of negative feedback, and their chapter touches on a series of oppositions and dimensions which are capable of providing a more informed framework for discussing classroom issues. These include explicit *versus* implicit feedback, positive *versus* negative evidence, and the signaling of errors *versus* provision of data.

Both Pine and Richards point out the need to move beyond the investigation of generally facilitative effects involving global measures of input and language acquisition. Such approaches, with their lack of clear hypotheses and reliance on *post hoc* explanations, have been largely unsuccessful in specifying the mechanisms by which language learners engage with and make use of the input available to them. It seems to us that even much of the best-informed current educational practice draws on a restricted body of research which underestimates the complexity of the language acquisition process and both overestimates the strength of evidence for the effectiveness of certain interaction styles and also fails to distinguish between different domains of language and different stages of development. Pine in particular regards the real benefits of input research as being a means for making inferences about processes and mechanisms rather than discovering what is generally facilitative. In fact, it is only when the mechanisms which mediate the observed relationships between input and language development are understood that the research into input and interaction can be exploited by practitioners.

One advantage of research into the registers addressed to foreign and second language learners, or to the elderly for that matter, is that, unlike young children acquiring language, the recipients are able to reflect on their experiences and express their views. Wesche's chapter contains some important information for teachers, some encouraging and some cautionary. For example, unless clearly signaled by the teacher, some features of Foreigner Discourse, such as restating information in an alternative form, can be misinterpreted by learners as additional rather than alternative information. Similarly, Wesche provides a telling example of how elaboration in an attempt to make meaning more transparent can interfere with syntactic parsing. On the other hand, a large number of studies are referred to in which Foreigner Discourse is found to be facilitative in as far as comprehension is enhanced. In section 2.3 we discussed the possible implications of the effect of interlanguage as a major constituent of the learner's linguistic environment, pointing out the lack of a clear causal link between exposure to interlanguage and restrictions in learners' command of the target language. In both foreign and second language classrooms, it seems quite clear from Wesche's account that the advantages of engaging learners in small group and pair-work activities can outweigh any possible disadvantages of interacting with non-native speakers. Not only is participation in conversation increased when conversing with another non-native speaker, rather than with a native speaker in these situations, but conversations are more varied and there is more negotiation of meaning, with no evidence of increased error rates.

In general, evaluating classroom discourse from a perspective informed by the main body of parent–child interaction has not been particularly enlightening. The classroom situation diverges from the child's early linguistic environment in too many ways (e.g. number of interlocutors, age of children) for straightforward comparisons to be made. In particular, the ultimate aim of classroom interaction is likely to be very different from that of conversational interaction; teachers appear to be more concerned with facilitating various tasks and thinking processes, passing on information, or developing often unspecified language skills, rather than with language acquisition. It has been frequently claimed that classrooms where a teacher-dominated and overcontrolling atmosphere reigns, are not likely to be facilitative for learning, and much classroom analysis has been cited as alleged evidence for this. However, the question of what is, or is not, being facilitated and the evidence for any facilitation in the long term (i.e. the eventual level of academic achievement such as acquisition of knowledge, literacy, or verbal fluency displayed by children educated in largely teacher-dominated classrooms) is all but completely lacking.

Geekie and Raban's contribution to this area is to move away from global claims and to focus on a particular area where they have observed classroom interaction closely paralleling an aspect of early mother–child interaction. Their description of a particular teacher with her developing writers shows her using structured support for their tasks, and documents the gradual withdrawal of this support. One implication here is that general statements on the nature of classroom interaction should be avoided as they are bound to be oversimplified. Further research is required to investigate the likely facilitative nature of this type of structured support, and to examine whether teachers can, or should, be trained in providing it.

## 4.2    Intervention

What conclusions can be drawn from the research which will help professionals dealing with language-delayed and language-disordered children, and with profoundly deaf children acquiring spoken language? The lack of strong evidence for facilitative effects, combined with the dearth of information about what atypical children really need, seems to point to a conservative approach: we are really still far from knowing what type of intervention is needed. In addition, as Conti-Ramsden points out, when suggesting alternative interaction strategies, practitioners must not imply that parents are themselves failing to provide a good linguistic environment for their children.

However, research lags behind the needs of the practitioner, who must, in the meanwhile, assist such atypical children and their parents. It is clear that increasing understanding of the issues involved should certainly underpin future developments in intervention strategies, and should increase our sensitivity to the wide range of possible linguistic environments in which children successfully acquire language. Claims about possible unfacilitative environments have been made in the past; such claims have often been based on oversimplified assumptions and should now be avoided.

Understanding which functions are likely to be achieved by different features of child-directed speech is likely to be a valuable asset to future discussions. Gaining and directing attention has to be a feature of early interaction and can be achieved in various ways; Gallaway and Woll's chapter describes research which indicates that deaf parents may deal with this function differently from, and probably more effectively than, hearing parents of deaf children. Separating out this function and examining what is needed in an atypical situation is more likely to shed light on good intervention practices than global comparisons or the "scattershot" approach to find a so-called facilitative linguistic environment.

## NOTE

1 In this chapter, all references without dates are to the authors' contribution to this volume.

# References

Adams, C., and Bishop, D. V. M. 1989. Conversational characteristics of children with semantic–pragmatic disorder, I: Exchange structure, turntaking, repairs and cohesion. *British Journal of Disorders of Communication*, 24, 211–39.

Akhtar, N., Dunham, F., and Dunham, P. J. 1991. Directive interactions and early vocabulary development: the role of joint attentional focus. *Journal of Child Language*, 18, 41–9.

Aksu-Koç, A., and Slobin, D. I. 1985. The acquisition of Turkish. In D. I. Slobin (ed.), *The crosslinguistic study of language acquisition*, vol. I. Hillsdale, NJ: Erlbaum.

Allen, G. D., and Hawkins, S. 1980. Phonological rhythm: definition and development. In G. H. Yeni-Komshian, J. F. Kavanagh, and C. A. Ferguson (eds.), *Child phonology*, vol. I: *Production*. New York: Academic Press.

Andersen, E. S., Dunlea, A., and Kekelis, L. S. 1984. Blind children's language: resolving some differences. *Journal of Child Language*, 11, 645–64.

Anderson, B. J. 1979. Parents' strategies for achieving conversational interactions with their young hearing-impaired children. In A. Simmons-Martin and D. R. Calvert (eds.), *Parent–infant intervention*. New York: Grune and Stratton.

Andrews, V., and Bernstein Ratner, N. 1987. Patterns of maternal and paternal response to language-learners' verbalizations. Paper presented at the American Speech and Hearing Association Convention, New Orleans.

Arthur, B., Weiner, R., Culver, M., Ja Lee, Y., and Thomas, D. 1980. The register of impersonal discourse to foreigners: verbal adjustments to foreign accent. In D. Larsen-Freeman (ed.), *Discourse analysis in second language acquisition research*. Rowley, MA: Newbury House.

Au, T. K., and Markman, E. 1987. Acquiring word meanings via linguistic contrast. *Child Development*, 57, 217–36.

Austin, J. L. 1962. *How to do things with words*. Oxford: Oxford University Press.

Baetens-Beardsmore, H. 1990. The bilingual school for mixed populations: a case study. *Bilingualism in education: theory and practice* (Brussels Pre-Prints in Linguistics). Brussels: Vrije Universiteit Brussel.

Baker, C. L. 1979. Syntactic theory and the projection problem. *Linguistic Inquiry*, 10, 533–81.

Baker, N. D., and Nelson, K. E. 1984. Recasting and related conversational techniques for triggering syntactic advances in young children. *First Language*, 5, 3–22.

Bandura, A. 1977. *Social learning theory*. Englewood Cliffs, NJ: Prentice Hall.

270

Baran, J., Laufer, M., and Daniloff, R. 1977. Phonological contrastivity in conversation: a comparative study of voice onset time. *Journal of Phonetics*, 5, 339–50.

Bard, E. G., and Anderson, A. 1983. The unintelligibility of speech to children. *Journal of Child Language*, 10, 265–92.

Barnes, D. 1976. *From communication to curriculum*. Harmondsworth: Penguin.

Barnes, D., Britton, J., and Torbe, M. 1986. *Language, the learner and the school*, 3rd edn. Harmondsworth: Penguin.

Barnes, S., Gutfreund, M., Satterly, D., and Wells, G. 1983. Characteristics of adult speech which predict children's language development. *Journal of Child Language*, 10, 65–84.

Barton, M., and Tomasello, M. 1991. Joint attention and conversation in mother–infant sibling triads. *Child Development*, 62, 517–29.

Bates, E. 1976. *Language and context: the acquisition of pragmatics*. New York: Academic Press.

1979. Peer relations and the acquisition of language. In M. Lewis and L. Rosenblum (eds.), *Friendship and peer relations*. New York: Wiley.

Bates, E., Bretherton, I., Beeghly-Smith, M., and McNew, S. 1982. Social bases of language development: a reassessment. In H. W. Reese and L. P. Lipsitt (eds.), *Advances in child development and behavior*, vol. XVI. New York: Academic Press.

Bates, E., Bretherton, I., and Snyder, L. 1988. *From first words to grammar: individual differences and dissociable mechanisms*. Cambridge University Press.

Bates, E., and MacWhinney, B. 1979. A functionalist approach to the acquisition of grammar. In E. Ochs and B. Schieffelin (eds.), *Developmental pragmatics*. New York: Academic Press.

Bates, E., and MacWhinney, B. 1987. Competition, variation, and language learning. In B. MacWhinney (ed.), *Mechanisms of language acquisition*. Hillsdale, NJ: Erlbaum.

Bates, E., and Volterra, V. 1985. On the invention of language: an alternative view. Commentary on Goldin-Meadow and Mylander. In *Monographs of the Society for Research in Child Development*, 49.

Bavin, E. forthcoming. The acquisition of Warlpiri as a first language. In D. I. Slobin (ed.), *The crosslinguistic study of language acquisition*, vol. III. Hillsdale, NJ: Erlbaum.

Bee, H. L., Barnard, H. E., Eyres, S. J., Gray, C. A., Hammond, M. A., Spietz, A. L., Snyder, C., and Clark, B. 1982. Prediction of IQ and language skill from perinatal status, child performance, family characteristics, and mother–infant interaction. *Child Development*, 53, 1134–56.

Beebe, L. 1985. Input: choosing the right stuff. In S. Gass and C. Madden (eds.), *Input in second language acquisition*. Rowley, MA: Newbury House.

Bellinger, D. 1979. Changes in the explicitness of mothers' directiveness as children age. *Journal of Child Language*, 6, 443–58.

Bennett-Kastor, T. 1988. *Analyzing children's language: methods and theories*. Oxford: Blackwell.

Berko Gleason, J. 1973. Code-switching in children's language. In T. Moore (ed.), *Cognitive development and the acquisition of language*. New York; Academic Press.

1975. Fathers and other strangers: men's speech to young children. *Georgetown University Roundtable on Language and Linguistics*. Washington, DC: Georgetown University Press.

Berman. R. 1985. The acquisition of Hebrew. In D. I. Slobin (ed.), *The cross-linguistic study of language acquisition*, vol. I. Hillsdale, NJ. Erlbaum.

Bernstein Ratner, N. 1984a. Patterns of vowel modification in mother–child speech. *Journal of Child Language*, 11, 557–78.

1984b. Phonological rule usage in mother–child speech. *Journal of Phonetics*, 12, 245–54.

1986. Durational cues which mark clause boundaries in mother–child speech. *Journal of Phonetics*, 14, 303–10.

1988. Patterns of parental vocabulary selection in speech to very young children. *Journal of Child Language*, 15, 481–92.

1990. Maternal input and unusual phonological behaviour: a case study. Paper presented at the Fifth International Congress for the Study of Child Language, Budapest, July 1990.

Bernstein Ratner, N., and Luberoff, A. 1984. Cues to post-vocalic voicing in mother–child speech. *Journal of Phonetics*, 12, 285–9.

Bernstein Ratner, N., and Pye, C. 1984. Higher pitch in BT is not universal: acoustic evidence from Quiché Mayan. *Journal of Child Language*, 2, 515–22.

Berwick, R. 1985. *The acquisition of syntactic knowledge*. Cambridge, MA: MIT Press.

Bickerton, D. 1981. *Roots of language*. Ann Arbor, MI: Karoma.

1984. The language bioprogram hypothesis. *Behavioral and Brain Sciences*, 7, 173–221.

Bishop, D. V. M. 1982. Comprehension of spoken, written and signed sentences in childhood language disorders. *Journal of Child Psychology and Psychiatry*, 23, 1–20.

Bishop, D. V. M., and Adams, C. 1989. Conversational characteristics of children with semantic–pragmatic disorders, II: What features lead to a judgement of inappropriacy? *British Journal of Disorders of Communication*, 24, 241–63.

Bishop, D. V. M., and Mogford, K. 1988. *Language development in exceptional circumstances*. Edinburgh: Churchill Livingstone.

Bishop, J., and Gregory, S. 1985. Mothers and teachers looking at books with deaf children. *Child Language Teaching and Therapy*, 1, 149–61.

Bliss, L. 1988. Modal usage by preschool children. *Journal of Applied Experimental Psychology*, 9, 253–61.

Blount, B. G. 1977. Ethnographer and caretaker–child interaction. In C. E. Snow and C. A. Ferguson (eds.), *Talking to children: language input and acquisition*. Cambridge University Press.

Blount, B. G., and Padgug, E. J. 1977. Prosodic, paralinguistic, and interactional features in parent–child speech: English and Spanish. *Journal of Child Language*, 4, 67–86.

Bodner-Johnson, B. 1985. The deaf child in the family: interactions and school achievement. In I. G. Taylor (ed.), *The education of the deaf: current perspectives*, vol. I (Proceedings of the International Congress on Education of the Deaf). London: Croom Helm.

Bohannon, J. N., and Hirsh-Pasek, K. 1984. Do children say as they're told? A new perspective on motherese. In L. Feagans, C. Garvey, and R. Golinkoff (eds.), *The origins and growth of communication*. Norwood, NJ: Ablex.

Bohannon, J. N., MacWhinney, B., and Snow, C. 1991. No negative evidence revisited: beyond learnability: or who has to prove what to whom. *Developmental Psychology*, 26, 211–26.

Bohannon, J. N., and Marquis, A. 1977. Children's control of adult speech. Child Development, 48, 1002–8.

Bohannon, J. N., and Stanowicz, L. 1988. The issue of negative evidence: adult responses to children's language errors. *Developmental Psychology*, 24, 684–9.

Bohannon, J. N., and Warren-Leubecker, A. 1988. Recent developments in speech to children: we've come a long way, baby-talk. *Language Sciences*, 10, 89–110.

Bondurant, J. L., Romeo, D. J., and Kretschmer, R. 1983. Language behaviors of mothers of children with normal and delayed language. *Language, Speech and Hearing Services in Schools*, 14, 233–42.

Bonvillian, J. D., Orlansky, M. D., and Novak, L. L. 1983. Early sign language acquisition and its relation to cognitive and motor development. In J. Kyle and B. Woll (eds.), *Language in sign*. London: Croom Helm.

Bornstein, M., and Ruddy, M. 1984. Infant attention and maternal stimulation: prediction of cognitive and linguistic development in singletons and twins. In H. Bouma and D. Douwhuis (eds.), *Attention and performance*, vol. X: *Control of language processes*. London: Erlbaum.

Braidi, S. 1990. A theoretical framework for the interaction of input and syntactic principles and parameters in the formation of second language grammars. Ph.D. dissertation, University of Delaware.

1991. Reanalyzing input effects in second language acquisition from a universal grammar perspective. Paper presented at the Second Language Research Forum, Los Angeles, California.

Braine, M. 1991. What sort of innate structure is needed to bootstrap into syntax? Paper presented at the Workshop on crosslinguistic and cross-populations contributions to the theory of acquisition, Hebrew University, Jerusalem.

Bresnan, J. 1982. *The mental representation of grammatical relations*. Cambridge, MA: MIT Press.

Bridges, A. 1979. Directing two-year-olds' attention: some clues to understanding. *Journal of Child Language*, 6, 211–26.

1980. SVO Comprehension strategies reconsidered: the evidence of individual patterns of response. *Journal of Child Language*, 7, 89–104.

Bridges, A., Sinha, C., and Walkerdine, V. 1981. The development of comprehension. In G. Wells (ed.), *Learning through interaction: the study of language development*. Cambridge University Press.

Brill, R. G. 1969. The superior IQs of deaf children of deaf parents. *The California Palms*, 15, 1–4.

Brinich, P. 1980. Childhood deafness and maternal control. *Journal of Communication Disorders*, 13, 75–81.

Broen, P. 1972. The verbal environment of the language-learning child. *Monographs of the American Speech and Hearing Association*, 17.

Brown, J. S., Collins, A., and Duguid, P. 1988. *Situated cognition and the culture of learning*. Institute for Research on Learning, Report No. 88–0008, Bolt Beranek and Newman.

Brown, R. 1973. *A first language: the early stages*. London: Allen and Unwin.

1977. Introduction. In C. E. Snow and C. A. Ferguson (eds.), *Talking to children: language input and acquisition*. Cambridge University Press.

Brown, R., and Bellugi, U. 1964. Three processes in the child's acquisition of syntax. *Harvard Educational Review*, 34, 133–51.

Brown, R., and Hanlon, C. 1970. Derivational complexity and order of acquisition in child speech. In J. R. Hayes (ed.), *Cognition and the development of language*. New York: Wiley.

Brulhart, M. 1986. Foreigner talk in the ESL classroom: interactional adjustments to adult students at two language proficiency levels. *TESL Canada Journal*, special issue no. 1, 29–42.

Bruner, J. S. 1975. From communication to language: a psychological perspective. *Cognition*, 3, 255–87.

1978. Berlyne Memorial Lecture. Acquiring the uses of language. *Canadian Journal of Psychology*, 32, 204–18.

1983a. *Child's talk: learning to use language*. Oxford University Press.

1983b. The acquisition of pragmatic commitments. In R. M. Golinkoff (ed.), *The transition from prelinguistic to linguistic communication*. Hillsdale, NJ: Erlbaum.

1986. *Actual minds, possible worlds*. Cambridge, MA: Harvard University Press.

Bruner, J. S, Goodnow, J. J., and Austin, G. A. 1956. *A study of thinking*. New York: Wiley.

Bruner, J., and Haste, H. (eds.), 1987. *Making sense: the child's construction of the world*. London: Methuen.

Bryan, T. 1986. A review of studies on learning disabled children's communicative competence. In R. L. Schiefelbusch (ed.), *Language competence: assessment and intervention*. London: Taylor and Francis.

Budwig, N., and Wiley, A. 1991. The contribution of caregivers' input to children's talk about agency and pragmatic control. Paper presented at the Child Language Seminar, University of Manchester, March 1991.

Buium, N., Rynders, J., and Turnure, J. 1973. Early maternal linguistic environment of normal and nonnormal language learning children. *Proceedings of the 81st Annual Convention of the American Psychological Association*, 79–80.

Burger, S. 1989. Content-based ESL in a sheltered psychology course: input, output and outcomes. *TESL Canada Journal*, 6, 45–59.

Bygate, M. 1988. Units of oral expression and language learning in small group interaction. *Applied Linguistics*, 9, 59–82.

Bynon, J. 1968. Berber nursery language. *Transactions of the Philological Society*, 107–61.

Bzoch, F. R., and League, R. 1970. *Receptive–Expressive–Emergent Language Scale*. Gainesville, FL: Computer Management Corporation.

Carroll, S., Roberge, Y., and Swain, M. 1991. The role of feedback in adult second language acquisition: error correction and morphological generalizations. Manuscript, Modern Language Centre, The Ontario Institute for Studies in Education, Toronto.

Caselli, M. C. 1983. Communication to language: deaf children's and hearing children's development compared. *Sign Language Studies*, 39, 113–44.

Cathcart-Strong, R. 1986. Input generation by young second language learners. *TESOL Quarterly*, 20, 515–30.

Cazden, C. 1965. Environmental assistance to the child's acquisition of grammar. Unpublished doctoral dissertation, Harvard University.

1988. Environmental assistance revisited: variation and functional equivalence. In F. S. Kessel (ed.), *The development of language and language researchers: essays in honor of Roger Brown*. Hillsdale, NJ: Erlbaum.

Chadderton, J. H., Tucker, I. G., and Hostler, M. E. 1985. The responsiveness of mothers of young hearing-impaired children to their child's communicative initiations. *Journal of the British Association of Teachers of the Deaf*, 9, 36–44.

Chafetz, J., Feldman, H. M., and Wareham, N. L. 1992. 'There car': ungrammatical parentese. *Journal of Child Language*, 19, 473–80.

Chapman, R. S. 1981. Mother–child interaction in the second year of life: its role in language development. In R. L. Schiefelbusch and D. Bricker (eds.), *Early language: acquisition and intervention*. Baltimore: University Park Press.

Chaudron, C. 1982. Vocabulary elaboration in teachers' speech to L2 learners. *Studies in Second Language Acquisition*, 4, 170–80.

1983a. Simplification of input: topic reinstatements and their effects on L2 learners' recognition and recall. *TESOL Quarterly*, 17, 437–58.

1983b. Classroom foreign talk discourse: forms and functions in teachers' questions. In H. W. Seliger and W. H. Long (eds.), *Classroom oriented research in second language acquisition*. Rowley, MA: Newbury House.

1985a. Intake: on models and methods for discovering learners' processing of input. *Studies in Second Language Acquisition*, 7, 1–14.

1985b. A method for examining the input/intake distinction. In S. Gass and C. Madden (eds.), *Input in second language acquisition*. Rowley, MA: Newbury House.

1985c. Comprehension, comprehensibility, and learning in the second language classroom. *Studies in Second Language Acquisition*, 7, 216–32.

1988. *Second language classrooms: research on teaching and learning*. Cambridge University Press.

1991. Validation in second language classroom research: the role of observation. In R. Phillipson, E. Kellerman, L. Selinker, M. Sharwood-Smith, and M. Swain (eds.), *Foreign language pedagogy research: a commemorative volume for Claus Faerch*. Clevedon, England: Multilingual Matters.

Chaudron, C., Lubin, J., Sasaki, Y., and Grigg, T. 1986. *An investigation of procedures for evaluating lecture listening comprehension*. Technical Report No. 5, Center for Second Language Classroom Research/Social Science Research Institute, University of Hawaii at Manoa.

Chaudron, C., and Richards, J. 1986. The effect of discourse markers on the comprehension of lectures. *Applied Linguistics*, 9, 113–27.

Cheseldine, S., and McConkey, R. 1979. Parental speech to young Down's syndrome children: an intervention study. *American Journal of Mental Deficiency*, 83, 612–20.

Cheskin, A. 1981. The verbal environment provided by hearing mothers for their young deaf children. *Journal of Communication Disorders*, 14, 485–96.

1982. The use of language by hearing mothers of deaf children. *Journal of Communication Disorders*, 15, 145–53.

Chomsky, N. 1965. *Aspects of the theory of syntax*. Cambridge, MA: MIT Press.

1986. Changing perspectives on the nature of acquisition of language. Keynote address, Boston University Child Language Conference, October.

Clancy, P. 1985. The acquisition of Japanese. In D. I. Slobin (ed.), *The cross-linguistic study of language acquisition*, vol. I. Hillsdale, NJ: Erlbaum.

1986. The acquisition of communicative style in Japanese. In B. B. Schieffelin and E. Ochs (eds.), *Language socialization across cultures*. Cambridge University Press.

1989a. A case study in language socialisation: Korean wh-questions. *Discourse Processes*, 12, 169–91.

1989b. Form and function in the acquisition of Korean wh-questions, *Journal of Child Language*, 16, 323–47.

Clark, H. H., and Clark E. V. 1977. *Psychology and language*. New York: Harcourt Brace Jovanich.

Clarke-Stewart, K., Vanderstoep, L., and Killian, G. 1979. Analyses and replication of mother–child relations at two years of age. *Child Development*, 50, 777–93.

Clyne, M. 1968. Zum Pidgin – Deutsch der Gastarbeiter. *Zeitschrift für Mundartforschung*, 35, 130–9.

1977. Multilingualism and pidginization in Australian industry. *Ethnic Studies*, 1, 40–55.

1978. Some remarks on foreign talk. In N. Dittmar, H. Haberland, T. Skutnabb-Kangas, and U. Telemann (eds.), *Papers from the first Scandinavian–German symposium on the language of immigrant workers and their children*. Linguistgruppen, Ruskilde Universiteits Center.

Cohen, L., and Manion, L. 1985. *Research methods in education*, 2nd edn. London: Croom Helm.

Collis, G. 1977. Visual co-orientation and maternal speech. In H. R. Schaffer (ed.), *Studies in mother–child interaction*. London: Academic Press.

Constable, C. M. 1983. Creating communicative context. In H. Winitz (ed.), *Treating language disorders*. Baltimore, MD: University Park Press.

1986. The application of scripts in the organization of language intervention contexts. In K. Nelson (ed.), *Event knowledge*. Hillsdale, NJ: Erlbaum.

Conti-Ramsden, G. 1985. Mothers in dialogue with language-impaired children. *Topics in Language Disorders*, 5, 58–68.

1989. Parent–child interaction in mental handicap: an evaluation. In M. Beveridge, G. Conti-Ramsden, and I. Leudar (eds.), *Language and communication in mentally handicapped people*. London: Chapman and Hall.

1990. Maternal recasts and other contingent replies to language-impaired children. *Journal of of Speech and Hearing Disorders*, 55, 262–74.

Conti-Ramsden, G., and Dykins, J. 1991. Mother–child interactions with language-impaired children and their siblings. *British Journal of Disorders of Communication*, 26, 337–54.

Conti-Ramsden, G., and Friel-Patti, S. 1983. Mothers' discourse adjustments to language-impaired and non-language-impaired children. *Journal of Speech and Hearing Disorders*, 48, 360–7.

1984. Mother–child dialogues: a comparison of normal and language impaired children. *Journal of Communication Disorders*, 17, 19–35.

Conti-Ramsden, G., and Gunn, M. 1986. The development of conversational disability: a case study. *British Journal of Disorders of Communication*, 21, 339–51.

Cook, T. D., and Campbell, D. T. 1979. *Quasi-experimentation: design and analysis issues for field settings*. Boston MA: Houghton Mifflin.

Cook, V. J. 1985. Chomsky's universal grammar and second language learning. *Applied Linguistics*, 6, 2–18.

1988. *Chomsky's Universal Grammar*. Oxford: Blackwell.

1989. Universal grammar theory and the classroom. *System*, 17, 169–81.

1991. *Second language learning and language teaching*. London: Edward Arnold.

Corder, S. 1967. The significance of learners' errors. *International Review of Applied Linguistics*, 5, 161–70.

Corsaro, W. 1981. Communicative processes in studies of social organization. *Text*, 1, 5–63.

Cross, T. G. 1977. Mothers' speech adjustments: the contributions of selected child listener variables. In C. E. Snow and C. A. Ferguson (eds.), *Talking to children: language input and acquisition*. Cambridge University Press.

1978. Motherese: its association with the rate of syntactic acquisition in young children. In N. Waterson and C. Snow (eds.), *The development of communication*. Chichester: Wiley.

1981. The linguistic experience of slow learners. In A. R. Nesdale, C. Pratt, R. Grieve, J. Field, D. Illingworth, and J. Hogben (eds.), *Advances in child development* (Proceedings of the First National Conference on Child Development). University of Western Australia, Nedlands.

1984. Habilitating the language-impaired child: ideas from studies of parent–child interaction. *Topics in Language Disorders*, 4, 1–14.

Cross, T. G., Johnson-Morris, J. E., and Nienhuys, T. G. 1980. Linguistic feedback and maternal speech: comparisons of mothers addressing hearing and hearing-impaired children. *First Language*, 1, 163–89.

Cross, T. G., and Morris, J. E. 1980. Linguistic feedback and maternal speech: comparisons of mothers addressing hearing and hearing-impaired children. *First Language*, 1, 8–121.

Cross, T. G., Nienhuys, T. G., and Kirkman, M. 1985. Parent–child interaction in receptively disabled children: some determinants of maternal style. In K. E. Nelson (ed.), *Children's language*, vol. V. Hillsdale, NJ: Erlbaum.

Cruttenden, A. 1986. *Intonation*. Cambridge University Press.

Curtiss, S. 1977. *Genie: a psycholinguistic study of a modern-day 'wild child'*. New York: Academic Press.

Day, E., and Shapson, S. 1991. Integrating formal and functional approaches to language teaching in French immersion: an experimental study. *Language Learning*, 41, 25–58.

Day, R. (ed.) 1986. *Talking to learn: conversation in second language acquisition*. Rowley, MA: Newbury House.

De Villiers, J. 1975. Learning how to use verbs: lexical coding and the influence of verbs. *Journal of Child Language*, 12, 587–95.

1985. Limited input? Limited structure. Commentary on Goldin-Meadow and Mylander. *Monographs of the Society for Research in Child Development*, 49.

De Villiers, J., de Villiers, P., and Hoban, E. 1993. The central problem of functional categories in the English syntax of oral deaf children. In H. Tager-Flusberg (ed.), *Constraints on language acquisition: studies of atypical children*. Hillsdale, NJ: Lawrence Erlbaum.

DeCaspar, A. J., and Fifer, W. P. 1980. Of human bonding: newborns prefer their mothers' voices. *Science*, 208, 1174–6.

Della Corte, M., Benedict, H., and Klein, D. 1983. The relationship of pragmatic dimensions of mothers' speech to the referential–expressive distinction. *Journal of Child Language*, 10, 35–43.

Demetras, M., Post, K., and Snow, C. 1986. Feedback to first-language learners. *Journal of Child Language*, 13, 275–92.

Demos, V. 1982. The role of affect in early childhood: an exploratory study. In E. Tronick (ed.), *Social interchange in infancy: affect, cognition and communication*. Baltimore, MD: University Park Press.

Demuth, K. 1986. Prompting routines in the language socialization of Basotho children. In B. B. Schieffelin and E. Ochs (eds.), *Language socialization across cultures*. Cambridge University Press.

Derwing, B. 1990. Speech rate is no simple matter: rate adjustment and NS-NNS communicative success. *Studies in Second Language Acquisition*, 12, 303–13.

Dore, J. 1974. A pragmatic description of early language development. *Journal of Psycholinguistic Research*, 4, 343–51.

Doughty, C., and Pica, T. 1986. 'Information gap' tasks: do they facilitate second language acquisition? *TESOL Quarterly*, 20, 305–25.

Dromi, E., and Ringwald-Frimerman, D. 1990. The effects of input characteristics on lexical learning by hearing-impaired children. Paper presented at the International Conference for the Study of Child Language, Budapest.

Dunn, J. F., and Kendrick, C. 1982. The speech of 2- and 3-year-olds to infant siblings: baby talk and the context of communication. *Journal of Child Language*, 9, 579–95.

Dunn, J. F., and Munn, P. 1985. Becoming a family member: family conflict and the development of social understanding in the 2nd year. *Child Development*, 56, 764–74.

Dunn, J. F., and Shatz, M. 1989. Becoming a conversationalist despite (or because of) having an older sibling. *Child Development*, 60, 399–410.

Durkin, K. 1987. Minds and language: social cognition, social interaction and the acquisition of language. *Mind and Language*, 2, 105–40.

Early, M. 1985. Input and interaction in content classrooms: foreigner talk and teacher talk in classroom discourse. Ph.D. dissertation, University of California, Los Angeles.

Edmondson, W. 1986. Discourse worlds in the classroom and in foreign language learning. *Studies in Second Language Acquisition*, 7, 159–68.

Edwards, D., and Mercer, N. 1986. Context and continuity: classroom discourse and the development of shared knowledge. In K. Durkin (ed.), *Language development in the school years*. London: Croom Helm.

1987. *Common knowledge: the development of understanding in the classroom*. London: Routledge.

Ehrlich, S., Avery, P., and Yorio, C. 1989. Discourse structure and the negation of comprehensible input. *Studies in Second Language Acquisition*, 11, 397–414.

Eisenstein, E. 1979. *The printing press as agent of change*. Cambridge University Press.

Ellis, R. 1984. *Classroom second language development*. Oxford: Pergamon.

 1985a. *Understanding second language acquisition*. Oxford University Press.

 1985b. Teacher–pupil interaction in second language development. In S. Gass and C. Madden (eds.), *Input in second language acquisition*, Rowley, MA: Newbury House.

 1989. Are classroom and naturalistic acquirers the same? A study of the classroom acquisition of German word order rules. *Studies in Second Language Acquisition*, 11, 305–28.

 1991. The interaction hypothesis: a critical evaluation. Paper presented at the RELC Annual Conference, 1991, Singapore. To appear in the Proceedings.

 1992. Comprehension and the acquisition of grammatical knowledge. In R. Courchêne, J. Glidden, C. Thérien, and J. St. John (eds.), *Comprehension-based second language teaching / L'Enseignement des langues secondes axé sur la compréhension*. University of Ottawa Press.

Ellis, R., and Wells, C. G. 1980. Enabling factors in adult–child discourse. *First Language*, 1, 46–62.

Ellis Weismer, S. 1985. Constructive comprehension abilities exhibited by language-disordered children. *Journal of Speech and Hearing Research*, 28, 175–84.

Erbaugh, M. S. 1992. The acquisition of Mandarin. In D. I. Slobin (ed.), *The crosslinguistic study of language acquisition*, vol. III. Hillsdale, NJ: Erlbaum.

Erikson, A., and Simon, H. 1984. Verbal reports as data. *Psychological Review*, 87, 215–51.

Erting, C. 1987. The interactional context of early deaf mother–infant communication. Paper presented at the 1987 International Pragmatics Conference, Antwerp.

Ervin-Tripp, S. 1973. Some strategies for the first years. In T. E. Moore (ed.), *Cognition and the acquisition of language*. New York: Academic Press.

Estes, W. K. 1959. The statistical approach to learning theory. In S. Koch (ed.), *Psychology: a study of a science*, vol. II. New York: McGraw-Hill.

Faerch, C., and Kasper, G. 1986. The role of comprehension in second language learning. *Applied Linguistics*, 7, 257–74.

Farrar, M. J. 1990. Discourse and the acquisition of grammatical morphemes. *Journal of Child Language*, 17, 607–24.

 1992. Negative evidence and grammatical morpheme acquisition. *Developmental Psychology*, 28, 91–9.

Feldman, H., Goldin-Meadow, S., and Gleitman, L. 1978. Beyond Herodotus: the creation of language by linguistically deprived children. In A. Lock (ed.), *Action, gesture and symbol: the emergence of language*. London: Academic Press.

Ferguson, C. A. 1964. Baby talk in six languages. *American Anthropologist*, 66, 103–14.

 1971. Absence of copula and the notion of simplicity: a study of normal speech, baby talk, foreigner talk and pidgins. In D. Hymes (ed.), *Pidginization and creolization of languages*. Cambridge University Press.

1975. Towards a characterisation of English foreigner talk. *Anthropological Linguistics*, 17, 1–14.

1977. Baby talk as a simplified register. In C. E. Snow and C. A. Ferguson (eds.), *Talking to children: language input and acquisition*. Cambridge University Press.

Ferguson, C., and DeBose, C. 1976. Simplified registers, broken languages and pidginization. In A. Valdman (ed.), *Pidgin and creole*. Bloomington: Indiana University Press.

Ferguson, G. A. 1981. *Statistical analysis in psychology and education*, 5th edn. London: McGraw-Hill.

Fernald, A. 1984. The perceptual and affective salience of mothers' speech to infants. In L. Feagans, C. Garvey, and R. Golinkoff (with M. T. Greenberg, C. Harding, and J. Bohannon) (eds.), *The origins and growths of communication*. Norwood, NJ: Ablex.

1985. Four-month-old infants prefer to listen to motherese. *Infant Behaviour and Development*, 8, 181–95.

1989. Intonation and communicative intent in mothers' speech to infants: is the melody the message? *Child Development*, 60, 1497–1510.

1990. From preference to reference: affective and linguistic functions of prosody in speech to infants. Paper presented at the International Conference on Infant Studies, Montreal.

in press. Meaningful melodies in mothers' speech to infants. In H. Papousek, U. Jurgens, and M. Papousek (eds.), *Origins and development of non-verbal vocal communication: evolutionary, comparative, and methodological aspects*. Cambridge University Press.

Fernald, A., and Kuhl, P. K. 1987. Acoustic determinants of infant preference for motherese speech. *Infant Behaviour and Development*, 10, 279–93.

Fernald, A., and Mazzie, C. 1983. Pitch-marking of new and old information in mothers' speech. Paper presented at the Society for Research in Child Development, Detroit. [Reported in Fernald 1984.]

1991. Prosody and focus in speech to infants and adults. *Developmental Psychology*, 27, 209–21.

Fernald, A., and Morikawa, H. 1993. Common themes and cultural variations in Japanese and American's speech to infants. *Child Development*, 64, 637–56.

Fernald, A., and Simon, T. 1984. Expanded intonation contours in mothers' speech to newborns. *Developmental Psychology*, 20, 104–13.

Fernald, A., Taeschner, T., Dunn, J., Papousek, M., De Boysson-Bardies, B., and Fukui, I. 1989. A cross-language study of prosodic modifications in mothers' and fathers' speech to preverbal infants. *Journal of Child Language*, 16, 477–501.

Ferrier, L. J. 1985. Intonation in discourse: talk between 12-month-olds and their mothers. In K. E. Nelson (ed.), *Children's language*, vol. V. Hillsdale NJ: Erlbaum.

Fischer, M. A. 1987. Mother–child interactions with preverbal children with Down syndrome. *Journal of Speech and Hearing Disorders*, 52, 179–90.

Fletcher, P. 1985. *A child's learning of English*. Oxford: Blackwell.

Forrester, M. A. 1988. Young children's polyadic conversation monitoring skills. *First Language*, 7, 145–58.

Fortescue, M., and Olsen, L. L. 1992. The acquisition of West Greenlandic. In D. I. Slobin (ed.), *The crosslinguistic study of language acquisition*, vol. III. Hillsdale, NJ: Erlbaum.

Freed, B. 1978. Foreigner talk: a study of speech adjustments made by native speakers of English in conversations with non-native speakers. Ph.D. dissertation, University of Pennsylvania, Philadelphia.

  1980. Talking to foreigners versus talking to children: similarities and differences. In R. Scarcella and S. Krashen (eds.), *Research in second language acquisition*. Rowley, MA: Newbury House.

Frith, U. 1989. *Autism: explaining the enigma*. Oxford: Basil Blackwell.

Furrow, D., and Nelson, K. 1984. Environmental correlates of individual differences in language acquisition. *Journal of Child Language*, 11, 523–34.

  1986. A further look at the motherese hypothesis: a reply to Gleitman, Newport and Gleitman. *Journal of Child Language*, 13, 163–76.

Furrow, D., Nelson, K., and Benedict, H. 1979. Mothers' speech to children and syntactic development: some simple relationships. *Journal of Child Language*, 6, 423–42.

Gaies, S. 1977. The nature of linguistic input in formal second language learning: linguistic and communicative strategies in ESL teachers' classroom language. In H. D. Brown, C. A. Yorio, and R. H. Grimes (eds.), *On TESOL '77: teaching and learning English as a second language – trends in research and practice*. Washington, DC: TESOL.

  1981. Learner feedback and its effect in communication tasks: a pilot study. *Studies in Second Language Acquisition*, 4, 46–59.

  1982. Native speaker – non-native speaker interaction among academic peers. *Studies in Second Language Acquisition*, 5, 74–81.

Gallagher, T. 1981. Contingent query sequences in adult–child discourse. *Journal of Child Language*, 8, 51–62.

Gallaway, C., Hostler, M., and Reeves, D. 1990. The language addressed to hearing-impaired children by their mothers. *Clinical Linguistics and Phonetics*, 4, 221–37.

Gardner, R. C. 1983. Learning another language: a true social psychological experiment. *Journal of Language and Social Psychology*, 2, 219–39.

Gardner, R. C., Lalonde, R. N., and Pierson, R. 1983. The socio-educational model of second language acquisition: an investigation using LISREL causal modelling. *Journal of Language and Social Psychology*, 2, 1–15.

Garnica, O. 1977. Some prosodic and paralinguistic features of speech to young children. In C. E. Snow and C. A. Ferguson (eds.), *Talking to children: language input and acquisition*. New York: Cambridge University Press.

Garton, A., and Pratt, C. 1989. *Learning to be literate: the development of spoken and written language*. Oxford: Basil Blackwell.

Gass, S. 1988. Integrating research areas: a framework for second language studies. *Applied Linguistics*, 9, 198–217.

Gass, S., and Madden, C. (eds.), 1985. *Input in second language acquisition*. Rowley, MA: Newbury House.

Gass, S., and Varonis, E. 1985. Variation in native speaker modification to non-native speakers. *Studies in Second Language Acquisition*, 7, 37–58.

Genesee, F., Holobow, N., Lambert, W. E., and Chartrand, L. 1989. Three elementary school alternatives for learning through a second language. *The Modern Language Journal*, 73, 250–63.

Ghahremani Ghajar, S. 1989. The impact of 'foreigner talk' on comprehensibility. Internal research report, University of Ottawa.

Giralometto, L. E. 1988. Improving the social-conversational skills of developmentally delayed children: an intervention study. *Journal of Speech and Hearing Disorders*, 53, 156–67.

Gleitman, L. R., Newport, E. L. and Gleitman, H. 1984. The current status of the motherese hypothesis. *Journal of Child Language*, 11, 43–79.

Gold, E. 1967. Language identification in the limit. *Information and Control*, 16, 447–74. ·

Goldfield, B. A. 1987. The contributions of child and caregiver to referential and expressive language. *Applied Psycholinguistics*, 8, 267–80.

Goldin-Meadow, S. 1979. Structure in a manual communication system developed without a conventional language model: language without a helping hand. In H. Whitaker and H. A. Whitaker (eds.), *Studies in Neurolinguistics*, vol. 4. New York: Academic Press.

1982. The resilience of recursion: a study of a communication system developed without a conventional language model. In E. Wanner and L. Gleitman (eds.), *Language acquisition: the state of the art*. New York: Cambridge University Press.

Goldin-Meadow, S., and Feldman, H. 1977. The development of language-like communication without a language model. *Science*, 197, 401–3.

Goldin-Meadow, S., and Mylander, C. 1985. Gestural communication in deaf children: the effects and non-effects of parental input on early language development. *Monographs of the Society for Research in Child Development*, 49.

Goldstein, H. 1984. Effects of modeling and corrected practice on generative language learning of preschool children. *Journal of Speech and Hearing Disorders*, 49, 389–98.

Golinkoff, R., and Ames, G. 1979. A comparison of mothers' and fathers' speech to young children. *Child Development*, 50, 28–32.

Goody, J. 1977. *The domestication of the savage mind*. Cambridge University Press.

Goodz, N. S. 1989. Parental language mixing in bilingual families. *Infant Mental Health Journal*, 10, 25–44.

Goodz, N. S., Bilodeau, L., Amsel, R., and White, K. 1987. Parental language to children in bilingual families. Paper presented at the biennial meetings of the Society for Research in Child Development, Baltimore.

Goodz, N. S., Goodz, E., and Green, D. 1991. Mothers' and fathers' conversations with their young bilingual children. Poster presented at the biennial meetings of the Society for Research in Child Development, Seattle, WA.

Gopnik, A., and Choi, S. 1990. Do linguistic differences lead to cognitive differences? A cross-linguistic study of semantic and cognitive development. *First Language*, 10, 199–215.

Gopnik, M. 1991. Theoretical implications of inherited dysphasia. Paper presented at the workshop on crosslinguistic and cross-populations contributions to the theory of acquisition. Hebrew University, Jerusalem.

Goss, R. N. 1970. Language used by mothers of deaf children and mothers of hearing children. *American Annals of the Deaf*, 115, 93–6.

Greenberg, M. T. 1980. Social interaction between deaf pre-schoolers and their mothers: the effects of communication competence. *Developmental Psychology*, 16, 465–74.

Gregg, K. 1984. Krashen's monitor and Occam's razor. *Applied Linguistics*, 5, 79–100.

Gregory, S., and Barlow, S. 1989. Interactions between deaf babies and their deaf and hearing mothers. In B. Woll (ed.), *Language development and sign language, Monograph 1*, International Sign Linguistics Association. Bristol: International Sign Linguistics Association.

Gregory, S., and Mogford, K. 1981. Early language development in deaf children. In B. Woll, J. G. Kyle, and M. Deuchar (eds.), *Perspectives on British Sign Language and deafness*. London: Croom Helm.

Gregory, S., Mogford, K., and Bishop, J. 1979. Mothers' speech to young hearing-impaired children. *Journal of the British Association of Teachers of the Deaf*, 3, 42–5.

Grice, H. P. 1975. Logic and conversation. In P. Cole and J. L. Morgan (eds.), *Syntax and semantics*, vol. III. London: Academic Press.

Grieser, D. L., and Kuhl, P. K. 1988. Maternal speech to infants in a tonal language: support for universal prosodic features in motherese. *Developmental Psychology*, 24, 14–20.

Grimm, H., Shatz, M., Niemeier-Wind, K., and Wilcox, S. 1990. Culture-specific speech styles: different uses of modal expressions in German and American mothers and their two-year-olds. Paper presented to the Fifth International Congress for the Study of Child Language, Budapest, July 1990.

Grimshaw, J., and Pinker, S. 1989. Positive and negative evidence in language acquisition. *Behavioral and Brain Sciences*, 12, 341–2.

Håkansson, G. 1986. Quantitative aspects of teacher talk. In G. Kasper (ed.), *Learning, teaching and communicating in the F. L. Classroom*. Aarhus University Press.

Halliday, M. 1975. *Learning how to mean: explorations in the development of language*. London: Edward Arnold.

Hampson, J. 1989. Elements of style: maternal and child contributions to referential and expressive styles of language acquisition. Unpublished doctoral dissertation, City University of New York.

Hampson, J., and Nelson, K. 1990. Early relations between mother talk and language development: masked and unmasked. *Papers and Reports on Child Language Development*, 29, 78–85.

Hardy-Brown, K. 1983. Universals and individual differences: disentangling two approaches to the study of language acquisition. *Developmental Psychology*, 19, 610–24.

Hardy-Brown, K., Plomin, R., and DeFries, J. C. 1981. Genetic and environmental influences on the rate of communicative development in the first year of life. *Developmental Psychology*, 17, 704–17.

Harkness, S. 1971. Cultural variation in mothers' language. *Word*, 27, 495–8.

  1977. Aspects of social environment and first language acquisition in rural Africa. In C. E. Snow and C. A. Ferguson (eds.), *Talking to children: language input and acquisition*. Cambridge University Press.

Harley, B. 1984. The interlanguage of immersion students and its implications for second language teaching. In A. Davies, C. Criper, and A. Howatt (eds.), *Interlanguage*, Edinburgh University Press.

  1987. Functional grammar in French immersion: a classroom experiment. In B. Harley, P. Allen, J. Cummins, and M. Swain (eds.), *The development of bilingual proficiency: final report*, vol. II: *Classroom treatment*. Toronto: Modern Language Centre. The Ontario Institute for Studies in Education.

  1992a. Aspects of the oral second language proficiency of early immersion, late immersion, and extended French students at grade 10. In R. Courchêne, J. Glidden, J. St.John, and C. Thérien (eds.), *Comprehension-based second language teaching / L'Enseignement des langues secondes axé sur la compréhension*. Ottawa: University of Ottawa Press.

  1992b. Patterns of second language development in French immersion. *Journal of French Language Studies*, 2, 159–84.

Harris, M., Clibbens, J., Chasin, J., and Tibbitts, R. 1989. The social context of early sign language development. *First Language*, 1, 81–97.

Harris, M., Jones, D., Brookes, S., and Grant, J. 1986. Relations between the non-verbal context of maternal speech and rate of language development. *British Journal of Developmental Psychology*, 4, 261–8.

Hatch, E. 1974. Second language learning – universals? *Working Papers on Bilingualism*, 3, 1–17.

  1978a. Acquisition of syntax in a second language. In J. Richards (ed.), *Understanding second and foreign language learning*. Rowley, MA: Newbury House.

  1978b. Discourse analysis and second language acquisition. In E. Hatch (ed.), *Second language acquisition: a book of readings*. Rowley, MA: Newbury House.

  1983a. *Psycholinguistics: a second language perspective*. Rowley, MA: Newbury House.

  1983b. Simplified input and second language acquisition. In R. Andersen (ed.), *Pidginization and creolization as language acquisition*. Rowley, MA: Newbury House.

  1984. Theoretical review of discourse and interlanguage. In A. Davies, C. Criper, and A. Howatt (eds.), *Interlanguage*. Edinburgh University Press.

Hatch, E., Shapira, R., and Wagner-Gough, J. 1978. 'Foreigner-talk' discourse. *International Review of Applied Linguistics*, 39, 39–59.

Hawkins, B. 1987. *Scaffolded classroom interaction in a language minority setting*. Center for Language Education and Research, University of California at Los Angeles.

Heath, S. B. 1983. *Ways with words*. Cambridge University Press.

  1986. Sociocultural contexts of language development. In California State Department of Education, *Beyond language: social and cultural factors in schooling language minority children*. Sacramento: CSDE.

Heidelberger Forschungsprojekt. 1975. Pidgin Deutsch. *Sprache und Kommunikation ausländischer Arbeiter.* Kronberg/Ts.: Scriptor.

Henggeler, S. W., and Cooper, P. F. 1983. Deaf child–hearing mother interaction: extensiveness and reciprocity. *Journal of Paediatric Psychology*, 8, 83–95.

Henggeler, S. W., Watson, S. M., and Cooper, S. V. 1984. Verbal and non-verbal maternal controls in hearing mother–deaf child interaction. *Journal of Applied Development Psychology*, 5, 319–29.

Henzl, V. 1973. Linguistic register of foreign language instruction. *Language Learning*, 23, 207–22.

1979. Foreigner talk in the classroom. *International Review of Applied Linguistics*, 17, 159–65.

Hess, C. W., Sefton, K. M., and Landry, R. G. 1986. Sample size and type-token ratios for oral language of preschool children. *Journal of Speech and Hearing Research*, 29, 129–34.

Hickey, T. 1991. Mean length of utterance and the acquisition of Irish. *Journal of Child Language*, 18, 553–69.

Hirsh-Pasek, K., Golinkoff, R., Braidi, S., and McNally, L. 1986. 'Daddy throw': on the existence of implicit negative evidence for subcategorization errors. Paper presented at the Boston University Conference on Child Language Development.

Hirsh-Pasek, K., and Treiman, R. 1982. Doggerel: motherese in a new context. *Journal of Child Language*, 9, 229–37.

Hirsh-Pasek, K., Treiman, R., and Schneiderman, M. 1984. Brown and Hanlon revisited: mother's sensitivity to ungrammatical forms. *Journal of Child Language*, 11, 81–8.

Hirvonen, T. 1985. Children's foreigner talk: peer talk in play context. In S. Gass and C. Madden (eds.), *Input in second language acquisition.* Rowley, MA: Newbury House.

1986. Discourse structure in children's foreigner talk: indicators of willingnessto negotiate. In I. Linblad and M. Ljung (eds.), *Proceedings of the Third Nordic Conference for English Studies.* Stockholm: Almqvist and Wiksell.

1988. Monolingual and bilingual children's foreigner talk conversations. In A. Holmen, E. Hansen, J. Gimbel, and J. N. Jorgensen (eds.), *Bilingualism and the individual.* Clevedon, England: Multilingual Matters.

Hladek, E., and Edwards, H. 1984. A comparison of mother–father speech in the naturalistic home environment. *Journal of Psycholinguistic Research*, 13, 321–32.

Hoff-Ginsberg, E. 1985. Some contributions of mothers' speech to their children's syntactic growth. *Journal of Child Language*, 12, 367–85.

1986. Function and structure in maternal speech: their relation to the child's development of syntax. *Development Psychology*, 22, 155–63.

1989. Effects of social class and interactive setting on maternal speech. Poster presented at Society for Research in Child Development, Kansas City, Missouri, April.

1990. Social class, maternal speech and child language development. Paper presented at the Fifth International Congress for the Study of Child Language, Budapest, July 1990.

1992. Methodological and social concerns in the study of children's language-learning environments: a reply to Pine. *First Language*, 12, 251–5.

Hoff-Ginsberg, E., and Shatz, M. 1982. Linguistic input and the child's acquisition of language. *Psychological Bulletin*, 92, 3–26.

Hornstein, N., and Lightfoot, D. 1981. Introduction. In N. Hornstein and D. Lightfoot (eds.), *Explanation in linguistics: the logical problem of language acquisition*. London: Longman.

Horsborough, K., Cross, T., and Ball, J. 1985. Conversational interactions between mothers and their autistic, dysphasic and normal children. In T. G. Cross and L. M. Riach (eds.), *Issues and research in child development. Proceedings of the Second National Child Development Conference*. The Institute of Early Childhood Development and Melbourne College of Advanced Education, Australia.

Howe, C. 1980. Learning language from mothers' replies. *First Language*, 1, 83–97.

Hu, Q. in press. A study of common features of mothers' vocabulary. In J. Sokolov and C. E. Snow (eds.), *Handbook of research in language development using CHILDES*. Hillsdale, NJ: Erlbaum.

Hughes, M. E. 1983. Verbal interaction between mothers and their young hearing-impaired children. *Journal of the British Association of Teachers of the Deaf*, 7, 18–23.

Hughes, M. E., and Huntington, J. N. 1983. Subjective listener judgments of mothers' speech to normally-hearing and hearing-impaired children. *Journal of the British Association of Teachers of the Deaf*, 7, 48–9.

Hulstijn, J. 1982. Monitor use by adult second language learners. Ph.D. dissertation, University of Amsterdam.

1989a. Experiments with semi-artificial input in second language acquisition research. In B. Hammarberg (ed.), *Language learning and learner language* (Scandinavian Working Papers on Bilingualism). Stockholm: Centre for Research on Bilingualism, University of Stockholm.

1989b. Implicit and incidental second language learning: experiments in the processing of natural and partly artificial input. In H. Dechert and M. Raupach (eds.), *Interlingual processes*. Tübingen: Gunter Narr.

1990. A comparison between the information-processing and the analysis/control approaches to language learning. *Applied Linguistics*, 11, 30–45.

Hulstijn, J., and Hulstijn, W. 1984. Grammatical errors as a function of processing constraints and explicit knowledge. *Language Learning*, 34, 23–43.

Hunt, K. 1966. Recent measures in syntactic development. *Elementary English*, 43, 732–9.

Huntington, A., and Watton, F. 1986. The spoken language of teachers and pupils in the education of hearing-impaired children. *Volta Review*, 88, 5–19.

Huttenlocher, J., Haight, W., Bryk, A., Seltzer, M., and Lyons, T. 1991. Early vocabulary growth: relation to language input and gender. *Developmental Psychology*, 17, 236–48.

Hyams, N. 1987. *The acquisition of parameterized grammars*. New York: Springer.

Hylstenstam, K. 1983. Teacher talk in Swedish as a second language classrooms:

quantitative aspects and markedness conditions. In S. W. Felix and H. Wode (eds.), *Language development at the crossroads*. Tübingen: Gunter Narr.

Ingram, D. 1989. *First language acquisition: method, description and explanation*. Cambridge University Press.

Issidorides, D., & Hulstijn, J. 1992. Comprehension of grammatically modified and non-modified sentences by second language learners. *Applied Psycholinguistics* 13, 147–72.

Johnson, P. 1981. Effects on reading comprehension of language complexity and cultural background of a text. *TESOL Quarterly*, 15, 169–81.

Jones, C. P., and Adamson, L. B. 1987. Language use in mother–child–sibling interactions. *Child Development*, 58, 356–66.

Jöreskog, K. G., and Sörbom, D. 1978. *LISREL: analysis of linear structural relationships by the method of maximum likelihood*. Chicago: International Education Services.

Kamhi, A. G., and Masterson, J. J. 1989. Language and cognition in the mentally handicapped: last rites for the difference-delay controversy. In M. Beveridge, G. Conti-Ramsden, and I. Leudar (eds.), *Language and communication in mentally handicapped people*. London: Chapman and Hall.

Kaplan, C., and Simon, H. 1989. Cognitive science: an introduction. In M. I. Posner (ed.), *Foundations of cognitive science*. Cambridge, MA: MIT Press.

Katz, J. 1977. Foreigner talk input in child second language acquisition: its form and function over time. *Proceedings of the Los Angeles Second Language Research Forum*. English Department, UCLA.

Kavanaugh, R., and Jen, M. 1981. Some relationships between parental speech and children's object language development. *First Language*, 2, 103–15.

Kavanaugh, R., and Jirkovsky, A. M. 1982. Parental speech to young children: a longitudinal analysis. *Merrill-Palmer Quarterly*, 28, 297–311.

Kearns, K. P., and Salmon, S. J. 1984. An experimental analysis of auxiliary and copula verb generalization in aphasia. *Journal of Speech and Hearing Disorders*, 49, 152–63.

Kelch, K. 1985. Modified input as an aid to comprehension. *Studies in Second Language Acquisition*, 7, 81–9.

Kemler-Nelson, D. G., Hirsh-Pasek, K., Jusczyk, P. W., and Wright Cassidy, K. 1989. How the prosodic cues in motherese might assist language learning. *Journal of Child Language*, 16, 55–68.

Kenworthy, O. T. 1986. Caregiver–child interaction and language acquisition of hearing-impaired children. *Topics in Language Disorders*, 6, 1–11.

Keogh, B. K., and Hall, R. J. 1983. Cognitive training with learning disabled pupils. In A. Meyers and W. Craighead (eds.), *Cognitive behavior therapy with children*. New York: Plenum.

Killarney, J., and McCluskey, K. 1981. Parent–infant conversations at age one: their length, reciprocity, and contingency. Paper presented at the biennial meetings of the Society for Research in Child Development, Boston.

Klein, D. 1980. Expressive and referential communication in children's early language development: the relationship to mothers' communicative styles. Unpublished doctoral dissertation. Michigan State University.

Koenig, M. A., and Mervis, C. B. 1984. Interactive basis of severely handicapped and normal children's acquisition of referential language. *Journal of Speech and Hearing Research*, 27, 534–42.

Kramsch, C. 1986a. Interactive discourse in small and large groups. In W. Rivers (ed.), *Interactive language teaching*. New York: Cambridge University Press.

1986b. From language proficiency to interactional competence. *Modern Language Journal*, 70, 366–72.

1987. Socialization and literacy in a foreign language: learning through interaction. *Theory into Practice (Special Issue on Teaching Foreign Languages)*, 243-50.

Krashen, S. 1978. Second language acquisition and learning. Presentation to the Public Service Commission of Canada, Language Training Branch, Ottawa.

1980. The theoretical and practical relevance of simple codes in second language acquisition. In R. Scarcella, and S. Krashen (eds.), *Research in second language acquisition*. Rowley, MA: Newbury House.

1981. *Second language acquisition and second language learning*. Oxford: Pergamon.

1985. *The input hypothesis*. London: Longman.

1989. Language teaching technology: a low-tech view. In J. Alatis (ed.), *Georgetown Roundtable on Languages and Linguistics*. Washington, DC: Georgetown University Press.

1992. The input hypothesis: an up-date. In J. Alatis (ed.), *The Georgetown Roundtable on Language and Linguistics*. Washington, DC: Georgetown University Press.

Kuczaj, S. A. 1979. Influence of contractibility on the acquisition of the *Be*: substantial, meager, or unknown? *Journal of Psycholinguistic Research*, 8, 1–11.

1983. *Crib speech and language play*. New York: Springer.

Kyle, J. G. 1990. *From gesture to sign and speech*. Final Report to the Economic and Social Research Council. University of Bristol.

Kyle, J. G., Ackerman, J., and Woll, B. 1987. Early mother–infant interaction: language and pre-language in deaf families. In P. Griffiths, A. Mills, and J. Local (eds.), *Proceedings of the Child Language Seminar*, University of York.

Landau, B., and Gleitman, L. R. 1985. *Language and experience: evidence from the blind child*. Cambridge, MA: Harvard University Press.

Lapkin, S. 1984. How well do immersion students speak and write French? *Canadian Modern Language Review*, 40, 575–85.

Lapkin, S., Hart, D., and Swain, M. 1991. Early and middle French immersion programs: French language outcomes. *Canadian Modern Language Review*, 48, 11–40.

Larsen-Freeman, D. 1985. State of the art on input in second language acquisition. In S. Gass and C. Madden (eds.), *Input in second language acquisition*. Rowley, MA: Newbury House.

Larsen-Freeman, D., and Long, M. 1991. *An introduction to second language acquisition research*. London: Longman.

Larson, S., Ferrier, L. J., Chesnick, M., Liebergott, J., and Schultz, M. C. 1982. Tuning infant behaviours: evolution of mothers' directives. Paper presented to the American Speech Language and Hearing Association Convention, Toronto. [Reported in Ferrier, 1985.]

Lasky, E. Z. and Klopp, K. 1982. Parent–child interactions in normal and language-disordered children. *Journal of Speech and Hearing Disorders*, 47, 7–18.

Leonard, L. 1979. Language impairment in children. *Merrill-Palmer Quarterly*, 25, 205–32.

Levelt, W. J. M. 1975. What became of LAD? In W. Abraham (ed.), *Ut videam: contributions to an understanding of linguistics, for Pieter Verburg on the occasion of his 70th birthday*. Lisse: Peter de Ridder Press.

Levine, M. 1963. Mediating processes in humans at the outset of discrimination learning. *Psychological Review*, 70, 254–76.

Lewis, C., and Gregory, S. 1987. Parents' talk to their infants: the importance of context. *First Language*, 7, 201–16.

Lewis, M. M. 1936. *Infant speech: a study of the beginning of language*. New York: Harcourt Brace.

Liceras, J. 1985. The role of intake in the determination of learners' competence. In S. Gass and C. Madden (eds.), *Input in second language acquisition*. Rowley, MA: Newbury House.

Lieven, E. V. M. 1978a. Conversations between mothers and their young children: individual differences and their possible implications for the study of language learning. In N. Waterson and C. E. Snow (eds.), *The development of communication: social and pragmatic factors in language acquisition*. Chichester: Wiley.

1978b. Turn-taking and pragmatics: two issues in early child language acquisition. In R. Campbell and P. Smith (eds.), *The psychology of language*. New York: Plenum Press.

1984. Interactional style and children's learning. *Topics in Language Disorders*, 4, 15–23.

1987. Change and continuity in early language development. In A. J. Ellis (ed.), *Progress in the psychology of language*, vol. III. Hillsdale, NJ: Erlbaum.

Lieven, E. V. M., and Pine, J. 1992. Productivity in multi-word utterances: analytic and synthetic solutions. Paper presented at the 1992 Child Language Seminar, University of Glasgow.

Lieven, E. V. M., Pine, J. M., and Dresner Barnes, H. 1992. Individual differences in early vocabulary development: redefining the referential–expressive distinction. *Journal of Child Language*, 19, 287–310.

Lightbown, P. 1987. Classroom language as input to second language acquisition. In C. Pfaff (ed.), *First and second language acquisition processes*. Rowley, MA: Newbury House.

1992. Can they do it themselves? A comprehension-based ESL course for young children. In R. Courchêne, J. Glidden, C. Thérien, and J. St. John (eds.), *Comprehension-based second language teaching / L'Enseignement des langues secondes axé sur la compréhension*. University of Ottawa Press.

Lightbown, P., and Spada, N. 1990. Focus-on-form and corrective feedback in communicative language teaching: effects on second language learning. *Studies in Second Language Acquisition*, 12, 429–48.

Lipscomb, T., and Coon, R. 1983. Parental speech modification to young children. *Journal of Genetic Psychology*, 143, 181–7.

Livingston, S. 1983. Levels of development in the language of deaf children. *Sign Language Studies*, 40, 193–286.

Loncke, F., Quertinmont, S., and Ferreyra, P. 1990. Deaf children in schools: more or less native signers? In S. Prillewitz and T. Vollhaber (eds.), *Current trends in European Sign Language research*. Hamburg: Signum.

Long, M. 1981a. Input, interaction, and second language acquisition. In H. Winitz (ed.), Native language and foreign language instruction, *Annals of the New York Academy of Sciences*, 379, 259–78.

1981b. Questions in foreigner talk discourse. *Language Learning*, 31, 135–57.

1983a. Linguistic and conversational adjustments to non-native speakers. *Studies in Second Language Acquisition*, 5, 177–93.

1983b. Native speaker/non-native speaker conversation and the negotiation of comprehensible input. *Applied Linguistics*, 4, 126–41.

1985. Input and second language acquisition theory. In S. Gass and C. Madden (eds.), *Input in second language acquisition*. Rowley, MA: Newbury House.

Long, M., and Porter, P. 1985. Group work, interlanguage talk, and second language acquisition. *TESOL Quarterly*, 19, 207–27.

Long, M., and Sato, 1983. Classroom foreigner talk discourse: forms and functions of teachers' questions. In H. Seliger and M. Long (eds.), *Classroom-oriented research in second language acquisition*. Rowley, MA: Newbury House.

Lynch, A. 1988. Speaking up or talking down: foreign learners' reactions to teacher talk. *English Language Teaching Journal*, 42, 109–16.

Lyon, M. 1985. The verbal interaction of mothers and their pre-school hearing-impaired children: a preliminary investigation. *Journal of the British Association of Teachers of the Deaf*, 5, 119–29.

Lyster, R. 1990. The role of analytic language teaching in French immersion programs. *The Canadian Modern Language Review*, 47, 159–76.

Lytton, H., Conway, D., and Suave, R. 1977. The impact of twinship on parent–child interaction. *Journal of Personality and Social Psychology*, 35, 97–107.

McCartney, K. 1984. Effect of quality of day care environment on children's language development. *Developmental Psychology*, 20, 244–60.

McClelland, J. L., and Rumelhart, D. E. 1986. *Parallel distributed processing*, vol. II. Cambridge MA: MIT Press.

McConachie, H., and Mitchell, D. R. 1985. Parents teaching their young mentally handicapped children. *Journal of Child Psychology and Psychiatry*, 26, 389–405.

McConkey, R., and O'Connor, M. 1982. A new approach to parental involvement in language intervention programmes. *Child Care, Health and Development*, 8, 163–76.

McCormack, W. 1982. 'Foreigner talk' in social interaction. *The Ninth LACUS Forum 1982*. Columbia, SC: Hornbeam Press.

1984. Intonation and foreigner talk. *The Eleventh LACUS Forum 1984*. Columbia, SC: Hornbeam Press.

McDonald, J. L. 1986. The development of sentence comprehension strategies in English and Dutch. *Journal of Memory and Language*, 26, 100–17.

McDonald, L., and Pien, D. 1982. Mothers' conversational behaviour as a function of interactional intent. *Journal of Child Language*, 8, 327–58.

Macken, M. A., and Barton, D. 1980. The acquisition of the voicing contrast in Spanish: a phonetic and phonological study of word-initial stop consonants. *Journal of Child Language*, 7, 433–58.

McLaughlin, B. 1990. Restructuring. *Applied Linguistics*, 11, 113–28.

McLaughlin, B., Rossman, T., and McLeod, M. 1983. Second language learning: an information processing perspective. *Language Learning*, 33, 135–58.

McLaughlin, B., White, D., McDevitt, T., and Raskin, R. 1983. Mothers' and fathers' speech to their young children: similar or different? *Journal of Child Language*, 10, 245–52.

MacLure, M., and French, P. A. 1981. A comparison of talk at school and at home. In G. Wells (ed.), *Learning through interaction: the study of language development*. Cambridge University Press.

McNeill, D. 1966. Developmental psycholinguistics. In F. Smith and G. A. Miller (eds.), *The genesis of language: a psycholinguistic approach*. Cambridge, MA: MIT Press.

MacPherson, C. A., and Weber-Olsen, M. 1980. Mothers' speech input to deficient and language normal children. *Proceedings from the First Wisconsin Symposium on Research on Child Language Disorders*, 1, 59–79.

McShane, J. 1980. *Learning to talk*. Cambridge University Press.

McTear, M. 1985. Pragmatic disorders: a case study of conversational disability. *British Journal of Communication Disorders*, 20, 129–41.

MacWhinney, B. 1987. The competition model. In B. MacWhinney (ed.), *Mechanisms of language acquisition*. Hillsdale, NJ: Erlbaum.

  1991. *The CHILDES project: tools for analyzing talk*. Hillsdale, NJ: Erlbaum.

MacWhinney, B., and Bates, E. 1989. *The crosslinguistic study of sentence processing*. New York: Cambridge University Press.

MacWhinney, B., Leinbach, J., Taraban, R., and McDonald, J. 1989. Language learning: cues or rules. *Journal of Memory and Language*, 28, 255–77.

MacWhinney, B., and Snow, C. E. 1985. The Child Language Data System. *Journal of Child Language*, 12, 271–95.

  1990. The Child Language Data Exchange System: an update. *Journal of Child Language*, 17, 457–72.

Maestas y Moores, J. 1980. Early language environment: interactions of deaf parents with their infants. *Sign Language Studies*, 26, 1–13.

Mahoney, G., and Powell, A. 1986. *Transactional Intervention Program: teacher's guide*. Farmington, CT: Pediatric Research and Training Center (University of Connecticut Health Center).

Malone, M., and Guy, R. 1982. A comparison of mothers' and fathers' speech to their three-year-old sons. *Journal of Psycholinguistic Research*, 11, 599–608.

Malsheen, B. 1980. Two hypotheses for phonetic clarification in the speech of mothers to children. In G. Yeni-Komshian, J. Kavanagh, and C. A. Ferguson (eds.), *Child phonology*, vol. II: *Perception*. New York: Academic Press.

Malvern, D. 1991. Interpreting the type token ratio – a mathematical model. Poster presentation at the Child Language Seminar, University of Manchester, March 1991.

Mannle, S., Barton, M., and Tomasello, M. 1991. Two-year-olds' conversations with their preschool-aged siblings and their mothers. *First Language*, 12, 57–71.

Mannle, S., and Tomasello, M. 1987. Fathers, siblings, and the bridge hypothesis. In K. E. Nelson and A. van Kleeck (eds.), *Children's language*, vol. VI. Hillsdale, NJ: Erlbaum.

Mannon, T. 1982. 'Foreigner Talk' in social interaction. *The Ninth LACUS Forum.* Columbia, SC: Hornbeam Press.

1984. Intonation and foreigner talk. *The Eleventh LACUS Forum.* Columbia, SC: Hornbeam Press.

1986. Teacher talk: a comparison of teacher's speech to native and non-native speakers. MA thesis, University of California at Los Angeles.

Maratsos, M., and Chalkley, M. A. 1980. The internal language of children's syntax: the ontogenesis and representation of syntactic categories. In K. E. Nelson (ed.), *Children's language*, vol. II. New York: Gardner Press.

Marmor, G. S., and Petitto, L. 1979. Simultaneous communication in the classroom: how well is English grammar represented? *Sign Language Studies*, 23, 99–136.

Marshall, N. R., Hegrenes, J. R., and Goldstein, S. 1973. Verbal interactions: mothers and their retarded children vs. mothers and their non-retarded children. *American Journal of Mental Deficiency*, 77, 415–19.

Martinez, A. M. 1987. Dialogues among children and between children and their mothers. *Child Development*, 58, 1035–43.

Masur, E., and Berko Gleason, J. 1980. Parent–child interaction and the acquisition of lexical information during play. *Developmental Psychology*, 16, 404–9.

Matey, C., and Kretschmer, R. 1985. A comparison of mother speech to Down's syndrome, hearing-impaired and normal-hearing children. *Volta Review*, 87, 205–13.

Meadow, K. P., Erting, C. J., Bridges-Cline, F., and Prezioso, C. 1985. Interaction of mothers and deaf infants in the first year of life. In I. G. Taylor (ed.), *The education of the deaf: current perspectives. Proceedings of the International Congress on Education of the Deaf*, vol. I. London: Croom Helm.

Meadow, K. P., Greenberg, M. T., Erting, C., and Carmichael, H. 1981. Interactions of deaf mothers and deaf pre-school children: comparisons with 3 other groups of deaf and hearing dyads. *American Annals of the Deaf*, 126, 454–68.

Mehan, H. 1979. *Learning lessons: social organization in the classroom.* Cambridge, MA: Harvard University Press.

Meisel, J. 1975. Ausländerdeutsch und Deutsch ausländischer Arbeiter. *Zeitschrift für Literaturwissenschaft und Linguistik*, 18, 9–53.

1977. Linguistic simplification: a study of immigrant workers' speech and foreigner talk. In S. Pit Corder and E. Roulet (eds.), *The notions of simplification, interlanguages and pidgins and their relation to language pedagogy. Actes du V$^{ème}$ Colloque de linguistique appliquée de Neuchâtel.* Geneva: Droz.

Michalski, R. S., Carbonell, J. G., and Mitchell, T. M. (eds.) 1983. *Machine learning: an artificial intelligence approach*, vol. I. Palo Alto, CA: Tioga Press.

(eds.) 1986. *Machine learning: an artificial intelligence approach*, vol. II. Los Altos, CA: Morgan Kaufman.

Miller, P. 1986. Teasing as language socialization and verbal play in a white working-class community. In B. B. Schieffelin and E. Ochs (eds.), *Language socialization across cultures*. Cambridge University Press.

Mills, A. E. 1983. *Language acquisition in the blind child: normal and deficient*. London: Croom Helm.

Mills, A., and Coerts, J. 1990. Functions and forms of bilingual input: children learning a sign language as one of their first languages. In S. Prillewitz and T. Vollhaber (eds.), *Current trends in European Sign Language research*. Hamburg: Signum Press.

Moerk, E. L. 1976. Processes of language teaching and training in the interaction of mother–child dyads. *Child Development*, 47, 1064–78.

1983. *The mother of Eve – as a first language teacher*. Norwood, NJ: Ablex.

Mogford, K., Gregory, S., and Keay, S. 1979. Picture-book reading with mother: a comparison between hearing-impaired children at 18 and 25 months. *Journal of the British Association of Teachers of the Deaf*, 3, 43–5.

Mohan, B. 1986. *Language and content*. Reading, MA: Addison-Wesley.

1991. LEP students and the integration of language and content knowledge structures and tasks. Paper presented at the National Research Symposium on Limited English Proficient Students' Issues, Washington, DC.

Mohay, H. A. 1982. A preliminary description of the communication systems evolved by two deaf children in the absence of a sign language model. *Sign Language Studies*. 34, 72–90.

1986. The adjustment of maternal conversation to hearing and hearing-impaired children: a twin study. *Journal of the British Association of Teachers of the Deaf*, 10, 37–44.

Moores, J. M., and Moores, D. F. 1982. Interaction of deaf mothers with children in the first months of life. In *Proceedings of the International Congress on Education of the Deaf, Hamburg, 1980*, vol. I. Heidelberg: Julius Gross.

Morgan, J. 1986. *From input to complex grammar*. Cambridge, MA: MIT Press.

Morgan, J. L., and Newport, E. L. 1981. The role of constituent structure in the induction of an artificial language. *Journal of Verbal Learning and Verbal Behaviour*, 20, 67–85.

Morgan, J. L., and Travis, L. L. 1989. Limits on negative information in language input. *Journal of Child Language*, 6, 531–52.

Murphy, A. D., Johnson, J., and Peters, J. 1990. Fine-tuning of utterance length to preverbal infants: effects on later language development. *Journal of Child Language*, 17, 511–25.

Musselman, R., Lindsay, P. H., and Wilson, A. K. 1988. The effect of mothers' communication mode on language development in pre-school deaf children. *Applied linguistics*, 9, 185–204.

Nelson, K. 1973. Structure and strategy in learning to talk. *Monographs of the Society for Research in Child Development*, 38, 1–2, serial no. 149.

1981. Individual differences in language development: implications for development and language. *Developmental Psychology*, 17, 170–87.

Nelson, K. E. 1977a. 

*Psychology*, 13, 

1977b. Aspects of language children's syntax acquisition. *Developmental*

1980. Theories of the child ... ition and use from age 2 to 20. *Journal of the American Academy of ... hiatry*, 16, 584–607.

... n of syntax: a look at rare events and at

necessary, catalytic, and irrelevant components of mother–child conversation. *Annals of the New York Academy of Sciences*, 345, 45–67.

1981. Toward a rare-event cognitive comparison theory of syntax acquisition: insights from work with recasts. In P. Dale and D. Ingram (eds.), *Child language: an international perspective*. Baltimore, MD: University Park Press.

1987. Some observations from the perspective of the rare event cognitive comparison theory of language acquisition. In K. E. Nelson and A. van Kleeck (eds.), *Children's language*, vol. VI. Hillsdale, NJ: Erlbaum.

1989. Strategies for first language teaching. In M. L. Rice and R. L. Schiefelbusch (eds.), *The teachability of language*. Baltimore, MD: Brookes.

Nelson, K. E., Carskaddon, G., and Bonvillian, J. 1973. Syntax acquisition: impact of experimental variation in adult verbal interaction with the child. *Child Development*, 44, 497–504.

Nelson, K. E., Denninger, M. M., Bonvillian, J. D., Kaplan, B. J., and Baker, N. D. 1984. Maternal input adjustments and non-adjustments as related to children's linguistic advances and to language acquisition theories. In A. D. Pellegrini and T. D. Yawkey (eds.), *The development of oral and written languages: readings in developmental and applied linguistics*. New York: Ablex.

Nelson, K. E., Heimann, M., Abuelhaija, L. A., and Wroblewski, R. 1989. Implications for language acquisition models of children's and parents' variations in imitation. In G. E. Speidel and K. E. Nelson (eds.), *The many faces of imitation in language learning*. Berlin: Springer.

Newhoff, M., and Browning, J. 1983. Interactional variation: a view from the language disordered child's world. *Topics in Language Disorders*, 4, 49–60.

Newhoff, M., Silverman, L., and Millet, A. 1980. Linguistic differences in parents' speech to normal and language disordered children. *Proceedings from the First Wisconsin Symposium on Research in Child Language Disorders*, 1, 44–57.

Newport, E. L. 1977. Motherese: the speech of mothers to young children. In N. J. Castellan, D. B. Pisoni, and G. R. Potts (eds.), *Cognitive theory*, vol. II. Hillsdale, NJ: Erlbaum.

1984. Constraints on learning: studies in the acquisition of American Sign Language. *Papers and Reports on Child Language Development*, 23, 1–22.

Newport, E. L., Gleitman, H., and Gleitman, L. R. 1977. Mother I'd rather do it myself: some effects and non-effects of maternal speech style. In C. Snow and C. A. Ferguson (eds.), *Talking to children: language input and acquisition*. Cambridge University Press.

Newport, E. L., and Meier, R. 1985. Acquisition of ASL. In D. I. Slobin (ed.), *The crosslinguistic study of language acquisition*, vol. I. Hillsdale, NJ: Erlbaum.

Nienhuys, T. G., Cross, T., and Horsborough, K. M. 1980. Child variables influencing maternal speech style: deaf and hearing. *Journal of Communication Disorders*, 17, 189–207.

Nienhuys, T. G., Horsborough, K. M., and Cross, T. G. 1985. A dialogic analysis of interaction between mothers and their deaf and hearing pre-schoolers. *Applied Psycholinguistics*, 6, 121–39.

Nienhuys, T. G., and Tikotin, J. A. 1983. Prespeech communication in hearing and hearing-impaired children. *Journal of the British Association of Teachers of the Deaf*, 7, 182–94.

Ninio, A. 1992. The relation of children's single word utterances to single word utterances in the input. *Journal of Child Language*, 19, 87–110.

Ninio, A., and Bruner, J. 1978. The achievement and antecedents of labelling. *Journal of Child Language*, 5, 1–15.

Nwokah, E. E. 1987. Maidese vs. motherese: is the language input of child and adult caregivers similar? *Language and Speech*, 30, 213–37.

Ochs, E. 1982. Talking to children in Western Samoa. *Language in Society*, 11, 77–104.

1985. Variation and error: a sociolinguistic approach to language acquisition in Samoa. In D. I. Slobin (ed.), *The crosslinguistic study of language acquisition*, vol. I. Hillsdale, NJ: Erlbaum.

1986. Introduction. In B. B. Schieffelin and E. Ochs (eds.), *Language socialization across cultures*. Cambridge University Press.

Ochs, E., and Schieffelin, B. B. 1984. Language acquisition and socialization: three developmental studies and their implications. In R. Schweder and R. LeVine (eds.), *Culture theory: essays on mind, self, and emotion*. Cambridge University Press.

O'Connor, E. F. 1972. Extending classical test theory to the measurement of change. *Review of Educational Research*, 42, 73–97.

O'Connor, J. D., and Arnold, G. F. 1961. *The intonation of colloquial English*. London: Longman.

Olson, D. R. 1977. From utterance to text: the bias of language in speech and writing. *Harvard Educational Review*, 47, 257–81.

Olson, S. L., Bayles, K., and Bates, E. 1986. Mother–child interaction and children's speech progress: a longitudinal study of the first two years. *Merrill-Palmer Quarterly*, 32, 1–20.

Oshima-Takane, Y. 1988. Children learn from speech not addressed to them: the case of personal pronouns. *Journal of Child Language*, 15, 95–108.

Pankhurst, J., Sharwood-Smith, M., and Van Buren, P. (eds.), 1988. *Learnability and second languages: a book of readings*. Dordrecht: Forris.

Parisi, D. 1983. A three-stage model of language evolution. In E. de Grolier (ed.), *Glossogenetics: the origin and evolution of language*. Chur, Switzerland: Harwood.

Parker, K., and Chaudron, C. 1987. The effects of linguistic simplification and elaborative modifications on L2 comprehension. *University of Hawaii: Working Papers in ESL*, 6, 107–33.

Peck, S. 1978. Child–child discourse in second language acquisition. In E. Hatch (ed.), *Second language acquisition: a book of readings*. Rowley, MA: Newbury House.

Peters, A. M. 1983. *The units of language acquisition*. Cambridge University Press.

1985. Language segmentation: operating principles for the perception and analysis of language. In D. I. Slobin (ed.), *The crosslinguistic study of language acquisition*, vol. II. Hillsdale, NJ: Erlbaum.

Peters, A. M., and Boggs, S. T. 1986. Interactional routines as cultural influences upon language acquisition. In B. B. Schieffelin and E. Ochs (eds.), *Language socialization across cultures*. Cambridge University Press.

Petersen, G. A., and Sherrod, K. B. 1982. Relationship of maternal language to language development and language delay in children. *American Journal of Mental Deficiency*, 86, 391–8.

Peterson, C., and McCabe, A. 1992. Parental styles of narrative elicitation: effect on children's narrative structure and content. *First Language*, 12, 299–322.

Petitto, L. 1988. 'Language' in the pre-linguistic child. In F. Chesses (ed.), *The development of language and language researchers*. Hillsdale, NJ: Erlbaum.

Phillips, J. R. 1973. Syntax and vocabulary of mothers' speech to young children: age and sex comparisons. *Child Development*, 44, 182–5.

Pica, T. 1987. Second language acquisition, social interaction, and the classroom. *Applied Linguistics*, 8, 3–21.

1991a. Foreign language classrooms: making them research-ready and researchable. In B. Freed (ed.), *Foreign language acquisition research and the classroom*. New York: D. C. Heath.

1991b. Classroom interaction, negotiation, and comprehension: redefining relationships. *System*, 19, 4, 437–58.

1992. Communicating with second language learners: what does it reveal about the social and linguistic processes of second language learning? In J. Alatis (ed.), *The Georgetown Round Table on Languages and Linguistics*. Washington, DC: Georgetown University Press.

Pica, T., and Doughty, C. 1985. Input and interaction in the communicative language classroom: a comparison of teacher-fronted and group activities. In S. Gass and C. Madden (eds.), *Input in second language acquisition*. Rowley, MA: Newbury House.

Pica, T., and Long, M. 1986. The linguistic and conversational performance of experienced and inexperienced teachers. In R. Day (ed.), *Talking to learn: conversation in second language acquisition*. Rowley, MA: Newbury House.

Pica, T., Young, R., and Doughty, C. 1987. The impact of interaction on comprehension. *TESOL Quarterly*, 21, 737–58.

Pienemann, M. 1984. Psychological constraints on the teachability of languages. *Studies in Second Language Acquisition*, 6, 186–214.

1989. Is language teachable? Psycholinguistic experiments and hypotheses. *Applied Linguistics*, 10, 52–79.

1992. Teachability theory. In *Language acquisition in the classroom*. Language Acquisition Research Centre, National Languages and Literacy Institute of Australia, University of Sidney.

Pine, J. 1990. Individual differences in early language development and their relationship to maternal style. Unpublished Ph.D. thesis: University of Manchester.

1992a. The functional basis of referentiality: evidence from children's spontaneous speech. *First Language*, 12, 39–55.

1992b. Maternal style at the early one-word stage: re-evaluating the stereotype of the directive mother. *First Language*, 12, 169–85.

Pine, J., and Lieven, E. V. M. 1990. Referential style at thirteen months: why age-defined cross-sectional measures are inappropriate for the study of strategy differences in early language development. *Journal of Child Language*, 17, 625–31.

Pinker, S. 1979. Formal models of language learning. *Cognition*, 3, 217–83.

1984. *Language learnability and language development*. Cambridge, MA: Harvard University Press.

1988. Learnability theory and the acquisition of a first language. In F. S. Kessel (ed.), *The development of language and language researchers: essays in honor of Roger Brown*. Hillsdale, NJ: Erlbaum.

1989. *Learnability and cognition: the acquisition of argument structure*. Cambridge, MA: MIT Press.

Plomin, R., and DeFries, J. C. 1985. *Origins of individual differences in childhood*. Orlando, FL: Academic Press.

Plunkett, K., and Marchman, V. 1991. U-shaped learning and frequency effects in a multi-layered perceptron: implications for child language acquisition. *Cognition*. 38, 43–102.

Pollard, C. 1985. Head-driven phrase structure grammars. Unpublished doctoral dissertation, Department of Linguistics, Stanford University.

Porter, P. 1983. How learners talk to each other: input and interaction in task-centered discussions. Paper presented at TESOL Conference, Toronto, Canada.

Post, K. 1992. Maternal provision of negative evidence in a rural community. Unpublished doctoral dissertation, Harvard Graduate School of Education.

Power, D. J., Wood, D. J., and Wood, H. A. 1990. Conversational strategies of teachers using three methods of communication with deaf children. *American Annals of the Deaf*, 135, 9–13.

Power, D. J., Wood, D. J., Wood, H. A., and MacDougall, J. 1990. Maternal control over conversations with hearing and deaf infants and young children. *First Language*, 10, 19–36.

Price, P. 1984. A study of mother–child interaction strategies with mothers of young developmentally delayed children. In J. Berg (ed.), *Perspectives and progress in mental retardation* (Sixth Congress of the International Association for the Scientific Study of Mental Deficiency). Baltimore, MD: University Park Press.

1989. Language intervention and mother-child interaction. In M. Beveridge, G. Conti-Ramsden, and I. Leudar (eds.), *Language and communication in mentally handicapped people*. London: Chapman and Hall.

Prinz, P. M., and Prinz, E. A. 1985. If only you could hear what I see: discourse development in sign language. *Discourse Processes*, 8, 1–19.

*Profiling and partnership: a summary of views expressed through working groups at the 1991 Initial Teacher Training Conference for modern language teacher trainers held at Stoke Rochford Hall, from 10th to 12th September*. 1991.

Pye, C. 1983. Mayan telegraphese: intonational determinants of inflectional development in Quiché Mayan. *Language*, 59, 583–604.

1986. Quiché Mayan speech to children. *Journal of Child Language*, 13, 85–100.

1992. The acquisition of K'iche' Maya. In D. I. Slobin (ed.), *The crosslinguistic study of language acquisition*, vol. III. Hillsdale, NJ: Erlbaum.

Radford, A. 1990. *Syntactic theory and the acquisition of syntax*. Oxford: Blackwell.

Ready, D., and Wesche, M. 1992. An evaluation of the University of Ottawa's sheltered program: language teaching strategies that work. In R. Courchêne, J. Glidden, J. St. John, and C. Thérien (eds.), *Comprehension-based second language teaching / L'Enseignement des langues secondes axé sur la com-préhension*. University of Ottawa Press.

Reid, K. 1988. Learning and learning to learn. In D. K. Reid (ed.), *Teaching the learning disabled*. Boston, MA: Allyn and Bacon.

Remick, H. 1971. The maternal environment of linguistic development. Unpublished doctoral dissertation, University of California, Davis.

Retherford, K. S., Schwartz, B. C., and Chapman, R. S. 1981. Semantic roles and residual grammatical categories in mother and child speech: who tunes in to whom? *Journal of Child Language*, 8, 583–608.

Rice, M. 1990. Preschooler's QUIL: Quick incidental learning of words. In G. Conti-Ramsden and C. E. Snow (eds.), *Children's language*, vol. VII. Hillsdale, NJ: Erlbaum.

Richards, B. J. 1987. Type/token ratios: what do they really tell us? *Journal of Child Language*, 14, 201–9.

  1990a. *Language development and individual differences: a study of auxiliary verb learning*. Cambridge University Press.

  1990b. Predictors of auxiliary and copula verb growth. Paper presented at the Fifth International Congress for the Study of Child Language, Budapest, July 1990.

  1990c. Access to the agenda: some observations on language development research and its relevance for the practitioner. *Australian Journal of Remedial Education*, 22, 16–20.

  1991. Investigating relationships between maternal input and rate of children's language development: a reanalysis of Yoder. *Journal of Speech and Hearing Research*, 34, 347–50.

Richards, B. J., and Gallaway, C. 1993. Input and interaction in child language acquisition. In R. E. Asher and J. M. Y. Simpson (eds.), *The encyclopedia of language and linguistics*. Oxford: Pergamon.

Richards, B. J., and Robinson, W. P. 1993. Environmental correlates of child copula verb growth. *Journal of Child Language*, 20, 343–62.

Rogoff, B. 1990. *Apprenticeship in thinking*. New York: Oxford University Press.

Rogoff, B., Ellis, S., and Gardner, W. 1984. Adjustment of adult–child instruction according to child's age and task. *Developmental Psychology*, 20, 193–9.

Rondal, J. A. 1977. Maternal speech to normal and Down's syndrome children matched for mean length of utterance. In E. Meyers (ed.), *Quality of life in severely and profoundly mentally retarded people: research foundations for improvement*. Washington, DC: American Association of Mental Deficiency.

  1980. Fathers' and mothers' speech in early language development. *Journal of Child Language*, 7, 353–69.

Rosen, C., and Rosen, H. 1973. *The language of primary school children*. Harmondsworth: Penguin.

Roth, F. 1984. Accelerating language learning in young children. *Journal of Child Language*, 11, 89–107.

Roth, P. L. 1987. Temporal characteristics of maternal verbal styles. In K. E. Nelson and A. van Kleeck (eds.), *Children's language*, vol. VI. Hillsdale, NJ: Erlbaum.

Rūķe-Draviņa, V. 1977. Modifications of speech addressed to young children in

Latvian. In C. E. Snow and C. A. Ferguson (eds.), *Talking to children: language input and acquisition*. Cambridge University Press.

Rumelhart, D., and McClelland, J. 1986. On learning the past tense of English verbs. In J. L. McClelland and D. E. Rumelhart (eds.), *Parallel-distributed processing: Explorations in the microstructure of cognition*. Cambridge, MA: MIT Press.

Ryan, M. L. 1978. Contour in context. In R. N. Campbell and P. T. Smith (eds.), *Recent advances in the psychology of language*. New York: Plenum Press.

Sachs, J., and Devin, J. 1976. Young children's use of age-appropriate speech styles in social interaction and role-playing. *Journal of Child Language*, 3, 81–98.

Sachs, J., and Johnson, M. 1972. Language development in a hearing child of deaf parents. Paper presented at the International Symposium on First Language Acquisition, Florence, Italy.

Sato, C. 1986. Conversation and interlanguage development: rethinking the connection. In R. Day (ed.), *Talking to learn: conversation in second language acquisition*. Rowley, MA: Newbury House.

Savic, S. 1980. *How twins learn to talk*. New York: Academic Press.

Scarborough, H. S., Rescorla, L., Tager-Flusberg, H., Fowler, A. E., and Sudhalter, V. 1991. The relation of utterance length to grammatical complexity in normal and language-disordered groups. *Applied Psycholinguistics, 12,* 23–45.

Scarborough, H., and Wyckoff, J. 1986. Mother I'd still rather do it myself: some further non-effects of 'motherese'. *Journal of Child Language*, 13, 431–7.

Scarcella, R. 1983. Discourse accent in second language performance. In S. Gass and L. Selinker (eds.), *Language transfer in language learning*. Rowley, MA: Newbury House.

Scarcella, R., and Higa, C. 1981. Input, negotiation, and age differences in second language acquisition. *Language Learning*, 31, 409–37.

1982. Input and age differences in second language acquisition. In S. Krashen, R. Scarcella, and M. Long (eds.), *Child–adult differences in second language acquisition*. Rowley, MA: Newbury House.

Schachter, J. 1986. Three approaches to the study of input. *Language Learning*, 36, 211–25.

Schaffer, H. R. 1989. Language development in context. In S. von Tetzchner, L. Siegel, and L. Smith (eds.), *The social and cognitive aspects of normal and atypical language development*. New York: Springer.

Schaffer, H. R., and Liddell, C. 1984. Adult–child interaction under dyadic and polyadic conditions. *British Journal of Development Psychology*, 2, 33–42.

Schieffelin, B. B. 1979. Getting it together: an ethnographic approach to the study of the development of communicative competence. In E. Ochs and B. B. Schieffelin (eds.), *Developmental pragmatics*. New York: Academic Press.

1985. The acquisition of Kaluli. In D. I. Slobin, (ed.), *The crosslinguistic study of language acquisition*, vol. I. Hillsdale, NJ: Erlbaum.

Schieffelin, B. B., and Ochs, E. 1983. A cultural perspective on the transition from prelinguistic to linguistic communication. In R. M. Golinkoff (ed.), *The transition from prelinguistic to linguistic communication*. Hillsdale, NJ: Erlbaum.

(eds.) 1986. *Language socialisation across cultures.* Cambridge University Press.

Schlesinger, H. S., and Meadow, K. P. 1972. *Sound and sign: childhood deafness and mental health.* Berkeley: University of California Press.

Schmidt, R. 1990. The role of consciousness in second language learning. *Applied Linguistics*, 11, 129–58.

Schwartz, R. G., and Camarata, S. 1985. Examining relationships between input and language development: some statistical issues. *Journal of Child Language*, 12, 199–207.

Schwartz, R. G., Chapman, K., Prelock, P. A., Terrell, B. Y., and Rowan, L. E. 1985. Facilitation of early syntax through discourse structure. *Journal of Child Language*, 12, 13–25.

Searle, J. 1969. *Speech acts: an essay in the philosophy of language.* New York: Cambridge University Press.

Seitz, S. 1975. Language intervention: changing the language environment of the retarded child. In R. Koch, F. de la Cruz, and F. Menolascino (eds.), *Down's syndrome: research, prevention and management.* New York: Bruner/Mazel.

Selinker, L., Swain, M., and Dumas, G. 1975. The interlanguage hypothesis extended to children. *Language Learning*, 25, 139–51.

Sharwood-Smith, M. 1986. Comprehension versus acquisition: two ways of processing input. *Applied Linguistics*, 7, 239–55.

Shatz, M., and Gelman, R. 1973. The development of communication skills: modifications in the speech of young children as a function of the listener. *Monographs of the Society for Research in Child Development, 38* (5, serial no. 152).

  1977. Beyond syntax: the influence of conversational constraints on speech modifications. In C. E. Snow and C. A. Ferguson (eds.), *Talking to children: language input and acquisition.* Cambridge University Press.

Shatz, M., Hoff-Ginsberg, E., and MacIver, D. 1989. Induction and the acquisition of English auxiliaries: the effects of differentially enriched input. *Journal of Child Language*, 16, 141–60.

Shockey, L., and Bond, Z. S. 1980. Phonological processes in speech addressed to children. *Phonetica*, 37, 267–74.

Shute, B., and Wheldall, K. 1989. Pitch alterations in British motherese: some preliminary acoustic data. *Journal of Child Language*, 16, 503–12.

Simon, H. 1962. The architecture of complexity. *Proceedings of the American Philosophical Society*, 106, 467–82.

Sinclair, J. McH., and Coulthard, R. M. 1975. *Towards an analysis of discourse: the English used by teachers and pupils.* Oxford University Press.

Skehan, P. 1989. *Individual differences in second-language learning.* London: Arnold.

Skinner, B. F. 1957. *Verbal behavior.* New York: Appleton-Century-Crofts.

Slobin, D. I. 1973. Cognitive prerequisites for the acquisition of grammar. In C. A. Ferguson and D. I. Slobin (eds.), *Studies of child language development.* New York: Holt, Rinehart, and Winston.

  1985a. Crosslinguistic evidence for the language-making capacity. In D. I. Slobin (ed.), *The crosslinguistic study of language acquisition*, 2 vols. Hillsdale, NJ: Erlbaum.

(ed.). 1985b. *The crosslinguistic study of language acquisition*, 2 vols. Hillsdale, NJ: Erlbaum.

1988. From the Garden of Eden to the Tower of Babel. In F. S. Kessel (ed.), *The development of language and language researchers: essays in honor of Roger Brown*. Hillsdale, NJ: Erlbaum.

(ed.) 1992. *The crosslinguistic study of language acquisition*, vol. III. Hillsdale, NJ: Erlbaum.

Smith, C. B., Adamson, L. B., and Bakeman, R. 1988. Interactional predictors of early language. *First Language*, 8, 143–56.

Smith, N. V. 1989. *The Twitter Machine: reflections on language*. Oxford: Blackwell.

Smoczyńska, M. 1985. The acquisition of Polish. In D. I. Slobin (ed.), *The crosslinguistic study of language acquisition*, vol. I. Hillsdale, NJ: Erlbaum.

Snow, C. E. 1972. Mothers' speech to children learning language. *Child Development*, 43, 549–65.

1977a. Mothers' speech research: from input to interaction. In C. E. Snow and C. A. Ferguson (eds.), *Talking to children: language input and acquisition*. Cambridge University Press.

1977b. The development of conversations between mothers and babies. *Journal of Child Language*, 4, 1–22.

1981. Social interaction and language acquisition. In P. Dale and D. Ingram (eds.), *Child language: an international perspective*. Baltimore, MD: University Park Press.

1983. Saying it again: the role of expanded and deferred imitations in language acquisition. In K. E. Nelson (ed.), *Children's language*, vol. IV. Hillsdale, NJ: Erlbaum.

1986. Conversations with children. In P. Fletcher and M. Garman (eds.), *Language acquisition: studies in second language development*, 2nd edn. Cambridge University Press.

1989. Understanding social interaction and language acquisition: sentences are not enough. In M. H. Bornstein and J. S. Bruner (eds.), *Interaction in human development*. Hillsdale, NJ: Erlbaum.

in press. Understanding social interaction and language development: sentences are not enough. To appear in M. Bornstein (ed.), *Social interaction and cognitive development*.

Snow, C. E., Arlmann-Rupp, A., Hassin, Y., Jobse, J., Joosten, J., and Vorster, J. 1976. Mothers' speech in three social classes. *Journal of Psycholinguistic Research*, 5, 1–20.

Snow, C. E., and Ferguson, C. A. (eds.). 1977. *Talking to children: language input and acquisition*. Cambridge University Press.

Snow, C. E., and Goldfield, B. 1983. Turn the page please: situation-specific language acquisition. *Journal of Child Language*, 10, 551–69.

Snow, C. E., and Hoefnagel-Höhle, M. 1982. School-age second language learners' access to simplified linguistic input. *Language Learning*, 32, 411–30.

Snow, C. E., Perlmann, R., and Nathan, D. 1987. Why routines are different: towards a multiple-factors model of the relation between input and language acquisition. In K. E. Nelson and A. van Kleeck (eds.), *Children's language*, vol. VI. Hillsdale, NJ: Erlbaum.

Snow, C. E., van Eeden, R., and Muysken, P. 1981. The interactional origins of foreigner talk: municipal employees and foreign workers. *International Journal of the Sociology of Language*, 28, 81–91.

Sokolov, J. L. 1988. Cue validity in Hebrew sentence comprehension. *Journal of Child Language*, 15, 129–55.

  1990. Conversational interaction and competition in child language. Doctoral dissertation, Department of Psychology, Carnegie Mellon University.

  in press. Parental imitations and implicit negative evidence in a multiple factors framework. *Journal of Child Language*.

Sokolov, J., and MacWhinney, B. 1990. The CHIP framework: automatic coding and analysis of parent–child conversational interaction. *Behavior Research Methods, Instruments and Computers*, 22, 151–61.

Spada, N., and Lightbown, P. forthcoming. Instruction and the development of questions in L2 classrooms. *Studies in Second Language Acquisition (Thematic Issue)*, 15.

Speidel, G. E. 1987. Conversation and language learning in the classroom. In K. E. Nelson and A. van Kleeck (eds.), *Children's language*, vol. VI. Hillsdale, NJ: Erlbaum.

Staats, A. W. 1974. Behaviorism and cognitive theory in the study of language: a neopsycholinguistics. In R. L. Schiefelbusch and L. L. Lloyd (eds.), *Language perspectives: acquisition, retardation, and intervention*. London: MacMillan.

Stark, R. E., and Tallal, P. 1981. Selection of children with specific language deficits. *Journal of Speech and Hearing Disorders*, 46, 114–22.

Stern, D. N., Spieker, S., Barnett, R. K., and MacKain, K. 1983. The prosody of maternal speech: infant age and context related changes. *Journal of Child Language*, 10, 1–15.

Stern, D. N., Spieker, S., and MacKain, K. 1982. Intonation contours as signals in maternal speech to prelinguistic infants. *Developmental Psychology*, 18, 727–35.

Sternberg, R. 1984. *Mechanisms of cognitive development*. New York: W. H. Freeman.

Stoneman, Z., Brody, G. H., and Abbott, D. 1983. In-home observations of young Down syndrome children with their mothers and fathers. *American Journal of Mental Deficiency*, 87, 591–600.

Swain, M. 1985. Communicative competence: some roles of comprehensible input and comprehensible output in its development. In S. Gass and C. Madden (eds.), *Input in second language acquisition*. Rowley, MA: Newbury House.

  1988. Manipulating and complementing content teaching to maximize second language learning. *TESL Canada Journal*, 6, 68–83.

Swain, M., and Lapkin, S. 1986. Immersion French in secondary schools: 'the goods' and 'the bads'. *Contact*, 5, 2–13.

Swisher, M. V. 1989. The language-learning situation of deaf students. *TESOL Quarterly*, 23, 239–57.

  1990. Conversational interaction between deaf children and their mothers: the role of visual attention. In P. Siple and S. Fischer (eds.), *Theoretical issues in sign language research: psychology*. University of Chicago Press.

Swisher, M. V., and Christie, K. 1989. Communication using a signed code for

English interaction between deaf children and their mothers. In B. Woll (ed.), *Language development and sign language, Monograph 1, International Sign Linguistics Association*. Bristol: International Sign Linguistics Association.

Taylor, P. 1992, October 2. Silenced with sentences of correction. *Times Educational Supplement*, p. 24.

Terrell, T. D. 1990. Foreigner talk as comprehensible input. In J. E. Alatis (ed.), *Georgetown University Round Table on Languages and Linguistics*. Washington, DC: Georgetown University Press.

Tiegermann, E., and Siperstein, H. 1984. Individual patterns of interaction in the mother–child dyad: implications for parent–child intervention. *Topics in Language Disorders*, 4, 50–61.

Tingley, E. 1990. The effects of maternal depression on symbolic interaction between mothers and their young children. Unpublished doctoral dissertation, Boston University.

Tizard, B., and Hughes, M. 1984. *Young children learning*. London: Fontana.

Tomasello, M., Conti-Ramsden, G., and Ewert, B. 1990. Young children's conversations with their mothers and fathers: differences in breakdown and repair. *Journal of Child Language*, 17, 115–30.

Tomasello, M., and Farrar, M. J. 1986. Joint attention and early language. *Child Development*, 57, 1454–63.

Tomasello, M., Farrar, J., and Dines, J. 1983. Young children's speech revisions for a familiar and an unfamiliar adult. *Journal of Speech and Hearing Research*, 27, 359–63.

Tomasello, M., and Herron, C. 1989. Feedback for language transfer errors: the garden path technique. *Studies in Second Language Acquisition*, 11, 385–95.

Tomasello, M., and Mannle, S. 1985. Pragmatics of sibling speech to 1-year-olds. *Child Development*, 56, 911–17.

Tomasello, M., Mannle, S., and Barton, M. 1989. The development of communicative competence in twins. *Revue Internationale de Psychologie Sociale*, 2, 49–59.

Tomasello, M., Mannle, S., and Kruger, A. C. 1986. Linguistic environment of 1- to 2-year-old twins. *Developmental Psychology*, 22, 169–76.

Tomasello, M., and Todd, J. 1983. Joint attention and lexical acquisition style. *First Language*, 4, 197–212.

Tucker, I., Hughes, M. E., and Glover, M. 1983. Verbal interaction with preschool hearing-impaired children: a comparison of maternal and paternal language inputs. *Journal of the British Association of Teachers of the Deaf*, 7, 90–8.

Tudor, I., and Hafiz, F. 1989. Extensive reading as a means of input to second language learning. *Journal of Research in Reading*, 12, 164–78.

Valdman, A. 1981. Sociolinguistic aspects of foreigner talk. *International Journal of the Sociology of Language*, 28, 41–52.

Valian, V. 1990. Null subjects: a problem for parameter-setting models of language acquisition. *Cognition*, 35, 105–22.

van Lier, L. 1984. Analyzing interaction in second language classrooms. *English Language Teaching Journal*, 38, 160–9.

 1991. Inside the classroom: learning procedures and teaching procedures. *Applied Language Learning*, 2, 29–68.

Van Valin, Jr., R. D. 1992. Competing theories, extraction restrictions and the logical problem of language acquisition. Paper presented at the Conference on the Reality of Linguistic Rules, Milwaukee, WI.

Van der Lely, H. J. K., and Harris, M. 1990. Comprehension of reversible sentences by specifically language-impaired children. *Journal of Speech and Hearing Disorders*, 55, 101–17.

Vandell, D., and Wilson, K. 1987. Infant's interaction with mother, sibling, and peer. *Child Development*, 58, 176–86.

Vanniarajan, M. S. 1988. Importance of input in second language acquisition. Unpublished MA thesis, University of Ottawa.

VanPatten, B. 1987. On babies and bathwater: input in foreign language learning. *Modern Language Journal*, 71, 156–64.

1988. How juries get hung. Problems with the evidence for a focus on form in teaching. *Language Learning*, 38, 243–60.

1990. Attending to form and meaning in the input. *Studies in Second Language Acquisition*, 12, 287–301.

VanPatten, B., and Cadierno, T. 1992. Explicit instruction and input processing. Unpublished manuscript, The University of Illinois at Urbana-Champaign.

1993. Input processing and SLA: a role for instruction. *Modern Language Journal*, 77, 45–56.

Varonis, E., and Gass, S. 1982. The comprehensibility of non-native speech. *Studies in Second Language Acquisition*, 4, 114–36.

1985. Native/non-native conversations: a model for negotiation of meaning. *Applied Linguistics*, 6, 71–90.

Vignola, M.-J., and Wesche, M. 1991. Le savoir-écrire en langue maternelle et en langue seconde chez les diplômés d'immersion française. *Etudes de linguistique appliquée*, 82, 94–115.

Voegelin, C. F., and Robinett, F. M. 1954. 'Mother language' in Hidatsa. *International Journal of American Linguistics*, 20, 67–70.

Volterra, V. 1983. Gestures, signs and words at two years. In J. G. Kyle and B. Woll (eds.), *Language in sign*. London: Croom Helm.

Volterra, V., and Caselli, C. 1985. From gestures and vocalisations to signs and words. In W. C. Stokoe and V. Volterra (eds.), *The Third International Symposium on Sign Language Research*. Silver Spring: Linstok Press.

Vygotsky, L. 1978. *Mind in society: the development of higher psychological processes*. Cambridge, MA: Harvard University Press.

Wagner-Gough, J., and Hatch, E. 1975. The importance of input data in second language acquisition studies. *Language Learning*, 25, 297–308.

Warren-Leubecker, A., Bohannon, J., Stanowicz, L., and Ness, J. 1986. New evidence about negative evidence. Paper presented at the Teachability of Language Conference, Kansas City, MO.

Watkins, R. V., and Pemberton, E. F. 1987. Clinical applications of recasting: review and theory. *Child Language Teaching and Therapy*, 3, 311–28.

Watson-Gegeo, K. A., and Gegeo, D. G. 1986. Calling out and repeating routines in Kwara'ae children's language socialisation. In B. B. Schieffelin and E. Ochs (eds.), *Language socialization across cultures*. Cambridge University Press.

Weber, S., and Tardiff, C. forthcoming. Culture and meaning in French immersion kindergarten. In L. Malavé and G. Duquette (eds.), *Language, culture, and cognition: a collection of studies in first and second language acquisition for educators in Canada and the United States*. Clevedon, England: Multilingual Matters.

Wedell-Monnig, J., and Lumley, J. M. 1980. Child deafness and mother–child interaction. *Child Development*, 51, 766–74.

Weir, R. H. 1962. *Language in the crib*. The Hague: Mouton.

Weist, R., and Stebbins, P. 1972. Adult perceptions of children's speech. *Psychonomic Science*, 27, 359–60.

Weistuch, L., and Byers Brown, B. 1987. Motherese as therapy: a programme and its dissemination. *Child Language Teaching and Therapy*, 3, 57–71.

Wells, C. G. 1978. What makes for successful language development? In R. Campbell and P. Smith (eds.), *Recent advances in the psychology of language*, vol. III. New York: Plenum.

  1980. Adjustments in adult–child conversation: some effects of interaction. In H. Giles, W. P. Robinson, and P. M. Smith (eds.), *Language: social-psychological perspectives*. Oxford: Pergamon.

  1981. *Learning through interaction: the study of language development*. Cambridge University Press.

  1985. *Language development in the pre-school years*. Cambridge University Press.

  1986a. *The meaning makers: children learning language and using language to learn*. Portsmouth, NH: Heinemann.

  1986b. The language experience of five-year-old children at home and school. In J. Cook-Gumperz (ed.), *The social construction of literacy*. Cambridge University Press.

  1986c. Variation in child language. In P. Fletcher and M. Garman (eds.), *Language acquisition: studies in first language development*, 2nd edn. Cambridge University Press.

Wells, G., and Montgomery, M. 1981. Adult–child interaction at home and at school. In P. French and M. MacLure (eds.), *Adult–child conversation*. New York: St. Martins.

Wells, G., and Robinson, W. P. 1982. The role of adult speech in language development. In C. Fraser and K. Scherer (eds.), *The social psychology of language*. Cambridge University Press.

Werker, J. F., and MacLeod, P. J. 1989. Infant preference for both male- and female infant-directed talk: a developmental study of attentional and affective responsiveness. *Canadian Journal of Psychology*, 43, 230–46.

Wesche, M. 1989. Les diplômes de l'immersion: implications dans le domaine de l'enseignement du français. *The Canadian Journal of Higher Education*, 19, 29–41.

  1992. French immersion graduates at university and beyond: what difference has it made? In J. Alatis (ed.), *Georgetown University Round Table on Languages and Linguistics 1992*. Washington, DC: Georgetown University Press.

Wesche, M. B., and Ready, D. 1985. Foreigner talk in the university classroom. In S. Gass and C. Madden (eds.), *Input in second language acquisition*. Rowley, MA: Newbury House.

Wexler, K., and Culicover, P. 1980. *Formal principles of language acquisition.* Cambridge University Press.

Wexler, K., and Manzini, M. R. 1987. Parameters and learnability. In T. Roeper and E. Williams (eds.), *Parameter setting.* Dordrecht: Reidel.

White, L. 1985. Is there a logical problem of second language acquisition? *TESL Canada Journal*, 2, 29–41.

1987. Against comprehensible input: the input hypothesis and the development of second language competence. *Applied Linguistics*, 8, 95–110.

1989. *Universal grammar and second language acquisition.* Philadelphia: John Benjamins.

1990. Implications of learnability theories for second language learning and teaching. In M. Halliday, J. Gibbons, and H. Nicholas (eds.), *Learning, keeping and using language: selected papers from the Eighth World Congress of Applied Linguistics.* Amsterdam: John Benjamin.

1991. Adverb placement in second language acquisition: some effects of positive and negative evidence in the classroom. *Second Language Research*, 7, 133–41.

White, L., Spada, N., Lightbown, P., and Ranta, L. 1991. Input enhancement and L2 question formation. *Applied Linguistics*, 12, 416–32.

White, S. J., and White, R. E. C. 1984. The deaf imperative: characteristics of maternal input to hearing-impaired children. *Topics in Language Disorders*, 4, 38–49.

Whitehurst, G., and Vasta, R. 1975. Is language acquired through imitation? *Journal of Psycholinguistic Research*, 4, 37–59.

Willes, M. 1981. Children becoming pupils: a study of discourse in nursery and reception classes. In C. Adelman (ed.), *Uttering, muttering: collecting, using and reporting talk for social and educational research.* London: Grant McIntyre.

1983. *Children into pupils: a study of language in early schooling.* London: Routledge and Kegan Paul.

Wolff, P. 1964. Observations on the early development of smiling. In B. M. Foss (ed.), *Determinants of infant behaviour*, vol. II. London: Methuen.

Woll, B., and Kyle, J. G. 1989. Communication and language development in children of deaf parents. In S. von Tetzchner, L. S. Siegel, and L. Smith (eds.), *The social and cognitive aspects of normal and atypical language development.* New York: Springer.

Woll, B., Kyle, J. G., and Ackerman, J. 1988. Providing Sign Language models: strategies used by deaf mothers. In G. Collis, A. Lewis, and V. Lewis (eds.), *Proceedings of the Child Language Seminar.* University of Warwick.

Wong Fillmore, L. 1976. The second time around: cognitive and social strategies in second language acquisition. Unpublished Ph.D. dissertation, Stanford University, San Francisco. Newbury House.

1979. Individual differences in second language acquisition. In C. J. Fillmore, D. Kempler, and W-S. Y. Wang (eds.), *Individual differences in language ability and language behaviour.* New York: Academic Press.

1989. Teachability and second language acquisition. In M. L. Rice and R. L. Schiefelbusch (eds.), *The teachability of language.* Baltimore, MD: Brookes.

Wood, D. J. 1980. Teaching the young child: some relationships between social interaction, language and thought. In D. R. Olson (ed.), *The social foundations of language and thought*. New York: W. W. Norton.

1982. The linguistic experiences of the prelingually hearing-impaired child. *Journal of the British Association of Teachers of the Deaf*, 6, 86–93.

Wood, D., Bruner, J., and Ross, G. 1976. The role of tutoring in problem-solving. *Journal of Child Psychology and Psychiatry*, 17, 89–100.

Wood, D. J., and Middleton, D. J. 1975. A study of assisted problem solving. *British Journal of Psychology*, 66, 181–91.

Wood, H. A., and Wood, D. J. 1984. An experimental evaluation of the effects of five styles of teacher conversation in the language of hearing-impaired children. *Journal of Child Psychology and Allied Disciplines*, 25, 45–62.

1992. Signed English in the classroom, IV: Teaching style and child participation. *First Language*, 12, 125–45.

Wood, D. J., Wood, H. A., Griffiths, A. J., Howarth, S. P., and Howarth, C. I. 1982. The structure of conversations with 6–10-year-old deaf children. *Journal of Child Psychology and Psychiatry*, 23, 295–308.

Woods, A., Fletcher, P., and Hughes, A. 1986. *Statistics in language studies*. Cambridge University Press.

Woollett, A. 1986. The influence of older siblings in the language environment of young children. *British Journal of Development Psychology*, 4, 235–45.

Wulbert, M., Inglis, S., Kriegsmann, E., and Mills, B. 1975. Language delay and associated mother–child interaction. *Developmental Psychology*, 11, 61–70.

Yoder, P. 1989. Maternal question use predicts later language development in specific-language-disordered children. *Journal of Speech and Hearing Disorders*, 54, 347–55.

Yoder, P., and Kaiser, A. 1989. Alternative explanations for the relationship between maternal verbal interaction style and child language development. *Journal of Child Language*, 16, 141–60.

Young, R. 1988. Input and interaction. *Annual Review of Applied Linguistics*, 9, 122–34.

Zobl, H. 1985. Grammars in search of input and intake. In S. Gass and C. Madden (eds.), *Input in second language acquisition*. Rowley, MA: Newbury House.

# Author Index

# Subject Index

affective factors 144–5, 147, 149, 152, 212, 263, 264, 265
  in second language 224, 234, 241, 263
American English 150
Arabic 149
Association Internationale de Linguistique Appliquée (AILA) 5
attention, management of 35, 60–1, 68, 109, 122, 126, 139, 145–6, 147, 149, 152, 161, 169–70, 190, 263, 264, 269
  with deaf children 201, 206, 210–11, 213, 214–15, 218
atypical language learners 6, 11–12, 76, 77, 82, 83, 93, 95, 100–1, 103, 183–96, 257–9, 268
  differences in interactions with 184–5, 186
  *see also* deaf children

Baby Talk (BT): *see* child-directed speech
behaviorism 38, 50
Berber 136
blind children: *see* atypical language learners
boundary marking 141–2, 148, 234
Bridge Hypothesis 69, 111–25 *passim*, 254
Bristol Language Development Study 157–8
British English 150
buffering 11–12, 195, 258

child-directed speech (CDS)
  absence of 53, 54–5, 59–63, 77, 110, 150, 151, 258
  *see also* deaf children, absence of input to
  amount of 9, 69, 126–7, 128, 205, 210, 212
  conversation-eliciting features of 28–9, 114, 123, 124, 264
  determinants of 18–19, 200–2, 205
  effects of 9–11, 20–37, 42, 52, 74–106, 109–11, 120, 124–31, 142–6, 152, 189–90, 191, 200–2, 265

features of 15–17, 39, 109, 111, 113–14, 122, 149–50, 152, 205, 255–7
functions of 16–20, 109, 135, 140–6, 152, 212, 260–5
in bilingual families 117–18, 255
phonetic aspects of 60, 135–8, 142–52, 206, 254, 256, 263
prosodic aspects of 60, 135–6, 139–52, 206, 254, 257, 263
simplicity of 16–22 *passim*, 75–6, 135, 137–8, 143, 185, 201, 261–2
universality of 149–52
*see also* crosscultural issues; crosslinguistic issues
variability in 19, 20
vocabulary 114–15, 199
*see also* affective factors; attention, management of; boundary marking; clarification; correction; directiveness; directives; environmental effects; expansion; extension; fathers; feedback; focus marking; Foreigner Discourse; imperatives; intonation; labeling; negative evidence; nonverbal interaction; older children; pauses; pitch; polyadic contexts; questions; recasts; referent matching; repetition; responsiveness; scaffolding; segmentation; semantic contingency; siblings; solidarity; styles of interaction; tuning; tutorial prompts; voice onset time
Child Language Data Exchange System (CHILDES) 8–9
Chinese 65, 66, 150
chunks: *see* rote learning
clarification 25, 27, 30–2, 135, 137, 144, 137–8, 149, 152, 262, 264, 265
*see also* questions, clarification
classroom discourse 6, 80–1, 153–7, 164–80, 126, 206–8, 260, 268
  and the development of meaning 156–7

Printed in the United Kingdom
by Lightning Source UK Ltd.
109761UKS00001B/124